Elizabeth Warnock Fernea teaches English and Middle Eastern Studies at the University of Texas at Austin. She has produced a number of films about the lives of Arab women and is the author of the bestselling *Guests of the Sheik*, as well as *A Street in Marrakech*, *A View of the Nile*, and with her husband, Robert A. Fernea, *The Arab World: Forty Years of Change*. She lives in Austin, Texas.

Elizabeth Warnock Fernea

In Search of Islamic Feminism

¤¤¤¤¤¤¤¤¤¤¤¤¤¤¤¤¤¤¤¤¤¤¤¤¤¤¤¤¤¤¤¤¤

One Woman's Global Journey

ANCHOR BOOKS
A DIVISION OF RANDOM HOUSE, INC.
New York

FIRST ANCHOR BOOKS TRADE PAPERBACK EDITION, DECEMBER 1998

The Library of Congress has cataloged the Doubleday hardcover edition as follows:

Fernea, Elizabeth Warnock.
In search of Islamic feminism: one woman's global journey / by
Elizabeth Warnock Fernea. — 1st ed.
    p. cm.
Includes index.
1. Muslim women—Islamic countries. 2. Women in Islam—Islamic
countries. I. Title.
HQ1170.F48 1998
305.48'6971—dc21   97-27121
CIP

ISBN 0-385-48858-0

Book design by Paul Randall Mize

www.anchorbooks.com

Printed in the United States of America
10 9 8 7 6

By 1997, Bob and I were fortunate enough to have been blessed with three grandchildren: Isabel Andrea Colorado, Maya Elizabeth Colorado, and Weston Creekmore Fernea. It is to them that this book is dedicated.

Contents

Acknowledgments

The idea of this book was first suggested to me by Martha Levin, publisher of Anchor Books. "Something about Islam, B.J., which is your interest," she said, "and something about feminism, which is my interest." I was hesitant, partly because I had just returned from the Middle East and was doubtful about possibilities for finding any new feminist trends, and partly because it seemed more appropriate, in this day and age, for such a book to be done, not by me, but by a Muslim woman. Martha responded that the perspective of an American feminist with long-standing interest in the Muslim world might be useful for an American audience, a view with which my longtime agent, Gloria Loomis, enthusiastically agreed. And so I set out, and over two years of traveling, discovered that the realities of Muslim women's lives today have far surpassed the discourse about those lives with which we have been presented in the West. Thank you, Martha, thank you, Gloria, for your encouragement.

In this effort, I owe thanks to many other people. Hospitality was extended by Leila Abouzeid, Roberta Micallef, Akile Gursoy, Taghreed al-Qudsi and Shafeeq Ghabra, Aziza al-Hibri, Bill and Andrea Rugh, Randa Sha'ath, and Tom Hartwell. For other kinds of friendly assistance, appreciation to Sue Buret, Deborah Kapchan, Ferial Ghazoul, Hesna Mekdashi, Anne Johnson, Lora Berg, Lamia al-Gailani, Asma al-Gailani, Ronda Aboubakr, Judy Blanc, Esther Raizen, Rita Giacoman, Eileen Kuttab, Saif and Zeinab Abbas Mohammed, Eleanor Doumato, Donald Powell Cole, Basima Bezirgan, Halit and Gulper Refiq, Pat Ivey, Leila Ahmed, Suad Joseph, and Margaret Ann U'ren. Special thanks to longtime friend and former editor Sally

Arteseros. To my old friends in the village of Al Nahra, Iraq, who welcomed me and asked for new copies of *Guests of the Sheik,* the book in which they appear, I can only say how wonderful it was to be able to briefly renew our friendship after forty years of separation.

Colleagues at the University of Texas at Austin, where I teach, have been supportive, including James Garrison, chairman of the Department of English; Abraham Marcus, director of the Center for Middle Eastern Studies; and good friends at the Center, Annes McCann-Baker, Deborah Littrell, Marjorie Payne, and Diane Watts. The University Research Institute gave me a one-semester grant to allow me to write, and a fellowship from the National Council on U.S.–Arab Relations made the Saudi Arabia trip possible. Research assistants included Sharon Doerre, Jennifer O'Connor, Mary Karam, Amal Chagumoum, Carl Hershiser, and Nafiz Aksehirlioglu. My children, Laura Ann, David, and Laila, and my daughter-in-law, Kim, read and soundly(!) critiqued various chapters. I thank them, and I thank Virginia Howell and Geraldine Behrens, who made the manuscript readable. Rob McQuilkin and Siobhan Adcock at Anchor Books shepherded the material through the editing and publishing processes and I am grateful for their assistance, as well as for their patience. But it is to my husband, Robert Fernea, that I owe the greatest debt. Critic, companion, questioner, he helped me shape the experience of this journey, both intellectually and emotionally, into the book that follows. Any errors, however, are my own.

Austin, Texas
September 1997

Introduction

This is the story of a journey, from Austin, Texas, to Portland, Oregon, to the Middle East, North Africa, Central Asia, and back again. It began as a search for Islamic feminism, but over the months and years, has become a meditation about the nature of feminism, what it means to me, my family, and to my friends in East and West. Feminism. Equality between men and women. Is it possible? Rebecca West once wrote that the problem between men and women constitutes the rock on which civilization will either split asunder or survive, with honor. Feminism is the newest human effort to deal with that problem, and its basic premise is that in considering the rights of men and women, their physical differences should not affect the way they are treated legally, socially, or politically. This conviction has been viewed by many as universally applicable. I wanted to see whether my Muslim friends agreed, whether their own women's movements operated on a feminist premise, or whether they saw their own struggles for rights as different from women's movements in the West.

It is easy to forget that feminism is a very new idea in the world, an idea that has come into existence in my own lifetime. I was reminded of this when I talked with old friends at the fiftieth reunion of our Jefferson High School class, in Portland, Oregon. The class of 1945. In 1945, when I was a senior in high school, my father would read aloud to us each day from the newspaper. For those were stirring times. Freedom from tyranny. Freedom from want. The Holocaust had been stopped, a racist dictator unseated. Europe was reborn. It was very exciting. Full of possibilities. I had a scholarship to Reed College, in Portland, Oregon, and, most exciting of all, Bobby Bolton was coming home from the South Pacific. He had enlisted in the Marines when he graduated from Central Catholic High School. He had continued to write to me and the tone of his letters recently—well, I decided not to mention this to my parents. And of course all that was still the man's choice.

Nineteen forty-five. More than fifty years ago. I don't remember anything in those inspiring end-of-conflict speeches about women, except that women were told they were lucky, they no longer had to work hard in the shipyard factories as they had during the war. They could now go back home and care for their children and their husbands, who had recently returned from battle. In fact, I don't remember thinking about women and women's rights at all. I was too full of thoughts about Bobby Bolton.

My memories are no different from those of my female classmates. When we compared notes at our fiftieth Jefferson High School reunion none of us could remember thinking about such issues. Women had the vote. They were going to college. They had good jobs, thanks to the war; going back to the home so veterans could have jobs seemed right—and temporary. The suffragettes were ancient history. Feminism was an ideology yet to be born. The first wave of new ideas about such matters was called women's liberation; at the reunion my friends and I talked about what that had meant to us at the time. Liberation from what? Men? Heaven forbid, we didn't want that. We wanted to have equality of course, choice in decision making, of course, and equal pay for equal work. Some of us were embracing the new birth control methods. Wasn't that liberation? Wasn't it part of progress?

Even in 1956, when I married Bob Fernea, a cultural anthropologist, and went with him to the Middle East, no one had yet articulated what we call today feminism. My mother counseled me about "our" (that is, Western) responsibilities to the women of other lands who were not so fortunate as we were. Middle Eastern women qualified as "women of other lands"; it was well known, or at least believed by many, that Middle Eastern women, like Chinese women and Indian women, were in grave need of our help. Chinese women had their feet bound painfully, Indian women were expected to throw themselves on their husbands' funeral biers, and Middle Eastern women were kept indoors and made to wear the veil. In those days, my mother also wore veils, on her hats. But she patiently explained the world of difference that lay between her starched spotted black veil of net and the heavy veils Middle Eastern women had to wear, veils so heavy that she said, "they couldn't even see to walk."

"Women's rights" was the working phrase I carried with me to Iraq in 1956, where I lived for two years in a small village with women who did indeed wear the veil, but who did not particularly want me to enlighten them, and were not interested in Western ideas about women's rights. This was hard to explain later to my mother and my high school and college friends. What did I mean? Had I failed? Had those Muslim ladies brainwashed me? Of course, in those days saying anything positive about Arabs or the Arab world was suspect in our circles of liberal friends. I found that I was also at odds with old friends when I tried to explain that the women I knew in the Iraqi village felt their lives were reasonably full even though they covered themselves with abbayahs when they went out of their houses, and lived much of their lives separate from men other than the members of their families. Even though we were proud of our Western society and its values, other modes of life existed, I said; we should respect them because they weren't all necessarily evil, only different. After all these years, I still remember the strange looks I received from friends I thought I knew well. They changed the subject. Silenced, I sat down and wrote, over four years, my first book, *Guests of the Sheik*. Thus began forty years of writing, teaching, lecturing about, and filming Middle Eastern women—a lifetime, really. Our three children were born in Egypt. Bob and I learned to speak colloquial Arabic and brushed up on our French. We have lived for more than twelve years in the Middle East, and still return regularly for shorter stays.

The book that follows is an attempt to look at Middle Eastern women today and ask once more that simple, or not so simple, question, the woman question. How are women doing? What does feminism mean to them? To me? To all of us in the West? Are feminist ideas helpful? Does feminism work across class, geographical, and cultural boundaries? Are its tenets universal? Do other forms of feminism exist—Islamic feminism, for instance? Forms that we don't understand because we don't read Arabic or Persian or Turkish?

I set out to try to answer those questions by going on a journey, a sort of pilgrimage. After forty years, did people still believe the stereotypes my mother had articulated about Middle Eastern women? Some of the books and media reports suggested they did. But I told myself that countries, like people, don't stand still. The Middle East is the center of near-catastrophic economic and social change, and new information might be jarring those remaining Western stereotypes.

So I embarked on my journey, traveling to countries like Egypt, Iraq, and Morocco, where I had lived for many years and knew the language; to countries where I had close friends such as Turkey, whose women believe they started the women's movement in the Middle

East; to Kuwait, a Gulf kingdom recently ravaged by the Gulf War; to Saudi Arabia, birthplace of Islam; to the West Bank and Israel, where I had lived while producing two films about peace possibilities; to Uzbekistan, one of the Central Asian republics, a non-Arab Muslim country recently freed from Russian rule.

I also set about traveling in my own country. No Muslim students graduated with me from Jefferson High School in 1945; there were very few Muslims in the United States then. The only thing I knew about Muslims was what I had learned in the Catholic Church, where I was reared: Islam started out as a heresy, the priests said, was battled by the Crusaders, and was still around in "foreign parts." But in 1996, six to eight million Muslims practiced their religion in America.

The world has changed in fifty years. The end of World War II marked the beginning of the atomic age, and people would never be as sanguine again about the future of the human race as we were in our years at Jefferson High School. While we were singing the class song in June 1945, the seeds of anticolonialism had already been sown in the Middle East as well as in Asia and Africa. Struggles for independence were underway in North Africa, and the British policy in Palestine had only exacerbated the problems between Palestinians and Israelis caused by the refugees from the Holocaust seeking refuge in the promised land. In 1948, while I was at Reed College, the state of Israel came into being. Egypt's King Farouk abdicated in 1952; as Bob and I sailed into Alexandria harbor in 1956 on our way to Beirut and eventually Baghdad, President Nasser had just nationalized the Suez Canal, enraging European shareholders. So we were not allowed to disembark, and hence missed seeing what we were told was the "real" Alexandria, so eroticized in Lawrence Durrell's novels.

The Iraqi monarchy fell in 1958, one month after we left for home, and the bloody battle for Algeria, already in progress, would last until 1962. The unrest, the struggles, the revolutions were marked by bombast and rhetoric and promises by the new leaders. And all those promises discussed women's role. It was to be a priority for the new governments.

Ideas travel. In the Middle East, the prospect of freedom from want and freedom from tyranny appealed to everyone, rich and poor, male and female. Hence in the 1950s when I came home, I explained to my high school friends that although Muslim women were not interested in my views about "women's liberation," their lives were improving through education. When we lived in Egypt, I could see the same thing happening there, a process that continued into the seventies. With OPEC came the widening of the gulf between rich nations and poor nations in the Middle East, and the disappointment that greeted the failure of people's raised expectations for economic and social improvement. The idea of Islam began to replace the ideas of modernism and development and westernization. For after all, what had westernization and modernization, women's struggles for equality, and economic development plans done for people in the Middle East, Africa, and Asia? It hadn't brought peace and prosperity, nor freedom from tyranny.

Islam on the other hand signified legitimacy, identity outside the Western sphere. Islam meant origins, heritage, tradition, all those things that had been devalued during the colonial period. Islam was the only shared identity of people that predated Western European colonialism. Some Western reports suggested that the new Islamism had laid waste to the signs of progress for women reported in the fifties: education, political rights, social choices. Was this to be believed?

For again, with the rise of religious rejuvenation came a reaction against the West in Middle Eastern societies. One of the key issues was that of women's place. Were women supposed to run about the streets in mini-skirts and low-cut blouses, smoking and drinking, fornicating freely, forsaking their families and their religion? Or were they to remain in their traditional honorable position as heart and soul of the family, the basis of all society? The new style of Islamic dress, or *hijab,* made headlines around the world, as it seemed to indicate that women were indeed retreating behind the veil. Who was to decide how women should dress? What would my mother have said? My father? Neither was fond of smoking and drinking and fornicating and low-cut blouses—my father was a Scotch Presbyterian minister's son, my mother a Polish Catholic. But they also believed that women were people who should have choices and rights. Somewhere in the middle of those questions, a kind of compromise is what I think they would have suggested if they were alive today.

But how are Middle Eastern men and women answering the question? That was the purpose of my journey. I wrote to old and new friends in the Middle East, told them what I wanted to do, and asked for their help. I hoped to interview different kinds of women—and men—as well as officials, and to ask the woman question. I offered to lecture and show my films. What did these people think about feminism? Was there a movement toward Islamic feminism? Could there be such a thing?

The inquiry I proposed was not an in-depth study, such as sociologists undertake when they prepare questionnaires and analyze the results, or as anthropologists do when they live for months or years in a single small community. But I would be acting as a participant observer, wherever I was, relying on my friends and their friends to help fill in background. I was heartened to receive welcoming answers to my letters, so I set off in 1994. In the course of my travels and in the writing, I have tried to keep my own Western values, my own ideas of feminism, out of the endeavor. But they turn up, not only in my interviews, but in the questions put to me by Muslim women themselves. For I discovered, as I traveled and lectured, that many of them already knew my work and had questions to ask *me*. Thus the experience became more reciprocal than I had expected, and I began asking questions of myself, of my own convictions, questions that became part of the journey and its chronicling.

Bob and I grew up in a different world from our children—two daughters and a son, who were born in Cairo, went to school in Morocco, and have spent most of their lives in the United States. They take for granted many of the things I was just beginning to discover in 1945: relations between women and men need improvement; other cultures are just as legitimate as ours. Our children—and their children—also take feminism for granted, I think, and their lives reflect their understanding and knowledge of the movement's achievements: a struggle for rights, yes, but also the creation of a new vision of the world, the legitimacy of a woman's view as well as a man's view, a vision which has begun to change human thought and attitudes— toward science, art, the self. How Muslim women are reacting to these multiple aspects of the feminist dream is the subject of the book that follows.

A Note on Transliteration

The Arabic language has no capital letters, so transliterating it into English poses problems. In this book, the following guide has been used: for names of people, such as Samiha al-Khalil, the al- is lower-case. For places, such as the village of Al-Nahra, the Al- has been capitalized. Although Webster's Collegiate dictionary gives "Koran" for the sacred book of Islam, we have followed academic usage: "Qur'an."

Finally, people's names throughout the Arab world vary, as the dialects vary. Transliterated names appear as the people themselves prefer—i.e., Leila (not Laila) Abouzeid, and Hassan El-Ebraheem (not al-Ibrahim).

In Search of Islamic Feminism

ONE

❑❑❑❑❑❑❑❑❑❑❑❑❑❑❑❑❑❑❑❑❑❑❑❑❑❑❑❑❑❑❑

Uzbekistan

I PEERED OUT the window of the Lufthansa plane at glistening
fields of snow, stretching away and sloping upward in the dim
moonlight as far as I could see. The only artificial lights were those of
the plane as it slipped and bumped along the runway, past rows of
other airplanes topped with heavy caps of snow, dark, unmoving
planes that clearly had not been flying anywhere for some time.

"Madame," said my seatmate, a polite Spanish gentleman, "those
fields. They are the steppes of Mother Russia. You have heard of the
steppes?"

"Oh yes," I replied. What else could I say? I doubted that he would
be interested in my memory of Omar Sharif striding across the snowy
plains in *Dr. Zhivago,* or my reactions to the descriptions of the steppes
in nineteenth-century Russian novels. We had already exchanged basic
personal information on the flight from Frankfurt.

"You are going to meet your family in Tashkent?" he had asked.

And when I had replied that no, I was going to Uzbekistan at the
invitation of the National Institute of Arts and Literature to give some
lectures in comparative literature and women's studies, he had turned
around in his seat and stared at me.

"I'm a professor," I had said half-apologetically. Why was I being
apologetic? Perhaps because I realized that I did appear somewhat
anomalous, a middle-aged lady traveling alone into the steppes of
Central Asia on a cold winter evening. "And you?"

"A UN mission to the natural gas companies," he replied.

"What are we doing here?" I asked, as we came to a shuddering
slippery stop near what was clearly an airline terminal.

"A brief stopover in Alma-Ata," he answered.

This was not what my ticket indicated, but before I could say anything, my seatmate spoke up.

"You can't count on the schedule," he said. "Weather, you know. Look at the bright side. You now have a chance to see another country, Kazakhstan, known I think in America as Cossack land." He smiled at his bon mot.

Down the icy airplane steps we filed, onto the moonlit snow-covered walkway, and into the transit lounge, certainly a euphemism for the crowded, dimly lit room, where, as my eyes became accustomed to the gloom, I saw that the seats were all occupied. Nowhere to lounge. Many people were also asleep on the floor, their heads resting on lumpy pieces of luggage. It was cold! My Spanish gentleman friend placed himself against one of the marble pillars which held up the ceiling, and gestured to me to do the same. I did, situating my hand luggage around my legs, for warmth as well as safety. I straightened up. After all, it was only going to be forty-five minutes. Less than an hour. Good to stretch my back after sitting on the plane.

Time passed. It was cold. My watch told me that we had been here for more than two hours. I tried to stretch my stiff legs. And I asked myself what I was doing here, in the dawn of a Cossack day, halfway around the world from my family and my comfortable house in Austin, Texas. A week ago, the idea of a trip to Uzbekistan, one of the new Central Asian republics, to talk to women and learn about feminism and Islam, sounded exciting and intriguing.

My son, David, married and a new father, had asked me, the night before I departed, whether I was not a little too old for such an arduous trip. I had denied this, vehemently.

Now I was having doubts. I was cold and hungry, and stiff from standing. In another moment I was gripped with anxiety. How would I know when and if the Lufthansa flight was going to depart? I knew no Russian and no Kazakh and no Uzbek, and nothing was announced in English as far as I could hear. Maybe the plane had already gone? I looked around the lightening lounge for my fellow passengers: the Spanish gentleman; a Pakistani man with a graying beard and a gray caracul hat; a tall blond, Scandinavian; an Armenian engineer; a middle-sized man with a frayed American raincoat. They were still waiting, like me. At least I now had a seat, near the sign that said BAR. But the bar was closed.

The Spanish gentleman came over to explain that the fog was too dense for the plane to go to Tashkent. Our plane was going back to Frankfurt! Frankfurt! What about us?

"We are a small number, madame," said the Spanish gentleman sadly. "Lufthansa promises that Kazakh Air will take us later this afternoon."

Kazakh Air! What on earth was that? As though to dispel my rising doubts, a smiling Lufthansa agent moved among us, distributing Milky Way chocolate bars, two to a passenger. He was young and thin, and wore thick steel-rimmed glasses.

"Tea!" he cried. "Tea for Tashkent passengers!" And guided our small group into the lounge's newly opened bar. In the surreal early light of day, we sat down, Spanish, Swedish, Pakistani, Armenian, and American gentlemen—and me. The samovar was steaming. We drank scalding tea and ate chunks of stale pound cake and munched our Milky Way bars. It was wonderful! "Ah," said the Spanish gentleman. "Not unusual—such incidents in these Central Asian flights. Everything has changed since independence!"

"But how?"

"The central planning is all gone," he said, "and there is no discipline, no organization. The private sector . . ."

"The free market, you mean?" interposed the Swede.

"The free market cannot be free if there is nothing to market."

"Hear, hear!" said the Armenian engineer, his first words. "I will say that in my country, the so-called free Armenia, there is free market but no milk for babies."

"How are women doing?" I asked politely.

All eyes turned to me. The American gentleman, an ecologist, actually laughed.

"I suppose you are a feminist then?" he said. "American style?"

"Yes," I said firmly, and explained again why I was here, to give lectures and learn about feminism in the republic of Uzbekistan.

The Spaniard intervened, with a smile. "Women here are fine, just fine, madame," he said. "Better than in many countries of Europe. Really it's true," to my surprised look. "Equal rights were established under the Russians, you know."

Push on, I told myself. Push on.

"But now," I said, as sweetly as I could, "with Islam coming back, how are women doing?"

The Pakistani said smoothly, "You may not realize it, madame, but Islam provides women with many rights—economic rights, political rights, much better, I think, than you have in America, where you must fight for your rights."

"And besides," added the Spaniard, "this talk about Islam returning is premature. Uzbekistan is a secular society. The Russians got rid of Islam and Judaism and Christianity and every other kind of religion that was there."

"Yes," agreed the Pakistani. "Razed the mosques, and the churches, and the synagogues, to the ground. Terrible! Terrible!" Then he subsided and buttoned his coat up to the collar. We were all cold.

Ten hours later, as we sat, transfixed by fatigue in the bar, now chilly with the approach of night, the Lufthansa agent appeared. "Come please quickly," he said. "You are to be taken by Pakistan Airlines, now on runway. But against rules. Must come now! Now!"

We had been lucky. Pakistan International Airlines does land at Alma-Ata, en route to Islamabad, though it is not allowed to pick up passengers or indeed to fly to Tashkent. But our Pakistani colleague was a friend of the director of the Airlines and behind his mild, bearded manner was, apparently, a firm desire to attend his meeting in Tashkent. I had been placed beside him in the comfortable jet seats, and I thanked him profusely for his intervention.

"Islam states firmly that one must befriend strangers," he murmured.

Was he being ironic? I realized I did not care. The long hours I'd already spent in the Alma-Ata airport were more than enough.

A beautiful Pakistani stewardess in a russet wool sari appeared before us. "We will now recite a prayer in Arabic," she announced, "a prayer that the Prophet Muhammad, may peace be upon him, always uttered before embarking on a dangerous journey. We know also you will appreciate the fact that Ramadan, the month of fasting, has begun. We will not be serving refreshments. *Ramadan karim.*"

I sat in my seat, grateful if hungry, and when the prayer was finished, I turned to thank the Pakistani once more. But he had closed his eyes. Islam, for better or worse, might not be functioning in Uzbekistan, but clearly was alive and well in Pakistan, both on the ground and in the air. Two hours later we landed in Tashkent, where, wonder of wonders, no snow and ice lay on the ground. My search for Islamic feminism had apparently begun.

Why are you going to Uzbekistan? Many of my colleagues asked this question, colleagues who had, over the years, become accustomed to my traveling to the Arab world, where Bob and I had lived and done research, written books, made films. I had told them about my new project, a search for Islamic feminism. What could Uzbekistan offer to such a project? In fact many saw the trip as an academic boondoggle, a journey that had nothing to do with research, but was just an excuse for a sponsored adventure.

I had been invited to Uzbekistan through the good offices of Roberta Micallef, one of my Texas graduate students. She was there doing research for a Ph.D. in comparative literature, and had suggested that the National Institute of Arts and Literature invite me. Would I be kind enough to give a lecture or two on women's studies in the United States, or on some aspect of translation or comparative literature? How could I refuse? It was an unusual opportunity to visit a non-Arab Muslim country, an area that had been more or less closed to independent travelers for more than sixty years, since the Soviet Union moved into Central Asia and transformed these small ethnic enclaves into "Soviet Socialist Republics."

Turkmenistan. Uzbekistan. Tajikistan. Kyrgyzstan. Kazakhstan. The very sound of the names reverberated through my romantic head. I had grown up reading travel accounts of faraway places, for my father was addicted to such works. His own travels took him west and north at a time when Midwesterners like himself seldom left their small-town homes. The book I remember was called *The Royal Road to Romance* and it had wonderful glossy color pictures of places I had never heard of and never thought I would see.

"Uzbekistan," our travel agent had said to me. "Where is it, B.J.?" Beverly Redwine had been writing tickets for Bob and me for years. She was an inveterate traveler herself. "But not to places like this," she amended.

Uzbekistan was eventually pinpointed and flight paths traced. But the maps were not helpful. They had been made during the Cold War, when Russia was pictured as a great Red presence covering half of Europe, Asia as far south as Turkey and the Black Sea, and east to China, north to Siberia.

We had heard of Siberia. But the southern center of greater Russia was where Central Asia lay, an enormous area now divided into five separate republics.

American ignorance of Central Asia was partly a product of the time in which we lived, for that ignorance was not shared by peoples of earlier eras when Central Asia was an important crossroads and trade route, a natural resource base that had been fought over and carved up by conquerors like Genghis Khan and Tamerlane. Archaeologists think that long before becoming the focus of East-West rivalry, in the so-called "Great Game" of the nineteenth century, Central Asia had been a center of trade and of civilization, one of the oldest inhabited areas of the world, with history traced back at least five thousand years.

Today the great game of attempting to dominate Central Asia continues. Almost as soon as the Soviet Union collapsed, businessmen descended from many parts of the West and the East. When I sat in the Lufthansa transit lounge in Frankfurt in March 1994, waiting for the ill-fated Alma-Ata–Tashkent flight, a group of European parliamentarians was also waiting. They were bound for Alma-Ata, the Swedish gentleman told me, to observe and report on the first open elections to be held in Kazakhstan. Their choice of Kazakhstan for study was hardly an accident. Chevron Oil Company had set up headquarters there; contracts to develop the local oil reserves had already been signed by Kazakh leaders and Chevron officials. In Uzbekistan, people had begun to refer to the area as Chevronistan, half sneeringly, yes, but also half jealously. Oil was big business, after all, and its presence assured the new republic of considerable revenues in the not too distant future.

My other reason for visiting Uzbekistan was a serious and considered one. In my search for Islamic feminism, I was planning to visit countries where Bob and I had lived and worked for long periods of time—Egypt, Morocco, Iraq—or countries where we had spent shorter periods of time, but also had close friends to help with the research—Turkey, Kuwait, Israel/the West Bank. That seemed an obvious and legitimate approach. But I had never visited the other Muslim nations, where, contrary to general belief, more Muslims live than in the Arab world: China, Indonesia, Africa, the Philippines, as well as Central Asia. Roberta's invitation was therefore an opportunity to see how Islam was practiced in a non-Arab Muslim country, a country where Islam had been outlawed by colonialist rulers for three generations.

It was true that in the beginning of Russian rule over Uzbekistan the czarist regime was interested only in the area's vast natural resources, not in "meddling in local affairs." That meddling began after the Bolshevik Revolution of 1917, when the Russian revolutionaries saw their mission as one "to free the Central Asian peoples from the bonds of feudalism."

The Communist revolution was also, of course, a secular revolution. Just as religion became discredited in Russia, with the suppression of the Orthodox Church, so were Islam and Judaism frowned upon in Central Asia, where, as my Pakistani traveling companion had pointed out, mosques and synagogues were destroyed, as well as churches. The evidence of a vibrant Islam that had flowered since the eighth century was almost eliminated; only the great monuments like the Registan in Samarkand were left standing, restored as "cultural artifacts," as tourist attractions for Russians who traveled in search of both exoticism and warmer weather. To replace everyday buildings, Soviet administrators began to build secular memorials which stand to this day—the Lenin Monument, the People's Friendship Theater.

Now, of course, just as the Soviet monuments were being renamed, the secular institutions were in the process of being reevaluated. This was the area I was eager to explore. Would the secular laws stay on the books or would the nationalist officials move to reestablish Islamic law, and particularly Islamic family law, which regulates the structures which affect women's identity, status, and welfare: marriage, divorce, child custody, inheritance, and polygyny? The battle over secular vs. religious family law had been fought and was continuing to be fought in many Muslim countries. What was happening here in schools, in the workplace? And what about that central issue which, in the West, had become a symbol for women's status in Islamic lands—the issue of dress? Would the new Uzbek woman be forced to wear the veil? How were Uzbek women handling those problems? Did they consider themselves feminists?

My journey to Uzbekistan was a research trip, but also a personal adventure.

The long, dismaying hours in Alma-Ata began to fade in the warm Central Asian welcome offered by Roberta, her graduate student colleague Michael and his wife Monica, and the Uzbek poets, writers, and officials I began to meet. It turned out almost immediately, however, that there would be no need for me to give lectures. No need at all. But we needed to personally thank the official who had invited me!

"Welcome to the new republic of Uzbekistan," said the director of the National Institute of Arts and Literature. "We have arranged visas for you to visit the beautiful historic cities of Samarkand and Bokhara. This will perhaps be more interesting to yourself than giving lectures." I thanked him. Roberta and I moved on, out into the thin winter sunshine, along the paved streets, toward the central cultural square of Tashkent, where museums and institutes and libraries stood on each side of a grassy median, where trees, and pruned bushes, bare now, would add shade and beauty in the spring.

"We're walking on the Silk Route, B.J.," said Roberta. "The very road. Isn't it exciting?"

"Would you come with me to Samarkand and Bokhara, Roberta?"

"Yes, I want to. I haven't been yet. And you could probably interview women there."

"I'd like to."

"And I'd like to invite Vera, my Uzbek friend, the scientist I told you about."

"Vera? A Russian name for an Uzbek? I thought all Uzbeks were anti-Russian, or at least anticolonialist Russian."

"Yes," agreed Roberta. "But they lived side by side for years, these people. Bound to make a few friends. That's why Vera is named Vera— after a dear Russian friend of her mother. It's complicated to explain."

And I'm so ignorant, I thought. The opportunity to come here was sudden and I knew almost nothing about Central Asia, except *The Royal Road to Romance,* some brief historical accounts, and memories of the old legends of exotic Samarkand and Bokhara. I knew no Russian and no Uzbek. Here Arabic, French, and English were of little use. I felt lucky to be here at all, and I thanked Roberta once more for arranging my invitation. "You must remember to tell me, Roberta," I added, "when I sound too stupid."

Roberta laughed. "You're older than I am, B.J., and Uzbeks respect age, and you're my professor and that's a big deal here." She stopped. "So I can't tell you in public, but I will tell you in private, B.J.—when you sound . . . uninformed."

Slowly I began to realize that my Alma-Ata conversations with the Spanish gentleman, the Armenian engineer, and the Pakistani official had been a better introduction to Uzbekistan than I believed at the time. They had talked about change, about confusion, about chaos. At first glance, Tashkent, the capital city within which I walked, did not appear disordered or chaotic. On the contrary. People moved purposefully to and fro, there were no beggars, except an old Russian man at the entrance to the subway; stores were open, traffic moved briskly. On the surface, the symbols of the socialist republic had been efficiently and easily replaced by those of an independent nationalist state. The Lenin Museum was now the National History Museum. The statue of Karl Marx, which had dominated the great park beneath my window on the eighth floor of the Uzbekistan Hotel, had been replaced by one of Amr Timur, Uncle Tamerlane, reviled earlier as a cruel feudal despot, now lionized as the great-great-grandfather of modern Uzbekistan.

But as the days passed, I felt that, not surprisingly, the country was experiencing problems as it shifted from central planning to a form of capitalism. How did I know?

My breakfast in the Uzbekistan Hotel, for example. Guests were offered a choice of thin rice porridge (not bad), or brown bread (stale), with a curl of butter (rarely) and a small spoonful of prune jam on a tiny white saucer. The coffee varied from brown water to a reasonable brew to nothing at all. For several days there was no sugar.

And one morning, seeing a Japanese guest served two boiled eggs, I pointed and asked for some.

The waitress shook her head no.

I pointed again to the Japanese gentleman, who was happily dipping his stale brown bread into the runny egg yolk. It looked scrumptious. "Two!" I said, holding up two fingers. "He had two!" She shook her head again and when I refused to be mollified, called the headwaiter, a white-shirted gentleman whose black trousers were much too tight around his bulging waistline.

"No egg more, madame," he said in heavily accented English. "Yes, maybe tomorrow?" He smiled, showing bad teeth.

I subsided, thinking that I would get down earlier tomorrow, before the eggs were gone. Perhaps I was focusing too much on relatively trivial details and failing to see the big picture. But the big picture also had problems.

Roberta's and Michael's description of the currency crisis several months earlier was an ominous sign of trouble brewing on a national scale, and I began to think that the complications of the national scenario were reflected in everyday life at the Uzbekistan Hotel. For the hotel, according to the 1993 Cadogan guide to Central Asia, was, "At $120. per night for a double room, the best in the country and the second most expensive in Central Asia." And there was no sugar for coffee? Clearly something was not working. Further, a good barometer of inflation was the actual cost of my room, not $120 per night as in 1993, but $55 per night in 1994. In one year, the value of the dollar had more than doubled. And the Uzbek *som* had accordingly fallen.

My room was adequate, though small, but, as Roberta pointed out, "no one would steal the towels." They were faded and worn. But clean. The bathroom was also clean, though old and scarred by use. But it seemed I was fortunate to have found a berth, albeit small, in the Uzbekistan Hotel. Hotel rooms were scarce, and housing was at a premium in Tashkent, as many Uzbeks were moving from country to city, in search of employment in the new industries the government had promised. Roberta said she felt lucky to be sharing a sublet apartment with Michael and his wife Monica. And she pointed out that the thin rice porridge and stale bread I found less than palatable at the hotel might be viewed as luxuries by poor people in both country and the city.

I vowed to myself I would stop complaining, and offered to cook dinner at the apartment—mushrooms with potatoes and eggs. The meat was said to be not only horribly expensive but horribly tough.

My culinary skills had, it seemed, been touted to Michael and Monica, and Michael produced a bottle of Russian champagne to drink with our meal; it was inexpensive and quite good. I unwrapped dessert—four oranges in tattered newspaper, purchased on the street, out of sight of Roberta and Michael, who had insisted they were too expensive at one dollar each.

In the pleasant aura following the oranges and champagne, Monica decided to take me on ideologically.

"So just how would you define a feminist, B.J.?"

I took her seriously, and tried to talk about equality, and choice, and opportunity.

"Well," said Monica crisply. "They all say they have that here, but they don't."

Michael interposed, "Well, at least we do, my dear. We do the laundry and shopping together. Equal rights."

"Oh, Michael, come on. I mean, Uzbek women. They just stay home. They never go out. If you look at them on the street, they have this cowed look."

"Tell me more," I urged. "What about some of the women you know, for example?"

Monica did not respond. Roberta said, in the silence, "It's hard to meet Uzbek women—and men. . . ." Then, gathering herself together, she asked Michael to accompany us back to my hotel.

"No, really, don't bother, I'll take a taxi."

"Not safe," asserted Michael, putting on his coat. "Really, B.J., not safe."

Monica came to life. "In this feminist country women are not safe? Not really!"

"Not safe for men or women alone after dark," answered Michael gently.

"Especially," added Roberta, winding a scarf around her neck, "people like us, who look like rich foreigners." Economic uncertainty. Political jockeying. Social confusion, in this new nation which only became independent in 1991.

How was I going to learn about Uzbek women if they were so hard to meet? "Don't worry, B.J., I have made you some appointments," said Roberta. "But first we must observe International Women's Day."

The next day we did so, beginning with television. The new Uzbek television corporation presented special programs, including interviews with Uzbek women from city and country. The President of the

republic spoke about the crucial role of women in national development. Husbands were urged to take flowers to their wives as a sign of
love and respect. The State Women's Committee, appointed by the
President, appeared on a talk show, well dressed and coiffed, to discuss
the fortunate situation of Uzbek women. According to the members
of the committee, all Uzbek women were happy and contented. No,
they said in answer to a question from a woman in the studio audience,
Uzbek women did not need help from Western women, and particularly not Western women who called themselves feminists. Feminism,
said one of the ladies with a toss of her smooth head, was unnecessary
here (Roberta was translating this loosely as it appeared on the screen).
Feminism, she said, in the way Westerners define it, is seen here as very
bourgeois; Uzbek women have gone far beyond feminism. The nation
has wonderful laws for women, equal pay for equal work, equal education, equal health care, equal access to divorce. "Uzbek women are far
luckier than Western women," concluded the spokesperson for the
group, a large lady in a beautiful mauve suit and fashionable shiny
black pumps. The audience burst into applause.

Monica laughed derisively. "Yeah, sure," she commented, and
turned off the television.

"Is that all true?" I inquired.

"Well, in some ways it is," temporized Roberta.

Monica frowned. "Roberta, you are being brainwashed here by
your Uzbek nationalist friends. Don't listen to her, B.J."

Roberta did not reply. She stood up and reached for her coat and
her flowered shawl. "Let's go. It's late," she pointed out. I had
bought us all tickets for the special Women's Day Concert at the
Alisher Navoi Theater, which was set for four o'clock. "Come on,
Monica."

The theater is named for the writer Alisher Navoi, who lived in the
fifteenth century and is considered the father of Uzbek literature. It
appears that the Soviets attempted, in this theater, to create a monument which would serve as a bridge between the heritage of Muslim
Uzbekistan and the new goals of the Soviet Uzbek republic. The
building does indeed incorporate elements of functional worker-type
architecture: square no-nonsense lines, a useful colonnaded facade
where theater-goers may purchase tickets at the box office, out of
wind, rain, and snow. But Muslim-style stalactites top the roof and
beautiful tiles border the building, spelling out slogans from Leninist
works, rather than verses from the Qur'an, as is usual in such mosaic
decoration.

An American critic named Arthur Sprague is said to have described this theater as combining elements of a small-town American bank with the excesses of a frivolous Muslim East. Since the architect is the same Russian who designed the Lubianka Prison and Lenin's Mausoleum, the American's reaction to the Alisher Navoi Theater may be understood as cultural bitterness. But for the crowds who pushed into the theater for International Women's Day, these architectural elements were less important than the comfortable crimson plush seats, the well-lighted ample stage, and the admirable central heating.

The concert, like the theater itself, proved to be a strange mélange of East and West: tenors and sopranos singing arias from *Carmen* and Italian romantic tunes like *"O Sole Mio."* Classical ballet pas de deux à la Bolshoi were interspersed with Uzbek folk dances. But the audience loved it all, including the speeches marking the day dedicated to women, and the encores provided after thunderous applause. The socialist commitment to art as expression of a people came through in the high quality of the performance, the talent of the singers and dancers, the lighting, the settings, and the costumes.

It was clearly an occasion. The women had shed their dark and serviceable coats at the cloakroom and emerged in bright dresses: violet, green, scarlet, as well as trusty black, decked with colorful scarves, fur stoles, jeweled belts. And the price of admission was well within the range of people's pocketbooks, said Roberta. All four of the tickets I purchased cost less than a single orange.

"Not bad," Monica admitted. "I enjoyed it. Thanks, B.J."

The official buildings which dominate the city of Tashkent, Uzbekistan's capital, speak not of its culturally diverse past but of one influence, and one only: Russian, the Soviet socialist variety of functionalism.

"They used the 1966 earthquake as an excuse to get rid of all Uzbek structures," said Ergash Orimer bitterly; as an Uzbek historian and linguist, he had been working with the exchange students and he offered to take me on a tour of his city. Roberta and Michael came, too.

A man in his sixties, Orimer wore a worn navy blazer and a smart gray fedora on his head, a head which bulged oddly on one side. I inquired about his wife, but Roberta did not translate my question. "He is very traditional," she said. "His wife stays at home."

"So Monica is right about Uzbek women being suppressed?"

"Well, yes and no," temporized Roberta and hurried to catch up with Orimer, who was leading us through a crumbling ruin of mosque and *madrasahs*, or schools called the Bokhara complex. He was very proud, obviously, that the complex was being renovated by the new government. He indicated the small part of the school which was already in use, where white banners bearing Qur'anic suras in green script, fluttered in the garden.

I asked what kind of religious instruction was involved and in what language. Ergash explained that the curriculum was standard, with one course in religion added.

"We have fallen behind," he said, "in our tradition, in our knowledge. We've been living in concentration camps for so many years, practicing our traditions in secret. Everything was in Russian, all business, now we must relearn the language of our grandfathers—Uzbek—and of our religion—Arabic."

"What about traditions related to women?"

Ergash looked at me, amazement showing in his eyes. "They are fine, women," he said. "Islam provides good rights for women. Thus we do, too. It is religious practice and language where we are behind."

We walked together over the broken cobbles of what must have been a wide avenue between the ancient buildings, leaving behind the little school with its white and green banners.

"You see, madame," Ergash said, "we will work with other Muslim countries to restore our heritage. President Mubarak of Egypt has offered a hundred scholarships to Uzbeks who wish to study at Al-Azhar."

Roberta pointed out that Ergash was fasting. He was the only Uzbek I met during my entire stay who was faithfully observing Ramadan, the religious month of fast.

"And your wife?" I persisted.

"She fasts at home," he answered shortly. "Now we will go to the market. For I must buy the food for our family's meal when we break the fast. My wife does not go out for this purpose. It is my job. It is men who cook the meat."

"What?"

Roberta smiled. "I'll explain later, B.J."

And that, it seemed, was the end of the conversation. We were in the great market, built by the Russians to bring "order" out of the "chaos" of the old-fashioned bazaar that had served Tashkent traders and buyers from all over Asia for hundreds of years.

"Order" meant clearing out the itinerant peddlers and constructing a four-story cement building, with areas assigned to specific merchants: meat, vegetables, fruits, dairy. But despite the strict assignments of space, the small traders still sat or stood outside the cement market: women with a few vegetables piled on a small piece of flowered cloth; men wheeling carts of sundries like ribbons, buttons, hair bows, batteries, cigarettes. The peddlers were illegal, it seemed, and dashed away when the market police appeared on their regular inspection tours, only to return an hour or two after the police had departed.

Ergash was instructing the butcher exactly how to cut up the chunk of lamb he had purchased. We waited and followed him along to the displays of smoked and dried fish.

Ergash paused. "We don't buy fish," said Roberta.

"Why not?"

"Remember Chernobyl?"

"Yes, of course."

"Many people have strange skin conditions and growths," said Roberta. Her eyes, like mine, were inadvertently drawn to the lump under Ergash's smart fedora. "And scientists think it comes from left-over fallout. Fish swim in the rivers and their flesh is very porous." She sighed, and looked down to avoid staring at poor Ergash, who was talking to the fishmonger. "I used to love this fish."

Ergash shook our hands. "I leave you here, Madame le Professor," he said, smiling. "Be good to Roberta. She is a hard worker." He winked and Roberta smiled. "My wife awaits me, and I must cook the meat."

We were left to wander through the rest of the market, past the dairy section where slabs of butter the size of small television sets were guarded by old women, knitting furiously and seeming uninterested in purveying their goods. Other old women hovered over clay pots of sour cream, yogurt, honey, sat by bricks of white cheese, offered us baskets of what looked like bonbons but turned out to be dried yogurt balls, ready to pop in one's mouth on the spot (I decline after a whiff!) or take home to reconstitute with water.

"Is it like the markets in other Islamic countries where you've lived, B.J.?"

"Yes, in the sense that the Russian colonialists have tried to organize and control the market." I remembered the French organizing central markets in Marrakech and Casablanca, in Cairo. "But what they're selling is so different."

"How?"

"Well, lots of preserved things, like that," and I pointed to the jars of cherries, peaches, figs, walnuts even. "And some of these vegetables I've never seen before in my life. The fresh fruits look good, too."

"But it all costs a lot," Roberta said shortly. We passed a section of what appeared to be salads, of carrots and eggplant presided over by oriental matrons, their heads bound up in scarves. "They're Korean."

"Korean."

"Yes," said Roberta. "The market reflects history, but the Korean market is a sad history. These are the people that the Russians forcibly removed from the eastern borders, in case they might rebel against Soviet rule. They've been making salads like this for years and now people think of it as native Uzbek food."

We headed away from the market to meet Vera, Roberta's young scientist friend, who, she said, would explain to me the real situation of Uzbek women.

"Is she a feminist?" I asked.

"Wait and see," Roberta answered. "We'll take the subway, okay?"

I replied that I was happy to take the subway, the only one in all of Central Asia. Uzbeks had already told me many subway legends and stories, most of them true, according to Roberta. The central myth concerned the patriotic heart of Comrade Sharaf Rashidov, the Uzbek-born Soviet-appointed ruler of Uzbekistan in the thirties and forties. Each year, instead of sending Moscow all the revenues from the bountiful Uzbek cotton harvest, he held back a portion. Year after year he salted away these ill-gotten gains, and eventually had enough to build the Tashkent subway.

The subway, then, was seen as the triumphal utilization of bad money for good ends, and Roberta and I had been traveling on it regularly, for it was clean, cheap, and ran on time. Further, each station offered an artistic memorial to significant events in the long history of Uzbekistan. Independence Station was the newest and brightest, lit by great cut-glass chandeliers, like a Paris ballroom. At the People's Friendship Station, seals of all the former Soviet Socialist Republics had been fashioned out of metal, enameled, and set into the walls of the station, occupying spaces that in the London and New York subways were given over to advertising. And then there was Roberta's favorite, Petacor, or Cotton Picker, celebrating Uzbekistan's place as the world's fourth-largest producer of cotton. Mosaic tiles formed giant stylized cotton blossoms—blue, for the sky, explained Roberta, yellow for the sun, and white for the cotton blossom itself.

We got off to meet Vera at the most dramatic of all the subway stations, Cosmonaut, dedicated to the conquest of space. As we left the train, we emerged into an atmosphere of subdued light reflected from the dark luminescent green walls. Stone faces loomed out of the semidarkness, silver and black, remarkable lifelike portraits of past and current scientists. I felt I could be at the bottom of the sea, or in the dark of unknown space, viewing the surfaces of alien planets, glimpsing the lights of distant moons and dim stars.

"Hello! Hello!" A small figure in dark jeans and a purple quilted parka bobbed up beside us on the subway platform. "Here you are, Roberta! How do you do, B.J.?"

Vera. She smiled, a cheerful smile, showing two gold teeth. Her hair was short and black, her eyes almond-shaped.

"So you're the scientist?" I said nonsensically. Could this small, cheery creature in her purple parka really be the scientist Roberta had described? A microbiologist, specializing in the venom of spiders, with several published papers to her credit, who held a full-time research position at the National Research Institute.

Vera smiled again. "That's me."

"And you are a feminist?"

Vera looked serious. She wrinkled up her almond eyes. "A feminist? No." She shook her head. "I don't think so. No need."

"No need?"

"Well, I'm paid the same as men in my same job," she pointed out. "And my husband Saidollah is very good to help with the children, they call this something in America, Roberta?"

Roberta looked at her questioningly.

"Sharing the work between a man and a woman?"

Roberta smiled too. "Ah yes. Division of labor."

"Like Marx said," smiled Vera happily. "Well, every woman is like this. Everyone must work, help each other." This seemed to confirm the account of my earlier traveling companions, and even the ladies of the State Women's Committee: Uzbek women had equal rights. So was this what I should write about, and forget Monica's doubts?

But then there was the case of Valentina V. Tareshkova, the first Russian woman cosmonaut, the first woman in space, and a scientist in her own right. She was memorialized in the Cosmonaut Station. We walked along, while waiting for our train, looking at the portraits of scientists who prepared the way for the leap into space: people like the philosopher Avicenna of Bukhara, and Ulu Beg, the fifteenth-century Uzbek astronomer. At the very end was Valentina, carved, like the other scientists, in high relief, lighted from behind to shimmer toward us, as if emerging from the sea.

"Now what about that?" I asked, pointing to Valentina.

"Well, she is a great scientist. She is a woman. Be happy!"

What seemed curious to me, I said to Vera, was that the scientists were depicted with their books, their tools, their astrolabes and compasses. Except Valentina. Valentina was holding a bouquet of white flowers. Flowers!

"Yes, yes," said Vera. She smiled, humoring me. "You are always looking for the mistake in us. I think you Americans do that. But why not look for something that is not a mistake?"

The train had still not arrived, and Vera walked us along the platform to a portrait that was not of any specific person: it was a human face, of androgynous cast, surrounded by numbers and abstract images.

I stood before it, puzzled.

"This is, do you think maybe," said Vera in her soft voice, "the human mind? All men and all women. The same. They have the same . . ."—she gropes for a word—"idea, imagination?"

Roberta nodded. "But I still wonder, Vera," she said, "and probably B.J. does too, why give Valentina the flowers rather than a compass or a book?"

Vera just laughed, a light musical laugh, as befitted such a small, winsome person.

"Who knows?" she replied airily. "We look at Valentina and at this imagination, and we . . . hope in the future?"

"What do you think, B.J.?" she asked me as we boarded the subway together.

In Marx Square, we all alighted once more and headed up the steps toward the Uzbekistan Hotel, walking along the broad avenue beside the park. My questions, Monica's doubts, and Vera's answers returned to me. The women here did not look downtrodden or cowed, at least no more so than the men. True, they did not seem to smile or laugh much; they seemed essentially businesslike, adequately dressed in sober warm clothing designed to ward off the last chill of winter. No veils. Only occasionally did a woman pass us wearing a head scarf that Roberta identified as truly "Uzbek"; a square of bright stripes, reds and green and blues, shot through with silver threads which glinted in the weak sunlight. But no veils. Hats, yes, to keep out the cold wind. I wore one myself.

"You see, B.J., everybody works here," Vera went on. "Men. Women. We have to. No other way to live. Yes, Roberta?"

Roberta nodded agreement.

"But who takes care of the children?" I asked.

"The state of course. From one year. It is good care."

"How much does it cost?"

"Cost?" Vera looked surprised. "No cost. How could there be cost?

Government says we must work, so they must help with children. Of course."

Roberta looked at me and smiled broadly. "Try that one on at home," she said.

Vera looked questioning, and Roberta tried to explain to her about the high cost of day care in the United States. Vera didn't believe it.

"In America? The rich country? Not possible. Why don't women stand up for their rights?"

Why not indeed? Good question. Over to you, Vera.

When we were both silent, Vera relented a little.

"Well, when children are in school, it is harder here."

"How?"

"We must be there when they come home." She sighed. "We can't. Saidollah and I both are in the lab all day. So . . ."

"So what do you do?"

"We brought my cousin from the village to live with us. She goes to school and helps. Many people do this."

"What if you had another baby?"

Vera set her mouth in a firm line. "No more children," she said. "Not possible."

"But what if you get pregnant?"

"Abortion. Abortion is free. Everybody does it."

I could think of nothing to reply.

At the hotel, we sat and had coffee. Vera smiled and rose. "We will invite you soon," she said. "My husband Saidollah will make *osh,* our national dish."

Roberta explained that men always make the *osh.*

Vera smiled. "Saidollah makes very good *osh.* . . . You will see."

Curiouser and curiouser. The men cooked, the state provided free child and health care, the women got abortions on demand. Men and women worked side by side. So there must not be any card-carrying feminists for me to interview, let alone Muslim feminists.

"Oh yes there are," smiled Roberta. "I am making you some more appointments."

The Flame is the title of a shocking documentary film about Uzbek women setting themselves on fire, either committing suicide or maiming themselves in a horrible way. Some Western commentators have suggested that the women are immolating themselves because the new national Uzbek government, turning to Islamic practice after half a century of Soviet secular domination, is forcing them to wear the traditional veil once more. Therefore, the self-immolation is seen as a feminist act against patriarchy. Hedrick Smith, the Pulitzer Prize–winning journalist, offers another explanation in his book *The New Russians*. Women, he states, are given tough jobs with long hours and poor wages. Self-immolation is their form of protest against forced labor. But what a terrible form of protest, harming the protestors more than those being protested against!

I hoped to meet and interview the filmmakers, the Uzbek husband-and-wife team of Razika and Shukhrat Makhmudov, and ask them what they thought about the awful phenomenon they had filmed, whether they saw this self-immolation as political, social, or religious protest. Was it really a statement against new Islamic oppression of women, or was it some other kind of symbolic act, like the Buddhist monks burning themselves alive in South Asia to protest the Vietnam War? For I could find nothing in the writings or the practice of Islam to condone such a self-destructive act.

The Makhmudovs, it turned out, were famous in Tashkent, well known to Roberta's friend Ikram, who had worked for the BBC when British producers came looking for stories. *The Flame* was clearly a story. The Makhmudovs sent word that they would be happy to meet me and show the film at their home.

English speakers are at a premium in the new Uzbekistan, and I was fortunate to have four translators with me that day. Roberta, Ikram, and Michael and Monica, who wanted to meet the Makhmudovs and had asked to accompany us to the meeting.

Tashkent was still very cold. It was late March and warmer weather was forecast, but the trees in Amr Tamerlane square outside the hotel were still bare and black; people continued to bundle up on the street and in the subway. I donned all the layers I had: turtleneck over trusty long underwear; then a blouse, a sweater, skirt and jacket, and my raincoat with its zip-in lining. Roberta, Michael, and Monica were similarly bundled and layered, but Ikram seemed indifferent to the cold, and wore only a thin coat over his turtleneck and trousers. Later, I had to silently applaud Ikram as I spent several embarrassing moments unwrapping myself after we had climbed the twelve flights of stairs to the centrally heated Makhmudov apartment. Roberta, Monica, and Michael were in the same predicament. But how could we know that the Makhmudovs not only had central heating but comfortable antique furniture, fine old Bokhara rugs, and a magnificent view of the city of Tashkent.

Mr. Makhmudov offered us biscuits and small dishes of almonds while his wife poured tea from a gleaming samovar. They appeared to be energetic, lively, middle-aged, and charming, though of course I could not understand a single word they said.

I was introduced as an American feminist filmmaker who had produced documentaries about Middle Eastern women. Mrs. Makhmudov looked at me, spoke to her husband, and they both laughed.

"What did she say?" I asked.

Michael smiled, a bit embarrassed. "She said you don't look like an American filmmaker."

The Makhmudovs both wore dark corduroy pants and turtlenecks. My gray flannel suit and earrings were perhaps too formal? Too grandmotherly? I considered a reply.

"Revolutionaries only wear pants?" I ventured.

When this was translated, they both laughed again. "No, no, but the only ones we see in the movies don't look like you."

Mrs. Makhmudov asked about my Egyptian film, *A Veiled Revolution*. I told her a bit about the situation in Egypt, but this was not why we had come.

"I have heard about *your* films," I said, "and would very much like to see them."

He nodded. "Only *The Flame*, I presume. That's all the Western visitors want to see, something horrible about women."

No, no, I protested, and explained that I was always looking for documentaries to be shown in the United States. "I'd like to see several."

The two consulted. Mrs. Makhmudov poured us some tea. Wonderful tea that seeped into my bones. Mr. Makhmudov produced several videos. While he was inserting the first, *A Sufi Saint*, into the machine, I turned to look out the wide windows against which we were sitting. The view was worth that twelve-story climb; the city spread out before us, in its carefully planned panorama of squares and parks and public buildings. But unfortunately what dominated the view was not so splendid: row after row of cement-block, utilitarian apartment houses, now aging, the bright paint on their decorative cement tracery flaking away, spotted with mildew. In the distance, a few trees raised bare branches beside the boulevards where Roberta and I had walked along the old Silk Route from China, which in the past had perambulated across Central Asia, toward Istanbul, Baghdad, Damascus.

The Flame, which was shown next, was ninety minutes long, and was horrendous. We all sat, silent and mesmerized in the warm room, but by the time the credits rolled, I felt I knew no more about the issue than I had when I came through the Makhmudovs' double mahogany door.

It was a good documentary, well shot and edited, as one might expect from two honor graduates of the Moscow Film Institute. Fine footage of women working in the fields, in the factories, wearing head scarves, but no veils. The filmmakers interviewed women who tried to commit suicide but failed, interviewed doctors who treated the terrible burns of the women who had survived.

Newspaper reports flashed on the screen told the audience that 364 cases of women immolating or trying to immolate themselves were reported in a six-month period during 1988 and 1989. But nothing in particular was happening then, said the Makhmudovs. The independence of Uzbekistan was not declared until 1991. Islam was not mentioned once. Nor was forced labor. "When a woman dies like this, part of the country dies," said a doctor, toward the end of the film. Everyone agreed.

"So why are they doing this? And are they still doing it?" I asked.

"No, as far as we know, they're not."

"So why then?"

"You have to listen to what the women say in the interviews," said Mrs. Makhmudov gently.

I had. Perhaps the translation was faulty, but I didn't think so. Ikram and Michael and Monica and Roberta had all been listening, carefully translating, sometimes correcting each other.

I thought back to what had actually been said. The interviewer (Mrs. Makhmudov) asked several questions. Did the woman want a divorce and was she unable to get one? No. Need an abortion and husband refused? No. Husband beating her? No. Why then? Depressed, said one. Kidney problems that wouldn't go away, said another. Just felt bad, said a third. Tired of working so hard, said a fourth.

The women interviewed certainly did not look rich and contented, like the ladies of the State Women's Committee who had appeared on television on International Women's Day. These women came from villages and small towns, not from the big cities. They worked hard in factories and in the fields, and they looked older than their years. No nice potent American vitamins and estrogen for them.

But if one is poor and depressed, does one expose oneself to terrible pain by setting fire to oneself?

I posed this to the Makhmudovs. They looked at each other and shook their heads.

"Maybe it's—something here, in this country?" I asked.

"They think it might be cultural." Michael translated the answers. "They say there might be some traditional pattern associated with fire that comes to these women's minds when they are depressed and contemplating suicide."

"Do the Makhmudovs really think that?"

A long discussion ensued in Russian and Uzbek among Michael, Roberta, and the Makhmudovs. Ikram sat on the floor and kept objecting, first quietly, then louder.

"Ikram?" I queried.

"I do not agree with them, B.J. I don't think it is in our hearts here. Who would be so cruel?"

"What about suttee?" I asked. Ikram looked bewildered. I explained the old Indian tradition of the widow throwing herself onto the burning pyre of her dead husband. I had heard this custom defended as both traditional and appropriate, since there is no structural place in Hindu society for a widow.

Both Makhmudovs listened in amazement when this was translated.

"India is *not* our spiritual ancestor," said Mrs. Makhmudov forcefully. "Maybe it is severe depression or despair?" she said, through Michael. "We are not sure."

I could think of nothing to reply. Despair, certainly. But what a terrible response to that despair. I turned, fidgeting in the uncomfortable silence and saw that night had fallen. The view behind me had become a dark plain, punctuated only occasionally with points of light. It was time to leave. The five of us donned coats, scarves, and hats, thanked our hosts, and made our way slowly down the twelve flights of stairs, guiding ourselves by holding onto the wall and each other, as the landing lights were burned out.

"So what is *The Flame* about, then?" asked Monica. "I thought it was all about women's oppression or Islam forcing them to veil or something. Now everyone says it's not. What would a feminist say, B.J.?"

"Things are different here than in America."

"But that's no excuse. That cultural difference business. Oppression is oppression."

"They're doing it to themselves, though," observed Ikram, in his slow, heavily accented English, "are they not, Monica?"

"Oh, Ikram," answered Monica, "don't be silly. They are clearly pressured to do it by something outside—like men."

"Are they really?" Michael queried.

"Michael, don't get me started all over again."

Roberta, always the mediator, interrupted.

"I'm hungry," she announced. "They only gave us nuts and tea."

"Dinner's on me," I put in heartily, "with thanks for all your good translations."

"So you have figured out the answer to these women's problems, B.J.?" asked Ikram.

I shook my head. "No, Ikram, I haven't."

We ended up on the top floor of the Uzbekistan Hotel, where a Japanese restaurant was advertised, "with entertainment by lovely Japanese ladies. Payment in dollars only."

We ate reasonably good and very expensive Japanese food, presented in exceedingly small portions. Ikram seemed puzzled by the contents of the sushi. So was I. Could it be the rice porridge from breakfast recycled with a parsley wreath? But none of us were puzzled about the nature of the entertainment, a procession of erotic Japanese dancers. As one small plump woman gyrated on the circular stage, moving a red balloon from one naked breast to the other and then down to her waist, Michael laughed aloud.

"You think they're feminists, Monica?"

Monica looked furious. "Don't say anything more, Michael!"

But I could not resist. "Well, they're clearly enjoying themselves, so maybe they are a special kind of Japanese feminist."

Roberta swallowed a giggle.

Perhaps we were all upset by our day watching women burning in *The Flame*.

Marfua Tokhtakhodzhaera is a self-declared radical feminist. She had published some articles in the West and I was anxious to meet her. Roberta and I set off for our appointment at the Institute for Restoration of Cultural Monuments, where Marfua worked as an architect. We took the subway to Petacor Station and then walked for a quarter of an hour past various empty lots, clean of debris; here socialist discipline seemed still to be in force. Along Alisher Navoi Street, named, like the theater, after the father of Uzbek literature, official-looking dun-colored buildings were interspersed with small bright shops, offering new services like copy and fax machines, and cellular phones. Abai Street, named after a twentieth-century Uzbek writer, led us to the institute itself, another official-looking dun-colored building set in a garden which boasted, in the rear, the beautiful blue-domed fifteenth-century mausoleum of Yunus Khan.

Three flights up was the office where we found Marfua poring over architectural plans on a drafting table set under the window. She came forward to greet us and introduced her assistant, a young dark-haired woman named Fatima, in a black skirt and long-sleeved sweater. A *sotto voce* word from Marfua, clearly the mentor, led to Fatima's excusing herself. I heard the word "tea" exchanged.

"This is my current project, very exciting," said Marfua, indicating the plans and watercolors on the table. "We are restoring the garden near Samarkand which surrounds the mausoleum of our national hero, Tamerlane. Very exciting," she repeated, and her eyes sparkled as she thumped the table gently. She obviously enjoyed her work, this tall, imposing woman, not too young, her dark hair stylishly cut, wearing fine black wool trousers and a matching tunic decorated around the neck with a gold thread in a pattern of small flowers.

She looked me up and down, and I felt somewhat dowdy in my raincoat and dark suit, which had the virtue of helping me melt into the sober Uzbek crowd but was not much of a walking advertisement for Western elegance.

"Do you know Fatima Mernissi, the Moroccan feminist?" she asked immediately.

I nodded, and she rushed on. "I met her at a feminist conference in Lahore, Pakistan, about women's crises. My clothes are from there, a present, aren't they beautiful?"

We agreed. Roberta then explained what I was doing. "My professor hopes to write about possibilities for Islamic feminism."

A short laugh from Marfua. "Not possible. Not possible," she repeated. "Not here. No."

"Why?" I asked. "Does Islam not allow it?"

Marfua shook her head in irritation. "This is not an Islamic country, madame."

"It's not?"

"In name perhaps, but Islam is not known or practiced here for many years. We are a secular country really." She paused. "You should write about secular feminism, isn't that what you have in the United States? How our secular feminism articulates with yours? What is this Western fascination with *Islamic* issues? Are they afraid of us? Poor us?" She laughed a little.

Fatima reentered, bringing a tray of tea and biscuits.

"Fatima is my assistant," explained Marfua. "I am training her. These days there is no money to study abroad. I was lucky enough to do graduate work in Moscow and then spend a month interning with an architectural firm in Boston. So you see I have Boston English."

She smiled engagingly. Her English was very good indeed. So was the tea. Fatima left us and I took a second cup of tea. The slices of lemon were paper-thin, the sugar coarse and gray, but the cups and saucers were of very thin, old bone china.

I decided to open the interview with a provocative question, since Marfua was clearly up to it. "Would you say then that there are no problems for women here?"

Marfua paused, her teacup in midair. "Let me begin in another way to answer your question," she said. "You do not know much about Uzbekistan, but your friend Roberta does. This society is in a difficult period, a period of transition, and this makes it difficult for both men and women."

Where was she heading? She drank her tea, set the cup down in its beautiful saucer.

"Furthermore, as a new republic," she continued, "the leaders of the country want to put a good face on everything. So of course there are no problems."

She smiled delightedly and looked to me for assurance. I looked at Roberta, who looked doubtful.

"No problems," I repeated.

"No problems," Marfua stated again, "or at least, my American friend, this is the image they wish to purvey to the wider international society. They say, and many ladies of Uzbekistan with so-called feminist tendencies will say, that we have everything we need. We don't need help."

"Yes," put in Roberta, "they always refuse help. The cultural attaché at the United States embassy asked whether there were any books the universities needed. The answer was no, we have everything we need."

I took a deep breath, and tried to change the direction of what seemed to be turning into a lecture. But then, I asked myself, why shouldn't Marfua lecture me, an arrogant American imperialist feminist who knew nothing about the country but felt impelled to criticize it. I told myself I just wanted to learn. Without realizing it, I found I had said just that.

"Yes, yes," said Marfua, kindly, but a bit impatiently, "I realize that you just want to learn. That's what all Westerners say. And what is your next question?"

"The laws, what about the laws? Everyone tells me that the laws are great, giving equal rights to men and women. Is that really true?"

Marfua waved a graceful hand. Her cheekbones were high, her skin was ivory; she had wide eyes. A good-looking woman. "Do you have children?" I suddenly found myself bursting out.

"Yes, I have one daughter. I am divorced. I support my aged mother and my daughter. And you?"

"Three, all grown. One grandchild," I added proudly. "So my husband and I are grandparents!"

She peered at me, then said, in what she meant I'm sure to be an admiring tone, but it came out patronizingly, "You seem to look quite well for a grandmother." She paused. "Ah, America! Wonderful food. Vitamins. Good for health and appearance." She smiled. It was a genuine smile and I smiled back. "We would all like what you have in America . . ." she said, adding mischievously, "But not your laws about women and men. We prefer ours."

"Are they really that equal?" Roberta interposed.

"Yes, yes, they are wonderful—yes. That is true. But the law is one thing, dear friends, and what happens every day to people is something else."

"Such as?"

"Just what I've been saying to you, my dear. Health issues. Poverty. Family violence. Men want women to stay at home, but of course they can't. Difficult. Yes. Times are getting strange. We don't know what will happen with education, with wages."

"What about religion? Will that create difficulties?"

"Perhaps. But that is not the real problem."

"What is? What is the real problem?" I persisted.

Marfua was silent. The light was fading outside her office window, the gray sky blurring into the gray landscape, and dimming the branches of leafless trees. Our tea was cold. She moved over to the crowded bookcase. "I am trying to find some of my articles to give you," she said, pulling out a folio. "Maybe dear Roberta can translate—some in Russian, some in Uzbek."

"Thank you."

"And I have written a book they wish to publish in the West. Would you perhaps carry it out for me? It is called *Daughters of the Amazons.*"

"Yes, of course. I'd be glad to."

Daughters of the Amazons, I thought. Good title.

"We have a great heritage," said Marfua. "We are strong women here. We must fight against people who wish to reduce us to mere mothers. Women are more than mothers . . ."

"Of course," said Roberta, "we'd agree, wouldn't we, B.J.? Women are people, too."

"The self. The self, that's it, what is needed, a sense of self," said Marfua.

Roberta said we should go, and I rose.

"Thank you," I said, and offered my hand. "If you want to give me the manuscript now . . ."

"No, I will bring it to the hotel next week. I must copy it some-where. All the copy machines are broken down and no parts to fix them. Of course we need things!" Marfua's voice rose, then she re-laxed and shook hands good-bye.

At the stairwell, she stopped us.

"I have not answered your question," she said to me. "I have been thinking. What is the real problem for women? What can feminism do? What can I do? I don't know. The problem for women and men is very complicated, it has many sides. Things are changing fast here. You can see that, even as a tourist. Yes, Roberta wants to get going before dark. Five years ago we wouldn't have worried—everyone safe under iron-fist socialism—everything except what—choice? Self? Perhaps that is what I wish to stress to you both for us here in Uzbekistan and for feminists in America. The self. We are *more* than wives and mothers, yes? Yes. It is the self that is the issue. We must learn to nourish the *self.*"

Marfua shook her head. "But it's hard—for us and for you, too, I think, even with all your Western affluence and ideas about equality."

We had already started down the stairs before she added, "Do come back. Come back and see me before you go home to your wonderful America."

Samarkand

Samarkand. Bokhara. Legendary cities of song and story, out of bounds to Western travelers during most of my lifetime. Alexander the Great visited Samarkand in the fourth century B.C. and rhapsodized, "Everything I have heard about the beauty of Samarkand is true, except that it is even more beautiful than I could have imagined."

Two thousand years later, Fitzroy MacLean echoed Alexander's praise, singling out the "tiles, of vivid blue and deep turquoise, alabas-ter . . . jasper . . . courtyards and gardens, great heaps of fruit in the bazaars."

I had never dreamed I would get to Samarkand and Bokhara but here I was, en route, thanks to the National Institute of Arts and Literature of Uzbekistan. Both Marfua and the Makhmudovs had urged me to explore the differences between women's lives in Tash-kent and in other parts of Uzbekistan. Roberta and Vera had come along to help me look for ancient magic and new freedoms.

I was not traveling by camel or elephant, it was true, but I was on my way, at least that was what I was told, on a knockabout, crowded, tired old bus with hard wooden seats that seemed to stop at every lamppost and cluster of houses. The milk run on the road to Samarkand. As people got off or on, Roberta, Vera, and I finally managed to maneuver ourselves into neighboring seats. This was useful so they could interpret for me, in case I missed an important request like "Please get up, madame, so I can get out of this bus!"

The landscape did not whiz by, we were traveling so slowly, so there was plenty of time to eye the clusters of row houses along the highway which seemed to be a principal feature of the scenery. Identical gray one-story structures, they were "collective farms," said Vera. Occasionally one could see beyond the houses to barns and poultry sheds, to muddy enclosures housing a cow or a donkey. I wondered about farm women, collective-farm women. "We will ask," promised Roberta.

Creaking purposefully if jerkily along, the bus passed rows and rows of leafless trees, some recognizable even to me as apples or almonds or apricots, but the most common I did not recognize at all. Small, stunted, set in ditches slightly below the level of the road, these trees had been pruned ruthlessly into the shapes of fans.

"Mulberry trees," whispered Roberta across the aisle. "Silk, B.J.!"

Ah yes. Mulberry trees. Grade school geography class came back to me, my wonderful sixth-grade teacher, Miss Forster, showing us pictures of pale, rather disgusting-looking worms.

"They're silk worms, class," chirped Miss Forster. She explained that the worms chomped on mulberry leaves, and eventually spit out the threads that people then gathered and wove into blazing bolts of colored silk, still in demand throughout the world for blouses and skirts and dresses and shirts!

Perhaps it was the influence of those rainbow silks, or the fabled colors of the monuments we were about to see, or even Samarkand's position southwest of Tashkent along the lush Zerarshan River, but the people on this bus looked different from the sober, dark-coated citizens of Tashkent. Over shirts and trousers, for example, men wore *charpays,* long blue quilted robes piped in printed silk and knotted around the waist with multihued belts or sashes. They sported small four-square hats, black or blue, decorated with traceries of white braid. The women's black full-length coats fell open to reveal flowery dresses over flowery pantaloons, orange, sea green, blue, crimson. And the pantaloons had cuffs of velvet and embroidered silk cleverly designed to draw the eyes of potential admirers to the shapely ankles of their wearers.

"They only wear the black coats in winter," Roberta said. Her seatmate was pulling up her striped scarf, and in the process tossed her head to reveal a long braid and dark hair curling over her forehead and down to her eyes, outlined with kohl. Those eyes shone above distinctive high cheekbones. Just like Vera's.

"We come from a village near here," said Vera. "The women of my family dressed like that."

"And you, too?"

She smiled. "More or less, till I went to Tashkent, to the university."

"Your family had a collective farm, like these we're passing?"

"Yes."

"And was it a problem for your family?"

Vera looked at me. "Why a problem?"

I recounted the news stories I had read about problems the Soviets had encountered in trying to force peasants into collective groups.

"Yes maybe. But no problem for us. We were already one."

I was puzzled.

Vera started over again. "Roberta told me you lived in Iraq with your husband, in a village, and there was a big tribe."

"Ye-es . . ." Where was she going with this?

"Well, isn't a tribe kind of collective?" she said. "My father and his brothers had all been farmers on the land together for a long time. So when the Russians came, my father and his brothers signed to be collective and farm together. Didn't change. And then, you see . . ." Vera stopped.

Roberta and I and everyone else in the bus followed her gaze to the front, where an elderly man in green robes was being ceremonially helped up the steep steps. His turban was white, his beard was long and white, and he carried a long white cloth bag on each green-robed arm. Three women rose from their seats and gathered their dark coats around them, to cover their silk dresses and pantaloons. The old man eased onto the front side seat of the bus, occupying places for three, as though it were his right. The bus started again while he burrowed in one of his white cloth bags and produced three small shiny red apples, one for each of the women who had apparently done their good deed for the day by giving him a place to rest.

"He's a hodja," Vera explained.

Her voice carried and the holy man, in the act of closing his bag, looked up and threw us a piercing glance. Then followed a series of strange motions by his old gnarled hands which I could only assume was some formula for warding off—what? Evil as personified by Vera, a good Uzbek girl speaking English and not covering her head with the gold head scarf? Or evil as personified by me, maybe an infidel, old but impertinent (yes, I was staring at his bony face and fierce eyes). Who knew what the old man was doing or thinking? But Vera and I, like schoolgirls, cast down our eyes, and across the aisle, Roberta, her head properly covered by her flowered shawl, smothered a smile.

After such a ritual rebuke, we could scarcely be surprised that the bus took us to the wrong side of Samarkand (population four hundred thousand), and that we had to search for a long time to find a taxi to take us to the hotel recommended by Roberta's friend. Then the hotel was closed, and we ended up at another hotel, where the pompous desk clerk refused us rooms.

"Your Uzbek friend does not have proper identification," she said to us in bad French.

"But I am from here," Vera kept repeating. "They are the foreigners, not me."

"Why are you here without your husband?" said Madame the Desk Clerk, a large woman in a black dress, jeweled eyeglasses on a ribbon around her neck. She offered rooms to Roberta and me, "but without your friend. She does not have proper papers. I cannot."

"No, thank you," I said. "Not without our friend."

"I will call the guide that Michael knows," Roberta said, "and arrange something else."

But the phone did not connect. After five tries, Roberta gave up. I saw she was beginning to look worried. Something had to be done, she said. We couldn't sleep here on the sofa in the lobby, women didn't do that; Madame would certainly not allow it. And the door kept opening to admit one boisterous group of men after another who looked like traveling salesmen. They eyed us and poked each other and laughed or looked beyond and around us as they made their way into the crowded restaurant at the end of the hall, from which floated loud raucous laughter and music distinctly reminiscent of good old Egyptian belly dancing.

We were good feminists, were we not? Maybe we could sleep on the street? No, said Roberta. It is dark and cold, and very dangerous. She tried to reach Michael's friend again. The phones were still not working. It was now nearly 10 P.M.

"What should we do, B.J.?" Roberta said anxiously.

"I'm not sure."

Then, quite unexpectedly, I had an inspiration. Wasn't this a culture where public shaming was the worst thing that could happen to one? It was worth a try. Nothing else was working.

So, when the next group of businessmen entered, I marched purposefully up to the desk and said loudly in English, "You are treating us shamefully. Shamefully! Are we to sleep in the street? We will not leave until our Uzbek friend is given a room. Shame! Shame!"

Madame fluttered her ringed hands and tried to shut me up, but the men had heard (it would have been difficult for them not to hear since I was standing not more than two feet from them). A somewhat grizzled and elderly man in a heavy Tashkent-type overcoat asked what was happening. Madame did not reply. The grizzled gentleman then came over and asked Vera. She told him. The details of his response were unintelligible to me, but his emotional reaction was clear. He gathered the rest of his group and marched back to Madame at the desk.

After a long consultation, Madame made her way over to our sofa, her jeweled glasses bouncing against her bosom. She cleared her throat. "Ahem! These very kind gentlemen have offered to appeal in your name to the police officer who handles hotel permits and rules. He lives in this hotel. This man will go to ask him."

I inclined my head in what I hoped was a frosty gesture of acceptance. Vera said thank you in Uzbek and the grizzled gentleman called for the elevator and disappeared. If we had not been so tired and cold, the situation might have been amusing. But it was not amusing. We had stepped out of line, two Western females traveling alone, without men accompanying us. This, it seemed, was the first sin. No equal rights nonsense here. What was worse, we had brought along a third female, a native of Uzbekistan, married but also without her husband. In our innocence, we had thought Vera would enjoy the trip and would also serve as an informal guide. A mistake. She was not a guide, she was a scientist. We were treading on guides' turf. And with dollars. All kinds of rules had been broken, but most of them seemed to concern the behavior considered proper for a woman in supposedly egalitarian Uzbekistan.

After what seemed a very long quarter of an hour, a bell sounded, the elevator doors opened, and our grizzled savior-cavalier reappeared. He was escorting a tall man in a gray-green uniform who wore stars on his epaulets, a revolver at his belt, and a large luxuriant mustache on his upper lip, which was carefully waxed at the tips. We stood up as the men approached. Madame fluttered over and introduced us.

The police officer rocked back on his heels and reached for the elderly cavalier's arm to steady himself.

I realized the man was so drunk he could hardly stand up.

A pretty little speech by the police officer, stammering and swallowing, was repeated clearly by our cavalier and then translated into English by Vera.

We were most welcome, it seemed. Two American ladies. One Uzbek lady. Most welcome.

Roberta, Vera, and I smiled and nodded our thanks.

But the police officer wasn't yet finished. After a couple of false starts, he got out part two of the pretty little speech. As a sign of the importance of tourists to Uzbekistan in these new, nationalist times, the rule that all Uzbeks, men and women, must carry special identification papers at all times, was suspended in our honor.

"Thank you very much," I replied, "for all of us. We appreciate your help."

The police officer burped loudly.

Our cavalier frowned.

Madame offered us tea and the keys to the rooms.

We nodded our thanks. Our cavalier took the police officer firmly by the elbow and escorted him back into the elevator.

Up in our pleasantly heated rooms, with crimson silk bedspreads over the heavy quilted cloth comforters, we were exultant. We had arrived finally in Samarkand and we had a place to sleep. The shame of it was, of course, that we owed it all not to our stalwart feminist consciousness, but to a man. My mother would have taken it in stride, I realized. Her maxim was that gentlemen must help women. Very simple.

The next morning Roberta finally got through to Michael's friend, the French-speaking guide, who rescued us from Madame's clutches, seemed to have no problem with Vera's ID, found guides to *"les sites historiques"* and arranged for us to stay overnight in a private home, *"très élégante."* A private home, she explained, was much more appropriate for ladies traveling without men. Madame the Desk Clerk pointed out that since we had already paid for breakfast at the hotel, we might as well eat it there.

So we sat down in the restaurant, now empty of traveling salesmen and belly dancers, to a splendid breakfast of coffee and Samarkand blinis, thin pancakes wrapped around meat and vegetable mixtures and topped with dill-flavored thick cream.

Roberta noted that the only other person in the room was our grizzled cavalier, drinking coffee several tables away. He was singing softly to himself and glancing at us from time to time.

"What should we do?" I asked Vera. "Thank him?"

"No," she said, "we did that last night."

The waiter, in a grubby white apron, suddenly appeared at our table with a single lemon on a plate. We peered at it.

"From him," said the waiter, indicating our cavalier.

"Oh," said Vera brightly. "Thank you! And a knife, please."

The waiter produced a knife and Vera cut the lemon into thirds.

"Good with blinis," she said, taking her third of the lemon and squeezing it over her vegetable blini.

We followed suit, then turned and nodded our thanks.

Our cavalier kept on singing.

"I think he's attracted to you, Roberta," giggled Vera.

"No, to B.J."

I shook my head. "I think he likes Vera. After all, he got her a room."

Suddenly Vera's face changed and she smiled. "You know what he's singing? It's an old Uzbek song which says, 'You must always respect women'!" But she added, "I think we should leave quickly before he decides to invite us for lunch!"

Our host family in Samarkand consisted of Nadar (an exile from Georgia), his wife Emma (Russian, but of Greek descent), and Amelie, Emma's daughter by her Russian first husband. The language was Russian, not Uzbek, and Vera was the translator here.

"Here we are!" Emma flung open the door to a tidy second-floor flat, then opened another door before us. "Your room, ladies!"

Vera and Roberta and I stared at a veritable fantasy of gold and white—curtains edged with shiny golden ribbons; a vast bed with a gold and white canopy, bedspread, and throw pillows. The mantel of the small fireplace was decorated with engravings, in gold-leaf frames. The lampshades were encircled by gold braid, and even the crystal chandelier boasted golden drops.

"We thought you would like this. It is Amelie's bridal room. For when she will marry."

"I will not marry," boomed Amelie from the door. Dark-haired, stocky, and taller than her mother, she wrung our hands in friendly fashion. "Don't listen to my mother. I am thirty years old, too old."

"Oh, Amelie," protested Emma. Maneuvering Amelie out and down the hall, she said, "I'll be back with towels and we will see you in our dining room at seven!"

Vera and Roberta and I eyed the golden bed and burst out laughing.

Dinner was good; the conversation was even better after we had passed through the first stiff and uneasy stage. Like Madame the Desk Clerk at the Samarkand Hotel, Emma and Nadar and Amelie were clearly puzzled by us. The American tourists they had heard about did not travel with an Uzbek friend and certainly did not speak Uzbek, as Roberta did. So they finally asked outright what we were doing in

Samarkand and how we could afford to pay our airfare all the way from America.

I explained that I was writing a book about Muslim women, and I was also Roberta's professor. Roberta told them about her research into Uzbek literature. Vera was our friend, whom we had invited to come with us.

The next stage of conversation involved Texas. The very name fascinated them. So I delivered a short lecture on the natural resources of the state of Texas: oil, beef, oranges, rice, cotton.

"Cotton?" echoed Nadar. "Like Uzbekistan?"

"Like Uzbekistan," I answered.

Nadar shook his head, then perked up. "What about cowboys?" he asked. I delivered another short speech about cowboys, using as material my own son David's experiences as a cowboy in Texas and Montana.

"Your son is a cowboy?" Amelie repeated.

"Not now. He was."

After some conversation back and forth, Vera finally said, to me, "They don't understand how your son could be a cowboy and then after that go to university. Here, if you're lucky enough to pass the exams, you go to university. If you drop out, too bad, that's it."

I felt obliged to discourse on the virtues of an open educational system. But there was little response, as everyone was now busily eating. A laden table. White radishes vinaigrette, carrot and eggplant salad, tomatoes with hot pepper and zucchini; spaghetti with sauce; rice; meatballs in sour cream, and special cheese breads, like large light yellow biscuits. A feast.

"The bread is Emma's own recipe," Nadar told me proudly.

"Tell us about your work here in Samarkand," I said.

Emma's lively middle-aged face was framed by short, curly salt and pepper hair. She announced that she was a notary public.

"Much more important position here than in America, I think," offered Roberta, "because people can't do anything without official stamps on every single piece of legal paper: car deeds, rental receipts, birth certificates, permits to do this or that, so Madame Emma"—with a smile at our hostess—"can make or break people."

"That's how I met Nadar," Emma said, looking at him fondly while helping herself to more meatballs.

"Please tell us," said Vera.

Nadar was an independent cabdriver who had immigrated to Uzbekistan from Georgia after the divorce from his first wife. To work as a cabdriver in Samarkand, he had to have several permits, including an official stamp for his car. And Emma was the notary he visited to ask for that stamp. He fell in love at first sight.

"I kept going back to her again and again," he continued, looking at her fondly. "And one day she said, 'What are you doing here? I stamped your certificate long ago,' and I answered that I just wanted to come and look at her and that's how it started."

"Eight years!" announced Madame Emma.

"And what is Amelie's work?" I turned to the daughter, who had been silently eating her way through the tourists' feast.

"Amelie is a pediatrician at the government hospital."

"Would she be willing to talk to me about women's issues, so I could learn and record this in my book?"

"With pleasure."

"What do you think are the greatest problems facing Uzbek women today?"

Dr. Amelie waited until Vera had finished translating my question.

"Poverty," she answered. "Malnutrition. Bad diet. Bad water."

"Here, in Samarkand?"

"It's worse in the countryside, but yes, even to some degree here in the city." She went on, as Vera rushed to catch up with her words. "The children all have rickets because they don't have anything to eat but bread and tea. So do their mothers. They do eat potatoes on the farms if they're lucky, and sometimes cabbage. But no fruits, no other vegetables."

"No meat at all?"

"Once or twice a year, on the feasts."

Vera put in, "You know, B.J., that is true in our village. Some people had only potatoes all the time, and even me. After my kids, all my teeth went. If you're poor, you don't have gold caps like me. You just don't have teeth."

"I would like to ask Amelie about Islam and its effect on women," I said.

"Islam? What does that have to do with it?" asked Emma.

"Well, er . . ." I replied, trying to think quickly so that Vera and Roberta could translate quickly, "laws about marriage and divorce, religious ideas about woman's place . . ."

"No, no," said Dr. Amelie. "You have it all wrong in the West. You are fortunate, with good food and good water and good medical care. . . ." She was speaking so fast now it was hard for Vera to keep up, and her voice was rising. "You have the luxury of worrying about things like that—ideas about women and their place in the world."

Vera tried to break in, but Amelie held up her hand. "I know what the lady is getting at," she insisted. "I read women's magazines and health magazines, about women's ideas in the West that they call feminism. Now what on earth is *that?*"

I sensed the heavily sarcastic tone before Vera translated the words for me.

"Amelie, Amelie," her mother interrupted.

"What is that, feminism?" Amelie repeated, her words tumbling out, Vera translating. "Feminism, I tell you, is a luxury of rich people. If you don't have enough to eat and you're sick, do you think you care about anything except getting enough to eat, trying to get well? Here everyone has to work, men and women, there is no choice, you work or you don't eat."

Amelie paused and her mother spoke up. "My child," she said, "about women and men, dear, it's not just that they need food, it is the way men *think* about us."

Amelie snorted and took another helping of meatballs and sour cream. She looked at me accusingly.

"And as for us, madame, here in this house we are all employed professional types, we have a nice apartment, right, you think we eat like this every night? No, my friend, this is only show for tourists. And you're the first ones. Where are all those tourists who are going to make us rich?" Amelie asked scornfully, looking around the table.

Emma rose to clear the plates. Nadar tried, jovially, to change the subject.

"Ask the American lady from Texas to tell us about jazz," he said.

I tried my best.

"But is it fun?"

"Fun?" I looked at Vera. "Fun?"

"Yes," she answered, "that's the word he means."

"It's fun to listen to, maybe to dance to."

"But you do not yourself play an instrument?"

"No, no." I couldn't help smiling, "But my husband used to play the trombone and he still plays the piano."

Nadar nodded, seemingly content.

Madame Emma brought in dessert, and Vera translated her announcement.

"This is a special dessert madame is offering. Not on menu given to guide. Because she likes you and Roberta and wishes to celebrate Uzbek-American friendship."

We looked at the goodies set out before us on crystal plates.

"This is fig jam," said Madame Emma. "And this is my specialty, very special, grape and walnut preserves."

The dessert was rather strange, but delicious, especially when washed down with the sweet red wine Nadar offered. We toasted Uzbek-American friendship; Nadar toasted his dear wife, then the couple toasted each other and became flushed and happy.

"Amelie will soon marry, I think," said Nadar, laughing a bit.

"Nadar," cautioned his wife.

But the repast seemed to have had an effect. Amelie's mood had changed and she smiled tolerantly at the two middle-aged lovebirds.

"Marriage is good for some people," she admitted, "like you. But not, I think, for me. And that is all I wish to say."

She rose from the table and we took the hint to thank Emma and retire to the gold and white bridal chamber.

Our guide to the wonders of Samarkand was a tall, slim young man named Marat, whose eyes were bright and whose teeth were bad. In his stilted but clear schoolboy English, he explained as we set out that he was an aficionado of science fiction and wished to discuss the American series called *Star Trek*. He had seen episodes of *Star Trek* and *Star Trek: The Next Generation* on videos available in Uzbekistan.

Roberta smiled and explained that in America, such people were known as "Trekkies," and I was one of them.

"You, madame?" Marat looked at me in some amazement. But after we had exchanged a few questions and answers about Captain Kirk, Captain Picard, and Data, he apparently decided I was indeed a Trekkie, and began to give me his views on the plausibility of the scientific suppositions in which Mr. Gene Roddenberry believed.

Wandering through the incredible monuments of Samarkand, I was not surprised that Marat was interested in science fiction. The miles of tiles, blue and turquoise, red and gold, that constituted the complex of mosque and religious schools known as the Registan were spectacular enough against the gray people-level pedestrian housing developments of Samarkand to make me feel I was part of a surreal, out-of-consciousness adventure, or perhaps experiencing the virtual reality of *Star Trek*'s Holodeck. Even the materialist Vladimir Lenin had pronounced the fifteenth-century Registan as a "treasure of art and ancient culture" and had issued a decree in 1918 that it should not be bulldozed, but preserved and put on show for "the edification of the masses." The three great madrasahs or religious schools are positioned around a vast medieval courtyard of smooth cobblestones. Together with the mosque, they rise 180 feet into the air, their mammoth spectacular arches and domes of gold testifying to the power and the artistic vision of the descendants of Tamerlane.

Not a monument enthusiast myself, I nevertheless could not help but be impressed as we sat, four miniaturized human beings, on the narrow stone steps leading to the fountains and the courtyard of this architectural triumph. Marat sat with us for a moment, then led us away to the bookstalls, where he looked for his favorite science fiction authors, "to complement the American *Star Trek* tale."

The Shah-in-Zenda mausoleum complex is another surreal arrangement, sometimes called the Stairway to Heaven, for its medieval cobbled walkway stretches up and up, past cells where ancient monks lived, past small prayer nooks and mosques, past revered tombs of holy personae. The most important of all is the mausoleum of Qasim ibn-Abbas, a cousin of the Prophet Muhammad, who is supposedly buried here, and whose tomb is a place of pilgrimage for Muslims from all over the world. Other mausoleums date from Tamerlane's time.

Marat was a secularist. He was not impressed.

"This place is often a good set for filmmaking," he said.

As we walked up the Stairway to Heaven, I noticed many niches cut into the stone walls, some of which were blackened and sooty.

"Do people light candles in memory of the deceased, or set fires?" I asked. "Is that some kind of Islamic ritual? We light candles in Christian churches. Even the Russians used to do that."

"Well, not Muslims," replied Marat. "But people here are close to the Persian border, and maybe they think of the belief of the holy man Zoroaster."

"Fire worship?" asks Roberta.

"No, no, the power of fire to purify, that is it."

Then I asked him about the film, that shocking film we had seen, *The Flame*. Was that what it was about, the power of fire to purify?

Marat shook his head vigorously. He had heard about the film, but did not believe it was a true story.

"Life for everyone is hard here," he said. "Men and women both. Maybe people become depressed and sad at life, but they don't *burn themselves up.*" He looked upset.

"But the women in the film were Muslims," I persisted. "Did that fire idea have anything to do with Islam at all?"

"No, no," protested Marat. "Has nothing to do with it. Fire idea is not Islamic." He tried to smile. "More like science fiction."

But none of us smiled.

In the afternoon we visited the mosque of Bibi Khanum, Tamerlane's Chinese wife, and also the famous observatory built on a hilltop above the city in the fifteenth century by Ulu Beg. Ulu Beg was

Tamerlane's grandson and his studies in astronomy are now immortalized in the Tashkent subway.

"Both Ulu Beg and Bibi Khanum have as their problem Islam," said Marat.

"Oh, come on, Marat," temporized Roberta.

"Russian guides say this," he insisted earnestly. "Ulu Beg killed by religious fanatic who did not like science. Bibi Khanum killed by religious fanatic who did not like women. All because of Islam religion."

"That's what the Russians say," said Vera. "But what do Uzbeks say?"

Marat looked at Vera, and answered seriously, "Well, I think they are right about Ulu Beg. Bibi Khanum I don't know."

Bibi Khanum. Any Western researcher examining women's history in Central Asia, and particularly Islamic history, cannot fail to notice the tale of Bibi Khanum, the woman around whose life and death swirl many myths. Interestingly, the myth differs markedly depending on whether it is told in the East or West.

The only matter on which all writers agree is that the Bibi Khanum mosque is one of the largest mosques ever built anywhere. From that point on the chronicles vary. Some suggest that the building was the idea of Bibi herself; she wished to raise a colossal monument to welcome her royal husband on his return from a conquering foray into India between 1398 and 1399. Other accounts insist that the mosque was Tamerlane's idea, and that Bibi had nothing to do with it. He built it between 1399 and 1404 at enormous expense, utilizing an army of artisans, general laborers, and elephants. The mosque was named after Bibi Khanum, his favorite. If the latter tale is true, then the "myth" of Bibi Khanum's martyrdom on the altar of Islamic cruelty to women, a myth which has reached into Western feminist folklore, makes no sense at all.

"But whether it's true or not, B.J., the storytellers love the tale of Bibi Khanum," said Vera. "Don't they, Marat?"

"Yes," agreed Marat. "Yes." He smiled at her.

"So tell us the different versions," urged Roberta.

Marat lounged against one of the broken pillars standing near the entrance to the half-ruined mosque.

"Okay," he said, and with a look at me, "here is virtual reality à la *Star Trek,* madame. Best version, beloved by audiences."

Virtual reality, beloved by audiences, has Bibi as the initiator of the project. She so adores her husband that she hires the best architect in the world to design and build this special mosque. The best architect in the world, however, turns out to be young and handsome and falls madly in love with the beautiful Bibi. He finishes his work, but refuses pay; he asks only for one kiss. Bibi, at first refusing, finally relents, with the understanding that he can kiss her but only through a silken cushion.

"But," said Marat, lifting a finger to hold our attention, "the love of the architect was so great and so hot that the kiss passed through the cushion like a flame and left a love bite on Bibi Khanum's cheek. When Tamerlane came riding back from India on his elephant, he saw the bite on his beautiful wife's cheek and fell into a royal anger."

He paused dramatically.

"And how does the story end?" I asked.

Marat smiled. "Three choices for endings," he said.

Ending one: The architect kills himself because he cannot ever have Bibi Khanum for his own. Tamerlane kills Bibi Khanum, accusing her of being unfaithful [look at that bite!].

Ending two: The architect sees Tamerlane returning across the plain on his elephant, so he climbs to the top of his glorious building, and angels carry him off to heaven. [He did not sin; he just kissed a cushion.] Bibi Khanum welcomes her husband, and that is that.

Ending three: The architect kills himself because he cannot ever have Bibi Khanum for his own. Bibi Khanum, using all her wiles, explains the whole unfortunate situation to Tamerlane. [How could I know that his passion could pass through a cushion, and besides, my dear husband, you didn't have to pay him anything.] Tamerlane forgives Bibi Khanum, and they live happily ever after.

"So what version does the audience choose?" I asked.

Marat smiled. "A good question, madame. If the listener is Russian or English, they like number one. If they are Uzbek, they like two or three."

"Which ending do you like, Marat?" asked Vera. Despite her lumpy purple coat and her short cropped black hair, she, too, was beautiful, with those high cheekbones, the almond eyes, the wild rose complexion.

He looked at her.

"I like number three," he answered.

Early the next morning, Emma came to the gold and white bedroom to tell us that the buses to Bokhara had been canceled for at least three days, because of a shortage of gasoline. We looked at each other, but before we could begin to think about this catastrophe, she smiled and suggested that Nadar drive us.

"He has gasoline saved up for these occasions," she said. "And the cost will not be *much* more, especially for American ladies. And he is an excellent driver. Safer for ladies to go that way."

So we left Samarkand in state as the rain began to come down, happy to be in the relative comfort of Nadar's Georgian car, now licensed to drive passengers in Uzbekistan. Dr. Amelie had gone to work before we were even out of bed, so we had to leave our greetings and good-byes with her mother.

If we had had any doubts about the veracity of Emma's announcement, they were soon dispelled by the number of trucks and cars simply standing by the roadside, their drivers still sitting in the cabs.

"They're all out of gas," said Nadar.

"But what can they do?"

"Wait," answered Nadar. "We do a lot of waiting in this country, madame."

Bokhara

The Jefferson High School girls' choir was called the Treble Clef, to which one was admitted only after auditioning, first as soloist, then as part of a trio. I was exultant to be accepted when only a sophomore and I sang with pleasure for three years. We were in demand to sing not only for school assemblies but also before community groups like the Elks Club, the Daughters of the Eastern Star, the Knights of Pythias, and the Shriners. In our white blouses, navy skirts, and navy vests with the Jefferson blue and gold seal on the breast, we often were applauded so heartily we had to provide encores. (We were giving free concerts, we were enthusiastic teenagers, and our voices were not too bad.) A favorite encore, time after time, was "Allah's Holiday," a song with slightly atonal chords suggesting foreign climes, and an opening verse which I remember to this day.

> Sound of tinkling cymbal
> Sound of girls at play,
> Sound of splashing fountains . . .
> Allah's holiday!

What did this song mean? None of us knew or cared, really; we were only concerned with keeping the atonal three-part harmony on pitch. But as I read the lines now, they seemed to be saying that on the holiday of Allah, the Muslim God (who is different from the Christian God), young women (and presumably their patriarchal tyrant boss, who maybe played the cymbals) frolicked together in a beautiful garden where fountains splashed and music tinkled. Shades of the *Arabian Nights,* and the "Tale of the Porter and the Three Girls from Baghdad." Here of course is the genesis of a legend which had become a stereotype in the West long before my high school days in the 1940s. And if one reads modern accounts of Muslim women written by Western women, one can conclude that nothing has changed. Women are still in chains, religious if not actual, and they're still in the harem, symbolically if not physically.

The history of Central Asia does nothing to dispel this stereotype. Women are seldom mentioned unless they are important queenly figures like Bibi Khanum, and the reason cited by Western observers is that women were hidden in the harem, and due to Eastern mysogynistic thinking, their names were not to be mentioned in public. One can argue in response that in the long history of the Western world, women were also absent from the written accounts, until very recently.

But Eastern women, like Western women, turn up as central characters in tales and oral stories. And such stories are still told in the squares of the Central Asian cities. Women are also present, if invisible, in the magnificent embroideries and silks and carpets that have carried the name of Bokhara to the far corners of the globe, even today. My mother was most impressed by the small lovingly framed piece of Bokhara embroidery which we were given as a present by Egyptian friends.

"Think how long that would take, what patience," she had said, admiring the stylized crimson blossoms, hand-sewn on a cream ground with stitches so small they could not be seen by the naked eye.

My mother's sisters, Mary and Celia, had both been accomplished seamstresses, but my mother had rebelliously resisted the tatting and crocheting lessons that were de rigueur for young women in the early twentieth century.

"Keeps women quiet but doesn't improve the mind," was her tart explanation, but her criticism was not taken lightly. My aunt Mary insisted that *her* mind had not suffered. "One could do both," she said, "if one wanted to."

"Women also wove the beautiful rugs we see," said Raissa, our guide, who had responded to Roberta's Samarkand friend's call. Raissa had met us at the Ark, the citadel of Bokhara, where Nadar had faithfully delivered us in a blinding rainstorm. The Ark is both famous and infamous in Bokhara as a fortress, a dungeon, and a place of public execution. Not the pleasantest introduction to the city, but Raissa had explained that everyone knew the Ark, so we could not miss each other if we met there.

A Tartar lady of some charm and intelligence, Raissa had been an Intourist guide under the Russians, and thus was in a good position to step into the role of an independent, free-enterprise tourist guide. She knew four languages and all the monuments in Uzbekistan, she explained. Because Roberta had mentioned my interest in women's issues, she had cleverly organized her lectures and her sightseeing around that interest. "But the embroidery was very hard work, like the carpet-weaving, and poorly paid. In fact," she argued, warming to her task, "names like Silk Route are a kind of cover for the feudalism of the past."

"Feudalism as in Russia before the Revolution?" interspersed Roberta.

"Yes, yes," responded Raissa, and returned to her main theme, slightly altered to include a larger share of women's interests. This theme was that the glamour of historical Bokhara's power and opulence masked both the terrible poverty of the peasants, especially women, and the cruelty of the rulers who clapped people into dungeons for no apparent reason, or even cut off their heads in the public square!

"But I thought Bokhara was famous for scholars," said Vera. "That's what my father said."

"That's true," Raissa answered, with a careful look at her Uzbek compatriot. "But who learned? Not the people, only the rich and powerful. Omar Khayyám, Avicenna, yes. But mostly men of a high class. No women, especially not here in this famous madrasah."

"Here?" I looked around the slightly decrepit square. To get out of the light drizzle of rain, we had stopped under an overhang of blue tiles that shielded the entrance to the vast madrasah, or religious school, one of a series of schools and mosques built around the cobbled courtyard.

"Learning, yes," went on Raissa, agreeing with Vera. "For everybody, no. In 1832, there were more than three hundred schools in Bokhara, with fifteen thousand *men* learning." Raissa looked triumphant. "So, you see, madame, why we are somewhat happy about the Russians."

Vera looked startled.

Roberta repeated, "Happy?"

We had not heard of anyone who was happy about the Russians, past or present. As ex-colonial rulers, they were reviled and being encouraged to depart.

"Because of the family," said Raissa. "The structure of the domestic group has changed. We are mother, father, children. Not man with many wives. The Russians did some small good for us."

We emerged at the sacred pool, marking the crossroads where several covered bazaars used to stand in the center of the city, offering goods to traders from around the world. "This bazaar is the only one left. Is being restored," announced Raissa, with a wave of her hand at the domes of stone turning dark with rain.

"Look, B.J., there is the laughing hodja!" Roberta cried. And there indeed was a statue of Nasr ed din Hodja, the famous wise fool of Middle Eastern legends and a subject of some of Roberta's own academic research. Three times as large as life, sitting on his bronze donkey and laughing!

Raissa was not interested. "Is not Russian," said Raissa. "Not Islamic. Come now to the bazaar, out of the rain."

Laughter in general and this Hodja in particular were unusual elements to find in the center of this medieval city, famed for serious study. But there Hodja was, known for his subtle put-downs, in aphorism and joke, of power and authority, whether feudal or socialist. I took Roberta's picture with the laughing Hodja, and Raissa indulged us. We were tourists with ideas of our own, it seemed.

I hurried to catch up with Raissa. I was anxious to tell her an aphorism from Texas that I had just remembered. It was about woman's place, too.

"My son tells me that among Texas men, the saying is that a man values his horse first, his dog second, and his wife third. What do you think about that stereotype of Western men and women?"

Raissa, polite, considered. "Not the same, madame. Here we have long ages of history behind us. You are a new country. Not the same to compare the two."

We lunched in an eighteenth-century merchant's house, the Faisolah Khudair mansion, another relic of the past that the new government was restoring, to show off to tourists like Roberta and me.

"Be careful," cautioned Raissa, as I nearly stepped into the well! We stumbled through broken steps and rubble to a wing that still retained its earlier panache. These must have been the rooms where the old merchant received guests from Persia and China and Turkey. The rooms were painted and paneled, the walls of inlaid wood, dark and light, set into a series of arches, arches repeated in the doors and the windows. Flowers were the dominant decorative theme in the room where we sat on piles of flower-patterned rugs against pillows covered with cotton printed with red flowers of the traditional Bokhara design. A flowered curtain was hung over the door leading to a still-ruined room, held up, incongruously, by an old piece of rope, knotted on both sides.

Time and thought had gone into the menu, clearly, for though the ubiquitous Korean salads were there, so was smoked chicken, fresh dill, round wheat bread, and beef and onion stew. But it was the fruit that was surprising, smoky yellow grapes, pomegranates artfully cut in fours and spread out like flowers to be plucked.

"Well," I said to Roberta, "if as we saw in the market, Uzbeks can keep melons fresh all winter in hanging gourds, maybe they have another process for pomegranates and grapes."

Entertainment followed lunch. We were treated to a kind of Uzbek fashion show. The lady of the house, who with her painter husband was the curator of the mansion, asked for a model. Roberta and I were not the right size and shape for showing off the traditional Uzbek's woman's costume, which was, according to Raissa, "forbidden under the Russians."

Vera agreed to be dressed in the native dress of her own past, and stood on the Bokhara carpet, giggling a bit self-consciously, while the lady of the house brought out a series of garments.

"They were all worn together," she told us, "and they were worn every day. By the rich ladies, that is."

First over Vera's jeans and sweater went a long dress of multicolored heavy silk, an adaptation of the traditional Bokhara *iqat* pattern, fuchsia and white and green. The cotton sleeves were white and green and long enough to completely cover Vera's hands. Another dress, deep blue silk, followed, and then a wide gold brocade headband like a flapper's headgear was placed over Vera's short dark hair and tied in the back.

"The traditional lady had long, black hair, not so short," Raissa said.

"But I like my hair short," answered Vera crisply. She was beginning to exhibit some irritation with the process, though Roberta and I were moved again and again to say how beautiful she looked in the costume. For the layers of traditional clothing, and the colors—green, fuchsia, deep blue—complemented Vera's complexion; she was gradually being transformed from modern scientist into a figure from a Persian miniature.

Vera must have felt this, for she said suddenly, "My father and mother wanted me to wear something like this when I married Saidollah." She wrinkled up her nose under the heavy brocade headband. "I said no."

"But it is beautiful," said Roberta.

"And it is our heritage," put in Raissa.

Vera shook her head. "Yes, but I refused. I wore a white dress like you, Roberta, when you married Bjorn."

Even as she spoke, the lady of the house lowered over the gold brocade the *paranja,* a wide strip of black stiff horsehair which covered the face and formed a forehead-to-ankle veil. This was held in place by a second headband of black cotton with stout ties.

"I can see you," said Vera, "but you can't see me."

"That was the idea," Raissa remarked tartly, and rather surprisingly, given her insistence about how Russian destruction of tradition had improved the position of women.

Vera was moving in place, a bit restless. "Okay, that's enough," she said.

But the lady of the house had not yet finished. Over Vera's protestations, she was garbed in the last layer, a hooded coat of heavy silk, darker than any of the other garments, fastened in front. The final transformation had taken place. A shapeless mass of black had replaced the Vera who stood before us in jeans and sweater only a few moments ago.

From the muffled depths came a small voice. "Okay, let me out now."

"At least it must have been warm in winter," I offered, to cover the awkward moment as Vera shook her head and turned away from the garments as they were folded up on the arm of the lady of the house.

Raissa and the dresser spoke to each other, eyed Vera. Vera was not properly appreciative of the dress ritual, it seemed. Perhaps it was too close to her own experience, whereas it was just set-up play for Roberta and myself. But Raissa's and the lady of the house's attitudes were harder to explain. They wanted to provide an exotic spectacle for which tourists would pay, but they also were displaying a certain ambivalence toward this aspect of the Uzbek past. Yes, that old tradition was bad for women. Yes, in many ways it signaled the servitude of women. And yet, as proud members of a new nation, they were supposed to be appreciative of their heritage, warts and all. Could they revive some elements of that heritage, but not all? Perhaps they had not yet worked this puzzle out.

Raissa still seemed to be thinking of the uneasy costume drama as she led us, in the rain, to the summer palace of the last Emir of

Bokhara, Said Alim Kahn. The palace, much larger and more preten-
tious than the merchant's house, had been turned into a museum.

"You see, madame, those clothes. The women didn't go out very
much, but when they did, they had to be covered so no one would
treat them disrespectfully."

I was not ready to engage Raissa on this topic, so I kept silent.

"Shall we look at the palace?" Raissa asked brightly.

Roberta smiled. "Is it heated?" Even she was reacting to the freezing cold and the rain that would not stop, and perhaps also to the
coldness between Vera and Raissa.

"I don't know. We will see," replied Raissa.

We were led into the palace itself, where one could view ancient
costumes like those Vera had just shed, and velvet boots (shown with
practical rubbers like the ones my father used to wear on rainy days).
Also embroideries. Chinese vases. More elaborate women's head-
dresses involving turbans and jewels and feathers and brocade. Russian
bronzes. A half-finished suite of rooms for the Czarina, who promised
to come and visit the Emir, but never did. And the "white" salon, all
carved plaster and inset mirrors.

"A beautiful place to live, no?" Raissa turned to me, smiling.

"But not for women, I think," said Roberta softly. "I mean, this is
the harem, isn't it?"

"No, it's the white salon, as you see," replied Raissa primly. "Very
famous work." We strolled through the white salon and out into the
garden. Here there were fountains, shrubs, and trees, bare now, but
presumably pleasant when in bloom. On Allah's Holiday, maybe? For
near the garden was the bathhouse with a large pool nearby.

"Here, they say," continued Raissa, "the ladies of the Emir's harem
used to frolic on sunshiny afternoons in the summer. It is a *summer
palace,* you know."

Beside the pool stood an elaborate wooden gazebo, as high as a
military watchtower, with a dozen steps up to a covered platform
framed by carved wooden arches.

"Here," said Raissa, "the Emir would come to sit on a pleasant day
to watch the harem ladies swimming in the pool."

Her voice had changed. The half-wondering, slightly irritated tone
was gone. She was back to the text of her lecture. "Always beside the
Emir was a basket of apples."

"Apples?" I echoed.

"Apples," repeated Raissa.

Roberta, Vera, and I stared up the steps to the gazebo tower.

"If one of the maidens' beautiful forms pleased his eye, the Emir would, it is said, toss an apple into the pool." Raissa picked up a small stone from the walk and demonstrated. The stone plopped into the black water with a small splash and ripples spread out, creating circles and ever-larger circles on the surface of the dark rain-pocked pool.

"And whoever caught the apple," she finished, "would have the honor of the Emir's company for the evening."

Vera snorted. Raissa looked at her sharply. Roberta was silent, and I adjusted my scarf up over my head against the slow, steady fall of the rain.

Raissa seemed to pull herself up. She took a deep breath. "So now you can understand, my friends, what we mean when we speak about the great benefits that the Russians have brought to women of Uzbekistan in 1927."

"I thought the Bolsheviks took over here in 1920," I said. "What happened between 1920 and 1927?"

"Opposition by men," replied Raissa briskly. My question had obviously been asked many times before, and she was ready for it. "The men did not wish the laws to change. They did not wish women to be independent. Because when women become independent, the men lose power."

"And what happened to the Emir?" asked Roberta.

Raissa looked up at the watchtower. "He had to flee," she said, "because the Bolsheviks wanted to arrest him as an example of feudal despotism." She spoke the last word in three syllables, slowly, like a charm or a prayer. "He fled to Tashkent, then to Istanbul. The Russians changed the laws about men and women. Since 1927, our women are much more contented."

From a door in the harem, an old woman emerged, like a ghost from the past. But this woman was real enough. She was selling embroidery. I bought two dresser scarves at outrageous prices, unable to argue with her plea and the sight of her cracked and swollen hands.

"Come, we must go," urged Raissa, "or we will become really wet."

We walked back through the bare gardens to the gate, in an increasingly heavy downpour. The rutted street had turned to mud and we were delighted to see an old car awaiting us, and in the driver's seat Raissa's obliging husband, Anatoly, in his black Greek fisherman's cap and layers of coats. Car and chauffeur were necessary equipment for Raissa in her new tourist business.

"It is all in the family," Raissa explained. Her husband spoke to her in Russian and patted her arm. She smiled.

From the streaked window of the old car, I could still see the harem watchtower above the wall, but as we splashed forward, it was soon obliterated in the gray mists of rain. Yes, things had definitely changed in the structure of the family in Uzbekistan, and in the expectations of women.

No more swimming in the harem pool.

No more girls for apples.

And no more *paranjas,* head-to-ankle veils. At least officially. But were they coming back, those veils, in a different style, as Western observers had suggested? I hadn't seen any yet. I would have to ask again.

We thought we had planned our trip rather cleverly to use time to the best advantage, by making a circle from Tashkent to Samarkand, Samarkand to Bokhara, and then the night train from Bokhara back to Tashkent. With berths and blankets. It was an old-fashioned Wagons-Lits coach, Roberta said, and we had paid well for the reputedly comfy berths and blankets. Raissa was to travel back with us, to attend to business in Tashkent, so we had taken an entire compartment—four berths.

The train was set to depart at nine, but Raissa and Anatoly insisted on coming to pick us up two hours early. "The rain, the rain," explained Raissa merrily. "Good for the mulberry trees, but not for the tourists."

We chugged along the muddy side roads, I was waiting for the moment when we would simply roll onto the paved highway and then whiz along to the station when the car suddenly stopped.

"We get out here," said Raissa.

"Here?" I peered out the door into the rain. In the distance one could hear the whistle and chug of trains, and one could see tiny lights. But it was very far away. Very far indeed.

Roberta and Vera and I tumbled out with our baggage. Anatoly gave us each an umbrella, and shook our hands warmly in farewell. I peered out at those distant lights and wondered.

"She must know, B.J., she's from here," said Roberta in a low tone, clearly wondering, too.

"Here we go, down the slope, it is much faster," Raissa instructed us. "Take hands and follow me."

We followed her lead, holding hands tightly and slipping down the muddy hill.

"We're going to land in the ditch!" I cried.

Raissa trilled back, "Of course, that is the idea, we will walk in the ditch. Not yet full of water."

What could we do but follow her lead? Roberta and Vera and I trudged along in the ditch, between the muddy banks, single-file, carrying umbrellas, shifting our baggage back and forth from hand to hand. It seemed hours before the lights of the station came closer; then we saw to our dismay that the train stood on the other side of another deep ditch!

"Up we go, and down we go." Raissa cheered us on.

For several moments I could see nothing except the muck below and Raissa's stout dark form in front of me, and I began to wonder whether I might ever see my family again. My bag slipped and Roberta pushed it back into my hand. How could I possibly get to the top of this slippery hill, down the other side, and up another?

"Come, come," chided Raissa. She had gone up and down, but we were still stuck at the bottom of the last ditch. "Up, my friends, up!"

"Well, B.J.," began Roberta.

"Well, Roberta," I began.

And Vera saved us all, by calling to a large chunky man above, on the lip of the ditch. What she hollered I have no idea, but the man braced himself on the top, reached down, and grabbed me and my bag. We went up one after the other, hauled up by Vera's savior, and stood, panting and muddy, on the platform.

"Oh, Vera," I said, trying to catch my breath. "Thank him."

"I have," replied Vera airily.

The night train from Bokhara to Tashkent. It has a wonderfully adventurous ring. I kept reminding myself of that romantic connotation during the next hour. For we clambered onto the train to find our supposedly reserved compartment full. A large family was already ensconced, enjoying a late supper, which was spread out over the built-in window tables and onto a tablecloth across the occupants' laps. Shouting began. To no avail.

The porter was nowhere to be seen.

"He has been bribed!" cried Raissa hotly. "He will pay!"

"I do hope so," sighed Roberta. "I suppose I could survive standing up all night, but I don't want to, Raissa."

"And we paid for the compartment," put in Vera. "A lot."

Raissa pulled herself up again, in that characteristic guide lecturing stance. "Gather luggage around," she instructed. "Do not move from this corridor. We will stand here until the train starts and then I will arrange everything."

We sat down on our luggage, dispirited and tired from the long muddy trek. Not the romantic journey we had dreamed of at all. And outside the hubbub on the platform continued. Raissa had disappeared. None of us spoke. I doubted that Roberta or Vera really believed that Raissa could sort it out; I certainly didn't believe she could win over the surly-looking male porters.

In a scream of wheels, the train lurched forward. The whistle sounded, that long, sad whistle of trains that carries across plains, and cuts through mountains, and now was barely muffled by the steady beat of the rain. The train began to move, the stationmaster shut the door of our carriage, and we were off, sitting on our luggage in a mucky corridor on the night train to Tashkent.

"Look!" whispered Vera in my ear.

There at the end of the corridor was an official-looking man with a peaked hat, leading a smiling Raissa down the corridor. While we watched, jerking back and forth on our luggage as the train rocked faster and faster over a very bad railway bed, the family in our compartment was evicted, screaming and shouting, but evicted, and they departed, carrying their supper with them, a man carrying a sausage, a woman holding several loaves of round bread, a second woman trailing the tablecloth behind her. A third clutched a baby. Two men followed. How had so many people gotten into that small compartment?

We stood up to move our bags into the miraculously emptied space, but Raissa held up her hand peremptorily. "Not yet!" she ordered. "They must first clean up. Cheap sausage smelling on floor. Other bits of things. Wait. Wait!"

We waited. The missing porter appeared, looking somewhat cowed, swept out the compartment and wiped the windows, the tables, and the leatherette seats. *Then* we were allowed to enter.

"Well done, Raissa," said Roberta warmly.

"Yes, yes," Vera and I chimed in.

"If one is not willing to fight, one gets nowhere in any society," pronounced Raissa, offering us dates and nuts and bottled water.

We settled in for sleep on the newly made-up beds, Vera and Roberta, as the youngsters, in the top bunks, Raissa and I below.

The train rocketed and bumped through the darkness. Even though the shades were up, there was nothing to see, for rain slashed at the windows, and the vague shapes whizzing by could have been houses, or trees or barns, it was impossible to guess. The clouds hung low, blotting out the moon and the stars.

I tried to close my eyes and think of my comfortable house in Austin to which it appeared I might after all return. I thought of my children and my beautiful granddaughter, Isabel. I tried to think of the train trips I had taken as a child, with my father and brother in the top bunk, my mother and me below, looking at the moving moonlit landscape above the wonderful string sacks that hung below the window and held our shoes and our toilet kits. Those trips seemed calmer and safer than this one, somehow. But of course I was a dependent then, and someone else, fortunately my compassionate parents, made the decisions.

But I could not sleep. I thought of Bokhara, the harem and the apples in the Emir's pool. I thought of Vera in her gold brocade headband and the dreadful dungeons by the Ark, where we had first met Raissa. I tossed and turned, trying to be quiet, until I realized that Raissa was also awake, and was talking to me in low tones. "We don't want to wake the girls," she said.

We talked about our marriages and our children. Raissa had two children, a boy in the university and a girl of twelve.

"I am lucky in my marriage," she whispered. "Anatoly and I would like more children, but we do not have the money to do that."

She was in her forties, she said. No, she did not yet dye her hair, though many of her friends did.

And how did she manage to have only two children? I asked. Didn't she sleep with her husband?

An indrawn breath. "Of course. But then I have an abortion. I've had five."

"Five?" My voice rose.

"Shhh, you'll wake the girls," cautioned Raissa. "Yes, five. What else to do?"

"There is no other kind of contraception?"

"No, none."

We were silent. The train ground along the tracks.

The insistent spitting sound, I realized, was the rain beating against the window. Abortion as contraception? It was hard to contemplate.

Raissa whispered, "I hear that you are interested in women's issues. All of us are interested in women's issues; they affect everyone—men, women, children. It is not only we women who are affected."

"I can see that, Raissa. But you say that the Russians liberated women from the old system, which was bad?"

Raissa considered. "Yes," she said, "and no. I think it is not so simple."

"No?"

"No. Yes, Russia liberated Uzbek women to work alongside men and be paid equally. Women *had* to work to make the new Soviet industries and farms work. So it wasn't exactly liberation."

"And?"

"And so women had jobs outside the home. How wonderful. Just like men. Do you not in America know what that has meant? It's not liberation. It's double work. Work outside home. Work inside home."

"What about the laws, though. Equal divorce, marriage, etc."

"Yes, yes," Raissa admitted. "But the world does not change so easily, like a machine on wheels of oil. No. Divorce is legal and equal for men and women."

"So what is the problem?" I whispered back.

"The problem is dowry."

"I thought that was forbidden," I offered.

Raissa laughed softly. "Do you in America never do that which is forbidden?"

I subsided.

"Families wish to give their daughters large gifts. That is to say, dowry. Money. Gold. Household goods. Beds. And so forth. But in a divorce if dowry has been given, it must be returned. People don't want to give back the dowry. Big trouble. Because the witnesses at the wedding are also responsible. If dowry isn't given back by groom's family, then witnesses must pay. Nice, huh?"

I made an unintelligible sound.

"You are right. Benevolent socialist government always makes sure everybody pays. You give dowry. You take the chance. Because dowry is illegal."

"Difficult," I murmured.

"And in America?"

"Divorce is easy, or relatively easy," I said, "but men don't want to pay for children, so children suffer."

"You see," replied Raissa. "Man and woman. That is the big problem of the world."

My eyes were getting heavy. But I felt it would be rude to fall asleep now.

Raissa reached across the aisle and touched my shoulder gently. I had the feeling that if I could see her, she would be smiling at me in a patronizing way. Tourists must sleep, she would be thinking.

"I know you wish to sleep now, my friend, but before you do, I forgot to tell you final and most important job of Uzbek woman under Russian Soviet socialist government. Work outside home, work in home, and then guess what?"

"What?" I was at a loss.

"The third job, which was supposed to make up for the difficulties of the others and be a great pleasure, was"—she paused dramatically—

"to sleep with their husbands." Her voice rose and I found myself shushing her just as she shushed me.

"But," she said, "they couldn't relax and enjoy themselves because they were always afraid of getting pregnant!"

She patted my arm. "So write in your book, my friend, that Uzbek women need contraceptives more than they need anything else! Now sleep!"

We disembarked at the Tashkent Station in bright sunshine. It was only eight o'clock and I invited Roberta, Vera, and Raissa to breakfast at the Uzbekistan Hotel. Vera declined with thanks, and set off for her lab.

In the dining room of the Uzbekistan Hotel, Raissa's formidable self came to the fore. She did not seem at all like the whispering woman who shared confidences with me in the last hours of the night on the train from Bokhara.

First, she called the waiter and ordered eggs and *toast*. Who would have dreamed that toast was available?

"And don't tell me there are no eggs," she said.

The headwaiter opened and shut his mouth.

"But while you are preparing the eggs, you can change this table-cloth. It is disgraceful."

She began to pick up the grubby white tablecloth and he, realizing she was serious, called a busboy to change our linen.

"Then we want juice and coffee."

The man looked haggard. "No juice."

"No juice." She paused. He looked anxious. "Very well. I can see there might be no juice. There would be an excuse for that." He relaxed, only to be brought up short as she shouted, "But there is no excuse for dirty tablecloths. What kind of impression do you think this makes on American tourists?"

Several people at nearby tables looked around.

"Bravo, Raissa!" I said, and meant it.

The eggs came. They were perfectly cooked. The toast was hot. The cloth was white. I looked at Roberta and we both smiled and shook our heads.

"Uzbek women!" said I.

"I told you they were formidable," said Roberta. "Are they feminists, B.J.? Is Raissa a feminist?"

Raissa did not deign to respond. She drank her coffee in a ladylike way, and called for a second cup.

□ □ □ □

Ramadan, the month of fasting, ended with the feast of Iid al-Fitr, the feast celebrated with enthusiasm throughout the Arab Muslim world. In Uzbekistan, however, little public interest was apparent. People's enthusiasm, Roberta declared, was reserved for Nowruz, the pre-Islamic festival commemorating the New Year. By the time Roberta and Vera and I had returned to Tashkent, the drab utilitarian city had been dressed up for the New Year. All along Uzbekistan Street, in front of the public buildings and monuments, giant pink, yellow, and blue flags moved gently in the soft breeze that signaled the end of winter and the beginning of spring. Between those celebratory sweeps of color up and down and around the squares hung the blue-, white-, and green-striped flag of independent Uzbekistan, with its crescent and rows of stars. At the Palace of Culture, workmen were setting up small wooden booths, with cupolas and arched windows painted pink and green, in designs of flowers, "like old Central Asian cities," Roberta said. And indeed the booths did look like the traditional sections of the cities from which we had just returned. Samarkand, Bokhara. In the booths food would be sold, puppets would cavort, musicians and dancers and storytellers would hold forth.

"Telling stories like Bibi Khanum and jokes from Hodja?" I suggested.

"Yes," said Roberta. "You should stay, B.J."

Vera said that I must come to dinner before leaving. "Saidollah will make *osh,* like I told you."

Michael, Monica, Roberta, and I traveled on a bus for a long time, then transferred to an old-fashioned clanging street car to the end of the line. Another twenty-minute walk took us to the gray cement workers' apartment blocks, out near the old Russian airplane factory, where Saidollah and Vera had a small flat. We brought Russian champagne and the last of the chocolate bars I had purchased in the Frankfurt airport. Roberta said, "It's a good gift, B.J. Chocolate is hard to find."

In the narrow living room we sat in a row on layers of flowered padded comforters, against cushions covered with the same cotton. Facing us was a built-in breakfront cabinet with bookshelves, drawers, and the wedding china. In one glassed-in section stood the wedding pictures, Saidollah tall, dark, and serious in a tuxedo, Vera in a Western-style flared white dress just as she had described to us in Bokhara. They looked at the camera with wide-open eyes, anxious, unsmiling. Vera wore a crown of white flowers.

We were given a tour of the flat while Saidollah put the final touches on the *osh,* the pièce de résistance that in its round aluminum pot occupied two burners on the family's small gas stove.

Aidan, Vera's sixteen-year-old cousin, was introduced. "She has come from the village to go to school and help us," said Vera. She was working with Vera's and Saidollah's son Alisher, aged seven, and Nargeeza, the nine-year-old daughter, to frost a cake Vera had made for dessert. I noticed the torn wrappers from my chocolate bars; the gift chocolate I brought for *them* was being made into a special treat for *us,* the guests—a lightning-like reciprocity.

The kitchen was the center of the apartment, with bedrooms, bath, and living room arranged off of it. The cramped feeling of the narrow spaces was mitigated by the balcony, which stretched around the flat and faced outward to a view of other flats and a few trees.

"We sit out on the balcony sometimes when the children are in bed," said Vera. "Whenever we have a moment to ourselves." She laughed. "Whenever that is!"

Saidollah called us and we sat down, ourselves as guests on one side of the table, Saidollah, Vera, Aidan, and the children opposite.

Cousin Aidan indicated to me that I should begin.

"You're the oldest, B.J.," joked Roberta. "Sign of respect."

Aidan made a place for the dish of the evening, its steam rising from the food heaped on an enormous blue-flowered platter.

Osh. The national dish of Uzbekistan. As I admired the fragrant pile of rice, carrots, and meat, I privately told myself that it closely resembled the pilafs or rice specialties that I was fortunate to have eaten over the years in many Arab countries, in many hospitable households such as this one. The children watched as I dug into the festal dish and I found myself making extravagant appreciative sounds. But my enthusiasm was not faked. The *osh* was excellent.

"Saidollah, it is wonderful," I murmured.

But Saidollah was modest, like any first-rate cook. It was not his best effort, he explained, because he had to hurry it. He was only able to start cooking after he got home from his laboratory at the National Research Institute.

"*Osh* should cook all day," he said, "so the tastes of meat and onions and carrots and lots of cumin, salt, and pepper mix together very well. That is the first part, and it is quite easy . . ."

"Yes," laughed Vera, "even a woman can do that."

Saidollah frowned slightly. But his good nature returned and he warmed to his culinary description, now in Uzbek. "The next part is crucial. A lot of garlic. A *lot* . . ." Michael was translating and smiling at Saidollah; they were obviously good friends.

"What do you mean by a lot?" I asked, thinking that I would love to try and duplicate *osh* when I got back to Texas. Maybe Bob would even like to try cooking it!

Aidan rose and returned with a large bulb pod of garlic. "Like this, madame," said Saidollah in carefully accented English. . . . "Many like this, five, six." I opened my eyes. "Five, six?" "Or even more," smiled Saidollah.

So I was arrogant in thinking that *osh* was just like Iraqi rice. This dish was different, with a particularly Uzbek cast, not to be confused with other pilafs.

"And the *osh* should then cook slowly all day over a very slow fire until the garlic is soft and permeates everything. I did not have time for that. I am sorry. You must come back."

"This is still very good."

"Yes, Saidollah, don't make excuses," smiled Michael. "We're eating a lot. That should tell you."

Michael was right. We were all eating far too much. No matter what Saidollah said, this was the best meal I'd had in Uzbekistan.

The conversation turned to Aidan, a small girl with a round face and dark eyes, who told us that her secondary school in Tashkent was much better than the village school.

"Aidan is considered very pretty in this society," Roberta said. "A round face like hers is celebrated in Uzbek poetry; the face of the moon, they call it."

"Not like mine," Vera smiled. "My face is too sharp."

Aidan realized we were talking about her and smiled shyly, looking first at me and then at Monica and Roberta. None of us qualified as "moon-faced," but then, as Vera put it, "you're not trying to get married here." She was joking, but Aidan watched her carefully.

Saidollah gave a short speech, which Michael translated. It seemed that Aidan's older sister might soon join them; she had been accepted at the elite Institute of Economics in Tashkent, the national center where diplomats and government leaders were groomed for leadership. The institute used to be free, but no longer; thus twelve members of the family contributed large sums of money so Aidan's sister, a brilliant student, would be able to attend. Equal education was available, therefore, for both men and women, but at a price.

"Liberation!" said Vera sarcastically. "They call this liberation! And you pay!" I am moved to point out that in America, everyone has to pay to go to college and university, and to places like Harvard, thousands and thousands of dollars.

Vera and Saidollah and Aidan and the children, to whom this information was communicated, simply didn't believe it.

"You're joking, B.J.," said Vera gently. "Isn't it a democracy there?"

But Monica, Michael, and Roberta backed me up.

"We learn in school that democracy is for all the people," enunciated Saidollah.

"Yes," said Michael. "You are right, Saidollah, and all the people decided that everyone should pay for education."

"So it is a democracy where people decide to pay, and then money is everything."

"You got it, Vera!" responded Michael.

We all wiped our hands on the white napkins and waited for dessert.

Alisher, sitting on his father's lap, asked, "Is America bigger than Uzbekistan, Papa?"

Saidollah nodded yes.

"How much bigger, Papa?"

Saidollah pointed to the world map on the wall, showing him where America was, a big irregular rectangle in the center of North America, and then Uzbekistan, a small canal-shaped country across oceans and continents in Central Asia.

Alisher looked at the map, then shook his head vigorously. "No!"

He was a slight dark-haired boy with a ready smile and his father's dark eyes. "Our country looks so small, Papa. It is *not* small! No way!"

Saidollah began to speak and Alisher turned to him. Roberta explained to me that Saidollah was trying to convince his son that quality (a good Uzbek) is much to be preferred over quantity (many not-so-perfect Americans).

Fortunately this discussion came to an end with the arrival of dessert—the chocolate cake. Aidan told us proudly that she and Nargeeza, using bits from the chocolate bar, had spelled out America on top of the cake. They'd run out of space, however, so she apologized for the arrangement.

"Does it make sense?" she asked.

When I looked at the cake, I saw this:

ca
AME
ri

"Yes, of course," I replied.

Everyone applauded the effort and Nargeeza smiled at us all.

"She will be a dancer I think," Saidollah offered. Was it the child's moon face of beauty, a face like Aidan's, that suggested that to him?

"No," said Vera firmly, "not a dancer. A scientist. Why not?"

This comment was evidently addressed to her husband, who felt bound to reply. And he said, through translators Michael and Roberta, that science is a whole life and raising children is a whole life, and it is hard for husband and wife to bring the two lives together. An eloquent argument for the division of labor between men and women, men in science, women in child-raising. But that seemed to be only the first part of his speech, addressed to me, Roberta explained later, as he had been told by Vera about my interest in women's issues. Saidollah concluded that "bringing the two lives together must be done in the world we all live in," and that he and Vera tried to do it, but it was not easy. "Aidan helps," he added, with a look at the gentle moon-faced cousin.

"But you help me, too," Aidan replied softly, which Roberta translated.

There was a short silence. We had all eaten well, and we were all moved, I think, by Saidollah's comments. Vera broke the silence.

"It is hard, the way we do it, Saidollah and I," she agreed. "But, you know, B.J., it is good. I don't know about America, but here the children know us both, they know we work hard and we care about them and we care about each other. Maybe that can be called"—she turned to Roberta for the exact phrase in English, and came up, triumphantly, with—"working liberation."

On my last day Marfua came to the Hotel Uzbekistan to deliver her manuscript, which I had promised to send on to ZED Press in London and to Lynne Rienner Publishers in Colorado. Roberta and I drank thick sweet Turkish coffee with her, around a scarred black wooden table in the hotel lobby. Such tables were at a premium in the lobby, which literally thronged with men. Most, Roberta said, were businessmen from all over the world come to try to sell their products to the people of this new Central Asian nation. But I also noted a trio of gentlemen in the robes and turbans of Egyptian religious leaders. "They are here for the end of Ramadan, to give lectures about Islam," Roberta whispered. "It was in the paper yesterday."

Several of the businessmen stared at us, as though willing us to get up and leave so they could sit down. But Marfua sat on, smoking and sipping her coffee.

"About feminism," she said to me, "you must not despair. Here we are trying. With workshops, with writings."

"But," I argued, "you yourself said, Marfua, that the State Women's Committee believes there's only one place for women—at home. If that is government policy, how can there be a place for feminism?"

She waved that idea aside with a contemptuous gesture of her cigarette. Outside the hallowed halls of the Institute for Restoration of Cultural Monuments, where she was a respected architect, Marfua looked much like many other tall, soberly dressed Uzbek women, except that she had cocked a bronze velvet beret over her stylishly cut black hair. "But isn't that true in the West?" she asked. "Don't conservatives want women to stay at home?"

"Yes, it's true," agreed Roberta.

"And does that stop people from working to improve women's condition?"

We both shook our heads.

"Well, then!" She took a last sip of her coffee and stubbed out her cigarette in the glass hotel ashtray. I thought to myself how Raissa would have disapproved of that ashtray—it was filthy!

Marfua stood up. Three men were hovering near us, presumably to snatch our table as soon as we had moved away. Marfua paid them no attention. "We work," she said. "We write." She tapped the manuscript, which now reposed on the table, significantly. "We must concentrate on the self, my dear friends, the self. Only when the self is fully developed, *humanly* developed, then we shall be free, all of us, no? Nourish the self."

"Yes," answered Roberta, smiling.

"And don't women have selves, like men, despite the State Women's Committee?"

"Yes, of course," I answered, and stood up with Roberta. The man with the cellular phone tried to nudge us out of the way so he and his clients could sit down. But Marfua stood her ground.

"We have selves," continued Marfua. "Men have selves, too. We must all work. And," she added, in a concluding sort of tone, "many men are with us in this effort."

I thought of Saidollah and Nadar and Anatoly, and nodded in response.

Marfua moved toward the door, and the men sat down.

But something still nagged at my memory.

"I agree with you, Marfua, but what about the fire business, women setting themselves aflame, how does that work in with our ideas about the self?"

Marfua stopped dead in the center of the lobby and glared at me.

"You've seen the Makhmudov film," she said. "All Westerners see it and that's all they remember."

"But it's very horrifying, Marfua, it's terrible," put in Roberta.

"And that is the only thing you will write in your book about Uzbek women?" she asked, accusingly.

"Of course not!" I found my voice rising. "But I can't get it out of my mind."

"Do you think we can?" By now, we are attracting curious glances from the milling crowd in the lobby, and I realized we were almost shouting and in English!

Marfua's beret bobbed up and down as she set about making points to me.

"Poverty!" She held up one finger.

"Ignorance!" She held up two fingers.

"Too many children!" She held up three fingers. "It must change! It *will* change. No more burning! We are working together to change things. You must help us!"

Her hand went up in the air, came down again.

"Take the manuscript, thank you, that will help," she said. "Goodbye."

The doorman, who, we had decided, was also a kind of government representative to check on the comings and goings of Uzbeks and foreigners, started at Marfua. She gave him not a glance, but headed down the steps, toward an old woman sitting on the curb, who was proffering fresh flowers. They looked like daisies and daffodils. Beyond Marfua's quickly moving figure in the bronze beret, I could see that the trees in Tamerlane's park were responding to the warmer temperatures. The bare black branches sported a haze of green, and in a far corner of the park, blossoms of pink could be seen. An almond tree, perhaps?

Three women stopped near the subway entrance. One held up a finger, then put down her shopping bags and took off her heavy dark coat. A violet dress appeared for a moment against the greening trees in the park before the ladies disappeared into the metro. Nowruz, the celebration of the new year, was next week, and would bring, the media proclaimed, greater prosperity and happiness to the citizens of independent Uzbekistan.

TWO

¤ ¤

Morocco

THE SAME FRIENDS and colleagues who had teased me about my "adventure" trip to Uzbekistan were asking me now why I was headed for Morocco. "Don't you know enough about Morocco by this time?" they asked, only half-jokingly. It was true that I was *supposed* to know a lot. Bob and I and our children, Laura Ann, Laila, and David, had spent the summer of 1971 in Casablanca, where Bob had run a study-abroad program for American students; we had lived in the old city, or medina, of Marrakech in 1971–72; I had written a book, *A Street in Marrakech* and made two documentary films in Morocco; I had been back for short visits on four other occasions. Why go back now?

Women, I answered. Maybe things were changing. How would we know from what we read in the Western media? Women everywhere were active, not passive. My colleagues were unconvinced. I wondered whether I really believed that the seeds of feminism might be germinating, unremarked until now, in the hard soil of the patriarchal Muslim society of Morocco.

But, I reminded myself, there was Fatima Mernissi, sociologist, feminist, a woman whose work and life I had always admired. She had recently published new work, both alone and as editor of a feminist collective in Casablanca. Surely she would have something to say about the status of her countrywomen.

Morocco's King Hassan II had recently appointed the novelist Leila Abouzeid to a commission purportedly "investigating the current practice of family law in Morocco." This, too, might be important to look into. Leila was also my friend.

Then there was Aisha bint Muhammad, who had started out in 1971 as our maid in Marrakech, and had gradually become my mentor and friend as well. She had helped me graft some Moroccan Arabic onto my Egyptian Arabic dialect; she had taught me how to cook *tajines,* those marvelous Moroccan stews; she had introduced me to women's religious life in the city; and she had served as a member of our Granada Television film crew in 1976. Aisha's current situation would be another basis for thinking about women's status in Morocco today.

There were many other reasons for stopping in Morocco on my pilgrimage in search of Islamic feminism. Since the nation stands on the western edge of the Islamic world, it has always been considered on the edge of that tradition as well. This is attributed to the widely held belief that North Africa was a relatively latecomer to Islam. But history shows a different picture. As early as the seventh century A.D., Muslim invaders converted the indigenous population, who purportedly were attracted by the new dynamic, egalitarian, and monotheistic religion. The Berbers joined the Islamic faith, and helped in the Arab conquest of Spain. But Arab political domination of the area did not really begin until 1100. Even then, the tribal peoples were not much excited about becoming part of an Arab state; they were more interested in maintaining their own freedom, and thus until the time of the French conquest, Morocco remained a collection of dissident tribal groups. Into modern times, historians and political scientists have noted a continuing tension between people of the *maghzen* (urban organized government) and people of the *bled* (the rural areas and tribal peoples).

The French attacked Algiers in 1830, an event that electrified surrounding areas. Moroccans fought along with Algerians in the famous battle of Isly, but the French won. Moroccans retreated to the rugged coastal highland and the inland mountains, and it was not until sixty-five years later that France succeeded in "pacifying," that is controlling, the people of Morocco.

Spanish, French, Portuguese, Berber, and Arabic. Just as these languages are the linguistic heritage of Morocco, so too are the customs and history of these peoples a reflection of this heritage. The legal system of modern Morocco is based on Islamic law, the sharia. But local customary law is also part of the tradition, and this has resonances from tribal law, as well as from Spanish and Portuguese custom; and the French penal code dominates the civil laws. Attitudes toward women come not only from Islam, but from earlier presences. For example: Morocco's southern borders are inhabited by Tuareg nomadic tribes, the blue men of the desert who dominated the area in the past. Herodotus mentions the Tuareg, whose men wear veils and whose women are seen as socially strong. Amazons, he calls them. Eventually the "Amazons" became Muslims, too, and incorporated Muslim law into their codes, but remnants of older laws and customs remain both in the Tuareg south and in the mountains, where Berber populations dominate. For example, a form of trial marriage is found in the High Atlas among the Ait Haddidou tribe. Here, during the annual moussem or festival held in the town of Imilchil, men and women come looking for mates. Divorced, single, young, middle-aged, they gather at Imilchil each year to look over the marriage prospects and perhaps find true love, or at least a reasonable marriage partner. The village notary public does a good business registering the unions formed during the moussem, but it is commonly understood that the couple can split up after a day or a month or a year. No cost, no hard feelings, no religious stigma.

This is very different from the traditional form of marriage in Islamic society, which involves an elaborate set of negotiations between the families of the bride and groom, negotiations which lead to a marriage contract, with a specified dowry to be given to the bride's family by the groom's family. Clearly Morocco has a different history and different customs. As Fatima Mernissi has said, the eastern part of the Islamic world has always been somewhat suspicious of Morocco. "We are far away," she points out. "Are we quite legitimate? We have been rebellious, we don't fit into the proper pattern . . . there is something faintly dissident about us. So what kind of Muslims are we?"

Given this history, one might expect Morocco to present a different face in terms of women's rights, women's movements, and, perhaps, in terms of modern feminism. I had not seen much evidence of feminism in my previous stays in Morocco. But I hadn't been looking either.

Leila Abouzeid, the novelist, had invited me to stay with her in Rabat, and I'd accepted the invitation with some reluctance. Would I not be intruding on the family? Would my presence not be burdensome economically? No, no, Leila had answered. "After all, I stayed with you in Texas, B.J., don't you remember?"

Yes, I remembered. Leila had come to the United States in the mid-eighties as a participant in the World Press Institute at the University of Minnesota. While in Minneapolis, she had called her old school friend and distant cousin Aziz Abbassi, a graduate student in linguistics at the University of Texas. Aziz was then single and he sought my husband out to explain that he had invited Leila to visit, but it would not be appropriate for her, a single woman, to move into his apartment.

"So I think Aziz is asking if she can stay with us," said Bob.

"Fine, I guess," I had responded.

We had a big house with empty bedrooms since our children had grown up and settled in homes of their own.

"Who is she?" I asked Bob.

"A cousin of Aziz, that's all I know, except he says she's a writer."

So Leila came and stayed and gave a lecture and, in parting, presented me with a copy of her first novel, *Am el Fil* in Arabic, titled *The Year of the Elephant* in English translation.

"I think you will like it, B.J.," she said. "It's about women's problems, and especially ordinary women's problems, just like you write about."

I thanked her. She smiled. Leila was a small, self-contained young woman with dark hair and eyes, and a quizzical look for the world. Her face was transformed by an occasional big, sunny smile.

"Now I have something else to ask you," she said abruptly. "It's not easy for me to do this."

"What?"

"Your film. *Some Women of Marrakech.*"

"Ye—es," I replied tentatively.

She cleared her throat. I steeled myself for what was to come, knowing full well the reaction of the members of the Moroccan diplomatic service to the film, both when it was shown in England, as part of the Granada *Disappearing Worlds* series, and in the United States, as one segment in the PBS *Odyssey* series. They were furious. The Moroccan ambassador in London had gone so far as to suggest that the producer/director and myself had staged the whole thing in our own living rooms.

"You know it has been much criticized in Morocco," began Leila.

"Yes, I know, but . . ."

She held up her hand. "That was one reason I wanted to meet you, because people told me you were a good person, and that the terrible things they were saying about you were not true."

I laughed, but it was not too funny, really. I had drafted letters for both Granada and PBS officials to reply to the official accusations. What bothered them most, the officials said, was a scene in the women's public bath. And I thought that probably the images of poor women in the film conflicted with the official public image of Morocco as a prosperous modern nation. It did no good to point out that the

Granada series was called *Disappearing Worlds,* and therefore purported to chronicle styles of life soon to be out of existence.

"So?" I managed to get out.

"So I would like to ask you if I could see the film before I leave." I looked at her, amazed. "You haven't seen it?"

"No, and neither has anyone else I know. They just criticize it," she said, and dropped her eyes. "So I want to see for myself."

"Of course, provided . . ."

"Yes?"

"Provided you tell me honestly what you think after you've seen it." She nodded, her smile gone. "Oh, I will," she promised.

That evening, dinner at our house was not a quiet affair. Perhaps dreading Leila's reaction to the film, and wanting to avoid embarrassing us both, I had invited three other people. The conversation was general and lively, and Leila seemed as animated and unconcerned as she had been before our morning conversation. Why was I so hung up on the criticism of this film? It had been an honest attempt on my part, as the ethnographer hired by Granada, to help present lives of women of several classes in Marrakech.

It could have been a better film, but it was not dishonest.

It was true that I felt the producer/director had already made up her mind about the image of women she wished to present. Her underlying assumption, like that of many Western feminists, was that Moroccan women were sequestered, oppressed, passive, and powerless, and should be a salutary warning to Western feminists. I partially agreed with her, but my basic assumptions were different. Oppressed, yes, but by poverty as much as by man's patriarchal heavy hand. Sequestered, sometimes, but not as in the harems of the Ottoman sultans. Passive, never! Powerless? Perhaps in public life; women had no formal political power that we, as Western observers, could see and document. But on the other hand . . . the picture was complex. Morocco was not the United States, it had its own traditions, both benevolent and mean-spirited. I had welcomed the opportunity to work on such a film, and I felt that in many ways the actual footage, the images of women themselves, defied easy stereotyping.

The bath scene was a good example. As a properly catechized Catholic girl, I was, of course, a prude. I certainly had no desire to parade naked in a bath with several dozen unknown women. No desire at all. Our film crew, all women, were British and even more prudish, so the idea of filming women in the public bath never occurred to us.

"Now you've seen the film, that's the background," I found myself explaining to Leila after the dinner guests had left. Bob had retired to bed, and Leila had settled herself on our living room couch, clearly ready for discussion. I was not going to get out of this easily. To cover my uneasiness, I began to babble on about the problems in making the film.

Leila sat on the couch, observing me, not saying a word.

"And the bath," I sputtered. "It was the women themselves who wanted us to film in there, can you believe it?"

Leila smiled slightly and nodded. "You asked them," she said. It was a statement, not a question.

"No, we didn't ask them, they asked us. Aisha said to me, how can you make a film about Moroccan women without showing us in the bath? We go there once a week. It's great fun. That's where we hear the news, think about brides for our sons, see our friends in relaxed surroundings."

"Yes, of course," said Leila dismissively. "And then . . . ?"

"Well." I thought back to the editing days in London. Dai Vaughn, the editor, was fascinated with the opening and shutting of doors, the metaphor of inside/outside. He was flummoxed, clearly, by the bath footage.

"What are we supposed to do with this?" He had gestured at the steamy sequence, which was literally steamy; the camerawoman, Diane Tammes, had real problems keeping her lens clear; the sound recorder, Marilyn Gaunt, had to keep going out of the bath to dry off the equipment.

"It's another inside/outside metaphor," I had offered. "These women are covered up all week, but one day out of the week, they're uncovered."

It sounded ridiculous, stated in that way. Melissa Llewellyn-Davies, the producer/director, said so out loud.

"And what about the women?" she had asked crisply. "Won't they catch hell from their husbands and brothers for showing up naked on Western television screens?"

This of course had occurred to me, but the ethical issue had been finessed, we thought, in several ways. First, we had rented the bath for the evening, so only the ladies we knew would be there. No strangers would be present. Second, when we had invited people, we had told them what to expect, and added that they should not come if they felt it would not be good for their reputations.

Dai, Melissa, and I had sat in the London editing room off Wardour Street and viewed the footage again and again.

"Amazing," was all Dai would say. "Amazing."

And as I sat there, I began to feel that with all the good will in the world, we might still have made a mistake. Surely some male relative might see it and take offense.

"Maybe we should cut it," I suggested.

By this time Dai and Melissa had decided we must have it.

"Then only show people from the back," I suggested. In fact, I had insisted and that was what we had done.

Leila said, "Ahem," interrupting my musings. I was back in Austin, waiting for the critical ax to fall on me and my well-meaning but faulty efforts to show women's lives as I thought them to be.

"I see now why people don't like the film, why they criticize it so harshly."

I swallowed. "Why?"

"Well, it shows real life, doesn't it? Life is hard for women, isn't it? And the film shows us that. So the leaders and critics don't want to accept that."

I stared at her.

Then she smiled. "So I think it is a good film, and when I go back to Morocco, I will write an article about it."

Two months later I got a thank-you letter and a clipping. Leila had indeed written an article about the film. "The only thing to criticize about this work is the fact that we in Morocco haven't done it already," she had written. "Instead of castigating Professor Fernea for her effort to show reality, we should be doing it ourselves."

"Yes," Aziz had said. "Leila is serious in asking you to stay with her in Morocco. You are her friend. She will be upset if you *don't* accept her invitation."

Leila's house in Rabat was on Rue Haroun al-Rashid, named for the caliph of eleventh-century Baghdad who appears as a character in the *Arabian Nights*. The caliph, it was said, regularly donned disguises and went into the streets on warm summer nights, to see for himself what was happening to the people of his capital city. It would have been relatively easy then to pass unnoticed on those narrow winding medieval streets. Not so on the well-lighted thoroughfares of modern Rabat. The name was the only exotic characteristic of Rue Haroun al-Rashid, which, like most Rabat streets, was relatively new and certainly newly paved, did not meander at all, and cut straight as an arrow from the broad Avenue de France beyond the palace of King Hassan II, to Rue Idris, where the National Lottery building stood.

Sober, square modern apartment blocks, four and five stories high, stretched along both sides of Rue Haroun al-Rashid, their gleaming white walls accented with black ironwork balconies. Crimson bougain-villea blossoms trailed over the black ironwork fences enclosing small green strips of grass and borders of oleanders. And lemon trees in dark pots graced the buildings' entrances, where wide marble stairs led to more marble in the foyers, the stone broken by banks of neat polished wooden mailboxes, six in Leila's building. The only jarring note in this smooth and elegant stretch of modern construction was an abandoned villa directly opposite Leila's house, a villa that Haroun al-Rashid might have recognized, large and dilapidated with towers and window shutters crazily askew. The fence was bent, and the peeling wooden gate was shut on a tangle of unidentifiable shrubbery and vines, hiding the remnants of what once must have been a large private garden.

"Someone is trying to buy that house," Leila commented, "but the heirs have not yet agreed. One son is in Spain, I think."

The apartment on Rue Haroun al-Rashid, where I was a guest, actually belonged to Fatiha and Abdul Hadi, Leila's older sister and brother-in-law. Both were successful and busy lawyers, and Abdul Hadi was the dean of the Moroccan lawyers association, the local equivalent of the American Bar Association. The apartment was their city pied-à-terre, for they actually lived in the country, nearly an hour outside Rabat, where they raised chickens and ducks and flowers and grew their own vegetables.

"The country is so much better for the chidren," explained Fatiha, greeting me at the flat that first day. "But we still have to keep a city schedule—work, school, home for lunch. Too much. So we got this place. Welcome!"

"But aren't I putting you out?" I asked.

Fatiha smiled. "We'll still come here for lunch," she said. "That's mostly what we use the flat for anyway."

I was given a tour of the new apartment, two bedrooms, two baths, dining alcove, kitchen and a long salon giving onto a ground-floor patio, its retaining walls plastered white like all the houses on the street, in fact, like all the houses in Rabat!

"Yes, yes, Rabat is the white city," Fatiha explained. "I know you lived in Marrakech, that's the red city. Fez is gray and green, but we are white."

"Like Casablanca," put in Leila.

The half-walls of tiles in every room, dark blue, green, and gold, reminded me of our own house in the Marrakech medina where we lived in the seventies; even the sculpted white plaster ceilings were the same, intricately carved designs that were considered passé twenty years ago.

"But now they're coming back," said Leila. "The King is behind the new movement to return to traditional crafts to produce our own goods. All the tiles are from here. Really, B.J."

I nodded and admired, pleased that the Moroccan government had seen fit to recognize and revive its own fine arts and crafts production. The dark mahogany door frames were also carved, and Rabati pile carpets covered the cold marble floor of the salon; the room where I had been invited to stay boasted a red Berber rug from the mountains.

Why were we staying here, one might have asked, instead of at the Agdal flat which Leila owned and where she usually lived with her unmarried sister Soad?

"You will have your own room here," Leila had said. "I know how important privacy is to people in the West. And also," she'd added, "the wiring is not strong enough at the other house for the electric heaters. I know, my friend, that you are used to *warm* rooms. And it's cold here in January."

Leila was very thoughtful. I was getting old enough so that the cold did indeed bother me, though my family says that it has always done so.

Rue Haroun al-Rashid. "Does it remind you of what the West thinks of the Arab world, B.J.?" Leila asked over a breakfast of bread, butter, honey, and café au lait.

"Mmm," I answered and took my coffee outside, to a small place on the back patio that was warmed by the sun at that early hour of the morning. The flat itself was beautiful, but freezing; it did not get the sun at all. The heaters helped a little.

"But it's wonderful in summer," said Leila, as though she had read my thoughts. I hovered in that patch of sun with my cup of coffee.

"You know, B.J., the *Arabian Nights* is also an important text for us," Leila went on. She stood at the kitchen door, facing me on the patio, in an apron, an onion in her hand, clearly already thinking of lunch and dinner. I shook myself, realizing that I was so obsessed with my cold feet that I was already becoming an inconsiderate guest and had stopped listening to my friend.

"Yes, Leila, I know," I replied briskly and came back to the kitchen where Leila began cutting up onions and garlic and tomatoes and cleaning a feathery bunch of cilantro. The sun was gone from the patio.

"You remember when we met in New York, B.J., by chance?"

"Yes, indeed." I poured myself another cup of coffee. It was at the Carlyle Hotel. I was having a drink with a friend and suddenly Leila and a group of Moroccans burst through the revolving doors of the lobby entrance.

"We were recording the *Arabian Nights* then, remember? The King had decided to make cassettes of it for all the Arab leaders as gifts on the feast of Iid al-Adha."

"And you were reading the role of Scheherazade," I said.

She smiled happily, wiping her eyes of onion tears. "It was such fun! The language is so beautiful!"

"And now you're reduced to cooking for a lady friend from Texas who wants to learn what's happening to Moroccan women these days."

"Yes, yes, but everything is interesting in its time and place."

Leila, as long as I had known her, would every so often make such pronouncements. They were always a bit surprising, since one did not expect ironic comments from this small, modest, dark-haired young woman with the gifted pen and the heart-shaped face. When I wrote the introduction to the 1989 English translation of her novel *The Year of the Elephant,* I had wondered whether the often sad narrative might be loosely autobiographical.

I said to myself that she would tell me if and when she wanted to. For between the cheerful smiles and the philosophical pronouncements were long periods of quiet, thoughtful, even morose reserve. She kept her own counsel, as my mother would have said, and chose carefully the moment to speak out.

Soad arrived and was introduced, a striking dark-haired girl, younger than Leila, with intensely white skin and sleepy dark eyes. She was perfunctory but correct in her greetings. And she might look young and sleepy-eyed to me, but Leila had said that Soad was a high-powered economist with the Ministry of Finance. Her turquoise earrings were gorgeous and her black suit well cut and fashionable over a silk print blouse. She was not married, and had no plans in that direction, said Leila.

We had a quiet dinner à trois, a delicious couscous with various vegetables, but the principal accompaniment was pumpkin, in spiced, succulent chunks! And then to bed. I was still exhausted after the recent flight, and silently thanked Leila for her consideration once more as I lay down on my comfortably hard single bed, fitted out with bright pink sheets, flowered pink pillow cases, and a heavy coverlet of double velour-finish wool, gray with black polka dots and pink flowers. The coverlet also brought back memories of Marrakech, where Bob and I had had a similar coverlet, green and yellow; the merchant had explained to me that the double layer of velour finish was a sure bet to keep out all the winter cold of Morocco.

Just before I fell asleep, I got up again to make sure I had turned off the expensive heater Leila had provided for my comfort, and I saw, as I drew back the heavy flowered curtains, a glimpse of the moon. Large and pale, it was rising over the courtyard, which glimmered white in the darkness of the winter night that had settled over Rue Haroun al-Rashid.

Interviews began, in English, French, Arabic. Leila said she would help with the Arabic; I could manage the French. Leila had taken seriously my stated desire to learn about women's issues in the new Morocco, and made a list of the people I must talk to: lawyers; judges; bank tellers; a librarian who had started a volunteer family and child counseling organization; writers; a high school teacher who asked me to speak to his class. "And we must try to reach the new members of Parliament," she added. "The very first Moroccan women elected!"

I had no idea that women had recently been elected to Parliament; I had read nothing about it in the Western media.

First, however, came commitments. I had agreed to give lectures at two universities—Moulay Ismail in the central Atlas city of Meknès, and Muhammad V, Morocco's oldest and most respected liberal arts faculty, in Rabat.

At Muhammad V University, I had been invited to a meeting of the women's studies steering committee, formed in 1994 to promote research on women's issues, sponsor lectures, and eventually to initiate courses. The multilingual group of women drifted in slowly, and we warmed our hands first on tiny cups of strong Turkish coffee, then on big flowered teacups of mint tea.

Dr. Fouzia Rhissassi had studied in England, written on Thomas Hardy, and was the driving force behind the group, which also included Dr. Amina Belabbas, whose specialty was French literature and who, not surprisingly, had studied in France. Dr. Fathiya Benalla, a slim stylish woman with reddish hair, taught Spanish literature and had done graduate work in Spain. Dr. Khadija Misdali taught philosophy and Islamic studies. She had studied in Morocco. She was the only one wearing a head scarf, one element of the new style of modest dress called *hijab;* it went well with her tweed suit and white blouse.

The faculty lounge looked much like a faculty lounge at any university. Round tables, decent but much used; banquettes covered in brown corduroy; a few upholstered chairs, also in brown corduroy; rattan chairs; and the luxury of a tea man taking orders.

Dr. Fouzia introduced me as an American professor of comparative literature who had written many books about Arab women and was now preparing to write a new one, on what was happening with Muslim women today, their problems, their prospects. She added that I was also a former director of women's studies at the University of Texas.

There was a short silence.

Our teacups clinked in our saucers.

I was a bit embarrassed by the long and complimentary introduction. So I tried to turn the conversation away from my own work.

"How did your women's studies group get started?"

I had apparently struck the right note, for the women all started talking and then stopped. Dr. Fouzia took the floor.

"We went to a conference on women at the university in Granada, Spain. That was in 1992. You have heard about it, no doubt."

"No."

"You must have heard about it. It was an important women's issues conference."

I shook my head, thinking how language and geography, as well as culture, intervene in any efforts to reach across boundaries. No, I had never heard about any conference in Granada.

"So I came back," continued Dr. Fouzia, "and called a meeting of anyone interested. These ladies responded enthusiastically." The group of women smiled self-consciously; Dr. Fathiya fingered her rings, clusters of large sparkling diamonds.

"Our first task," went on Dr. Fouzia, "was to prove to the university administration that we were serious scholars, not just women who should be home with the children."

I could not resist a smile, remembering similar battles we had fought at Texas not so long ago. The then dean of the college of liberal arts had received us in his office. "You girls," he had called us, the first steering committee of a proposed women's studies program.

We had been shocked at first by his put-down. "We don't want activism here. This is an academic institution," he'd said. We had explained earnestly that women's studies was academic, substantive scholarship in the new paradigms emerging in the sciences and social sciences as well as the humanities. He dismissed us. It had taken twenty years and a change in deans and presidents before the women's studies program at Texas had been given an independent budget.

The Moroccan ladies listened politely while I recounted the tale of our women's studies struggle at Texas. When I had finished, Dr.

Fouzia said, "I think you will see that our experience has been very different."

"How?" I asked.

"Well, it begins differently," she said. "We started a research group to compile a bibliography of studies done at the university on women's issues, from 1974 to the present. What we found was shocking!"

"Shocking?" I echoed.

"Yes, the papers had all been destroyed. When we went to the librarian, he explained there was no space to store them. History had been wiped out!"

I responded, "That's terrible! Terrible!"

"But," said Dr. Fouzia, "this catastrophe gave us, though we didn't realize it at the time, a wonderful opening to talk about the need for our program. Destroying history was a crime in a new independent nation like Morocco."

Dr. Fathiya took up the tale. "The rector and the dean were receptive to the idea of a research center, and they sent us to the minister of culture. He, too, was helpful."

"That's wonderful," I said. "But they didn't give you support to do all that, did they?"

"Yes. They did, they gave us money."

In America at least, money was always the key issue, for any support for women's studies meant taking that money from other academic programs. At a time of shrinking budgets, this was crucial. How had they done it here?

"But if there is opposition . . ." I began.

"We expected it," said Dr. Khadija, "and were surprised at the response. You know what the minister of culture said?"

"No."

"He said bravo! He said women should have more courage."

"Courage?" I echoed. "To do what?"

"To speak out, to document, to articulate what was unspoken in our society about women's issues."

I could not think of a response. The highest levels of Moroccan government were interested in women's studies, had funded a research center, were encouraging women to "have more courage," and on the other hand, in the so-called progressive West, our dean had sent us back to our classrooms empty-handed!

"But," I said, "I expect the King was not so excited about this plan."

The ladies looked from one to the other. They smiled at me. Dr. Fouzia called for more tea.

"The King," said Dr. Fouzia, "gave support also."

"Why?" The question was out before I could stop it; the surprise I felt must have shown on my face.

"Why? Wouldn't your American President and Congress give such support?"

"Well . . ." I launched into a brief description of foundation grants for funding new academic programs, like women's studies.

"No, no, B.J." It was Leila, who had been until now a silent listener to the discussion. "They mean real support, like from the President."

"Politically I don't think our President would find it such a great idea."

"Politically?" The ladies looked at each other again. The tea man emerged, and set down his worn tray full of teacups on the brown table. As I turned to pass the sugar to Dr. Fathiya, I noticed a lone gentleman, in proper professorial corduroy coat with leather elbow patches, sitting by the window, clearly listening intently to our conversation. As I looked, he quickly and ostentatiously rattled his newspaper and focused intensely on the top of a page. But from my vantage point, I could see that it was upside down!

Dr. Fouzia explained. "Politics. That's exactly why the King and the minister were interested in our plan."

"Politics?" I echoed.

"Yes. Political parties wanted the support of women, the King wanted women to get involved in government, to work on issues of public affairs. The King said, Morocco is a small country; we need all the people we have to work on the issues. Especially those who are educated. They will educate others."

We stirred our tea. I looked at Leila, who looked back at me. "You have surprised our American guest," she said.

"Yes," I said. "You have."

"Maybe Hillary Clinton needs more courage," said Dr. Amina. Her English was spoken with a French accent. "Why did she collapse? We were so disappointed. Where was her self-confidence?"

Where indeed? "She wanted to do the best for her husband, I think," I offered lamely.

Dr. Fathiya made a sound which might, if she had not been such an elegant lady, have been described as a snort.

"I think," said Dr. Fouzia, smiling, "we should talk a bit about strength. We all need it!"

"Sources of strength." I took out my notebook. "Do you mind if I write down some of this?"

"No, we'd be delighted. We want you to write in your book what you see and hear from Moroccans, not what foreigners tell you."

"Strength," I repeated.

Dr. Khadija spoke up. "Moroccan women are not stupid and backward," she said.

"Of course not," I responded. "For example, all of you are highly educated."

"Oh, it is not just that," said Dr. Khadija. "There are Moroccan men who think even educated women should not be in positions of public responsibility. Yet Islam does not make such statements. No, no, the Qur'an does not say that." She set down her teacup.

"Back to sources of strength." I was writing busily.

"Faith in God," from Dr. Khadija.

"Belief in oneself," from Dr. Fouzia.

"Recognition of the need to resist, and resist, and resist," from Dr. Fathiya.

Dr. Amina suddenly looked at her watch, muttered something excusing herself as she was late to class, and rushed out of the room. I looked at my watch too and I closed my notebook. The man by the window had folded up his newspaper and was trying to creep out. But Dr. Fouzia hailed him genially.

"Ahmed," she said brightly. "Did you find our conversation interesting?" Ahmed looked uncomfortable for a moment, then smiled.

"Very interesting, mesdames," he answered, and almost ran out of the room.

Dr. Fouzia turned to me. "May I ask you one more question?"

"Certainly." I tried to look intelligent, yet I felt that my mind was not focusing, but racing away in many different directions. The discussion had not gone at all the way I had expected.

"Will you kindly," said Dr. Fouzia, "explain what this term gender studies means? We read it all the time now in the women's studies literature. What is it exactly?"

"Oh, Fouzia, it's *genre*, as in literary genres, nothing else," said Dr. Fathiya.

"No, I don't think so," I said. "It's quite different. The word gender does not mean literary type, nor does it mean sex . . ."

The four remaining ladies stared at me.

I tried again. "I mean, men and women are physically different everywhere."

"Of course," they replied.

"That doesn't mean being a man or being a woman is the same

everywhere. Society shapes people differently. Gender studies is based on that idea."

The ladies regarded each other, then turned back to me.

"But," offered Leila, "this cannot work in Arabic, B.J. I mean, every word in Arabic has a feminine or a masculine ending. Nothing is without those endings. So everything is defined as either masculine or feminine. We don't have a neuter word."

I took a deep breath. "It's not neuter I'm talking about. Gender doesn't mean neuter."

"What does it imply then?"

"Cultures, different cultures, build or construct gender in particular ways. . . ."

I was greeted with a chorus of "No, no . . . Not possible."

But Dr. Fouzia's eyes lit up. "Are you speaking perhaps of androgyny in the sense that Virginia Woolf uses it?"

I shook my head firmly, maybe too firmly. "No, no. I'm talking about the way in which men's roles and women's roles may be constructed or shaped differently in different societies. Dress, language, expected work, and so on."

"Of course," agreed Dr. Fathiya. "We can see that. We dress differently from African women or Asian women. Maybe we do different kinds of work. But people are always men or women, masculine or feminine. I frankly don't see what all the fuss is about gender in the literature these days."

I was stymied, for the moment at least. What I meant by gender was not what they meant. Why wasn't my understanding of the word gender, and all it implied, comprehensible to these highly educated women scholars?

We rose and shook hands. Dr. Fouzia asked me for a lecture title and a date. I came up with *Cross-Cultural Research on Women: Problems and Possibilities*. They seemed pleased. I reflected as I walked out to the busy street with Leila that maybe writing this lecture would help me answer the women's studies steering committee's questions about gender, and also help me to organize and marshal my own ideas about women, and women's roles, and how I understood and perceived the feminist movement in my own country.

"Don't be deceived," cautioned Leila, as we walked back toward Rue Haroun al-Rashid, stopping for a moment at her own flat to pick up some clothing.

"Deceived? What do you mean? Deceived about what?"

"Not all Moroccan women are as self-confident and powerful as the ones in that group," she said.

"It's true, that committee does seem rather special."

"But still . . ."

"Still what, Leila?"

"You also should remember that belief in God and belief in yourself are also necessary for everyone. That is what Islam is about."

"Islamic feminism is about that too?"

"Yes, if we can call it that. But it's not new and from the West, as you speak about it. It is a very old idea."

"Well, Christianity and Judaism are also full of very old ideas about belief in God and belief in yourself," I returned, rather defensively.

Leila nodded. "Of course. That is what you believe. I understand. But they are different from Islam. Islam gives more rights to women than either Christianity or Judaism. I think that's why maybe you go on and on about our veils in your society."

"Yes?"

Leila laughed, a throaty infectious laugh that never failed to surprise me, seeming as it did to be at variance with her sober demeanor. "It's a good way to cover up the weaknesses in your own beliefs—it veils them neatly, so to speak." She gave me a mischievous sidelong glance.

I was silent. And almost as if to answer for me, the noon prayer suddenly sounded from all the minarets of the white city of Rabat.

"God is great! God is great!"

Five times a day all the citizens of the city, young and old, male and female, poor and rich, were reminded of that belief. The words and the sounds were woven into the texture of everyday life, work, leisure, love, travel, sport, sleep. I, too, had come to expect that call, for though I am not a Muslim, I was present in the city, in the environment of that belief, and whether I chose to or not, I would hear the call to prayer before dawn, then at dawn, at noon, at sunset, and at the fall of night.

"There is no God but God." In Christian environments, the pealing of church bells reminded visitors to cities that it was Sunday, the Christian day of prayer; bells rang also, tolling dolefully, in times of death. But the Muslim muezzin reminded people five times a day, every day, that they were in the constant presence of the one Deity. They could not ignore it.

The call reverberated in my head and then died away while Leila and I climbed the stairs to her cold salon in the Agdal district to make some telephone calls. (There was no phone in the Haroun al-Rashid flat so no clients could bother Fatiha and Abdul Hadi and their children while they were having lunch.)

As we reached the top of the stairs, the phone rang.

"Hello!" said Leila. After a brief conversation, she hung up and turned to me, her face alight. "When God wants something to happen, He arranges it," she said elliptically.

"What?"

"That was my friend, the computer whiz, calling to say he has finally figured out a way to print out the disks of my new book from my broken computer."

I'd heard about this computer. Brought home from America, it blew out when Leila plugged it into the socket in the Rabat flat. A disaster.

"The computer man will be here in a few minutes." She smiled. "I've been struggling to print out those disks for months."

Fifteen minutes later, while the computer whiz was manipulating the broken machine and Leila was serving tea to his wife, a software producer wearing *hijab,* the phone rang again. This time it was for me, a Texas student friend, Sandra Carter, who was in Morocco on a Fulbright dissertation grant. I had been trying to find her here and she said she had been trying to reach me for days, but of course did not know that I had been staying, not here, but in Leila's sister's flat on Rue Haroun al-Rashid. We were there just in time for her call!

I swallowed my supercilious smile at Leila's suggestion that the Deity arranges things. Instead, I invited Leila for lunch to meet Sandra. Leila nodded and accepted, but could not resist reminding me: "God is great!" She smiled. "Don't forget that, B.J." And she wagged a finger at me.

Lunch at the pied-à-terre that day was special. Fatiha had come home early from her law office to make paella, "in honor of you, B.J.," Leila explained. The whole family had gathered to look me over and say hello: Fatiha, her husband Abdul Hadi, Zakaria, the middle son, and Fawzia, her twelve-year-old daughter, who brought along a friend from school. Their oldest son was in Tunis, attending medical school there. Soad also turned up, and I was asked to explain my project again. I first brought out a copy of my earlier book on Marrakech, and then I passed around family pictures, to show, Leila laughed, "that I'm a real woman, not a gender woman."

For a moment I thought we were moving into the gender quandary again, but the children torpedoed that possibility by asking detailed questions about the family photos of my oldest daughter Laura Ann, her husband Alberto, our son David and his wife Kim, and then about the youngest, Laila the lawyer. But the biggest interest was in the computer, which was visible in the picture of Laila in her law office.

"Look, Mama," said Zakaria. "This is the kind of computer we need here in Morocco."

His father looked carefully at the picture as well. At least I thought that was what Zakaria was saying, since the conversation went on in both French and Arabic and the Moroccan Arabic was now hard for me to follow.

Over the excellent paella, the salad vinaigrette, and the sole meunière, a family discussion raged about the quality of men's and women's lives in Morocco. I use the word "rage" to reflect the spirit of the discussion, which was intense and spirited. Every member of the family was telling me how to write my book.

"You must first explain about the changes in the family law," said Fatiha.

"And interview some judges, to get their point of view," said her husband. "Because they are the ones who will implement the changes in the law."

"Oh yes," I answered. "That's one of the principal issues I want to write about."

"You should," said Soad abruptly, switching to French. Her contributions up to now had been in Arabic. I saw her comment in French as a gesture of friendliness to me, the first she'd made, and I was pleased. After all, she had not invited me to stay, her sister had, and she had been inconvenienced by having to move back and forth between flats.

"And," she added, "when you write *that*, don't forget to mention the work of Leila Abouzeid."

The entire family focused on Leila, who smiled, pleased. Clearly her family was very proud of her contributions on this crucial issue. It was King Hassan II himself who appointed her to the special commission formed in 1992 to evaluate *mudawana*, or Moroccan family law. The commission's mandate was to judge whether the current law fulfilled the spirit of the Qur'an or not, and to measure its effects on women, men, children, and the family. It was also empowered to make recommendations. The group's work was finished, the recommendations had been forwarded to a committee of religious scholars (all men), and the King's proclamation of reforms had been recently published and analyzed in the media.

"And is it a beneficial document for women, the King's new proclamation, I mean?"

Soad, Fatiha, Leila, and Abdul Hadi all began to talk at once and in rapid Arabic. Fawzia and her friend excused themselves and peeled off to the back bedroom to watch television. The daughter's look at her friend said clearly, "I've heard all this before. They'll be here for hours."

But Zakaria sat on, looking from one to the other: his mother, his father, his aunts.

"Well." Leila turned to me finally. "I'll give you the article I wrote, B.J., it was published in one of our daily newspapers. You can judge for yourself."

Fatiha ventured, "The changes will probably seem trivial to you, B.J., as a Westerner, but they are not."

"Tell her what you think, Abdul Hadi," suggested Leila.

Abdul Hadi considered. His son watched him carefully. He was a middle-sized man with an intelligent, open face. He hunched his shoulders under his gray pullover sweater and began, slowly, in French.

"In the past, as you know, madame, family law was administered by qadis, religious judges. Everyone knows that in the past these qadis tended to discriminate against women. Well"—he opened his hands toward us, almost apologetically—"they thought the modern world was full of sin and it was women's fault because they didn't stay at home like they're supposed to . . ."

"But how can they stay at home?" broke in Soad. "How ridiculous. They have to go out and work."

"Yes, yes, Soad, I'm trying to explain to Madame the mentality of these qadis, that's all." Abdul Hadi paused again. "Well, of course women have to go out and work, that's the name of the game these days. What I am trying to say now is that qadis really can't discriminate against women anymore, at least in terms of divorce proceedings because of the careful wording of the new law."

Zakaria smiled at his father proudly.

"I agree with you, my dear," returned Fatiha, "in general, that is . . ."

Laughter interrupted her, a relief from the intensity of the conversation. Legal reforms changing women's position affected the everyday functioning of the family, that basic cornerstone of Moroccan society, indeed of all Islamic societies. What the King had done, and what the qadis will do with the new *mudawana,* would have reverberations in everyone's life for years to come—men, women, children.

"But . . ." continued Fatiha. She was not to be stopped. "One must not be too cheerful about all this. We want Madame to tell it honestly in her book. And I think"—Fatiha drew a deep breath—"I think this idea that if the mother remarries she has to turn over the children to her ex-husband—that is bad! That is not a reform at all!"

"Hear, hear, Fatiha!" from Soad, in Arabic, but even I got the gist. Abdul Hadi nodded. He folded his arms across his gray sweater. "Yes, you are quite right, my dear."

Where to go from here? No one apparently wanted to think about the possibility of new reforms so soon after the painful process of trying to pass the last ones. We finished the succulent paella—shrimp, rice, peas. I noticed Soad savoring the mushrooms. The girls were called to clear the table.

"Still, I believe there is hope that child custody practices will improve," announced Fatiha, bringing dates and oranges to the table.

"Hope?" echoed Soad sarcastically. "You are joking, I'm afraid."

"Yes, hope," repeated Fatiha firmly. "In the past the qadis were very old. They were the product of a different era, the past. They are almost gone. The new qadis are young."

Abdul Hadi was peeling an enormous sweet Moroccan orange. "They are mostly young now, madame, Fatiha is right. We deal with them all the time in our law practice. I hope there is hope." He smiled at his bon mot.

"I think those new qadis remember what their mothers went through and they are much more open," said Fatiha.

Soad and Leila were silent.

"Papa, Papa, look at the time!" cried Fawzia. "We're going to be late getting back to school."

"Yes, yes." Abdul Hadi wiped his mouth on the linen napkin, then rinsed his hands and face at the small sink in the foyer. He groped in his tweed jacket for his car keys.

"Leila," he said, "we will arrange for B.J. to talk to a judge in the Court of Appeals, the highest court of appeals. Then she can ask those who are actually involved in these cases."

Morocco's national courthouse stood in the center of downtown Rabat. It was set in a small fenced garden, far enough back from Boulevard Muhammad V so that passersby could appreciate the grandeur of the pillared portico, and the imposing proportions of the four-storied neoclassic building. Nineteenth-century France as well as classical Greece and Rome had clearly participated in the design of the structure, and little of the Moroccan architectural heritage was evident. Yet the building was imposing in its own hybrid way.

The same French influence was apparent inside the building, where lawyers in black gowns with white fichus at their throats moved among the crowds of litigants, witnesses, and family members who filled the central courtyard, standing in knots outside the doors of the judges' chambers, talking, weeping, gesticulating, shouting. They were middle class, but also working class, from their dress.

"Plaintiffs," said Leila. "You can see from the crowd. There are lots of legal problems to be solved in Morocco today. Everyone is supposed to have a lawyer, of course. But some come without lawyers and demand to be heard. Justice, they shout!"

"And are they heard?" I managed to ask across the hubbub that slowly receded as we were escorted through the crowds, up the stairs to the second floor, which was strangely quiet.

"These are the judges' private chambers," explained Leila. "No one is allowed up here except the judges and their clerks—and now—us!"

"And the cleaning ladies," I added, a bit frivolously, but I realized I was nervous. Would my French be up to this important interview? Leila had promised to help. The two cleaning ladies, with mops and pails, motherly women in blue uniforms, white head scarfs, and those ubiquitous *ship-ship* on their feet, the step-in slippers named for their onomatopoeic quality—the clopping and shushing sound they made as they moved across the marble floors. The women looked curiously at Leila and me as we knocked on the judge's door and were admitted by her clerk, a young woman in a brown print djellaba and head scarf.

"Please." She invited us to sit down. "Madame the Judge is in a meeting. She will be with you soon." To Leila, she added, "You are the sister of Fatiha and the sister-in-law of Abdul Hadi?"

Leila nodded. The clerk smiled. We sat down in two straight chairs before Madame the Judge's neat desk. Very neat. An "in" box, an "out" box, a pen and pencil set. A blotter. That was all.

The clerk went back to her desk, which was perpendicular to the judge's desk, against the wall. This desk was covered with ledgers, large, black, oversized ledgers reminiscent of Dickensian illustrations, or old French films. But the young clerk used a ballpoint, not a quill pen, as she made entries in the open ledger before her. Above her desk was a shelf of books, large books—legal tomes I assumed from their carefully bound backs and gold lettering. More shelves of books filled the wall behind the judge's desk. Very carefully shelved. No dust anywhere.

A window to the right of Madame's desk looked out on the street. It seemed outré to rise and peer out the window, but I was tempted. I turned my attention instead to the row of coat hooks mounted on a strip of varnished wood by the door. There was a black top coat, and next to it what was obviously Madame's judgely robe. Dark green, fashioned like an academic gown, it was faced with lapels of darker green satin, and boasted a thin, long dark green satin tie, with tippets of white fur on each end. "But don't they wear hats? Or wigs?" I asked Leila.

"Oh, judges don't wear hats here or wigs or turbans like the qadis. We're just like you in the United States," said Madame Assia Oaulalou, who had come in, shut the door carefully, introduced us to her clerk Fatima, apologized for being late, and drawn up a chair to sit not at her desk, but more casually, between Leila and myself.

"In the Supreme Court, though," she added, "the men wear Moroccan dress, including a red tarbush or fez."

All this was pronounced in soft but exceedingly clear French.

"Leila, how are you? How is your family?"

"Fine. Everyone is fine."

"I see Fatiha and Abdul Hadi all the time, but not you and Soad."

She smiled at me, and explained that she and Leila had been in elementary school together, long ago.

Leila said, "Your brother is in Parliament now."

"Yes," answered Madame Oaulalou, "and my husband, too." She considered Leila for a moment, then added, "Why don't you run for Parliament, my dear? You would win, you know."

Leila shook her head. "I am flattered that you think so. But I don't think politics is my destiny, or my contribution to my country. Writing is."

"Ah yes, I've read your books." The judge added, "And I liked them a lot. They are about real life, not feminist fantasies."

I pricked up my ears. Feminist fantasies? What were they? Before I could ask, however, Leila had intervened to discuss the reasons we were here, taking up the judge's time, on such a busy morning. My project.

Madame Oaulalou turned to me, listening to Leila describe my purposes while at the same time watching me carefully. I was conscious of two things. My French was adequate. And I had dressed correctly for this meeting, my best charcoal gray suit, a burgundy blouse, a French silk scarf. I was glad that I had done so, for Madame the Judge, a plumpish woman with dark hair, was also carefully dressed. The short black boots, black tights, herringbone skirt, single strand of pearls gracing a beautiful black pullover sweater subtly punctuated with tiny black satin bows and jet beads—they were becoming, elegant yet dignified. And, given our discussion about gender with the women's studies steering committee at the university, the garb was distinctly feminine. No question of "neuter" here.

I found that I was tempted to ask where she got her sweater (Paris, I think) but decided such a question was unworthy of me. After all, I was supposed to be a serious scholar intent on substance, not style. I told myself to focus on the issues!

Madame Oaulalou had been a judge in the High Court of Appeals for a year, she said, but before that, she had worked as assistant to the president in the lower courts, which dealt with crises, with urgent lawsuits.

"Are you the only woman judge?" I asked.

Madame Oualalou giggled. "Oh no, madame. There are many women judges in Morocco."

My eyes widened. "But, but . . ." I stuttered. "There are no women judges at all in Egypt."

She smiled in a kindly way. "Yes, I know, but that is Egypt. There are many Muslim countries where women are not allowed to act as judges. We are not one of them. One must look carefully at the history and experience of each country by itself . . ."

I nodded humbly. "And not make generalizations about Muslim women." I finished her sentence.

"Exactly." She smiled at me, turned to Leila, said something in Moroccan Arabic which I found difficult to catch. Leila replied. Again I didn't understand.

"You have your book with you, B.J.," Leila said in English. "You might show it to her now."

Madame the Judge looked at the cover of *Women and Family in the Middle East: New Voices of Change,* a collection of articles by Western and Middle Eastern scholars, which I edited in 1985.

"This is Morocco on the cover," she noted. "Look at the variety of women's lives, even in this picture. I have to tell myself to take each case before me on its own merits first, *then* begin to look for general patterns."

I had been properly instructed by the Court, and I knew it. I tried another tack.

"My youngest daughter is a lawyer," I began. "She would be interested in knowing the percentage of women judges in Morocco."

Madame Oualalou considered. "At least twenty percent!" she replied.

I was once more surprised. "I think that figure is higher than in the United States."

"Yes," agreed Madame Oualalou. "When I was in the United States some years ago, I found that people did not want to believe me. So please write about it, madame, and stress how many judges we have who are women. God knows we have worked hard to reach this level."

I asked her about the new amendments to the *mudawana,* or family law, but she explained that she did not deal with those cases. Perhaps she could arrange for me to talk to a qadi. She made several phone calls, to no avail.

"The dockets are very full for the next two weeks." She apologized. "I'm sorry. You can tell how important the male/female issue is—it dominates the system. The qadis are overworked. But still, at this moment the law is too new. It would be difficult for the qadis to tell you anything now. It will take time to see if the new amendments make a difference in women's and men's lives. We hope they will, don't we, Leila?"

Leila and Madame the Judge launched into a long discussion about the relationship between the French civil code, customary Moroccan law, and sharia, or Islamic law. I was having difficulty following what, if anything, all this had to do with family law.

"But," I asked, "isn't Moroccan family law just a form of Islamic sharia law? This is what the books suggest."

"No, no." For the first time Madame Oualalou raised her voice. "Not at all. Family law is *based* on sharia law; after all, all our laws have some relation to Islamic law, but the *mudawana* is distinctly our own creation—judges and *ulema,* lawyers and thinkers, here in Morocco."

I found this somewhat confusing.

"Abdul Hadi and Fatiha can explain it to you," said Leila.

I had the feeling we had overstayed our time, but Madame the Judge insisted we must stay for coffee. She relaxed and talked about her education and her work: she was a specialist in cases involving grievous harm.

"It is my duty to decide who is responsible for inflicting that harm—who is legally responsible."

"And you enjoy your work?"

"Oh yes," she answered. "But my responsibilities are very heavy. I work at home as well as here. I have no children, you see, so my time is less taken up than it would be otherwise. And here judges have more authority than in the United States. We listen to witnesses, we make definitive judgments in serious situations."

We finished our coffee and rose. Madame did not stop us. But as she took my hand, she said, "May I ask you a favor?"

"Of course."

"You can put in your book that Moroccan women are coming along, but there is much work to do."

I nodded.

"But also, can you say this in a pleasant way? If women here in Morocco are not trained or do not all hold responsible positions like mine, it is not because of their biological differences from men."

I am puzzled again. "It's not?"

"No, it's because of their social position in the society. It's because of *class*. We have to keep struggling against that."

On Boulevard Muhammad V, Leila and I tried to cross, but the traffic was against us. Bicycles, taxis, and cars were struggling to move around this circle in front of the railway station, the hub of the wheel from which, as in Paris, many streets fanned out into the neighborhoods of the city. Everyone was on the way home for the two-hour lunch. Some, like government servants, might not return. But some would. After a substantial meal, the main meal of the day, the family would take a short siesta. Then, in late afternoon, the traffic would converge once more on this principal hub, as shopkeepers, students, lawyers, teachers, and judges like Madame Assia Oualalou returned to their offices, to work until dark, when the sounding of the call to prayer throughout the city announced that the sun had set on another day and that God is great.

"Now, B.J.," said Leila, "before we go any further with these talks—the *mudawana,* the Parliament ladies, and so on, we have to meet Latifa. Latifa Djebabdi. Without her none of this change would have taken place."

"Who is she?"

"A dynamic young woman. You will see. I will phone her this afternoon."

We were lunching in town, with Sandra Carter and Deborah Kapchan. Roast chicken in a small, dim, but agreeable restaurant across the crowded boulevard. I told them what Madame the Judge had said, that women's status in Morocco was basically a matter of class. Sandra looked puzzled. Deborah and Leila nodded in agreement. So what did this all mean? Clearly, I had to rethink some of my own preconceptions about the place of women in modern Moroccan society.

The American feminist movement is based on the central idea that socialization, not biology, determines the roles which men and women will play throughout their lives. Socialization is responsible for the way both men and women are treated in society. Gender is the issue. Women's roles, according to this theory, are constructed: they are not the result of biological differences between males and females. It is socialization that determines who gets power. Therefore, feminists believe, to assure justice and equality of power between men and women, one must work to change the ways in which children are socialized: at school, in the home, in the religious institutions, in the workplace. Hence one can begin to understand feminists' stubborn insistence on changing textbooks to include women, on insisting that women are not just "Mrs." or "Miss," that is, defined by their relationship to a man (father or husband), but "Ms.," something else. Not neuter. Not dependent. A person not beholden to either males or females. A person with power.

Socialization, then, is seen in the West as the key to female progress. Not biology. And as I began to ponder the issue of barriers to women's progress and how my Middle Eastern friends perceived those barriers, I began to wonder whether in Morocco, *class,* the position of the woman in the social structure of Moroccan society, did not operate in much the same way as gender socialization did in our own country. Was it class formation that kept women back?

That was what Madame Assia Oaulalou had said, a woman who occupied an important position in Morocco as a judge in the High Court of Appeals. Class. Not biological differences. I thought also of Dr. Fouzia Rhissassi, chair of the women's studies steering committee at Muhammad V University. Hadn't Leila said that all the women of that committee were members of the upper class or upper middle class? Didn't that contribute to their power in society?

Class, the idea of social class, wherein people are rated not on their intrinsic moral behavior or native talents but on their position in the social hierarchy, is a distasteful subject to most Americans. We tell ourselves that we are a classless society, that it does not matter where we come from, what our origins may be. What matters is present behavior, hard work, and achievement. And we dismiss the rigid judgments made on the basis of social class that are presented in early English novels. Who can forget the scene in Jane Austen's *Pride and Prejudice* when Lady de Bourgh visits Elizabeth Bennet. Lady de Bourgh is furious at the rumor that her nephew, Mr. Darcy, might actually consider marrying Elizabeth. She says:

> "[You are] a young woman without family, connections, or fortune. . . . If you were sensible of your own good, you would not wish to quit the sphere, in which you have been brought up."

And Elizabeth's controlled, but equally furious reply:

"In marrying your nephew, I should not consider myself as quitting that sphere. He is a gentleman; I am a gentleman's daughter; so far we are equal."

But Lady de Bourgh will not be gainsaid.

". . . But who was your mother? Who are your uncles and aunts?"

The social world of Great Britain has changed since Jane Austen wrote those lines nearly two hundred years ago. Revolutions have taken place, the two world wars, the Beatles, the new red brick universities which rival ancient Oxford and Cambridge. The system has been shaken, but in Britain class differences are still important, particularly when it comes to marriage. It is not simply the acceptance of individuals of one class by another—an upper-middle-class boy and a working-class girl, for instance. It is a web of customs and accents, the strands of polite behavior that connect people to one class, that bind them subtly to their origins, their roots. It is this web of class familiarities that often makes members of different British social classes uneasy together in intimate situations, that brings differences in social expectations sharply to life.

In America, we tell ourselves that none of this matters. And in many ways we are right. America is perhaps the only country in the world where the rags to riches route, plus hard work, has been romanticized to the point that it can overcome all other considerations, including class. We are a country, we say, founded on revolution; the feminist revolution is only one of many. But class is present, even in revolutions like the feminist revolution. How many working-class women sit on the board of NOW? Class determines goals, and membership, and long-term expectations—of the feminist movement and many other movements. How was this different from what was happening in Morocco?

I told myself that Morocco's political revolution is newer than ours in America, dating from the nationalist revolts of the 1930s and 1940s through the 1956 declaration of independence from France. The egalitarian message of the revolution has not fully become a reality in Morocco for half a century isn't long enough for substantial change to occur—and to last. And it may never be what its idealistic leaders projected. But the social system today is not the same as it was at the turn of the century, the system in which men and women knew their proper places according to wealth, gender, religious lineage, place of origin, and blood descent.

Just as natural disasters like earthquakes and floods have upset the stratigraphy of the Moroccan land itself, shuffling and confusing the orderly layers of lived civilization—pots, tools, jewelry, holy icons—so have recent political and social movements muddled the sacrosanct class differences of the past. Fighting a common enemy, the French, served to unite men and women of all classes, and after peace was made, the old boundaries were hard to rebuild to exactly the same proportions.

The manifestos of the new independent state of Morocco contributed to the social upheaval. Nationalist leaders promised the breakup of large landholdings, health care for all, equal pay for equal work, and free education from primary grades through professional and graduate school for students who could qualify on prescribed examinations. By the time we were living in Marrakech in 1971 and 1972, problems with this ideology had already surfaced. The stated national goal to provide free education for all was thwarted by shortages of teachers, books, buildings, and administrators. Educational leaders persisted. In 1988 one third of the entire national budget of Morocco was allotted to education, yet still the educational system was not equal for all. In a large city like Marrakech, forty was the average number of students in a primary school classroom. And poor children in the isolated mountain villages and small suburbs of the High Atlas were not as well prepared, and hence did not do as well on the crucial year-end examinations as did children in urban centers. By the nineties, rich parents sent their children to private schools or paid for home tutoring to make certain that their progeny would excel and go on to perpetuate the family's social status.

All this history was important to remember in trying to understand what was happening in Morocco. For despite problems, some of the old barriers had broken down for good. Women had done well, for the crucial national school exams were graded blind, without knowledge of sex. Leila and her sisters were good examples. Their father had been the *qaid,* leader of the entire area of Beni Mellal, far from the imperial cities of Fez, or Rabat, or Marrakech and Meknès, which had produced Morocco's elite for centuries. But Beni Mellal became important during revolutionary times as an area of resistance against the French. Leila's father had refused to cooperate with the colonial authorities and was imprisoned for his refusal. Leila's mother and the girls were forced to move several times, up into the mountains, into smaller and more remote villages where their presence would neither be noted nor seen as a threat by the French colonial authorities. After independence, Leila's father was a national hero. The family moved to Rabat, and all the girls went on to college. Fatiha had been first in her class throughout her academic career. She married Abdul Hadi, a member of an old and conservative Rabati family, which traced its genealogy back to the fall of Granada, in 1492.

"In the past, they would not even have known each other," Leila told me. "Beni Mellal girl marrying Rabati boy? Not likely. They met at the university."

And it was here, in the arena of marriage, the joining of one family to another according to a carefully thought out and negotiated contract, that "class" might be seen to be shifting, and where many people were trying to prevent that shift. Marriage was the key issue for women and men in the new Morocco, for everyone realized it was marriage, and the children who were born of that marriage, that would determine the way in which class, gender, and equality would be articulated and expressed in the future. Elizabeth Bennet and Lady de Bourgh would have, like Jane Austen, recognized very well what was happening and might have viewed with alarm some of the new alliances, while sympathizing with parents and children who were trying to find their way into new relationships, based not always now on class, religious lineage, place of origin, or father's descent line, but on common interests and hopes—and even romance!

"Don't you also have this problem in America, B.J.? Don't you worry about who your children marry?"

"Well," I replied briskly, "I trust them. They are good people. They have good judgment. If they find someone to marry who is also a good person, that is enough for me."

"And your husband Bob feels the same?"

"Yes, yes," I replied firmly. "Of course."

"And you don't worry at all what the grandchildren might turn out to be like?"

"Of course. But the environment they grow up in is also important."

Leila nodded. "There are many differences between our cultures," she said slowly. "This gender business, for example."

"I think gender is about society's attitudes toward males and females," I said. "I mean, men and women are different biologically, but don't people in Moroccan society have definite ideas about how men should behave? And women?"

"Of course," replied Leila. "Men should be strong and dominant. Women should be modest and retiring."

"But what about men and women who don't behave that way? What about men who are weak, whose mothers run them? Like your friend from the village who doesn't get married because of his mother?"

"Well, he's still a man, isn't he?" asked Leila with a trace of hostility.

"Yes, but does he behave the way the culture says he should? In some cultures, men are *supposed* to be modest and retiring."

Leila laughed. "I don't believe it!"

"Well, what if they're supposed to be modest? They're still men, aren't they? Biologically, I mean? This is what is meant by cultural constructions of gender roles."

Leila shook her head. "B.J., don't confuse me."

We had long talks like these over the excellent meals which Leila prepared for me and Soad: one day it was chicken cooked with onions and paprika; the next a *tajine* or stew of lamb with lemons and cardons (a vegetable related to the artichoke). Cardons were in season now and could be found among the rows of carrots and cauliflower, tomatoes and peppers in all the open markets we passed on Rue Muhammad V and on the street behind Rue Haroun al-Rashid. Vegetables and fruits were delivered daily from the country, from the rich plains and fertile valleys of this most fortunately endowed nation: no oil, but phosphates in the south were an exportable product, and there was enough agricultural produce to provide for the population, at least minimally, and enough for cash crops like oranges and fresh flowers to sell in Europe.

Leila asked me about many things: the women's movement in the United States, people's attitudes toward Malcolm X and Jesse Jackson, the continual flurry of media attention toward the "reintroduction of the veil."

"Is that the only thing people in America care about in terms of Muslim women?"

"Well, it makes news," I answered. "It's visually gripping!"

Leila was not amused. She said, "Such people have fixed ideas. They don't look at history, at what religious books say."

"I agree."

"Of course, B.J., *hijab* is the unspoken issue here."

I looked around me as we walked, and I saw very few women wearing the new style of modest dress, or *hijab*. There were some women wearing djellabas, with hoods and veils; some wearing djellabas and head scarves, but no garments and scarves specially designed and termed *hijab*, or the new "Islamic dress," as in Egypt.

"Would you say that woman is upper class or working class?" I asked as we passed an older woman wearing djellaba, plus hood and veil, such as my friend Aisha in Marrakech used to wear when she went to the market.

"Just from the djellaba and veil, one can't tell," answered Leila. "So you look at the quality of the djellaba—that one is old and worn—and her shoes, traditional slippers, also worn. Working class."

"And him?" A middle-aged man, all in white, a white djellaba like the King wore on feast days, with a loose white hood. He, too, wore traditional Moroccan slippers, but these were new.

"Well," said Leila, "a religious man, not poor, probably a professional religious person, an *imam* or a scholar. With religious people, class is harder to identify."

"Aha!" I cried. "So that's it!"

Leila looked at me sideways. We were walking down the Avenue de France, and my voice was a little loud. A woman in black holding a small boy by the hand turned around and stared at us. I lowered my voice and added, "Religion is the universal leveler, then, isn't it, the arena where class doesn't matter at all?"

That of course was the stated ideal of Islam. No economic, social, racial, or political qualifications were necessary to join the Umma, the world community of Muslims. All were welcome, provided they evinced a sincere intention and were willing to profess their faith: "There is no God but God and Muhammad is His Prophet."

"That's the ideal," Leila agreed. "It doesn't work out quite that perfectly. I mean, most Moroccans are Muslims, B.J. So Muslim or not, people still have doubts before they marry into a different social class."

"Can you really tell class by looking at people, even on the street like this?"

Leila nodded. "Most of the time, as I've just shown you. And even at the university, you saw, B.J., even though they all wear jeans and sweaters and skirts and jackets and sometimes a head scarf, they all know each other's background, who their parents are."

"How?"

"By the name of the family, the secondary school they come from, by their speech. Isn't it the same in America?"

"Yes, to some extent."

Leila smiled. "Of course. So why are you so interested if it is the same in your country?"

"I'm trying to figure out what we share and where our differences lie, I suppose," I answered. "So tell me more about these people we're passing. How can you tell what class they belong to?"

Leila humored me. "I see, it's a game," she said and then proceeded to pick out the signs and codes of class found in the dress of the passersby. The religious gentleman in the white djellaba we had passed earlier was not clearly one class or another. But a small man wearing a gray suit of material more appropriate for the summer months, and large heavy black shoes, "is a workingman dressing like a white-collar worker, maybe going for a job interview."

The brown-striped wool djellaba and skullcap on the man ahead of us signaled a man from the country, from outside Rabat. "He's not a likely marriage choice for any urban daughter," pronounced Leila, half-humorously.

"Oh, but look at him!" A man in a beautiful tweed jacket over a cashmere pullover, with sculpted hair above dark glasses, signaled, "rich and secure upper class," Leila said. "Look at the haircut. Lots of people are getting rich these days, so anyone can buy a tweed jacket like that, but the haircut means old money."

"What about that woman who looks a bit like your sister Soad?"

We both observed the young woman approaching us, slim with short black skirt and jacket, bright blue turtleneck, high heels, striding purposefully along, adjusting her handbag and her black leather briefcase as she went.

"Professional," pronounced Leila, "from the briefcase of course. Probably upper middle class or she wouldn't have the nerve to wear her skirt so short."

I glanced at Leila, realizing again that my friend always wore very modest skirts, like me (but I am much older), sweaters, jackets and scarves, but no head scarf.

"We need to talk more about *hijab* and why it is the unspoken issue," I said. "Why it's important, if it is."

"Yes, B.J. We'll do that when you talk at Moulay Ismail."

On a sudden impulse I turned to Leila. "You have to talk too."

"No, no," she protested.

"Yes, it will be much more interesting for the students to meet you and hear you as well as me."

"We-ell . . . what will Driss say?"

Driss Ouauicha, my old friend, was the associate rector at Moulay Ismail.

"I'll call him tomorrow and tell him. He'll be delighted."

Leila sighed, but she was smiling. "Well, if you want to," she temporized but I realized that she did want to speak, and was glad that I had asked her.

Rabat, Morocco's present capital, is an upstart city next to Meknès, Fez, and Marrakech. These three great imperial cities have been seats of leaders since the ninth (Fez) and the eleventh (Marrakech and

Meknès) centuries, the headquarters of rival sultans and chieftains who have fought over time for domination of Morocco's fertile and beautiful land. Meknès is also the site of the first rulers of the 'Alawi dynasty, ancestors of the present King, Hassan II, who has ruled Morocco since the death in 1961 of his nationalist father, the much-beloved King Muhammad V.

Thus it is hardly surprising that one of the first new universities launched after independence was established in Meknès, and named Moulay Ismail in honor of one of the founders of the King's dynasty. But it turned out there were other reasons for choosing Meknès.

In the beginning of my guest lecture at Moulay Ismail on "Images of the Middle East in nineteenth-century English literature," I mentioned the French "protectorate," which, according to my reading, had begun in 1912, when French troops defeated Moroccans in the battle of Sidi Othman.

"No, no," called out a student. "Here in Meknès we held out long after that."

Dr. Abdulla Majid Hajji, the class's regular professor, stood up to silence the rude student.

"No, no," I insisted. "Let him speak."

"We know," said the young man, "because our fathers and grandfathers told us, that here in the Meknès valley and the Middle Atlas, people held out until 1934!"

"So you see, madame," put in a pleasant girl, "here in Meknès we were only under French rule for twenty years, one generation."

"Our thinking is different," added another.

"Then let's talk about that," I said, "and how that affects the way you look at literature, both here and in the West."

Leila smiled from the front row. I sensed I had made the right decision in insisting she speak as well.

What the students were telling me was that French rule was a mere moment on the stage of Moroccan history; Meknès and the people of Meknès had been around for a thousand years; *their* own sense of self was far stronger than any French import could be and they wanted to talk about it and about the new Moroccan literary expression of that self. After an hour of spirited discussion, Dr. Hajji asked me to explain my book project, *In Search of Islamic Feminism*.

"We don't use this word, feminist," said a young woman. "It has bad connotations. It means we are borrowing someone else's culture."

"We don't want to do that," said another girl. "Why should we? We have our own culture."

"The only people who use this word are the fundamentalist women. They call themselves Muslim feminists. Like Nadia Abdul Yacine."

I was startled. "Why do they do that?"

In the buzz and murmur which followed, Dr. Hajji took charge. "Why do you think?" he asked the students.

The answers came from several directions.

"Maybe because fundamentalist women think that women should stay home and be feminine, and not like men, who are masculine?"

"Because they are trying to attract the media to their cause?"

"It's a way to get themselves asked to talk," put in another. "That way, the government men who control lectures will think they are talking about the West."

General uproar and laughter.

A girl at the very back had been wagging her hand for several minutes.

"Yes, Malika?" Dr. Hajji recognized her.

She stood up. "We are trying to find a word that will express our desire for women's rights."

"How about women's movement?" asked Leila, who was now standing with me and Dr. Hajji and participating in the discussion.

"No, no, no," from several students. "We need a new word. Our word."

I looked at Leila. But Dr. Hajji was pointing out that the class had ended a half hour ago and that we were due to lunch with Driss Ouauicha.

"But we can continue this later," said Dr. Hajji. "Our guest will show a film this afternoon in this room."

"About what?"

It was Leila who answered. *"Hijab* in Egypt. It's called *A Veiled Revolution."*

Moulay Ismail, who gave his name to the new university where I was a guest, ruled from 1672 until 1727, and is renowned for different things in different history books. Moroccans see him as a stable, energetic, and often forceful and cruel ruler. French history celebrates him not only because he signed a treaty of cooperation with Louis XIV in 1682 but because he had designs on aligning himself with the French in the time-honored way of such alliances: by marrying a princess of the blood. On behalf of Moulay Ismail, it is said the pirate Ben Aicha made representations to the French Minister Pontchartrain for the hand of Marie-Anne de Bourbon, later Princess de Conti. The books do not record Louis's exact answer to the emissary, but Marie-Anne never married Moulay Ismail.

The city of Meknès was built by Moulay Ismail halfway between Fez and Marrakech, supposedly because he wanted to keep an eye on possible centers of opposition. The monuments and mosques and the fifteen-mile city wall testify to Moulay Ismail's energy, but it was the stables and the granaries that impressed me most. The granary and the stables are both in the old imperial part of the town, through which we were ushered by our hosts on the way to lunch in a traditional palace turned restaurant. Looking at the vast two-story stone granary, with vaulted silos, and stout supporting pillars, one could see the good sense and farsightedness of Moulay Ismail. I only wished my aunt Mary, the only one of my aunts to stay on my grandparents' farm, had been with me. Aunt Mary had never gone to college but she would have been able to estimate, on the basis of the measurements of *one* of these vast silos, the number of bushels of grain in the whole enclave, and also the number of people who might be fed with such a store. Long before the invention of Butler's Bins, the American temperature-controlled silos, Moulay Ismail had created stone granaries to keep the crops free of rot and mildew. To feed all the King's horses and all his men. And if the stone silos were a silent tribute to Moulay Ismail's practicality, the stables were an indication of his grandeur. The *roua* (or stables) were built of vaulted stone; as one wandered through the great, empty, echoing rooms, with the octagonal tack room in the center, it was easy to believe, as the Arab historians write, that twelve thousand horses, the sultan's cavalry, were housed here.

Our historical tour and traditional lunch were cut short when Abdulla Hajji looked at his watch. The film was scheduled to begin in twenty minutes and arrangements still had to be made with a technician, since I had declined to set up the film.

"No," I had said, "I really would prefer not to. Projectors and I don't get along."

"Oh, B.J.," laughed Driss. "How can you pretend to be a feminist, then?"

He had a point. I should have learned to run various video and film projectors after producing six documentary films. But each setup was different, and I was already mystified by this one, which involved connecting the video to a special machine that played it into another machine which projected the image on the wall behind the machine!

Unfortunately, my fears turned out to be justified. The "technician" had skipped out. Maybe he didn't know how to manipulate the contraption either? But we had a crisis. The classroom where I had spoken in the morning was packed, and a long line of students stood outside the door. Driss looked alarmed.

"We will get a bigger room," he announced, and the viewing was moved, first to one big room, then to an even larger room. "Maybe by the time they sit down, the machine will be working."

Half an hour later, while different people fiddled with the complicated equipment, Leila and I were entertaining a restive crowd of several hundred students by talking about how the film was made, who funded it, the problems of filming in the mosque. Sadly, it began to look as though the showing would have to be canceled. Abdulla Hajji had risen to make that announcement, while a student and the technician's assistant continued to push buttons. I could never be sure what happened, but suddenly there on the screen was the opening image of my film, women in the mosque.

"Yaseen, wa Qur'an el Hakim," the women intoned.

A hush fell over the crowded room, a stillness that lasted until the final credits began to roll. Then hands shot up.

"Be careful," cautioned one of the English faculty sitting next to me, a European woman married to a Moroccan. "The *hijab* is the unspoken issue here. Didn't you know that? You should have stuck to Keats and Byron."

Leila stood up, too. "I will help you with the questions, B.J.," she said firmly.

As the question and answer session went on—and on—and on, far past the deadline of one hour, I was grateful for Leila's presence, for I was not a Muslim, after all; she was. And when the questions piled up, I often turned to Leila, who then would return, sura for sura, Qur'anic verse for Qur'anic verse, the justifications or admonitions about Islamic dress.

Here are some of the questions and comments on the film, which is a 1982 documentary made for Channel 4 London on the new style of women's dress in Egypt, called Islamic dress or *hijab,* a style which may include only a head scarf, or a long full gown and head scarf and sometimes a face veil.

"What is the level of education of the women you interviewed?"

"Why were Islamic scholars, the *ulema,* not interviewed and included in the film, as their pronouncements are the most important?"

"Why is the West so interested in this? We have a choice, to wear or not to wear; that's the real issue, not the cover itself."

"If the West is a democracy and allows choice, why do the French forbid Muslim girls to wear the head scarf to class?"

"Why didn't you interview more men?"

"The guy in the film is wrong when he says women should stay at home. The Qur'an tells women that they should contribute to society; that means getting an education, and working outside the home."

"Did the people in the film know that it would be shown in the West?"

"Don't you, personally, think the *hijab* is a nonissue?"

To that question, I returned, "What do you mean?"

"Just what I said. I can wear a scarf or not" (the young woman who asked the question was wearing a head scarf with her jeans and heavy pullover sweater). "But the real question is what do I do with my education, how I use it for myself and for society."

Then from a young man in the audience: Leila, why don't you wear a scarf yourself?

LEILA: I think it's the first step toward the isolation and segregation of women. Isolation leads to ignorance and other terrible things follow, things which affect women, men, children, the family.

THE YOUNG MAN: But how can you justify that if you are a good Muslim?

LEILA: I do what Muslims are supposed to do, fast, pray, go on pilgrimage, give to the poor, act as a modest woman.

THE YOUNG MAN: But the Qur'an says . . .

LEILA: The Qur'an doesn't tell me to cover my head, it says to cover up my beauty, the jewels of my beauty, which means my body, not my head. My head is already covered; can't you see?

THE YOUNG MAN: By what? You are not wearing a scarf.

LEILA: By my hair!

Applause and laughter from the audience.

The young man was not impressed: "We will talk later," he shouted, "and discuss Islam."

Leila said, "Yes, by all means. I welcome it. Do you have your Qur'an with you?"

Applause.

Dr. Hajji finally brought the discussion to an end. But even before the applause had died, the young man had pushed through the crowds to talk to Leila. Others joined him. The conversation was now all in Arabic.

"Well," said Dr. Hajji heartily, "what did you think?"

"I found it a very interesting and constructive occasion," I answered sincerely. "Thank you for arranging all this."

The European member of the faculty shook my hand and nodded.

Was she amused by my interest? Who knew? She leaned closer and said softly, "I told you so. It's not worth discussing."

I looked at her, startled and amazed. Not worth discussing? Then why is "it" *(hijab)* the unspoken issue? Why has the government cracked down on activists who talk about the Qur'an and the need to reinterpret it, the need to get back to "roots" and "identity"? Why are the students so engaged by the issue? Not worth discussing?

Clearly, the issue should be discussed. Of course, the discussion will run very differently here, for the Islamists or the fundamentalists or the reinterpreters have two strikes against them when they talk about creating an Islamic state. Morocco had long ago been declared, by its leaders, to be an Islamic state. King Hassan's titles include "Commander of the Faithful" and "Leader of Believers," and his dynasty traces its roots beyond Meknès to the south, to the 'Alawi from Sijilmassa near the desert. The 'Alawi were descendants of the Prophet Muhammad, who came to power on a program of piety, virtue, and poverty, reactions against the luxury and indolence of the then reigning Saadians (in Marrakech) and Merinids (in Meknès). Some critics now argue that the dynasty is approaching the same level of self-indulgence as their earlier foes, but the King, an intelligent monarch, has managed to withstand those criticisms. How? By appealing to the people, as he has done with the movement to reform family law, as he has done by increasing appropriations for education. Driss told me that of the 6,000 students in the faculty of arts at Moulay Ismail, 4,300 are supported partially or fully by government grants. The basis for grants? Merit and need, in equal proportions, said Driss.

The King also moved recently to quiet possible rumblings from a dissident Berber faction by authorizing for the first time the teaching of the Berber language in all of Morocco's schools, a move that amazed not only his own people but longtime Western students of the country. His support for the revival of traditional Moroccan arts and crafts—the tiles, silk-weaving, copper, brass, pottery, plaster work— was surely another effort to engage a number of segments of his population—patriotic Moroccans proud of their heritage, and small manufacturers who needed work. This move also served to discourage imports since Morocco currently imports more goods than it exports.

"The King is aware of the calamity going on in Algeria," said the husband of one of Leila's friends, a retired businessman, over dinner at his house. "He is taking very careful steps to be sure that it does not happen here."

"What about his support for the Israeli-Palestinian peace process?" I asked.

The elderly businessman pondered for a moment. "The King is not without ambition. I think he would like to see himself as the regional mediator. He set up the Casablanca conference not only to improve political relations but to improve economic relations with the rest of the Middle East. It won't hurt him in the West either. He thinks the economy is the key. And of course he's right!"

"Remember," Driss had pointed out earlier, when I had visited Moulay Ismail, "the students in the universities are not just here for a free lunch. They have to pass the baccalaureate exam to get here in the first place, and the first two years are not easy. Look at Texas! I remember someone there saying that thirty percent of the freshman class is *expected* to flunk out the first year. It's not that high here."

"Why?"

"Well, it's obvious, isn't it? Students know that to get ahead in Morocco today, you need an education, as much as possible. So most of them work very hard and we work with them."

I told him I was impressed with the students' English.

Driss smiled. "It's not easy!"

"And the number of girls. Do parents object to their girls going to the university and sitting in classes with boys?"

Driss had stood up and looked out the window of his spacious university office. He'd aged in this job—pulling together the faculty, students, parents, the financial resources to make a university where none existed before. He still taught one class, at 8 A.M., so he would have the day free to deal with university administration. He also edited a linguistic journal published in both Arabic and English, a substantive and serious journal he founded himself. He was dedicated and he had obviously done a good job at Moulay Ismail.

"Look here, B.J."

We both looked out at the courtyard of the Faculty of Letters, centered by a tiled fountain the color of sand with insets of black and white. The carefully planted grassy plots were turning brown because of the lack of rain. The square utilitarian buildings fronted on this court where students stood and talked, or sat on benches in the arcade. It looked like any university in session, except that a few girls wore long modest dresses and had covered their heads with scarves.

"What about those girls?" I said.

"You're interviewing me now, B.J.," said Driss, smiling.

"Yes."

"Well, of course a few people will always object to women's education. But remember your own statements about the importance of the family here. Women and men are both members of the family, and are expected to contribute to its continuance. You know that. So you know why most girls are at the university—and it's not just because of the glory of education."

"To get a better job, help support the family, find an educated husband?"

"All three," smiled Driss, "but the first two are the most important. Families still want to have something to say about marriage—about who they are adding to the family group."

Marriage, like family law and unemployment, was a crucial issue for women—but also for men, as Driss had reminded me. Coming from the West, we take for granted that in a battle between the good of the individual man or woman and the good of the family group, the good of the individual often takes first place. But in the Middle East, the balance tips the other way—toward the group. Marriage is the moment when group allegiance is tested: whether or not the daughter or son will agree to marry somebody who is an asset to the family group—its social and economic and political position. And men are pushed to marry someone their family wants, just as are women. All the way back to Rabat on the train, Leila and I talked about marriage.

"It's difficult these days—marriage," said Leila. 'Everybody talks about the necessity of marrying, but doing it is something else. Who to choose? Rich families don't want their sons to marry poor girls. But it works the other way, too."

"What do you mean? Poor families don't want their children to marry rich folks? How come? I would think they would welcome getting into the upper strata."

Leila paused. "Maybe it's easier if I give you an example, B.J. We have a friend. He is very important, very high in the government bureaucracy. Theoretically he could marry anyone, and any family would be happy to welcome him, despite the fact that he comes from a very poor family in a tiny village in the south."

Leila had already explained to me the importance of marriage in Moroccan society, something that I knew from other experiences in Egypt, Iraq, Lebanon. Marriage is a religious as well as a social duty for Muslims. Only when a man and a woman have married and borne children are they considered complete adults, and mature Muslims. Marriage and children bring status to women, but also to men. Of course this is still more or less the case in the United States, but no longer with the force that obtained when I was growing up in Oregon, fifty years ago. Times have changed in the United States, and if Leila and her sister Soad were any indication, it was beginning to change in Morocco.

"So why doesn't he marry?"

"His mother and father don't want him to marry a rich, urban girl from Rabat. Especially his mother is against it."

"Why?"

"The mothers are afraid of such girls, that they will take away their sons, that if there are children, they will be brought up in a snobby way, and they, the unimportant grandparents, will be scorned and ignored."

"It's a question of mothers devoting all their emotional energy to their sons, and then wanting to keep them."

"Yes and no. It's okay if they marry someone the mother likes. And it's not," said Leila slyly, "the Oedipus complex like Westerners who study Freud talk about. This is from the woman's side, the mother's side. What kind of complex would that be called?"

I was not certain, and said so.

We were both glad to be back on Rue Haroun al-Rashid. Leila and I were drinking mint tea after another of Leila's good meals: chicken with onions and paprika. Her sister Soad had retired to the television room. The meal had been cooked, like most of Leila's offerings, in a pressure cooker, an item that I had not seen in American households since my mother's time.

"It's hard to find one," Leila agreed. "A Moroccan woman I know who went to Texas with her husband and children says her husband threatened to divorce her because her cooking was so bad!" She laughed, a small, choking sound. "She came to me in tears, and finally we found her a pressure cooker at a garage sale! The garage sale saved her marriage!"

"Marriage," I repeated.

"Okay, B.J., get your notebook," said Leila.

I obliged.

"Yes, you can write that men are in charge of the system, but women hold all the cards . . ."

"How?"

"Not just in terms of having babies and cooking good meals. They can also throw up obstacles, especially boys' mothers can do this, but so can girls."

Leila went on to point out, very sensibly, that no girl would want to marry a man whose mother disliked her. "It's not worth it. Why should she? Mothers-in-law can do a lot of damage—or a lot of good."

"Can the woman really choose?"

"Of course. The Qur'an says so. There are always a few mean men and women, who are not properly Islamic, who will try to decide for their daughters. But these days girls with education can easily fight that. They have more cards than their mothers."

What are the cards women hold? Girls can bring improvement in the family's economic situation. An educated wife means the possibility of another salary, a higher standard of living—money!

In the past, said Leila, families married within the group, something that is borne out by studies across the Mediterranean. They did this to keep wealth in that group and to control the inheritance of the next generation. Blood ties, honor, and money were the issues in marriage.

"For people of Fez, of course, it's always been money more than anything else," said Leila, rather sardonically.

Money then, and who your father was. Blood. These days, Leila told me, things were changing. Blood and money and honor were still important, but other things were happening. Attitudes toward class were shifting, and education, common goals, joint religious faith, even love and romance were now seen as important for the creation of a lasting marriage. The divorce rate was high. Families wanted their children to stay together.

In the old days, an unmarried man or an unmarried woman were exceptions. Yet I had met several people during my stay in Morocco who were unmarried, including Leila and Soad.

"It is beginning to be okay," Leila allowed. "But those who stay unmarried tend to be economically self-sufficient and well educated."

Motherhood, a visible sign of status, health, and fertility in women, also brought power and respect, didn't it? Yes, Leila agreed to that.

"But it brings power for evil as well as good," she said, and told me a story of a distant cousin who was to marry a promising young man in Rabat's new private sector business community.

"Everything was set, but his mother took against the girl. The mother herself was uneducated, had never been happily married, and took out all her frustrations in overloving her son. She could see he loved this city girl, and she set out to stop the marriage. No one could believe that she had the power to do it, but she did. She married her son to a young village girl, wealthy and illiterate."

"My cousin was devastated," said Leila. "She really loved the guy. Then one month after the marriage it turned out the village girl was five months pregnant. Disaster for the mother—honor, blood, money all involved: she had put her power on the line, but was too stupid to figure everything out."

"So what happened?"

"They were divorced. The son never forgave his mother for ruining his marriage to my cousin and at the same time humiliating him by engaging him to a girl who was already pregnant."

"So did he marry your cousin then?"

Leila shook her head. "It was sad," she admitted. "But after that, no way. Public humiliation? Not possible. How could she have dealt with his family? No."

"He never married?"

"No. He married. But he never sees his mother. He's living in Rabat. His wife is very beautiful, and very rich—and very cold. It's too bad. No children. She only wants him for his position, I think."

"And your cousin?"

"Still not married. Doesn't want to, she says."

And what about you, I thought. And your sister? And the several professional women at the university who are, whether by choice or not, unmarried?

Leila answered my unspoken question. "Girls are getting prouder these days," she said. "They want to decide themselves. They don't want to compromise. Why should they? It's their life."

This sounded suspiciously to me like that old Western ideal individualism, so castigated in the Middle East for its "selfishness" and "egotistic" pursuit of self-happiness. And I said so.

Leila considered. "Well, my friend, again you are right, but not right. Yes and no. Life is complex. I agree that life sometimes has to be a compromise, but many women in Morocco feel their grandmothers were the victims of compromise, and their mothers, and it's time for a little consideration for themselves."

"How can they hold out against their fathers?"

By this time Leila and I were washing dishes in the kitchen. The pressure cooker was soaking in the sink. From the opposite apartment came the strains of some traditional Berber music—I recognized it finally as *ahwash*, the choral music of the High Atlas. The counterpoint of men's voices and women's voices singing together drifted across the court and through the open kitchen door.

"Beautiful music," I said, putting the flowered dinner plates in their proper places in Leila's well-organized enamel kitchen cupboard. "Have you heard it?"

"Oh yes," said Leila, wiping the marble drainboard and the white enamel kitchen table. "I once did a story for my radio program about that music—how men and women speak together through the music, and to the community, as well. Things were supposed to be clear and simple in those days. But when you listen to the music of the *ahwash* you know they were not."

"Disappointment in love, you mean, opposition to parents' choice of marriage?"

"Of course. You think in the West we don't have romance here? That's silly. All people have romance; it is a wonderful part of life."

"But money and education were not so important then?"

"Education is new. Money was always important. And class. Who your family is."

We stood in the kitchen, now clean and shining, ready for breakfast. Outside darkness filled the court, but the rhythms and voices of the *ahwash* continued.

"I once tried to explain in America about women," said Leila. "I think you were there, B.J. It was in Texas. They asked, would I rather be a man?"

I nodded.

"And I said that the question was silly. That made them mad. I would rather be a rich upper-class woman than a poor working-class man any day. And they said, even in an Islamic country, and I said yes. I could tell they thought I was crazy. But of course I was right. They just didn't get it. And I think feminists still don't."

"No, Leila, things are changing in America, too," I said. "Feminists now are very aware of money and class."

"But I never met a poor woman in any of my lectures," she said.

It was useless to argue further. But I decided that my pilgrimage should have another component: my search for Islamic feminism should be coupled with an explanation and support for the movement called Western feminism. We needed to improve our image abroad, especially with other women's groups, I told myself.

The Union de l'Action Féminin is, said Leila, the most effective women's movement in Morocco. I accepted her point of view, but I was inclined to look further at the list of more than a score of women's organizations, compiled by a women's interest group in Rabat.

"Most are small and useful," conceded Leila. "Special interests, too, like family and child counseling, the disabled, the arts, etc. But the Union de l'Action Féminin is a really active organization that works for *all* women."

I said nothing, but I'd heard this pitch before, in many countries, including the United States, where women's groups have proliferated. I thought of the National Organization for Women, the Texas Women's Political Caucus, La Raza Unida (the Mexican-American political action group), Planned Parenthood, the National Museum for Women in the Arts, Mothers Against Drunk Driving, the now defunct ERA. All were useful and helpful in some way, and needed support. But did any one of the United States organizations qualify as a "really active organization that works for *all* women?" That was a tall order.

We were headed to the office of the Union de l'Action Féminin, to meet Latifa Djebabdi, whom Leila had identified as an important figure in Moroccan women's efforts to improve their condition. Leila was driving. Soad had lent us her car, because the headquarters of the union was far from Rue Haroun al-Rashid. In fact, said Leila, laughing gleefully, if we just keep going on Rue Temara, where the headquarters was located, we would come to the Temara-Plage, one of the many fine beaches along the Atlantic coastline that Rabati residents enjoy in summer. And there was a forest nearby, of beautiful trees, said Leila.

"Why not?" I returned half-seriously.

It was a beautiful if chilly morning and the white houses and buildings of Rabat reflected the sunlight, which fell on the great palms and oleander bushes that decorated both the sides and the center median of the street.

"Rue Temara is really a boulevard in the French sense," said Leila. "Too cold for you?" she added, with a side glance at me and a little laugh.

Had my obsession with heat become ridiculous? Was I using too much electricity? How could I reciprocate? Leila wouldn't accept anything. I had managed to buy her lunch last week only because I paid the bill at the bar, before she knew what was happening.

The neighborhood we were entering was different from Haroun al-Rashid, I noticed, as Leila parked near the Hotel Dahir, the supposed site of the office of the union. Gas stations. Mechanics. Industrial shops, from which came the whine of welding and the pounding of hammers. Oily mud marred the sidewalk where we walked past buildings not in their prime, into the side streets where children played soccer, jumped rope. Teenage boys, *shebab,* in track suits and soccer jackets (white stripes on blue or red) stood near the mechanics, at the edge of the gas stations, drinking tea and coffee. Hanging out. Leila pursed her mouth as we passed them.

"Idle. Doing nothing."

I concurred. "We have them at home," I said.

"Here there are no jobs," explained Leila, "especially for young people who have not passed the *bac* exam."

"Gas stations don't hire such kids?"

Leila sniffed. "Yes, but these boys had higher aspirations. They thought they'd become office workers, managers. Spoiled. They're spoiled. They don't want to work in gas stations."

We stood in front of the house to which we had been directed by a mechanic who wore greasy overalls and a cheerful smile. The sign was there, but it was not Union de l'Action Féminin, but ADM (Association for Democracy in the Maghreb).

"No," said Leila. "This isn't it."

Further checking with the mechanic brought direction from one of the "spoiled" teenage boys.

"The Hotel Dahir is across the street," he said, pointing to the building near where we had parked the car. "The ladies group is in the hotel, but up five or six floors."

Good sign, I thought. The headquarters of this women's action group was known even to the young and idle boys, who seemed helpful and polite. I realized also that Leila had not been here before, either.

The Hotel Dahir actually occupied only part of what was a large office block. Yes, the Union de l'Action Féminin had a mailbox in the lobby, with its name clearly marked. Another good sign. It was there for all to see.

But when we finally reached the offices, sixth floor, end of the hall, I was not so sure. A suite of small offices, leading one into the other. The young woman who answered the door had long dark hair in a plait, jeans, and a very heavy wool tunic, not surprising, since it was so cold. We were ushered into a room and sat down at a table where, in a distant corner, five or six middle-aged women in djellabas and hoods were being given a lesson of some sort.

"Literacy classes," explained the young woman, Malika, who shook hands and offered tea. "Madame Djebabdi will be here soon. She is late. I'm sorry."

Leila and I sat politely. No question of removing our coats. Too cold. The stuccoed walls of the three visible rooms bore posters to be found around the world in centers like these; Women's Rights Are Human Rights; The Rights of the Child; International Women's Day. UNICEF posters. The blackboard being used by the literacy classes was reversible. On the side facing us were simple words in Arabic— bread, milk, price, time, when, where.

In an inner office, someone was speaking on the telephone. A shelf of books along one side, plus several periodicals, invited the ladies in the literacy class—and us—to read about women's issues.

The tea came, piping hot. I warmed my hands on the cup gratefully, noting out of the corner of my eye that Leila did the same. And I also noted that she was warmly dressed in layers, like me, tights, boots, skirt, blouse, sweater, jacket, scarf. Well, I thought to myself, if this was the most effective women's organization in Morocco, then they had a long way to go, remembering the computers and file cabinets and crowds of volunteers who answered phones and stuffed envelopes in some of the women's organization offices I had visited in America. The door banged and in burst Latifa Djebabdi.

"She is Berber," Leila had told me, "but she doesn't look Berber!" Whatever that might mean.

Latifa was taller than either of us, solid but not plump, black hair framing an intense face with high cheekbones. Her clothes were simple—black turtleneck and skirt, beige jacket, no makeup, no jewelry except a wedding ring. But her shoes were surprising—shiny black pumps with big bows! The only thing I knew about Latifa was the story that Leila had told me, about a press seminar in which Leila herself participated with several men and women journalists. Latifa was legendary for doing what she did there, said Leila, which was to speak longer than anyone else, interrupt constantly and rudely, and try to talk everyone down.

This tall woman looked mild enough to me. But then she began to talk very rapidly in French, and only by holding up my hand could I interrupt to ask whether I might write down her remarks.

"Of course," she said, "why else have you come? Yes, I know what you are trying to do, and I will try to answer any questions you have. First I must explain however the history and background of the union, and how we operate, so that your questions will be asked with some knowledge and therefore not waste time, yours or mine."

I nodded, writing rapidly. Leila was silent, drinking her tea and watching Latifa perform.

For it was a performance. Here was a woman so imbued with mission that she was like a steamroller. She talked about the beginning of the union, more than ten years before, and about its literacy classes and workshops, and about its publications. I asked about funding.

"Malika!" she called and Malika smilingly obliged with copies of a small newspaper, published in Arabic, and titled *The Eighth of March*.

"You see!" she said. "International as well as national overtones. The eighth of March is International Women's Day.

"And most of our funding comes from this newspaper," she continued. "It is cheaper to produce in this size because the paper for newsprint can be cut in half." She went over the paper, explaining some of the articles, about law, the arts, women's work, education, women leaders in Morocco. Though it was clearly a well-planned publication, designed to take advantage of the size of newsprint rolls and written for women, I still had difficulty seeing how this small paper could be the major source of their funding.

"How many copies do you print each month?"

"Twenty thousand."

"Twenty thousand?" In a country like Morocco with a population of twenty-eight million, where the literacy rate overall was just 50 percent, and for women 25 percent, twenty thousand copies of a specialized women's activities newspaper seemed incredible.

"And you sell them all?"

"Oh yes." Latifa smiled broadly for the first time. "I see you have a doubtful look on your face."

"How do you sell them all?"

"Malika!" Another call, and when asked, Malika explained that when the copies were ready, volunteers took armloads to every kiosk in Rabat.

"And the owners of the kiosks agree to take them?" I asked.

Now Malika smiled and exchanged a knowing look with the boss.

"We-ell, not always in the beginning. But if the kiosk owner doesn't agree, we just stand beside the kiosk and sell them ourselves. That was in the beginning. Now nearly every kiosk takes them."

And outside Rabat? "They are sent by mail to other cities, where union volunteers take them on to kiosks."

Vigorous nods from both women. In the corner, by the window, the middle-aged ladies had finished their reading lesson, and had gathered themselves up to leave.

"*Bslama,*" they chorused.

One lady, almost toothless, pulled up her veil to cover her face. Latifa looked disapproving. This must have been a regular game, as the woman pulled the veil down again, readjusted the neck of her djellaba, and smiled a toothy smile.

"Why not, my dear?" she asked. "I've worn this veil all my life."

"Ya, Ammi, it's your business," said Latifa, her eyes on the documents on the table, clearly not wanting to engage in an ideological discussion of the issue, perhaps because of my presence.

My heart softened a bit. Latifa was not all cold, icy determination. Could this really be the woman who launched the campaign to change the *mudawana,* or family law? Who was considered to be a radical feminist and a pest besides?

Latifa raised her head. Could she have read my mind?

"I am like the gadfly in Greek philosophy. I bother people. I make them angry."

"But politely, my dear, quite politely," interposed Leila, "except at the press seminar. What came over you?"

Latifa looked annoyed. If she were standing, not sitting, I had the feeling she might have stamped her foot.

"They weren't listening," she said. "They weren't *listening!* To the important issue I was raising about the presentation of women in the media."

"Yes, yes," said Leila, laughing a little. "But sometimes . . ." she shook her head.

"But sometimes . . ." repeated Latifa. Her head came up. "No. No. Leila, we must not think of that. Not *sometimes. Always* we must struggle to make people listen, even if they don't want to."

Well, I thought, perhaps this was indeed the woman who launched the campaign to change the *mudawana.*

"How did you do it, really?" I asked.

She did not even wait for me to identify what "it" was. Because she knew that all over Morocco she was given credit—and blame—for "it." What she did, she told me in rapid-fire detail, was to collect one million signatures on a petition to the King himself, asking him to consider reforms in family law, the laws crucial to women's lives, the laws regulating marriage, divorce, inheritance, child custody, and polygamy.

"But," she added, raising that long arm upward as though she were about to take the oath in a court of law, "I did not do it alone. We did it together, the members of the union, and their brothers and sisters and cousins and mothers and fathers and grandfathers and grandmothers. Everyone knew that the law was not working. Everyone wanted to change it—not just women alone!"

"And this petition was enough to convince the King that he should take the group seriously? He convened a committee of women . . . ?" I asked.

"Well, you can ask your friend Leila here about that. She was on the commission."

"It is a first step," said Leila slowly.

"Yes, a first step," agreed Latifa. "Not enough. We have much more work to do."

The two women nodded together, as though confirming some future plan.

Latifa excused herself, and came back with a handful of small trinkets which she presented to me: a pin and a key ring designed around the organization's publication title: *The Eighth of March.*

"No, no," I protested mildly.

"Yes, yes," she insisted. "I'm going to give you a bound copy of a year of the newspaper, for your university library," she said, "but these are for you, to show your women's movement friends in America that symbols are important, but action is more important."

Again, it had been a long interview. We were standing up, Malika was bringing two volumes of *The Eighth of March,* when Latifa broke into a happy smile.

"I did forget one thing," she said, and while Leila and I shifted from one foot to the other, she launched into a nonstop account of how the one million signatures not only jump-started the King's commission to reform family law, but served as a wake-up call to the political parties, which were then reorganizing for the 1993 elections.

"How did it do that?"

Latifa wagged a finger at me. She was a head taller than I and her moving finger, at the level of my forehead, flashed past my eyes as she spoke, conveying a blurred message rather than a clear call to "attention!"

"The political parties saw what was missing in their cadres: women!" Thus, Latifa said, "They added women to the slates of the major political parties. For the first time in Moroccan history, after thirty-seven years of independence, two women are sitting in Parliament."

"One last question." I fumbled with my original list. The interview had gone in many different directions, more interesting than my questions, but still there was something I had to ask.

"Do you consider yourself a feminist, Madame Djebabdi?"

She laughed. "Of course." Looking at Leila, she added, "And even if I didn't consider myself one, I have been made into one by the fundamentalists and the media, right, Leila?"

"Yes," said Leila. "Tell her, Latifa."

"When the reform commission was suggested by the King, there was an outcry among the fundamentalists. They mobilized in the mosques and wanted to condemn me, me, Latifa Djebabdi, to death. Because I was that awful thing, a feminist."

"How did you feel?" I asked. "How did you react?"

She stood up straight. I realized that handmaiden Malika and another young assistant were standing to one side, listening intently. She was respected and admired here, even if demonized in some quarters.

"I felt terrible," she said. "But I felt I could not show it. I am a Muslim too, you know. I knew they were demonizing me for their own ends, because we had one million people behind this association . . . And my family and my husband stood behind me."

She stiffened and seemed to lean forward as though to jab me in the chest. "Do you think the fundamentalists would have attacked us if we were one of those other little women's organizations with nice, well-meaning educated elite ladies in it? No, they attacked us because they saw that we were powerful. We have seventeen offices in Morocco and one in Paris."

"They are religious Muslims and saw you as against Islam?" I queried.

Latifa dismissed this with a toss of her head.

"Religion! They are not interested in religion. They are interested in power."

"But they didn't put you in jail or . . ."

"No," said Leila, taking up the tale. "The King intervened. He had not forgotten the problems in Algeria with religious fundamentalists. He basically told them to stop, that we were a country where free discussion was allowed, and they must be quiet and let the commission do its work. And they did."

"The business of calling people feminists is just playing with words," said Latifa. "It has a bad association with the West—free sex, drugs, all that. The religious fundamentalists are not against that. They *want* us to see the West as corrupt. What they are really against is women asserting their rightful place in Islamic society."

We were at the door now. "Islamic feminism?"

Latifa tried that one on. "Well, if you like, madame. Frankly, I prefer something like Islamic women's movement. Then we avoid the mudslinging. *Au revoir!*" Firm handshakes all around. The door slammed behind us.

"So what did you think, B.J.?" Fortunately, the car did not have a ticket and we still had an hour before lunch—we were to have a simple kufta today, I had been told, but a larger dinner.

"Impressive woman!"

"Yes," said Leila, "but don't do what they do in America, B.J., and give one person all the credit. She works hard, but she has hundreds of people who work with her and help her. What she said though is right. The union is a real association, not an organization founded by foreign women's groups or foundations or any group that has 'ism after their names."

"Yes, Leila."

"I mean it, B.J.," Leila responded. "It is not this individualistic business, Latifa Djebabdi is doing it, etc. Here it could not be done by one person. Her association is not just for show, it comes from the

Moroccan people. Believe me, I have seen many associations come and go. This is, how do you say in English, for real."

"Grass roots?"

"What does that mean in English idiom?"

I explained.

"Yes," said Leila, turning into Rue Haroun al-Rashid. "Grass roots." She smiled. "I like that idiom. Grass roots."

But when she tried to explain all this to Soad, it was not to her liking at all. They spoke in Arabic, so I was not certain of the nuances, but Soad was definitely not amused, or pleased, or contented. I thanked her for the use of her car; she nodded. She wouldn't speak French with me, I couldn't be sure why. Today, I tried once more. My French was not *that* bad.

Finally Leila said, "Soad thinks of you as a capitalist."

"Me?"

"Well," said Soad, in French, "you are a citizen of a capitalist country. And that system is so passé, it is ridiculous."

"I agree there are problems with it, but . . ."

"Passé," repeated Soad, "and exploitative as well. Unjust."

I launched into a discussion of mixed economic approaches, but Soad was not interested. She ate her lunch, and excused herself to rest before returning to the office.

Leila eyed me over the fruit. "So what do you think?"

I laughed shortly. "She doesn't like capitalists."

"She doesn't like capitalists . . . or Americans, I think."

Not much I could do about that. We cleared the table and rinsed the dishes. Leila washed, I dried. On the patio the old man, the *functionnaire* of the apartment house, was trying to clean out the garbage burner that ran outside from the top to the bottom of the apartment house.

"Stupid people from the country," he was muttering. "Stupid. They put all kinds of things down the incinerator, block it up, start fires."

Leila commiserated with him, as she selected from the crates of vegetables stored on the patio—tomatoes, carrots, eggplants, onions, peppers—what we would eat in the evening.

No servants here, as there used to be in her house when her mother was alive. "Not enough work, really," said Leila. "I decided to stay home and write and cook. Once in a while my sister's maid comes and cleans the house, and we pay her extra. It works out."

I considered at some length and in private our long and fiery interview with Morocco's so-called "demon feminist," "gadfly," or women's activist. She was clearly a strong woman, from Tiznit, she had told us, a small town near the southern border of Morocco, famed for its craftspeople who produced silver jewelry and inlaid weapons.

She had been, she said herself, an "ardent" member of the student movement in the sixties, the group which campaigned in the secondary schools and then the universities for greater democracy in politics, who became identified with the new left; eventually she became a member of the PLS, the Communist Party of Progress.

"Women's questions were secondary on all the progressive agendas," she had said, "for women were perceived as *dependents*. I began to see that role of women was central if any democratic change was to take place in Morocco."

This had all been a revelation to me because, in my years in Morocco before, in the seventies, I had never heard of women like Latifa Djebabdi.

"That's because there weren't any," said Leila. "All this really began in the late eighties. It's different, isn't it?"

"Yes," I answered. "Even when I was visiting here in 1988, I didn't sense all this activity around women's issues. People were still thinking in the old *foyer* mode—teaching poor women how to embroider, cook, read, write, etc. But politics? No."

What had happened? Western observers cited the rise of Islamic fundamentalism, a conservative movement in many countries to return to traditional roots, hallowed principles. Was this secular political resurgence a response to fundamentalism?

Early promises of a rosy future in postrevolutionary Morocco had not been fulfilled. Economics, despite Soad's rejection of capitalism, had not yet come up with a system that would eliminate the private sector. The public sector hadn't been able to do it all. There was rising unemployment, and, if the figures of Latifa Djebabdi were to be believed, 75 percent of Moroccan women were illiterate, despite thirty years of government-sponsored public, free, and supposedly compulsory education. Things were not working out the way the early leaders had hoped. The rich were getting richer, the poor were getting poorer, as is true in many Third World countries, and some First World countries as well.

Raised expectations. Unfulfilled expectations. I thought of the crowd of unemployed teenage boys by the gas station on Rue Temara; they were part of a vast army of unemployed or partially employed throughout Morocco. Figures were hard to come by, but several analysts suggested 30 percent. This of course was 30 percent of those Moroccans living in Morocco, and did not take into account the thousands of men (and some women) who had emigrated to Europe, set-tled in France and Belgium, even Italy, taking low-level service and industrial jobs and sending part of their salaries home to their families in Morocco. In 1982, an economic analyst estimated that 60 percent of the men in the Rif, the northern coastal area of Morocco fronting the Mediterranean, were away working in Europe.

Absent fathers. Absent sons. This meant women-headed house-holds, and a real shift in the patterns of authority in the traditional Moroccan family. No wonder the Islamic fathers were worried; the whole fundamentalist argument began indeed to look like a struggle for power, not only in political and economic spheres but in the family group, the basic unit of power.

Another factor affecting change was the youth of the electorate. Morocco had recently passed a new law giving eighteen-year-olds the vote. To celebrate this development, King Hassan had held a reception for selected youths.

"And what are the concerns of youth in Morocco today?" he is supposed to have said, over glasses of mint tea and pastries.

"The major issues for Morocco," the youth are supposed to have replied, "are the problems of women and the problems of the family."

King Hassan is a good politician. He has not stayed on the throne of Morocco for more than thirty years without meeting crises success-fully. The youths' expressed concerns, *plus* the million-signature peti-tion of the Union de l'Action Féminin, clearly gave him pause and helped him change his tactics on the subject of women. So he had appointed that commission, which included Leila, to look over family law. He then appointed a group of scholars to look over the women's report and send their views to him.

"No women sat on the second committee," said Leila. "It was mostly the *ulema*, the religious men. Still, we have had some impor-tant changes and it is a first step, as I keep telling myself."

So where was Islam in all this? My search for *Islamic* feminism had so far not produced any Islamic feminists, per se. But what did Islamic feminism actually mean? Latifa Djebabdi was Muslim, Leila was Mus-lim. Both were strongly in favor of women's rights, greater freedom, and equality. So were Dr. Fouzia, Dr. Amina, Dr. Khadija, and Dr. Fathiya of the women's studies steering committee at Muhammad V University. They were all Muslims. Were they feminists in the Western sense? I was beginning to wonder whether the Western term had any meaning here at all.

□ □ □ □

The first two women elected to the Moroccan Parliament had agreed to my request for an interview. "Wasn't their election in 1993 something of a milestone?" I asked.

"Yes," Leila replied. "It was. But really long overdue. We have been an independent nation for thirty-seven years; this is the first time women have been *elected* to Parliament."

"In Egypt . . ." I began.

"Yes, yes, I know about Egypt," interrupted Leila.

From her tone, I realized I was beginning to be a bore in comparing Morocco to Egypt. But still, when I made two films about Egyptian women in 1981, thirty-five members of the Egyptian Parliament were women.

"That was during Sadat's time," Leila conceded, "but remember, B.J., he *appointed* most of them."

"Leila, that's not true," I asserted. "Sadat reserved thirty seats for women, but they had to fight for those seats with other women."

"So it wasn't an open election, like here," Leila retorted.

"Well, okay, the seats were reserved for women, but both men and women voted."

Leila nodded and changed the subject. "Anyhow, B.J., you are very lucky to be able to interview *both* Moroccan ladies. And I would like to come with you, if I may. They are very historic."

"Of course. I'll need your help."

Leila smiled. "Your French is really okay now, though at the beginning a little shaky."

I smiled, too. That, from Leila, was a real compliment. It was true that my rusty French was embarrassing in the beginning but it had gotten better.

"It will never be as good as my children's," I said.

"Well, they went to a French school," she pointed out. "Poor Americans, they are so backward in terms of language, I feel sorry for them, it is really not good for the future of their country."

Leila of course was fluent in three languages—Arabic, French, and English—and also spoke some Spanish and Italian. In addition, she was widely admired throughout Morocco, because, although she spoke the distinctive Moroccan dialect perfectly, she had had a good education in classical Arabic, so her modern standard Arabic was understandable, "even," she used to laugh, "in Egypt, where they make fun of our dialect."

I had been instructed to dress with elegance for these interviews.

Well, yes. I had only two suits with me, but lots of scarves. I decided to wear my favorite scarf, a multicolored tapestry wool square from

Liberty of London. It was not only beautiful but warm! And since all the important ladies in Morocco seemed to buy their clothes in Paris, Liberty of London was a good match, I thought.

Leila looked me up and down, then nodded. I'd passed the test. I also noted with interest that she had dressed up a bit, too, knotting a soft paisley silk scarf at the neck of her black suit.

Leila had pulled some strings to get me an appointment with Madame Latifa Bennani-Smires, the member who had run on the Istiqlal Party ticket. This was the old "freedom party," which, with the passing of time, had become the party of the status quo, the bastion of men who had been in power for three decades, and who were not interested in relinquishing that power. Leila had worked in Parliament herself for several years, first as assistant to an early member then, in recent years, as an English translator. The Istiqlal Party was the one which had embraced and honored her own father for his contributions to Moroccan independence, through his resistance to the French rule and his years in prison for his views on independence.

We were off to the Houses of Parliament set back from Boulevard Muhammad V, another impressive building with a resemblance to French public buildings of the nineteenth century. This was not surprising, given that the entire city was built under the direction of General Lyautey, French governor-general of Morocco, assisted by French architects and urban planners.

Leila and I skirted around the front entrance, which was presumably reserved for state occasions and visiting dignitaries. We headed to a narrow door that gave onto the fenced rear court and was guarded by police with telephones, desks, and what looked like a fax machine. One of the guards, a bald-headed old man wearing a wrinkled winter black uniform, greeted Leila with delight.

My sense of the exchange (which was in Arabic) and Leila's recurring laughter was that the old policeman was asking whether Leila's welcome and altogether unexpected appearance meant that they would have the pleasure of welcoming her back into the fold of Parliament.

"No, no," said Leila, holding up her hand.

Despite these pleasantries, we had to give up our passports and wait in the lounge, across the back street, in a small building lined with hard benches and chairs. The waiting room for petitioners to cool their heels, no doubt. But we, too, after all, were petitioners.

Half an hour later, we were ushered into the office of Madame Bennani-Smires. She rose to meet us in her peacock blue silk djellaba, a pale red chiffon scarf around her head. She looked great, and I was secretly glad I was wearing my Liberty scarf.

Madame Smires was a small woman with petite features and thinning black hair; she looked quizzically at us. She was uneasy. Was it timidity, annoyance, or concern about being described in a book by a brash American writer/feminist, me, who was as old or older than she was? Probably the latter. Like all politicians, her words were actionable, for better or for worse. I had the feeling that without Leila she would not want to talk to me.

Madame Smires might look petite and sweet, but she took the lead in the interview. She noted that although she had just been elected to Parliament, she had been active in Istiqlal Party politics for many years; secretary for the party youth in Fez (very important, Leila noted in an aside); since 1981, member of the Istiqlal Party's central commission; in 1989, elected to the executive bureau of the party.

"I am one of only two women in the party councils," she said, rather softly, but her intention was clear: I am important, so you should listen.

I am listening, I thought, and would like to ask questions. But Madame Smires did not pause. She proceeded, again gently and rather slowly, but firmly and steadily so that it was not possible to interrupt.

I wrote busily in my notebook.

"Tea, please!" Madame Smires ordered, as an aide came in, another young woman in djellaba and head scarf. "You like our mint tea, madame?"

"Oh yes." Before I could continue, Leila explained that I had lived in Morocco with my family, that I had written books and made films about Morocco.

Madame Smires paused.

And in the pause I sat up and asked questions. What were her hopes for women? Did she feel that her position would be used to help women? If so, how? What were the problems of women?

For the first time she smiled.

"Many questions, madame." She looked at Leila, who nodded.

The tea came, and we stirred it while Madame considered her reply.

"The problems of women seem insoluble," she began. "Economic, social. The *process* of getting social and legal assistance to women is very complicated in this country, for many reasons. I want to simplify that process."

"But how can you do it?" I asked.

Madame Smires sipped her tea.

"We currently have no commission on women's affairs. I want to start one, so these problems can be looked at clearly in their own right, not in relation to national problems or men's problems."

I looked, as I felt, doubtful. Another bureaucratic institution in what was already a bureaucratically overloaded country did not seem the answer. Madame pushed on, but slowly, as though she were trying to convince herself.

"Well, let's look at divorce and women who want divorces," she said. "When they are divorced, the man is supposed to provide economic support for the wife, or at least the children. There's no central office that deals with that."

I said something about the problem of getting fathers to provide child support in America. What was the French expression for deadbeat fathers? There were state laws, I explained, but the laws had not, until recently, been valid across the country.

"We have laws here, too," said Madame Smires. "Very strict laws, supported by religious law, which all men say we should honor and abide by."

"Sharia," added Leila, "Islamic law."

"Yes," agreed Madame Smires, "but you know, Leila, the *mudawana*, or family law, is based on sharia, but it isn't precisely sharia. Yet both are clear on the responsibility of mothers and fathers for children; what actually happens is something different. We need a central place where these complaints can be handled."

"Are the new changes in the *mudawana* important or not?" I asked.

Madame Smires said in a firmer voice, "They may look trivial to you, a Westerner, whose laws supposedly protect women, and give them lots of things ours don't, but the changes in the *mudawana* are important. Don't you think so, Leila?"

Leila nodded silently. "A first step," she said in a low voice.

"We have to be persistent," said Madame Smires gently. "Like all laws, they have to be implemented." She paused.

I realized the interview might be at an end. Madame Smires was a busy person. But she had not yet stood up, as a polite gesture to really tell us to go, so I launched into my final questions. What about her? Her background? Her children? What would she stress if she were writing my book?

A glance at Leila. "Does she know about Fezzis?" asked Madame Smires, smiling. "She lived in Marrakech, after all."

"Something, maybe," said Leila. She looked a little puzzled. What was Madame Smires getting at?

"Well," she said. "I am from Fez. My family has been living in Fez for hundreds of years.

"Fez has always been a place of political action," she went on. "And you may not believe this to look at me now, but I joined the Istiqlal Party when I was fifteen years old. My husband is also involved in party affairs. We both did degrees in two languages—French and Arabic."

"You have children?" I was trying to take this down verbatim.

"Three." She smiled again. "They've lived with politics all their lives. We as a family are political, always have been political, that is what I'm trying to say. And now, in answer to your final question, may I give you a small lecture?"

"Of course," I answered.

"Feminists are fond of saying that women have the same problems, no matter where they live: equality, political decision making with men, organizing women's movements, keeping their womanliness in spite of the struggle."

"Do you believe that?" I asked.

"Yes, but surely each society has specific problems . . . Here we can't forget religion, illiteracy, the economic situation in rural areas."

"Can you do anything about that in your position?" I asked.

"I've been assigned to the committee on the economy. I will try."

"And what about Islam?"

"It's a religion with scholars and texts, like any other religion. We have women now who are educated in religious matters, who read the Qur'an, who explicate the texts. Are they feminists? I don't know. But this is new. These women still don't have, nor do we have, a clear perception of what religious women's roles in politics should be."

"Do you have any ideas?" I asked.

"Well," said Madame Smires, "I have as an adviser one of three women in Morocco who is considered knowledgeable in religious affairs. I ask her all the time about religious issues. We are working on a definition."

"Thank you for your time," I murmured.

She guided us to the door. In her peacock blue silk djellaba, she was barely up to my shoulder.

"Change is going on here, very fast change," she added, as we shook hands. She had a small, dry, firm hand. "Tell her, Leila."

"I will," said Leila. The door closed behind us.

"Well, what did you think, B.J.?"

"A bit cool at first, but she warmed up."

"Yes," said Leila, "she did. I was surprised. She is supposed to be quite distant and cold." She laughed. "Like all rich Fezzis."

Aha, I thought to myself. Class once more.

◻ ◻ ◻ ◻

Madame Badia Skalli, the Socialist Party candidate, was completely different. A tall, enthusiastic woman wearing glasses and a tweed suit, she took us on a tour of the Parliament building itself, the plaques on the walls, the assembly with its podium, its Moroccan flag, the crimson seats for the delegates.

"Isn't it beautiful—the mix of Moroccan and French styles?" she asked. "I feel so proud to be a member of this body," she went on, "so proud. It is wonderful to be able to have a voice in the affairs of my country. And I get paid for it, so I can take leave from my job at the university." (She was a professor of economics at the university in Casablanca.)

"This is very important to me," she explained, "for I am a widow, supporting my only son, who is studying in Fez. It's a family pattern, I guess," she said ruefully. "I was lucky to be born into an educated family, in the fifties in Kasba Tadla. My father worked there, though both parents were originally from Fez. Then my father died and my mother was left with seven children to bring up. I helped. Good training for politics!" She laughed.

"Tell me about Moroccan women in politics," I suggested.

"Oh, women in politics!" She repeated my question and I felt quite set up since my French really seemed to have become fluent in this interview. Practice?

Women had always been in politics, according to Madame Skalli. First in the home, then in the student movements in independence days, then in the political parties. "Women first ran in elections in 1962, can you believe it?"

"Sixty-two!" repeated Leila.

"Yes, but of course they didn't win then, and they didn't win in 1967, either. Why? The conservative ideology, Islam and all that; the men thought that the Qur'an said women shouldn't be in public parliaments, etc. What nonsense. The Qur'an specifically gives women the right to prophesy and participate in political and economic life. Isn't that politics? Of course it is, but today rather than the seventh century."

Madame Skalli sat forward in her chair. We were in her office now, drinking mint tea. The walls were hung with certificates of appreciation, a sura from the Qur'an, photos of family, a French Impressionist print.

"Democracy doesn't fall from the sky, madame," she said earnestly. "One has to learn it, practice it, struggle for it."

I wrote in my notebook.

"Oh dear!" she said and took off her glasses. "I sound so earnest. How boring!" She laughed.

"No, no, no," put in Leila forcefully. "You are right. We must work for it . . ."

"Like you did on the *mudawana* commission. A lesson to us all. How was it, Leila?"

"Interesting. Difficult." Leila's contribution to the King's commission to reform family law had been referred to everywhere we went.

"The changes were not as great as we hoped," remarked Madame Skalli. "That business about child custody returning to the father if a divorced woman marries again. No. Not good."

"It was a beginning," temporized Leila.

Madame Skalli nodded. She was fingering papers, drumming on the desk. "Well, I tell myself it is an important step, a positive move. For the first time, the King has responded to women, to real people, not just some abstraction. But still, how can that be, the father takes over the child if the woman remarries? How cruel! How unjust!"

Leila nodded. I wrote.

I brought up another subject. "Is child labor necessary to help poor families get by?"

Madame Skalli frowned. "No, it's a pretext for not doing anything about the economic situation. You haven't asked me, madame, but the biggest problem for Moroccan women is not divorce, or child custody, or Islam, but unemployment! Money!

"And they overloaded me," she continued. "I'm on all the women's concerns committees: social affairs, health, youth, and sports." She fumbled on her desk . . . "Oh yes, and the handicapped and the veterans. It's impossible to think of contributing seriously on all those fronts."

Leila was trying to catch my eye. We were due for lunch in half an hour, a long way across town. We must search for a taxi, hard to get at this hour.

"Thank you, thank you." Madame Skalli held my hand and shook it hard. "Remember. Unemployment is woman's greatest problem! Unemployment."

"But the laws . . ." began Leila.

"If they have money, they can hire lawyers to help them through the laws, Leila. But poor women, what are they to do? They are illiterate. That means they don't buy the newspapers and they can't read the classified job ads. It is terrible."

A last try. "Are you a feminist, Madame Skalli?"

She laughed, but not merrily. "If you look at what I believe and stand for, yes, probably. But that word, feminist, is a pejorative term in our society—it means all the bad things our conservative men can think of to call us, based on their media views of American TV shows like *Dallas* and *Dynasty*. So I never call myself a feminist."

"What do you call yourself?" I was interested.

"A member of Parliament!" she cried. "That is a real achievement. Fifteen years ago, the conservative Muslim men argued that the Qur'an would not allow women to vote. Ten years ago, they argued that they could not sit in Parliament with men. Today there are two of us women—not many, but a beginning."

I am dreaming I am in Marrakech. Somehow I know I am dreaming but the figures of my husband and my children, the details of their faces and their clothes, are so vivid I feel they are not figments of a dream, but real, reincarnated as they were twenty-five years ago. Bob stands against the door of the study in our courtyard, with its stained-glass fanlights over the green wooden doors. It was the center of our traditional medina house. His hair is long and thick. His hand is up in the air, for reasons I cannot fathom in the dream. Laura Ann, the oldest, is wearing a green print dress with full sleeves that I bought for her twelfth birthday: it is French and came from a shop in Gueliz, the so-called modern section of the city. David, his straight long blond hair recently cut, has his arm around his nine-year-old blonder sister Laila, who looks pained. Is he pinching her? The fountain splashes into its stone basin, the sun shines on the white walls of the courtyard, half-tiled in patterns of green and blue stars, and topped with hand-carved white plaster borders.

Somewhere there is a loud knocking.

"Answer the door," calls Bob.

But I cannot, frozen in that dream position which prevents one from moving.

While I stand there, the knocking goes on, and on. A mist is descending on the colored tiles on the courtyard, combining with the rising water of the fountain to create a cloud of steam.

The knocking goes on. "Answer the door," Bob calls again.

The children do not move. I cannot move. Bob does not move. The mist and steam swirl around the courtyard.

Suddenly Aisha comes out of the kitchen. She is wearing her house caftan, a worn blue and silver garment, the skirt pulled up and tucked into her belt, the sleeves rolled and kept in place by that complicated double set of elastics which Moroccan women cross over back, shoulders, and arms to keep their sleeves out of the dishwater.

Aisha holds her finger to her lips. "Don't open the door," she says softly. "It's the djinn trying to get in." She crosses the courtyard, closes and locks the two cupboards in the walls of the courtyard. It is in these cupboards, built over the ancient well of the house, that the house djinn or spirit lives, according to Aisha. But if the djinn is in the cupboards above the well, how can he or she be knocking on the door?

Louder and louder, the knocking continues and the mist envelops the dream courtyard.

"B.J.," someone is calling. "It's time for breakfast."

I woke up. I was in a narrow bed, not in our medina house of long ago. I was alone.

"Wake up, B.J.! It's Sandra."

Outside the window was the street, and across the street the colonnaded law courts of the city of Marrakech. It was 1995, not 1971. I needed some coffee. My children were in the United States, and so was Bob. The dream had faded, but I had a pretty good idea where it came from. Sandra Carter, Deborah Kapchan, and I had come to Marrakech, and today was the day I was going to look for and hopefully find my old friend Aisha. I had to find her. We had found her once, when Bob and I were briefly in Marrakech in 1993, but she had moved again, I was told. I had no address. The word was that she had been reduced to penury. What could I do? I had put together some money in an envelope that I planned to give to her. But first I had to find her.

Aisha was my age. She was a grandmother, too. Intelligent, illiterate, lively and hardworking, organized and humorous. Her father came to the city from a village near Marrakech to deal in grain. Aisha had lived in the city all her life. She had married, borne four children, and worked at cleaning people's houses when her husband was unemployed.

In the warm well-furnished offices of the Moroccan Parliament, women's unemployment had been defined as a serious problem, but it was an abstraction. For people like Aisha, unemployment was at the core of her life. She had done what she perceived to be all the right things, and it hadn't worked out.

"I am proud to be a Moroccan," she'd told me many years ago. "The new government gives free education to everybody. All my children are in school. Could that have happened if Morocco weren't free from the French? The French, who used to hit me when I was a little girl if I forgot to salute them in the streets?"

Then, I agreed with her. Education would be the same means of getting ahead in Morocco as it had been in the United States. My own mother was the first member of her family to graduate from college, though her mother, my grandmother, had been educated in Poland in the middle of the nineteenth century, something unusual for a woman at the time. That education had worked in her favor when the Germans invaded and took over my grandparents' estate; the Germans were impressed enough with an educated woman that they made her their children's governess. But that did not satisfy Grandmother Meshynsky; the family story is that she nagged Grandpa until he emigrated to the United States. Education, she told my mother, is the way to improve your lot in this world. I told Aisha that story and she sighed.

"I wish I could have gone to school," she said. But then she added, cheering up, "At least my children are. They will all do well, I know they will."

Her oldest son Saleh had done well. He had earned a college degree and held a good job teaching in the secondary school of Daoudiate, one of the city's western suburbs. Her second child, Najiya, although somewhat disabled as a hunchback, had also done well in school, passed her baccalaureate exam at a high level and was offered three teaching jobs, but none in Marrakech. She passed them up in favor of an office job in the city of her home—she did not want to leave her mother and her siblings. She had died suddenly in 1979.

The third of Aisha's children, Abdul Krim, was on the high school gymnastics team, bright, good-looking, but, it turned out, lazy. He was touted for his athletic skills and traveled to tournaments in Casablanca, but he did not pass the baccalaureate exams, and therefore was more or less unemployable, at least in jobs which he felt were worthy of his talents. Abdul Krim was waiting for the big offer, which was unlikely to come looking for him in a country like Morocco, with a growing population of hardworking competitive young people. For a while, he had served as a part-time physical education instructor in a primary school, but that had come to an end, whether because of the school or because of Abdul Krim, it was not possible to know.

And then there was the youngest.

"Ah, Youssef," Aisha used to say, "well, he is hardworking."

Youssef had quit secondary school to go to work in a bakery near their house. The bakery had gone bankrupt and closed; Youssef had essentially crossed himself off the list of school candidates, and was now eligible only for unskilled labor jobs, like his father.

Aisha continued to work cleaning people's houses—for American members of the Peace Corps assigned to Marrakech, for the staff of Daniel Wagner's project to study literacy in Morocco. She had worked for me when we made the film *Some Women of Marrakech*. But now the word was out that she was unemployed again. Why? More important, how was the family living? Where was Aisha getting the wherewithal to feed and house herself. And what about her two unemployed sons? Her husband had only recently died but Aisha had always been the principal provider in the family.

"Sorry I overslept." We were drinking the good coffee and eating the fresh rolls provided by the Hotel Imlil. Deborah had news.

"It looks like we can visit Aisha tonight," she said.

"Tonight?" My voice must have betrayed my apprehension about this excursion, for both Sandra and Deborah looked at me with concern.

"If you don't want to go, B.J.—" said Deborah.

"No, no, I want to go," I insisted, pouring myself more coffee. "It's just that I'm afraid of what I will find, and I won't know what to do."

"It's Ramadan," said Deborah sensibly. "Give her a present. That's all you can do."

She was right, of course. But I did feel responsible, somehow. And I also felt guilt. Why? Because I was able to travel back and forth between the United States and Morocco in relative comfort, because my children were grown and all held paying jobs, because I did not need to worry that my house would be sold over my head. For Aisha had written to me, after the film premiered in London. "Please help me buy a house. About ten thousand dollars should be enough."

I was not offended nor surprised by this letter. The outlay of cash expended during the filming—rent, food, transport, film, salaries—must certainly have led Aisha and her family to believe that we were at least millionaires. And if so, what was ten thousand dollars? A mere drop in the bucket of our untold wealth.

But I had to reply in the negative and tried to explain something about our income and our obligations. I am certain she had trouble believing my story about the costs of United States college tuition, for in Morocco, all college instruction is free if you pass the exams and get in. She did understand that we were taking care of our mothers, however. She had met Bob's mother, in fact, in 1971. Aisha had strong feelings about the duties of children to their parents, though it hadn't done her much good. We had come back to Marrakech several times and given her presents of money. But that did not solve Aisha's long-term problem of how to survive in old age, when she could no longer work. And I had the feeling that our presents of money were quickly appropriated by her unemployed sons. Deborah, who has been doing ethnography in Morocco since 1982, had told me about a large fare-well gift of money that was put together by staff members of the literacy project, who had been very fond of Aisha. Aisha had said thank you and then come back and cried that it had been stolen out of her shopping bag as she crossed Djemaa el Fna on her way home.

This did not wash with me. Although native New Yorkers regularly report muggings and robbings on their own streets, it was hard to believe that a Marrakshi would get robbed like that. Also, I remem-bered vividly the care with which Aisha secreted her money in a special pocket inside her djellaba. I could not believe that she would have carried money openly in her shopping bag and that someone had snatched it from her. Even in the unlikely circumstance that someone had, she would have clouted them hard, screamed and hollered, and brought policemen and passersby running. Thus I did not think that the person who took the money was unknown to Aisha. I suspected Abdul Krim had used it to buy himself a nice pair of trousers and a French shirt and gone to Gueliz to sit in the Renaissance café to "look for a job." Aisha might even have bought into that story, for she loved Abdul Krim dearly, and she knew how depressed he was.

Once, in 1984, I had offered to take Abdul Krim to the doctor because he was suffering from an unidentified malady.

"Don't waste your money," Aisha had said crisply. "I think he is suffering from a disease that a lot of young men have—no work. The government gave them schooling, and told them they'd get wonderful jobs and wear neckties, but there aren't enough of those jobs."

"And particularly if they haven't passed the bac," I put in.

Aisha stared at me, a wounded look in her eye. "Please, Elizabeth, he did very well."

This was a sore point and I should not have raised it. Aisha could not bring herself to believe that her pride and joy, Abdul Krim, who was so good-looking and upstanding and had his picture in the paper when the gym team went to Casablanca, had failed his bac. How could he? It must have been a mistake.

The plan for finding Aisha and then going to visit her had been complicated by the rituals of Ramadan. Abdul Rahman, the teacher husband of Deborah's friend Rashida, had actually traced Aisha to a small house somewhere in the endless narrow, twisting lanes of the Marrakech medina. But visiting was another matter. Abdul Rahman came to the Hotel Imlil and explained how we were to proceed.

"We should not visit during the day, madame," he pointed out, "because people are fasting and perhaps resting. At night, we should not go until after the iftar is finished, or Aisha will feel she has to feed us."

I nodded. "You're right, Abdul Rahman. I'm sure Aisha couldn't afford to provide food for all of us, and would feel obliged to. So why don't we go at night, about eight?"

Abdul Rahman shook his head. "No, no," he said. "Three women alone you cannot. It is a bad district."

"Even with all three of us together?" queried Sandra, amazed. "We're stalwart types, aren't we, Deborah, B.J.?"

"Yes . . ." I began, but Deborah interrupted me.

"We have to go along with whatever Abdul Rahman wants us to do," she said gently. "He's done all this arranging, and he feels personally responsible for us."

"I will accompany you," announced Abdul Rahman, "take you to the door of the house, and leave you there. And afterward, you must go to *our* house for dinner. Rashida wants to see you anyway, Deborah. And this will give you an excuse not to stay too long at poor Aisha's house."

So it was agreed. After iftar, Abdul Rahman would come to the hotel on his motorbike. He would find us a taxi and then, on his bike, lead the taxi to the street from where we would have to go on foot. "And of course I will be with you, all the time. Not to worry," he told Deborah.

My heart was filled with dread. Bits of my dream floated into my mind, and I kept hearing Aisha say, "Don't open the door. It's the djinn trying to get in." Clearly I was unable to let things lie; I was going to let the djinn in and who knew what would happen. But what else could I do? I felt I had to visit her, and see if I could help. On the other hand, I did not think I could bear to find Aisha on a crumbling floor, weak and sick, while her son Abdul Krim sported in the cafés. I could not bring myself to say this to Sandra or Deborah, but my anxiety must have been palpable, for Sandra patted me on the arm.

"It'll be all right, B.J.," she said. "Don't worry."

The night was dark and cloudy, an ominous sign for our journey. "Don't bring your purses," Abdul Rahman had insisted.

Not take our purses? Where on earth was Aisha living?

The journey in the taxi seemed to take forever, following Abdul Rahman in his black leather jacket, put-putting, then zooming ahead of us on his "mo-to." Into the medina, past the Bahia Palace, a right into the casbah, out of the casbah. Now we were in the Mellah. This was where Aisha had been living before. Even though it was dark, some landmarks loomed up in the streetlights; the old Jewish cemetery for example, on our left, the Hebrew sign still intact above the high wall and the gate, locked and barred against intruders. But we whizzed past the old turnoff to Aisha's 1993 house (which had seemed to us roomier, pleasanter than her old quarters on Rue Tresor) and went on, barreling into narrower and narrower streets until I had no idea at all where we were.

Stop. The taxi driver, who seemed rather to be enjoying the adventure, explained to Deborah, whose Moroccan Arabic was fluent, that we could go no farther. The streets were too narrow for the taxi. He would wait for us there.

Crowds of small boys surrounded us, as the taxi disgorged us on the shadowy broken lane. They did not seem aggressive, but curious, as well they might be. What were three mature foreign women doing here in the heart of the medina after eight o'clock at night?

Abdul Rahman was asking directions. Ah, I said to myself, maybe we wouldn't find her after all and we could just go back to the hotel.

Deborah had pushed her way through the crowd of boys to a narrow shop front between buildings.

"I'll buy some sugar," she announced. "For Ramadan, you know. It's a nice present."

She was right. I had forgotten. I had not lived here for many years.

The owner of the shop excused himself, and left us standing at the counter. He said he would be back in a minute.

"He's gone to his house to get the sugar," said Deborah.

"His house?" echoed Sandra.

Deborah smiled. "He said he doesn't keep much in the shop because of people around, unemployed—and maybe hungry."

We stood by the counter.

The crowd of boys and a few adolescents eyed us. There were maybe twenty, but it was hard to tell in the shadows. We stared ahead into the darkness.

"Here, madame!" The owner presented two cones of sugar wrapped in rough pink paper and Deborah paid him as Abdul Rahman motioned us to follow. Down the street, right into another, then left into another, and if possible, even narrower street.

I suddenly realized that we had lost the crowd of boys. The street was very quiet. Three low dark doors faced us, barely distinguishable as forms in the shifting gray shadows on the unlit street. My mind whipped back to the dream. Shadows—mists—the djinn? There were glimmers in the shadows. It was the stars, shining a faint light out of the low cloud cover above.

Abdul Rahman was pounding on the middle of the three doors, but no one answered.

He continued to pound, and I was again back in my dream, standing in the misty courtyard with my family, with someone pounding on the door and Aisha whispering to me, "Don't open the door—you'll let the djinn in—or out."

I looked up to the sky. Orion was there, very bright suddenly, defining the shape of a house across the street from where Aisha was supposed to be living. But the neighbor's house was not a house after all; the starlight picked out a pile of rubble, which might have been a house, long ago.

A voice answered from behind Aisha's dark door. Was the house so poor they could not afford electricity?

"Who's there?"

Abdul Rahman explained. "Elizabeth, friend of Aisha from America."

"My mother is not here." A man's voice, gruff, fuzzed with sleep.

"What? Where is she?"

"At the mosque. Gone to pray. Don't you know it's Ramadan?"

I smiled to myself in the darkness. Aisha was alive and well. She was not going to maunder about in her dark house; she would take the route open to her—the mosque, which was certainly a clean, well-lighted place.

"When will she come?" from Abdul Rahman.

"Don't know." The door opened a crack, but still no light showed. "Do you want to wait?"

Abdul Rahman turned to me.

"No, no." I realized I could not bear to go through the dark door and sit around in the gloom to wait.

"No, no," I repeated. "Can we come tomorrow, in the morning?"

"After ten," answered the voice. The door slammed, but not before Deborah had passed her cones of sugar to Abdul Rahman, who passed them toward the door. The man inside (Abdul Krim/Youssef?) stuck his arm through the crack in the door and took the sugar.

"Thank you," he muttered.

I looked up at Orion again, the belt glittering brightly still, and I breathed out, realizing I had been holding my breath for several seconds.

The crowd of boys was back. I heard them repeating, "Tomorrow, in the morning, after ten," but they stood back at a respectable distance. Abdul Rahman shushed them fiercely, and they subsided, but followed us to the taxi, where the driver, in his heavy gray turtleneck, lounged on the counter, chatting with the shop owner, who was young but tired-looking and wore a worn brown overcoat against the cold. Perhaps the driver was talking about us, though he knew little except that he picked us up at the Hotel Imlil and that Abdul Rahman, a teacher in Daoudiate, led us here on his motorcycle.

"Tomorrow," said Deborah. "Nine-thirty at the hotel. Do you want to pick us up or shall we call another taxi?"

"No, no, madame," said the driver, "I will pick you up."

Abdul Rahman bade us good night, after giving the taxi driver detailed instructions about how to get to his house, where his wife had asked us to dinner. He then zoomed off to his 9 P.M. appointment, having performed his charitable duty for the day. I was somewhat relieved. At least the dreaded moment had been postponed until the next day.

Abdul Rahman's and his wife Rashida's house was only a twenty-minute taxi ride from Aisha's narrow dark door but it might have been on another planet. Here, I thought to myself, is the emerging middle class of Morocco. A comfortable roomy house. Rashida, the hostess, pleasant and relaxed. She and Deborah were old friends. Two healthy children. Mehdi, the four-year-old, was a jack-in-the-box, who couldn't decide whether he loved or hated his baby sister, a placid six-month-old, cooing and talking to us and herself as she sat against pillows, cheeks pink, black tendrils of hair beginning to come down about her ears. Strains of Moroccan music drifted from the radio in the other room.

Deborah presented gifts. Mehdi was delighted with his soccer ball and jean jacket. Sandra and I looked at each other. We should have brought flowers—or something. I was so worried about seeing Aisha in collapse that I had forgotten my manners.

Rashida was warm and welcoming, creamy skin, black hair, a bit heavy from her last delivery, which was a Cesarean.

"My body's still not the way it was before she was born," Rashida was saying to Deborah, in Arabic and French. I got the drift, as did Sandra. "It takes a long time. They cut through the *muscles*. No, Mehdi." But she admonished him gently. He was playing peekaboo with the baby, a little too close to her face.

How did high school teachers like Rashida and Abdul Rahman, on small salaries, afford this house? I wondered. Did they have rich parents?

It seemed not, I realized when I posed the question.

"You have to buy the land from the government with cash and pay to put in the foundation of the house before you can get a loan from the bank," Rashida explained. "You know, Deborah, we saved up, Abdul Rahman and I, from the literacy project. We were so lucky to work on that."

I asked about the loan, hoping I was not being rude.

"You have to have collateral," said Rashida matter-of-factly. "You need to show that there is some property in your family." Rashida's family was certainly not rich, but they did own a small house in the medina. So did Abdul Rahman's family. Ownership. *Real* estate.

This is what my friend Aisha did not have. She owned a small piece of land in her natal village, but she did not own property in Marrakech. She had paid out rent for fifty years instead.

"We've eaten at the hotel, Rashida, we had tea," Deborah protested, but Rashida brought out a tray of "starters" anyway. It turned out to be *sfuuf,* a slightly different version from what I'd had in Rabat.

"How do I make it?" Rashida smiled and recited on her fingers, "Ground almonds, sesame, anise, fennel, butter, honey . . . oh, and ground peanuts. *That's* the difference. Rabatis don't put peanuts in."

The mint tea was served in embossed green tea glasses, poured out of a pewter silver teapot, from a great height.

Sandra watched, fascinated. "It's in the wrist!" she announced, and everyone laughed.

Deborah and Rashida talked of the past, of mutual friends. Sandra and I played with Medhi and the baby and looked around the room. Rashida noticed our gaze and explained that the house, like the street, was not yet finished. She showed us the salon, one steep flight up, which was certainly finished—a long, ample room, a prototype of the traditional Moroccan (as opposed to French/Moroccan) sitting room. Marble floor, pile carpets, tiles to mid-wall, white plaster frescoing from tile up to the ceiling. Long banquettes lined the walls, upholstered in shiny polished cotton, stripes of burgundy and white; the round wooden tables were intricately carved. Family portraits in silver frames: Mehdi as a baby, Rashida and Abdul Rahman's wedding picture, black-and white pictures of an old man in a turban, a woman in djellaba and hood.

"It's very beautiful," I told Rashida.

She nodded, holding the baby. She clearly thought so, too. Mehdi scampered from one table to the next, banging on each with his four-year-old hands.

"When we were living in Marrakech twenty-five years ago," I said, "the plaster work was dying out. A friend of my husband's came one morning and told us to come to Djemaa el Fna because two old men were up on a ladder repairing the stucco work on the wall of a mosque.

'You won't see it again, they are the last of the breed,' my husband's friend said."

"It's different now," said Rashida. "My generation has been to the old palaces and some of us grew up in the medina. We've learned about Moroccan history, about arts and crafts that are our heritage. We decided we wanted some of that."

Leila had told me of the King's support for the training of artisans in the old crafts—tiles, plaster, copper, brass, wood, pottery. If Rashida's house were typical of the new structures, the crafts had already developed a good market.

"The tiles are made in Morocco, too," said Rashida, "a real change."

"Yes," I answered, "it is." The tiles in our old house had been imported from Spain. The tiles that Aisha always said had walled in the djinn.

Dinner was over. It was time for the children to sleep. We found a taxi to take us back to the Imlil Hotel. Tomorrow surely we would find Aisha, I told myself, realizing also how I feared this meeting.

"The taxi has arrived, madame." The young clerk from the Hotel Imlil desk came to the breakfast room to tell us. No more postponing. No more delaying. Now.

The driver, in another pullover, this one striped with black collar and cuffs, insisted he knew the way to Aisha's house. He moved rapidly through the medina. The sun was shining, the streets didn't seem as threatening as they had in the dark. And the crowd of boys had gone, perhaps to school? Even they must know that the exams were the way to move out of this worn neighborhood.

The shop was our landmark, but the cab came to a stop just short of the turn, behind an orange barrier. The sign announced, in Arabic and French PUBLIC WORKS. Four workmen were staring into a hole in the street.

"Clogged drains," said the taxi driver. I peered over the barrier to see a fifth man actually in the hole, down far enough so that his shoulders were below street level and all we could see was his yellow hard hat. The four above ground were asking him questions, offering picks, ropes, a bucket.

"How old is this street?" Sandra asked.

I looked at Deborah. "Four hundred, five hundred years, maybe more," I ventured.

Deborah nodded. "Probably," she agreed.

No wonder the drains were blocked. I wondered when the last new drain was installed, as had recently taken place in a district near Rue Haroun al-Rashid, where many new middle-class Rabat houses are under construction.

The tiny street where we had stood last night and where Abdul Rahman had pounded on the door, was so narrow that Sandra, Deborah, and I could easily span it with our bodies' width. The pile of rubble illumined by the stars of Orion was indeed a ruined house; the rubble sloped backward, but small bits of gravel rolled forward continually and clunked onto the broken pavement under our feet.

The three doors were there. They stood close together, two stories high. The middle one had a small grilled window on the right of the second story.

"Didn't Abdul Rahman knock on the middle door?" My voice quavered and Sandra eyed me.

"Yes, B.J.," said Deborah and she proceeded to grab the knocker in both hands and bang on the door. It was a big knocker, metal with a rag wound round and round the place where the knocker hit the door and then tied above in a neat knot. Why, I asked myself, would Aisha tie a rag on the knocker? To muffle the banging? Or because the knocker was broken?

The door creaked open slowly, as though its hinge were lame. And there was Aisha, dear Aisha, older and grayer and slightly more frayed in her dress, but the lilting voice was the same.

"Elizabeth!"

We embraced, a long, hard embrace. Then Deborah.

"And Sandra, my friend, from Texas!"

"Sandra!" Aisha's voice was upbeat and resonant, as always, but seemed a bit breathy to me—respiratory problems?

"Come in. Come in."

A step or two was all it took to enter. I looked around me. Let's call it heartbreak house. We were ushered into the room on the left, which appeared to be the only room. We sat down against the wall on the single banquette. From where I sat, I could see opposite me the tiny narrow court, on two levels, open to the sky. The upper level was full of laundry, a skirt, a shirt, a scarf, a threadbare towel, hung on a drooping line to reach the sun. The court was half-roofed with tattered green plastic. There were no stairs, only a ladder placed against the mud-brick wall.

We were sitting on a bed which had been neatly made up, the threadbare gray blanket tightly tucked under. Aisha sat cross-legged opposite us on another low bed, one arm on her lap, her chin propped on her other hand so she could stare at us. A bit of gray hair peeped from under her head scarf, which had faded into a pleasant hazy color. Red cotton turtleneck, stretched out in the neck, under an old V-neck navy sweater, frayed on the edges. A long dark skirt, and a wraparound waist-high white apron, with a front pocket stitched on halfway down. I fixed on that pocket, thinking that I could put my offering envelope in it as we went out the door, and thus avoid the hands of Abdul Krim, who hovered in the cramped outer court, listening to the radio. He was playing Sting on a cassette recorder. The insistent beat reverberated around the shabby little house.

"Turn it down," called his mother.

He did so.

"Elizabeth," Aisha repeated.

"Aisha," I repeated.

I was afraid for a moment that I might cry, but I didn't. The place, after all, was scrupulously clean. The pitiful bits of laundry on the line under the tattered green plastic roof had clearly been scrubbed to within an inch of their long lives.

It was the smell. Not a smell of bad food or filth or garbage. No, the smell of poverty. A vague whiff of age and rot that emanated from the layers of cracked floors, the deteriorating wall plaster behind our heads.

"How are the children, Elizabeth?"

"Fine."

Before I could ask about her children, Aisha interrupted.

"Look at me," she said, "I've lost my teeth," and indeed she had, all of them on one side, nearly all on the other. What could I reply? My teeth would have been gone, too, without the expensive ministrations of my excellent dentist.

"Does it hurt?" I asked, nonsensically, for some bit of response was needed.

"Hurt?" Aisha tossed her head. "Hurt? Of course it hurts me, I don't like the way I look at all. But," she said, making a pun which was entirely appropriate as my Arabic vocabulary in Moroccan Arabic was limited to one word for "hurt," "it doesn't *hurt,* as in pain."

"What about Youssef?" I asked after the youngest son.

"Youssef? He's left home. You knew that. He's living somewhere in the medina, doing odd jobs, like his father did. I don't see him much."

"And Mustapha, your grandson? Saleh's son by his first wife?" Aisha rocked forward on her knees and smiled. "He's fine, is Mustapha. He failed this year, though, in secondary school. He didn't work hard," said his grandmother, with some asperity. "But at least he went back to school and he's promised me he'll try hard this year."

Saleh, father of Mustapha. I remembered when he, too, was unemployed, not because of his laziness, but because he marched in protests against the low wages and bad working conditions in the schools. An air of desperation hung over Aisha's house in those days, but he was reprieved, with his colleagues, when the King signed an order giving back all the jobs that had been taken away. And added money to improve the schools. Saleh's first wife, a hairdresser, had not been Aisha's favorite person. But now that had all changed. Saleh had divorced his first wife and married again; he had two small children.

"His new wife never comes here," said Aisha. "She is ashamed of us. She is not rich, but would like to be. But the first wife, she comes to see us now."

"Is she still in the beauty business?"

"No, she went bankrupt. Now she works as a housekeeper in a hotel in Gueliz. She's in charge of the girls who clean the rooms. She's a good girl. She brings Mustapha clothes and sometimes other things."

A hope for the future is Mustapha. One could see it in the brightness of Aisha's eyes, a light that faded as she turned to look at Abdul Krim, who had turned off Sting and stood in the narrow open doorway, staring at us.

Abdul Krim's attire was in marked contrast to the stark destitution of the house; he wore a very nice pair of gray wool trousers, and a long-sleeved pullover in a lighter shade of gray. Why all this sartorial display for us? Something was wrong. Abdul Krim was only four years older than my son David; he used to take David out to play soccer when we lived opposite Aisha on Rue Tresor. That meant he was in his late thirties. But his hair was thinning and gray; his face was gray; he was sepulchrally thin. Early age lines were etched deeply around his mouth; he had a sulky, discontented unpleasant air. I looked directly at him, and found that I would not put it past him to snatch my gift to Aisha out of my hands or hers. That was nonsense, I told myself. I turned back to my old friend, who was exchanging pleasantries with Deborah about mutual acquaintances and being told about Sandra's study—a history of Moroccan cinema.

"And Alta? Bob's mother?" She turned to me.

"She died in 1991. She was very old, Aisha, almost ninety-two."

Aisha raised a hand to her lips and muttered an invocation.

"Christians, Muslims, Jews, we all die," she said, as if in answer to my unasked question.

"She was very small," remembered Aisha, for Alta, who was only

five feet tall, lived with us for three months in Marrakech. She and
Aisha spoke not a word of each other's languages, but seemed to
communicate quite well in spite of it.

"Even smaller than me." She smiled. "But she was hard."

I nodded. Alta lived with us for four years before she died. It was not
easy.

"But," said Aisha, "Bob was hard on her, too." She cleared her
throat; the voice was a bit husky. "And the girls? David?"

I passed around pictures. Aisha's eyes were clearly going, as well as
her teeth, for she turned the pictures around, held them closer and
farther to get a good fix on them. Then she kissed the pictures. I
winced inwardly. Why was I wincing? Something about the gesture
bothered me.

To hide my feelings, I looked around. A few pinups above the door
where Abdul Krim glowered. TV stars? Moroccan singers? No one I
recognized. Aisha's family pictures had disappeared.

"This is David? So big? Bigger than his father!" Aisha laughed
delightedly. "Married?"

"Yes. With a son."

"Good, good," said Aisha, "and this is little Laila."

"She's thirty," I said, rather more loudly than I expected.

"No," said Aisha, and turned to Sandra and Deborah. "I knew her
when she was such a little girl, so small, so blond, a sweet girl. Thirty!"
She shook her head.

"All your children have work?" The key question she has waited
until now to ask.

"Yes, thanks be to God."

"What about Mr. Bob?"

"He's fine."

"Thanks be to God," she repeated.

"Yes, he's fine. He sends his best. He's lost his hair."

Aisha laughed, and looked more closely at his picture. "That's why
his head looks bigger." She giggled. "Bigger thoughts?" she suggested, mischievously.

Her old élan was welling up, even in this dim and depressing place. I
marveled at her spirit, and wondered how I would behave in a similar
situation. Feminism? What did we mean? What did we want? Surely
the first thing was a clean, well-lighted place in which to live, enough
to eat. What was it Aisha had said in the film? "What I want more than
anything in the world is a house of my own."

I took a deep breath and looked around once more. Not much to
see. The only item I remembered from the old place on Rue Tresor

was the armoire, which occupied the whole wall, the armoire which was part of Aisha's wedding dowry. The wood was a bit scuffed and in need of polish, but the full-length oval mirror in its center door was still intact and clean. The bed clothes were rough, but serviceable and clean, whatever colors they once bore ground down by use. The pillow supporting my back was too small and I found I was hitting my head on the gray crust of the plastered wall.

"You're fasting?" asked Aisha.

"No," we chorused and added politely. *"Ramadan karim."* ("Ramadan is good.")

"I'll make tea."

"No, no, don't bother."

"No bother." But she didn't rise, as in the old days.

"Thank you, Aisha," I said firmly. "We can't stay long."

She gave in, quite easily. Probably hadn't much tea. I marveled once more at Deborah's thoughtfulness in providing the pink-wrapped cones of sugar last night.

The family belongings stored on either side of the armoire were unidentifiable—corners of old cardboard boxes, folded linens, all covered carefully with a blue and white crocheted cover which gave a sense of organization to the meager collection. The crocheted cover had a hole or two in its blue scalloped border, but it, too, like the rest of the sad house, was sparkling clean.

"Hajja Kenza," said Aisha. "Have you seen her?"

"Yes, I stopped by the hotel." (It was once our house.) "She looks bad, but the place looks good."

Aisha made a face and waved her hand back and forth, in anger or annoyance or both.

"I haven't seen her," she said. "She didn't even come to pay condolences when he died." She still called her husband "he," even though he was dead. "When I think how I nursed that child of hers, Naima, like my own because she didn't have any milk." She reached down and grabbed her breast to make sure her meaning had been communicated across the barrier of my failing Moroccan Arabic. "When I think of that. That means she's related to me, and to Abdul Krim," she went on. "A milk tie. I told you about that."

"Naima has two daughters," I said.

"And who's their father?"

"Nobody knows."

Aisha shook her head, looked down, muttered.

"What?" asked Deborah.

Aisha looked at Deborah, at Sandra, at me.

"What is it, Aisha?"

"Oh well, we're all getting old," she began, then sat up straight. "I was saying to myself, so Naima's no better than what people said she was, and I never believed it myself until now."

She passed her hand over her half-toothless mouth; clearly she was sensitive about her appearance. And why not?

"I forgot Laura Ann." She asked for the pictures again. "This is her husband?"

"Yes, and her daughter."

"Very handsome husband," pronounced Aisha. "Good for Laura Ann. And a fine daughter too." Her good humor had returned.

Deborah said, "I would really like to visit Moulay Ibrahim one day, like B.J. did. Would you go with me?"

"Oh yes," said Aisha. "I will go with you anytime, De-bor-ah." Aisha pronounced each syllable carefully.

An excursion. Something to look forward to. Her face became more animated and she recounted in detail our adventure more than twenty years ago when we went to the moussem of Moulay Ibrahim, up in the mountains. A wet, muddy day.

"Bob went off by himself, do you remember?"

I nodded.

"But we went into the shrine with the women; remember that, Elizabeth?"

How could I forget? My fear of being unmasked and ejected as an infidel from the sacred place had been disregarded by Aisha, who literally dragged me by the hand through the crowd.

Deborah asked, "But how did you get her in past the guards at the zawiya?"

Aisha actually laughed. She was pleased with herself, pleased to have an audience. "Well, I agreed with them that she looked a bit odd, but I said she was from Fez, and we all knew how strange Fezzis were. And I agreed that she couldn't speak very well, but I told them that was her problem, her speaking, and she wanted the *baraka* ["blessing"] of the great Moulay Ibrahim so she could learn to speak more easily. And they let her in, of course."

"But, Aisha, later you took other Americans. What about them?"

"I just said they were all Egyptians, foreigners."

She laughed. Deborah laughed. And Sandra.

But Aisha was back to Hajja Kenza. "She's sick, you say. So what good is all her money?"

I could have answered that at least it allowed her to live in comfort in her last days, but I didn't say it.

"She owns five houses on that street now," she continued. I wondered how she knew this since she had not seen Hajja Kenza for years. "Your old house, and hers, and three more. And they wrote it up in her will. Half is Hajja Kenza's, and half is Naima's, so when she dies, no problem, Naima gets it all."

Aisha was now on the sore topic of Hajja Kenza's ingratitude, her perfidy, her insensitivity to other people's sorrows and problems.

"And they are like our relatives," she continued. "The milk tie is very important." She clutches her breast once more. "And they don't even come to see us."

I told myself it was time to go. As though reading my thoughts, Abdul Krim stepped forward.

"I need work," he said. "Find me work, madame."

"I'm sorry, Abdul Krim, I cannot do that."

"In America, I mean, not here." He had suddenly come to life, but it was not pleasant.

"But in America to get in and have a job, you must be able to speak English."

"I told you," from Aisha.

Abdul Krim glared at me, as if to say I could find him work if I wanted to! I was reading too much into his gaze, I knew, but I had to hold myself back from saying, Why don't you try here, why don't you have any get-up-and-go, why don't you at least take odd jobs like your little brother Youssef and stop sponging off your mother, letting her live like this while you shop for elegant French slacks? But I wouldn't say any of this. Aisha was also partly responsible because she had spoiled him over the years. But what could she do about it now?

We made as if to rise, and I asked about the village, the land.

"Oh yes, the land. The house is still there, my sister still lives in it. Most of the old men are dead. The young ones came to the city to find jobs. Not many jobs."

"Do you still get grain from your piece?"

"Yes, some. Last year's harvest was good. But no rain this year, it won't be much."

We embraced. Deborah and Sandra were out ahead of me, and I quickly shoved my offering envelope into Aisha's apron pocket and felt her hand close over it. Did Abdul Krim see? He was standing behind her. But what could I do if he did see? Nothing.

"Good-bye, Aisha."

"I'll be back," said Deborah.

"Greet Bob and David and Laura Ann and Laila," said Aisha. "Kiss them!"

The door slammed behind us, and the knocker with its bit of rag moved a little, back and forth, from the force of that slam. In the main street, the four men from the public works department were still staring into the clogged drain; they had dug out and expanded the cut in the street. Chunks of clay and stones and black earth were piled at the edges of the cut. The man in the yellow hard hat was even farther down into the hole. The foreman did not look happy.

Sandra burst into tears in the taxi, but my eyes remained stubbornly dry.

Deborah said, "We all feel sorry for Aisha, but you know she has worked and earned reasonable wages for years, from B.J., from me, from other foreigners. Where has that money gone?"

"That son of hers—his clothes . . ." Sandra sobbed.

"Yes, Sandra," I agreed, "but what can Aisha do? Throw him out? She loves him. She'd never do that."

Deborah said, "It's the problem of men and women again. Women can find jobs easier than men. Unemployed sons, husbands, that's hard on everyone."

We rode along in silence. I knew, as did Deborah, that many people in Morocco were as poor or poorer than my old friend Aisha, and it seemed there was little we could do about it, other than offer occasional tokens of help.

What would my American feminist friends make of this combination of circumstances? A deadbeat son, an odd-jobs son, a professional son with two wives and three children, and a grandmother who cared for the first wife's child? Life was complicated, and the house was tiny and sad. No wonder Aisha spent more time at the mosque than she used to. The mosque offered peace, and after the prayers were finished, moments to meditate on space and time and God and one's relationship to God. I reminded myself that Aisha was a shareefa, a descendant of the Prophet, and thus entitled to sit alone and undisturbed, in any mosque she chose. No one was likely to ask an old lady like Aisha to move on. We were both old ladies now. It was hard to believe. We had both had sorrows and fears and anxieties, in ourselves and in our families, but I had been luckier than Aisha.

"Why?" asked Sandra, wiping her tears as we headed out of the old city, and down Muhammad V Street to the Hotel Imlil. "Why are some people so visited with troubles and not others?"

Why, indeed. Leila Abouzeid might reply that when God wanted something to happen, He arranged it. But it seemed to me that Aisha had had far more than her share of this world's sorrows.

The rain began while we were traveling back to Rabat. We were told by the woman in our train compartment that yesterday the King had gone to the mosque with a delegation of religious dignitaries and they all prayed for rain. Last night, they said, the wind came up and it was still raining.

The express train rocketed along past villages, past small stations where rain poured down on the flower beds next to the platforms. In the larger towns, the wind whipped the tops of the palm trees, snatched bits of paper and plastic, the unrecyclable trash, out of the gutters and tossed them about. The buildings were smeared and spotted with rain. Water gleamed in puddles on the pavements; an old man stood on his balcony staring at the welcome sight, as though at a mirage. But it was not a mirage, it was a heavy pelting rain, beloved rain, as Aisha once called it. Perhaps she would get more grain from her land this year than she expected.

THREE

¤ ¤

Kuwait

THE KUWAIT AIRPORT is a sea of white marble, bright white lights, men in snowy white dishdashas and kaffiyehs, white-painted woodwork, glistening white marble floors. This comes as a shock. Somehow I was prepared for doom and gloom following the Gulf War. Coming from dark, cold Berlin, I had expected some similarities. Both are war-torn lands. Berlin, divided by war and political conflict fifty years ago, still bears the scars of that conflict. Kuwait, on the other hand, ravaged by war less than five years ago, is spotless, neat, newly refurbished, in mint condition. The visitor cannot believe there could ever have been a war here, that bombs had blasted the streets, that smoke from the burning oil fields had fouled the air and covered the houses with thick soot. It is as though it had never been.

I was alone, in the airport waiting for my friend Shafeeq al-Ghabra to pick me up, as arranged. I'd known Shafeeq for a long time and I knew he was very busy and often late for appointments. I stood in the lounge, watching people arriving and departing from Kuwait City, the capital city, and its gorgeous newly redone international airport. I seemed to be the only single woman waiting, so I was not surprised when a friendly helper approached me, a pleasant-faced Indian gentleman with a little official sign on his lapel, offering information, assistance, free telephone usage.

"We are service to strangers from Kuwait country itself," he said in lilting Indian-English.

"Thank you," I replied. "I am being met."

"So to help if help needed," nodded the Indian helper, and passed on.

But I noticed he did not approach the only other single ladies in the airport, a group of eight clearly foreign women who stood against the wall, also waiting. No one approached them, in fact. The crowds of smiling mustached fathers in white, holding children by the hand, the mothers in smart Western suits, the grandmothers in abbayahs, swirled around but did not look at that row of strange ladies isolated against the wall. They were small women, dark-haired, some with dark skin, wearing garments vaguely akin to saris, draped over shoulders and heads; one wore a pants suit, another a blouse and skirt. I edged closer to them; they looked bewildered, and then I saw why. They had huge paper labels pinned to their chests, like children who were sent on long journeys without their parents. The labels bore numbers, not names.

"Perhaps those ladies need help," I said to the Indian "helper," who was now circling again, smiling, his portable phone in his hand.

The Indian helper's smile faded. "Do not need help, they," he said to me in a tone that told me I should have known better. "Are guest workers, waiting for master and mistress, they."

He moved past me, a little too quickly, and I looked with real concern at that row of ladies, with numbers pinned to their chests.

They did not speak, even to each other, but stood awkwardly, clutching oversized purses and small plastic flight bags stamped with the logos of Asian airlines; Air India, Philippine Airlines. They did not know what awaited them, and neither did I, though I had read plenty about the difficult plight of guest workers in the Gulf, particularly the plight of women workers.

"B.J.! B.J.! B.J.!" It was Shafeeq, smiling broadly, his driver behind him. "Sorry I'm late. Ah, you know me . . ." He laughed, having seen my expression. "I came as quickly as I could."

Muhammad, the driver, nodded at me politely, took my handbag, and led us outside toward the car. Did he and Shafeeq cast quick glances at that row of ladies, lined against the wall like unclaimed baggage? Perhaps it was my imagination.

"We seem to get guest workers, more guest workers all the time," said Shafeeq, opening the door of his new Peugeot and stowing me inside. "So much to be done. A lot of building is going on. Many children being born . . ."

"And in need of nannies," I put in.

Shafeeq laughed. "You are right. And I can tell you do not want to talk about your flight or Berlin, you are already thinking of what you will write about those poor ladies against the wall . . ."

He had seen them, then, and he reacted, like me.

"Well?" We were very old friends, after all, and could launch into a conversation like this with no preliminaries, no how are your children, how is your family, how is Texas. Bob Fernea was a member of Shafeeq's dissertation committee at Texas, I was a member of his wife Taghreed's dissertation committee; we gathered round when their second daughter Zaina was born in Austin. They were like part of our extended family.

"Abuse is all you read about, right, B.J.?"

"Right!"

"There is bound to be abuse with so many thousands of foreign workers here. Nearly a million, they say. I have done research on this subject, B.J., although no one wants to discuss it at all. There *is* some abuse, but it is a small percent. Furthermore . . ."

"But . . ." I began.

"Let me finish, please. The worst cases are now coming out into the open, in the Kuwaiti press itself," he said. "That is good news. There have been strikes. There is talk now of establishing a commission to deal with the workers, for after all this is a national problem, a labor relations problem, right?"

"I'm glad to hear it," I answered.

"We will talk about it some more," he continued. "Now tell me about your plans, your program. How can we help?"

I had come to Kuwait on one leg of my journey in search of Islamic feminism. Political change was in the air when I had visited Kuwait in 1988, and events following the Gulf War/Desert Storm of 1991 seemed only to corroborate my earlier suppositions. The Emir of Kuwait had returned to his newly liberated country; emerging from a jet airliner, he had been videotaped as he kissed the ground of his native land and declared that democracy was the political model of the future. This led to fervent and enthusiastic demonstrations and celebrations and the granting of the vote to men. Women were surely next, journalists speculated, reminding readers that ten years earlier more than one hundred women had marched to Parliament supporting a bill for women's suffrage. Parliament had voted down that request twenty-seven to seven, with thirty-one abstentions. No bill had been introduced since. Surely now that the war was over and the Emir was talking about democracy, surely now was the moment when women would become voters like their husbands, fathers, and brothers. Kuwaitis were aware, like everyone else in the world, about the voting rights issue as a factor in a country's progress in the old-fashioned nineteenth-century sense. Certainly the vote, in feminist thinking, was a clear sign of improvement in women's condition.

"We have to catch up with other countries," a member of the women's social and cultural union had told me in 1988. "We are behind now. But we will do it! And soon!"

With that enthusiastic assertion ringing in my ears, I had assumed that a 1995 visit, four years after the war's end, would be an appropriate time to see whether Kuwaiti women had, as they said themselves, "caught up." But my friends Shafeeq and Taghreed soon disabused me of this hope.

"This is not the moment for women to vote, B.J. Not now," said Taghreed, after showing me around their new house in the Andalous district of the city, and serving me a delicious Taghreed-like meal: chicken with sumac and onions, rice and salad, sambooza, and dates and oranges and sesame cookies for dessert. Haneen, the older daughter, now fourteen, sat up and smiled as I praised her, her height, her new haircut, the Dr. Martens boots; Zaina hugged me before going off to do her third-grade arithmetic; and the new baby Yazen jumped up and down in his father's arms before being carted off to sleep by the nanny, Lucette.

"We're lucky, B.J.," said Shafeeq, as he set down our coffee on a round table in the family/television room. "We have two good helpers at home, and a driver, Muhammad, whom you've met. Do they look abused to you?" He half laughed.

"Of course not," I replied indignantly. "But that's because you treat them well, and pay them well, and everyone who knows you and Taghreed would expect that."

"Shafeeq, why are you going on and on about guest workers again?" Taghreed asked, slightly annoyed.

Shafeeq looked at me and smiled. "B.J. is very interested in their problems, Taghreed, and I'm trying to provide her with a lot of information so she can balance whatever she writes about us."

Zaina came back in to ask about a multiplication problem. Taghreed turned to help her, and Shafeeq said to me, "Politics, the political situation. For women."

"Yes," I said. "What happened to all this agitation for women's political rights that I read about, even in the *New York Times,* in 1991 and 1992?"

Shafeeq shook his head. "It's frozen in place. Not going anywhere."

"Why?"

Shafeeq sat back on the comfortable beige sofa, then leaned forward and spread his hands toward me as though to begin a lecture.

"Okay," he repeated. "I think this is what is happening. Before the war, lots of enthusiasm for women's vote. Not now. Why? The war has changed a lot of things."

"What has it changed?"

"People are reconsidering. They're splitting into groups, liberal, conservative, religious. The balance of power has moved and no one is quite sure in which direction we are heading."

"What has that to do with the women's issue?"

"Everything," replied Shafeeq, opening his hands again in an all-inclusive gesture. "One's position on women becomes the bell-wether—is that the right English word, B.J.?—by which all other positions are measured."

"So women take the rap again, for things they are not responsible for," I said.

Shafeeq nodded vigorously. "Precisely. I'm actually thinking of writing a column about this—"

"For Kuwaiti newspapers?"

"Yes, I do it regularly and for *Al-Hayat* in London, too."

"A lot of work," I offered.

"Yes," said Shafeeq, "but the money's not bad. The children's schools, travel, cars, it's all expensive."

I looked about me at the spacious stone house, the ultramodern kitchen, the tastefully eclectic collection of furniture and objets d'art, the cozy room where we sat with television, the VCR, a cellular phone, a laptop computer, the works.

Shafeeq was following my train of thought. "It looks good, doesn't it, B.J.? It *is* good. We are very proud and feel very lucky to be where we are after the trauma of the war. The house was not damaged, thanks be. But everything is expensive. The cost of living here is incredible."

"And they won't give women the vote," I said. "I know that seems like a nonsequitur, Shafeeq, but it seems so ironic. All this wealth, but no say in how the wealth is used."

"At least for women that is true," agreed Shafeeq. "But many men who were prevented before are now participating in the decisions of state."

"Let her go to bed, Shafeeq, more talk tomorrow," said Taghreed, and she led me upstairs. Zaina had given me her room and I lay down on a bottom bunk, after unpacking a bit, and moving the rows of stuffed animals unceremoniously to the bunk above me, where they sat forward, their button eyes wide open, Pooh Bear, Mickey Mouse, two well-used stuffed dogs. The white curtains in Zaina's little-girl room covered the one window, but even when I pulled the curtains back I could see only the top of the wall of the house next door and a swath of black sky.

In the next two days, I spoke with several men and women at Kuwait University, who unanimously agreed that the issue of women's suffrage was dead for the moment. Women were not pushing it. Men were not pushing it. Conservative secularists and religious fundamentalists seemed to be against the whole idea. Why? I asked. For many reasons. Some conservative secularists believe, I was told, that women are too emotional and thus lack the reasoning capacity to make intelligent political decisions. Some fundamentalists believe that the Qur'an specifically forbids women from participating publicly in political life. Even liberals, I was told, are against raising the issue at this time, because they fear that women will vote with the conservatives and that this will reduce the liberal bloc in Parliament. Rich, well-educated women, both liberal and conservative, are afraid that uneducated women will vote, not on their own, but according to what their husbands tell them to do.

"People are ashamed that women don't have the vote here," said Dr. Saif Abbas, chairman of the political science department. "They ask how we can claim to be making strides toward national modernity. But I have to tell you that many so-called liberals have mixed feelings on this subject."

"Such as?"

"Well, they think women should vote all right, but not participate in politics or hold office. Don't ask me why, B.J. That's just what they say."

Dr. Miriam Hassan, a professor of political science, had another point of view. "We still don't have strong grass-roots bases for women's participation in any aspect of public life," she said. "It is a novel and strange idea to many. Actually voting? Actually running for public office? The only women who are considered appropriate are the rich upper-class educated ones, and that would hardly be democracy, to give the vote to some women, but not to others."

"It's been done," I replied. "Blacks in the American South even after emancipation could not vote unless they paid the poll tax or passed a literacy test."

Dr. Miriam looked shocked. "We are beyond that here," she said primly. "But it will take some time before universal suffrage for both men and women is accepted and passed."

☐ ☐ ☐ ☐

Well, I thought to myself, what do I do now? The problem that had interested me, that I felt might have some relation to Islamic feminism, the issue of political participation, was turning out to be a no-show.

"Other things are more important at the moment," Taghreed said. "I know about your project, B.J., but since the vote issue is dead, why not look at women's problems today and see whether that might help give you and your readers in America some new insights."

"Like what kind of problems?"

"Marriage, divorce, inheritance."

I sighed.

Taghreed smiled at me. "The same old problems over and over again, right? But here there are some interesting variations. Are you up for a panel discussion on the problems of divorce in Kuwait?"

"Sure, of course."

"There's one tonight in the Meridien Hotel downtown."

Shafeeq looked up from his newspaper. "Who is sponsoring it?"

"The Committee for the Implementation of Sharia Law in Kuwait."

"Well, B.J., divorce is certainly an issue both for women and for Islam, so maybe that's a problem for Islamic feminists?"

Taghreed glared at him. "Don't make jokes about it, Shafeeq. This is serious."

"Yes, Taghreed. Yes, B.J. Okay, I agree this is a good way for you to see what's going on. There will be a lot of speeches in classical Arabic, though."

My heart sank, and I could feel my dismay showing on my face. My spoken colloquial Arabic, though rusty, was adequate, but classical Arabic had never been my forte—the language of the Qur'an, of the educated elite.

Bob, my husband, was a cultural anthropologist. We had spent our years in the Middle East living in villages—southern Iraq, Egyptian Nubia—and in the cities of Cairo and Marrahech, where the average person revered that great rich sonorous sacred language, *fusha* Arabic, but seldom spoke it.

Taghreed patted my arm. "I will help you, B.J.," she said. "Besides, I'd like to hear what is going on. I'm so busy with teaching and the children and the house I never have time for public lectures. Let's go!"

As we stepped out of the air-conditioned car into the parking garage of the luxurious Meridien Hotel, we were greeted by a soft, warm wind, a humid wind, the wind of late summer in Austin, Texas. But it was only April here in Kuwait. The routine in the parking garage seemed familiar, somehow: drive to the barrier, stop, take a ticket, click, the barrier rose and one proceeded into the echoing cement cavern where parking spaces were designated by broad yellow lines. The "exit" and "entrance" signs were in English as well as Arabic, no doubt as a courtesy to the foreign consultants, engineers, architects, and salesmen who streamed in and out of Kuwait every day, arranging (for princely sums) that postwar Kuwait will be at least (if not more) modern and convenient and high tech as was prewar Kuwait. But of course the obvious reason that those English signs seemed familiar was that the entire system of highways and parking garages was probably a product of American engineering, a subcontract with an American company. The overpasses that wound up and about the six-lane highways looked as though they had been modeled on the overpasses in Houston and Dallas.

But the burst of Arabic that reached us as we entered the hotel from the garage elevator, and the groups of men in long white garments or dishdashas, clicking their worry beads as they strolled across the central patio, signaled not Dallas, but the Arab world.

The patio was the ground floor of the Meridien, white marble like the airport, bounded by an ice cream parlor, complete with white iron chairs and tables, and a coffee shop where several men sat over tiny cups of Turkish coffee, looking at us, as we crossed toward the gleaming brass doors leading upward to the air-conditioned hotel itself. Unlike the women in abbayahs who were heading for the auditorium as we were doing, we were bareheaded, and were wearing suits and long-sleeved blouses. I told myself I was being ridiculous; why should these gentlemen in their snowy white dishdashas stare at us when they had for contemplation an entire circle of glittering boutiques, offering all the luxuries of France: Patek Philippe watches, Daniel Hechter suits, Chanel perfumes, Yves St. Laurent designs. (No wines of course, for here in Kuwait, alcohol was taboo, banned by the Qur'an.)

The circle of French boutiques made perfect sense, for the Kuwait Meridien was one of an international chain of French hotels. Hence it was also not surprising to find the lecture auditorium done up in blue and gold, colors of the fleur-de-lys, symbol of la belle France.

On the stage, large studio portraits of the Emir of Kuwait and the Crown Prince were positioned left and right against polished mahogany walls, and below the Crown Prince was a large easel bearing on a placard the title of the evening's program: "Divorce in Kuwaiti Law." The Meridien's blue-and-gold seal appeared on the blue velvet skirt of the speakers' table, and, as we headed into one of the rows, the speakers themselves climbed the stairs and sat down in their marked places: Dr. Haifa Abdul Kader, chair, in abbayah, one brown dress sleeve showing as she wrote something on a pad, her gold wedding ring flashing in the bright lights. All the other speakers were wearing Western dress, which was oddly dissonant with the abbayah-clad rows of women filling up the blue plush chairs, quietly, very quietly, for the floor was carpeted in deep blue pile.

The announced hour of the lecture, 8 P.M., had passed, but no one seemed much concerned. Women greeted each other as they moved into the rows of seats. Waiters were circulating, men in white jackets, dark pants, small black bow ties over white shirts, offering the members of the audience trays of gleaming crystal wineglasses. The choice was sparkling designer water, or orange, apple, tomato, or grapefruit juice. Three men in what I had come to recognize as Kuwaiti uniform, white dishdashas, white kaffiyehs, and black agals, entered and sat on the far side of the auditorium, almost out of sight. Aside from the first speaker, they were the only men in the room. Taghreed was greeting friends in the row ahead of us. I was introduced, and I smiled, shook hands, and then sat back and waited, savoring the aroma of sandalwood. So familiar, so wonderful. It seemed to be emanating from the abbayah of the old woman next to me. That scent brought back memories—the ladies of southern Iraq, the ladies of Egyptian Nubia—sandalwood soap, sandalwood perfume. Long ago, in Cairo, my friend Susan Spectorsky and I shopped in the Mouski for that scent, and we wore it happily for years, until our elite Egyptian friends told us it was not appropriate.

"Only peasants wear it, B.J., really. You can afford French perfume. Why don't you try Joy or Cabochard?"

The old lady squirmed in her seat, readjusted her abbayah. The scent of sandalwood swept over me again, and I was back in a Nubian village house, sitting on a striped crimson mat on the floor, drinking tea. David was in my arms, Laura Ann stood beside me, her hand on my shoulder. Other guests arrived, and my hostess, searching for more cups, opened the heavy wooden chest beside us.

"Mama! Smells good!" cried three-year-old Laura Ann, and she was right. The aroma of sandalwood filled the room.

"B.J.!" Taghreed poked me. I had been dreaming. I shook my head and focused on the podium where Dr. Muhammad Abdul Salam was about to speak. He was a professor of sharia or religious law, in the national law school, according to the program.

"Marriage," announced Dr. Muhammad in ringing tones. (He was indeed speaking classical Arabic, and Taghreed began to whisper translations in my ear at appropriate moments.) "Marriage is half of religion. Marriage is sacred." He sipped from a glass of water on the speakers' podium.

"God," he continued, "God has given man authority over marriage, since He understands the importance of marriage, and the necessity of a strong and reasonable guardian of that institution. God has therefore also given men authority over divorce, that splitting of the sacred bond that the Prophet finds distasteful. Why has God given men authority over divorce?" Dr. Muhammad took another sip of water. "Because men are more rational than women. Thus men will make the difficult decision to break the sacred bond of marriage not on the basis of emotion, but on the basis of reason. This is the substance of what Qur'anic law, the sharia, tells us about divorce, and this is the law which we must obey. For it is God's law, revealed to us through the Prophet Muhammad, may blessings and peace be upon him."

Dr. Muhammad went on, but I was losing the train of his argument.

"More of the same," Taghreed whispered to me.

"But what is he saying about Christian marriage?" I had distinctly heard those words.

"He says," Taghreed whispered, "that even the Christian priest says, in the marriage ceremony, 'What God has joined together, let no man put asunder.' "

The old lady with the sandalwood-fragrant abbayah said, "Shhh!"
We shushed.

Dr. Muhammad continued, however, so Taghreed wrote me a little note.

"The divorce law is a just law, based on divine understanding of differences between men and women."

I wondered silently what my mother would think of this argument. She was a good Catholic, and most good Catholics are against divorce. Would she have approved of the idea that anyone, any mortal being that is, male or female, could initiate a divorce? I doubted it.

Things have changed in the Catholic Church these days but not in this area; men and women may sue for divorce in civil court, but the Church still refuses to recognize that act.

Dr. Muhammad ended by blessing the audience, which now filled the auditorium, the great majority being women in abbayahs. There were still only those three men in the far corner, and only a few women, like Taghreed and myself, without abbayahs, in suits and blouses.

Speaker number two, Dr. Bedriya Awadhi, rose and adjusted a machine on the podium so the audience might view the screen, which was silently being lowered over the mahogany wall behind the speakers. Before the lights dimmed, two young women in abbayahs passed among us with handouts: statistical tables on the number of divorces granted in Kuwait in 1993 and in 1994.

Taghreed whispered to me that Dr. Bedriya was a very famous lawyer.

Dr. Bedriya stood before the microphone, pulling down the jacket of her cornflower blue silk suit, (no abbayah here). Her first act was to greet the audience, the chair, the third speaker, and finally Dr. Muhammad. Neither Taghreed nor I caught her remark, but from the way Dr. Muhammad inclined his head and smiled, we could assume that cordiality reigned on the platform. The three men in dishdashas on the far side of the room leaned forward expectantly. Two more men, also in dishdashas, and a girl in jeans and white shirt, all of them with large professional-looking cameras, approached the speakers' table, and began to snap photos.

"And the man in front is from one of the big Kuwaiti newspapers," said Taghreed. "He wants to interview you, B.J."

"He takes pictures and writes, too?" I asked.

"Shhh!" admonished the old lady again. She moved her sandal-wood-scented self up and down and rearranged her abbayah on the blue velvet seat.

Taghreed and I were quiet.

Dr. Bedriya called for the lights to dim. A hush fell over the audience as the statistics were flashed on the screen. Dr. Bedriya used a wooden pointer to clarify her charts. Even I, with my rusty Arabic, got the point. A sharp rise in divorce in the past year. The lights went on, and Dr. Bedriya began to lecture, quickly, urgently. I did not get much of what she was saying, but it was clear that she was refuting Dr. Muhammad's principal points. I did hear "rational being" and "Qur'anic law" and "man," and I leaned close to hear Taghreed's telescoped translation. Yes, I was right. Dr. Bedriya was saying, in essence, "I'm so glad to hear, Dr. Muhammad, that men are rational beings and that's why they are the guardians of the sacred bond of marriage. How come then that they have agreed to this scandalous rise in the number of divorces, particularly since you yourself have reminded us of the Qur'anic statement about the distastefulness of divorce in the eyes of God."

She went on. "Last year, eighty-one percent of marriages were dissolved in the first year, and this is among Kuwaiti citizens. Who is responsible for this sad state of affairs? Not women, since you yourself have pointed out that women cannot institute divorce, since they are weak and emotional creatures and therefore have been given no authority in such matters. What is happening here? What has happened to men's rational minds? To their sense of responsibility to maintain the sacred bond of marriage?"

Dr. Bedriya's voice was strong and resonant, and, given her data, her tone was less ironic than it could have been. The audience sat spellbound. She ended suddenly and unexpectedly, with a joke which I did not catch, but Dr. Muhammad smiled and the entire audience burst into loud applause.

"It wasn't a joke, B.J.," said Taghreed, speaking during the sustained clapping so as not to offend our neighbor. "She was saying that she did not want to upset Dr. Muhammad, who is, she knows, an esteemed jurist, and she hopes she did not offend him." Taghreed smiled. "She knows how to get along in this society, B.J., can't you tell?"

Our neighbor leaned around and frowned at us. We all sat back and waited for speaker number three to begin, a lawyer who wore no abbayah, but a silk suit, this one peach and cream. She addressed the practical aspects of divorce in Kuwait, the problems of the children, and what she called the hypocritical aspects. "Many people," she pointed out, "will get a religious divorce, but still stay together in civil marriage in order to get government benefits, which of course are greater for married people than for singles."

She was well spoken, but did not hold the audience with her eloquence as Dr. Bedriya did. And in the discussion, most of the queries were directed to Dr. Bedriya, who very diplomatically turned to Dr. Muhammad each time before answering.

"I'm stunned by what I've heard this evening. Where did you get those statistics?" asked Dr. Muhammad.

Dr. Bedriya read from her own handout. "Courtesy of the Kuwaiti Ministry of Public Records. It's written right here."

A ripple of laughter. The discussion went on and on. Many women rose to ask questions and to make short impassioned speeches. They spoke about inheritance, and about the public perception of the divorced woman as a castoff, a failure. I was pleased to hear that they knew about the new reformed family law in Morocco. Dr. Bedriya said she believed that the new law was good because it is "based on Islamic principles, on historic changes, and remained open to new challenges." A woman told the audience about support groups for women in troubled marriages; she handed out a sign-up sheet, and several women wrote their names. The three men on the side rose to inquire why men were not officially invited. "Men, after all, are half the situation." The photographers were still taking pictures.

Finally, the chairwoman raised her hands and invited everyone to a reception next door, in the hotel dining room.

"Ahlan wusahlan!" she said. "Welcome."

Our sandalwood-scented neighbor stood up and offered her hand. "I wanted to hear everything," she said. "That's why I shushed you. It was good, wasn't it?"

At the sumptuous buffet, served on still another blue-and-gold-draped table, I met Shareefa Khamees of the Islamic Presentation Center. Sister Shareefa, as she designated herself, approached me near the platter of dolma, where I was happily filling my plate, together with Taghreed and two other ladies in silk suits. They had been introduced respectively as Dr. Bedriya's sister and the first Kuwaiti woman to serve in the Ministry of Foreign Affairs. Sister Shareefa inserted her rather portly, abbayah-covered self into our group and cleared her throat. One could almost say that she interrupted our conversation, but it was done so gently one could not take offense. Dr. Bedriya's sister and the political pioneer lady melted away before Sister Shareefa's opening words.

"Why are you here?" she asked abruptly. "Are you from the American embassy?"

I hastened to explain, between mouthfuls of the delicious dolma and tiny spinach pies, my project on Islamic feminism. Sister Shareefa looked intrigued, surprised, startled. She turned to Taghreed, who confirmed my bona fides. Yes, I really was a professor at the University of Texas, in fact I had been Taghreed's own professor! Yes, I had written many books about Islam and the Arab world. And yes, they had been published by presses in New York and in Texas.

"Please come to our center," said Sister Shareefa, "so you can learn what the Muslim community is doing to help women."

"You would call yourself an Islamic feminist?"

Sister Shareefa shook her head vigorously, and her heavy horn-rimmed spectacles slipped down her nose. She pushed them back in place, and set down her plate, now empty.

"I am certainly a Muslim, and I think all Muslim women want to help other Muslim women, but we do not use that word. It is a Western word. It is not our word."

Where had I heard that before? I smiled brightly and said, "Thank you very much. I would like to come. What would be a convenient day?"

Sister Shareefa looked startled again. Perhaps her words were the standard hospitality phrases, not meant to be taken up so quickly. But she rallied. She conversed rapidly in Arabic with Taghreed, and we settled on two days hence, Thursday.

"At the mosque," she instructed, handing me her card. "And you will come with the professor, Dr. Taghreed?"

Taghreed nodded. Sister Shareefa nodded.

"You are welcome, Professor," she said, extending her hand. "Till Thursday." In the car, I examined her card, elegantly engraved in English and Arabic. The center is on the "lower floor" of the Al-Mulla Saleh mosque, "one of the most prestigious mosques in the country," Taghreed said. The telephone number was 24-ISLAM.

Two days later I sat in a straight chair, pencil poised over my blue notebook, in the brand-new-looking office of Sister Shareefa. Taghreed sat opposite me, in another chair, with Haneen, her fourteen-year-old daughter, beside her. Haneen had wanted to come with us, and her mother had said yes. "It's good for her to hear about what is going on with Muslim women here," she told me.

We were only five minutes late for our appointment, which was miraculous, said Taghreed, given that we had to find a legal parking place in the center of Kuwait City, in between the bright lights, the video and stereo stores, the display windows offering bolts of bright fabrics—silk, Lurex, shimmering satin. We had no problem finding the Al-Mulla Saleh mosque itself, since it was the only one on the street, towering above the Meridien Hotel, its minaret garlanded with white lights, which after dark cast illumination far up into the sky.

Sister Shareefa sat behind her desk, in front of a poster depicting a giant family tree, each branch and twig leafed with signatures—in different-colored inks and in many languages—Arabic, French, German, Russian, English.

She was a large, comfortable woman, whose motherliness was confirmed by the sudden appearance of her two-year-old son. He climbed into her lap and asked for a biscuit.

She gave him a biscuit, bussed him soundly, and called to an obliging younger woman who carried him out, happily chewing his cookie. Then she looked at me again, pushing her glasses once more up her nose. She seemed very uneasy.

"Was it your center that sponsored the debate on divorces in the Meridien Hotel?" I asked.

"No, no, that was the Committee for the Implementation of Sharia Law in Kuwait."

"But I thought sharia law was already in force here."

"No, no, only for family and religious affairs. The committee wants all law to be sharia law."

"And you are a member of the larger committee?"

"Yes." Crisp, no nonsense, no more information offered. I was grateful for Taghreed's and Haneen's friendly presences. The atmosphere in the neat office was stiff.

"Well," I opened brightly. "Tell me about the work of the committee, which I presume is the moving force behind this women's center?"

"Yes, it is," said Sister Shareefa. She started describing the history of the committee, and visibly relaxed. What had she thought I was going to ask her?

Of course she must have been aware of the Western media's long, conflictual historical relationship with Islam, and the more recent vilification of Muslims as "fundamentalists" or "terrorists." Could that awareness be at the root of her early discomfort with our conversation? I was having difficulty keeping up with her but a general pattern emerged. The committee started in 1978, with classes held in a neighborhood school for foreigners interested in Islam and the Arabic language. Men only. Charity projects were next, for poor Muslim communities in Africa. I debated asking whether the committee also aimed to convert the Christians and the Jews and the heathen. But before I could, she had launched into the events of the war, "which changed many things."

"Yes?" I looked up from my notebook, and Sister Shareefa was smiling at me.

"Many things, Professor, many things, and for us it was an important change. The committee expanded to include women's affairs"—she leaned forward to emphasize her next words—"women's affairs, not only for Kuwaiti women, but for other Muslim women. You may not know, but people of sixty-five nationalities live in Kuwait. And we try to help."

"How?"

Sister Shareefa launched into what must by this time be a standard lecture. Classes. One would expect that. Classes were a part of the feminist women's movement improvement package all over the world. Education was the way to forge ahead—to what destination was not always clear—but everyone in the world believed this. Literacy was crucial. And in Muslim countries literacy had even greater status, since the first word of the Qur'an exhorted the faithful to read! That word was even more powerful to believing Muslims since everyone knew that the Prophet Muhammad himself could not read or write, but he urged his disciples to do so.

"Classes? How many classes?"

Sister Shareefa smiled even more broadly. She was on solid ground now. Thirty classes per week, about five per day. Four or five hundred women attended. And the classes were all free.

"Any other activities specifically for women?"

"Guidance, marital counseling, legal counseling, child care." She leaned forward across the desk and pointed a kindly finger at me.

"And we work with all women, non-Muslims as well as Muslims."

"Even the guest workers?" I ventured, still seeing in my mind's eye that row of women against the airport wall with numbers pinned to their modest chests.

"Yes, yes. They need us *very much,*" she said. "We teach them Arabic, help them with their . . . er . . . household . . . er . . . problems." She glanced at Taghreed and asked her in Arabic whether she had made her meaning (domestic abuse) clear to me. Taghreed nodded yes.

"And we provide free child care for women who attend our classes."

Haneen was shifting in her chair. Sister Shareefa's little boy ran in again, laughing, having escaped the clutches of the pleasant-faced young woman who had taken him out earlier. Sister Shareefa picked him up once more, smiling.

"Boys are so naughty," she said jovially.

The office was very clean, very neat. Women had been moving back and forth past the door while we had been sitting and talking. My mind went back to the poor women at the airport, the maids and cleaning women and nannies and cooks. Certainly they were in need of counseling, of attention. But . . .

I hesitated for a moment, then asked myself why I was hesitating. Sister Shareefa was clearly a kind, intelligent hardworking woman; her goals were compassionate and just. Was I afraid of hurting her feelings? Why? I faced up to myself, my reluctance to push people. My socialization in the direction of excessive politeness was apparently still strong.

"Sister Shareefa," I began. "Do Kuwaiti women have any serious problems?" (What a ridiculous cop-out question, I told myself.) She and Taghreed and I were all at the Meridien Hotel debate on divorce. Of course they had problems, and she knew that I knew they did.

"Of course we have problems," said Sister Shareefa carefully. "Doesn't everyone? Don't women in America have problems? We have many problems, but they are not due, as you seem to believe in the West, to the presence of Islam. They are due to the *malpractice* of Islam."

Taghreed stared at me. Haneen was fidgeting again. Maybe I should try to end on a positive note.

We stood up. "Thank you for receiving us, Sister Shareefa. I know you are a busy woman. But I wanted to ask you, so I can write it down in my book for a Western women's audience, what you see as the benefits which Islam offers for women? What some might see as a kind of Islamic feminism?"

The question hung in the air. Sister Shareefa, who was also standing by now, looked up and down and around and finally said to Taghreed something which sounded like, "My English isn't good enough for this one. I will bring in an American woman Muslim to give her the proper answers to that important question."

She motioned to us to sit down again, and she came out from behind the desk to call out, "Fajr! Fajr! Let Fajr come here!"

Out of the bustle in the hall, a slight young woman emerged, and sat down beside me. This young woman, presumably Fajr, wore her ab-bayah, like Sister Shareefa, but unlike Sister Shareefa had bound her head closely in white, covering her neck; at her throat was the black nikab or face veil, its position indicating, Taghreed pointed out later, that this young American woman covered up completely as soon as she went outside the center onto the street.

The conversation went like this:

FAJR: Hello, peace be upon you. Where are you from in the States?
ME: Texas.
FAJR: I used to live in Battle Creek, Michigan, but now I am a Kuwaiti citizen.

(I said nothing, but I wondered. Knowing what I did about the difficulty of *anyone* born outside Kuwait after 1950 ever aspiring to Kuwaiti citizenship, I wondered how Fajr did it. While I mused, I realized she was telling me that she had been in Kuwait for five years, that she had four children, two were boys, two were girls. I saw that Haneen was staring at Fajr. I, too, was fascinated by the pale, pretty face, delicate features carved like an old-fashioned cameo, dark eyes. With a start I realized that she was very carefully and fastidiously made up.)

ME (trying to be hearty): How is your Arabic, Fajr?
FAJR: Unfortunately, it is still weak. I am not able to speak much.

ME (trying to conceal my surprise that after five whole years in Kuwait she knows little Arabic): Do your children speak Arabic?
FAJR: Yes.

Sister Shareefa interrupted in a "let-us-get-to-the-point" tone. She said, "Madame the Professor wishes to know what she should tell American audiences about the benefits which Islam provides for women."

Fajr sat up straight, readjusted her abbayah, which had slipped a bit, and covered the folds of a pretty flowery dress she was wearing underneath. She said in a loud, almost strident voice, a voice totally at odds with that delicate cameo face, "Islam! Benefits? Of course, Sister Shareefa. Women are treated with respect in Islam!"

Since I was sitting so close, perhaps my doubtful silent response to this was communicated to her through the air. She turned to me and shouted, "Respect! Respect! Respect!" almost as though I were hard of hearing.

Taghreed now intervened gently. "The professor understands that, I think," she said. "She has lived for many years in the Arab world and is a friend of Muslims."

Fajr turned away from me, and said in a voice that had returned to normal, "Here women are treated as women. Here women do not need to imitate men. Women expect respect from men."

"And do they always get it, respect, I mean?"

FAJR (again in that loud voice): Yes. Always. And men support them so they don't need to work. Their children are also supported.
ME: Yes, I know. Islam expects men to support their wives and children. But what about divorced women?
FAJR: The same. I am divorced. Everything is provided.
ME: Your husband lives here or in Battle Creek?
FAJR: Here. He is Kuwaiti. I came here with him, then divorced. But still, everything is provided.

From the other side of the room, Taghreed spoke rapidly in Arabic to Sister Shareefa, who nodded. Taghreed was objecting mildly to this blanket statement about the universal benevolence of men.

Fajr turned to them in confusion, and Taghreed said rather kindly in English, "I am just saying to Sister Shareefa that men do not always fulfill their obligations to their divorced wives and children." I knew she was thinking of her own sister, divorced years ago, who had to fight to get support for the children.

Sister Shareefa acknowledged the point, but added, "Yes, that is true in a few cases, but Islam expects all men to fulfill their responsibilities, just as it expects all women to fulfill their responsibilities."

Fajr ignored this exchange and plowed ahead on the general topic of Islam's benefits to women.

"Here we have many guest workers," she said surprisingly, "women who have been badly treated in their own countries. Here they are brought into loving families and treated as daughters. When they have witnessed the general respect that Muslim men give to women, they all convert to Islam!"

She shot me a triumphant look.

Haneen coughed loudly, and tried once more to catch my eye.

Sister Shareefa saved us all again. "I believe there are stories of abuse here, some of them true stories, and they are played up in the Western press. But believe me, Madame Professor, it is a small minority."

I did not contest the issue. I'd read the stories, I'd been listening to people here talk about the problem, and the possible solutions. Still I could not get that image out of my mind, the bewildered ladies at the airport with numbers pinned to their chests. At least Sister Shareefa's committee was trying to work with these guest worker women, which was more than any other Kuwaiti seemed to be doing.

The Islamic Presentation Center certainly deserved points for that. And they had also taken on Fajr, and her four children, far from Battle Creek, Michigan, and any support she might have received from her family there. Of course, Fajr could go back to Michigan. But if she did, according to Islamic law, she would have to leave her children behind. She obviously did not want to do that. Sister Shareefa, I thought, was the stalwart presence assuring Fajr of her rights, her maintenance, her dignity. She was a member, after all, of the Committee for the Implementation of Sharia Law, which gave her some authority with men as well as women.

Sister Shareefa presented me with a beautiful Qur'an, bound in dark green leather with gold letters in English. I thanked her. I turned to Fajr with a smile. But she did not smile. She looked at me fiercely and shouted, in my face, "Here in Kuwait I don't have to fight for my rights, like you do in America! Here they are given to me. Tell your audience that!"

I felt like reminding her that they were given to her thanks to the motherly prodding of Sister Shareefa, surely not a feminist in the Western sense, but a strong and kindly Muslim woman, a woman who now said to her, "Fajr, Fajr, don't upset yourself, my dear, there, there."

I held out my hand, and Fajr, after a momentary glance of blazing hostility, dropped her eyes. She said in a low voice, "Peace be upon you," and extended a thin, small hand, cold.

Shareefa smiled and patted her on the shoulder. She escorted us out, past the bustling classrooms, the bulletin boards, the groups of women, young and old, who were teaching or studying or counseling in the many rooms of this Islamic center. A young woman about Haneen's age, wearing a long-sleeved blouse and skirt, her hair hidden under a white head scarf, smiled and greeted me.

"I am Amina, Fajr's daughter," she said. "What is your name?"

"Elizabeth," I answered.

She leaned close and whispered in my ear, "In Battle Creek, my name was Mary Elizabeth." And she was gone.

"What was all that about, Mama?" Haneen burst out as we reached the street. "Really, that woman, so pretty, and can't speak Arabic? What's wrong with her?"

"We'll talk at home, Haneen," said Taghreed firmly.

"But I thought you said B.J. might like to see the Indian jewelry show at the Meridien? Let's go, Mama, please, please?"

"What do you want to do, B.J.?"

"Why not, if you have the time," I replied, thinking that I would like to reflect on the evening's conversations before discussing them with Haneen. Taghreed must have felt the same, for she agreed to a brisk walk to the hotel where we happily admired jewelry, and more jewelry, and I even bought some earrings for my daughter Laila's birthday before we set off into the night for the Andalous district— and home.

"You have to do your Arabic, Haneen," Taghreed reminded her. "The tutor comes tomorrow."

"Oh *yes*," said Haneen in a disgusted voice.

"Haneen . . ." said her mother warningly.

"Yes, I'll do it, Mama." She seemed to have forgotten the episode with Fajr and I found I didn't feel like discussing it either.

Shafeeq was still up, working on his laptop. A column was due the day after tomorrow.

"An interesting evening?"

Taghreed burst out laughing. "What would you say, B.J.? I frankly can't think of what to say."

"Interesting," I repeated. "Could we have tea before we sleep?"

"Yes, yes, some nice calming herbal tea," Taghreed agreed, and put on the kettle. Zaina was already in bed and the nanny and cleaning woman were asleep, as was the baby. But Zaina was not asleep. She appeared at the head of the stairs in her Mickey Mouse nightgown.

"Was it fun, Haneen?" she asked.

"Fun?" Haneen looked at her, at us. "Fun? No way. Go to bed, Zaina."

Zaina, younger sister to older sister, made a face and ran back up the stairs before Haneen could catch her.

How was I to describe Sister Shareefa? Certainly she and other believing Muslim women in Kuwait were working to improve the lot of their sisters and daughters and those in need of support—like Fajr. But they could not be said to subscribe to feminist tenets of equality between men and women. Sister Shareefa had said that it was not Islam itself that was unjust but the malpractice of the system. Yet even the ideal of the system presupposed that men were in charge of women—the Qur'an said so explicitly. This was a patriarchal, patrilineal system. Complementarity, not equality, of male and female roles was the foundation of that system. The complementarity was based on biological differences which were felt to determine men's and women's roles: man as leader and provider, woman as child—bearer and nurturer (*not* leader)—a far cry from Western feminist beliefs. Would Shareefa agree with my construction? I thought she would.

Andalous, a large district in northwest Kuwait City, where Shafeeq and Taghreed lived, had twelve blocks of houses, each with its own fenced small garden. The plots were allotted by the government to citizens who signed up when the land was opened for development. Taghreed and Shafeeq put their names on the list in 1976, when they married, and in 1987, when they returned to Kuwait with their new Ph.D.'s from Texas, they were assigned the land and began building. They were scheduled to move in during the fall of 1990, but the war stopped that. The house was finally finished in the fall of 1991, and Taghreed had been putting the finishing touches on it ever since. Today, we were off to buy potted plants at the big nursery, and to visit the Adiliyah all-purpose market, a cooperative grouping of stores which included a video rental store and a bank.

"Where's the dry cleaner?" I asked lightly, thinking of small similar groupings in the United States.

Taghreed answered me seriously. "There's one nearby, but it's a big problem, B.J. Most of the experienced dry cleaners left during the war."

"So what do you do?" I asked, thinking of the designer silks I'd seen on nearly every woman's back.

She laughed. "Well, as for me, I try to do it myself, but some ladies I know take their expensive dry cleaning with them when they go abroad!"

Truly a luxury economy, I thought, and an unbalanced one. Dry cleaning was not provided, but the range of consumer goods available in the cooperative was literally incredible. Taghreed bought in quantity for her household of eight people. They fed the driver, Muhammad, the cook/nanny Lucette, and Rozaleen, the cleaning lady, in addition to themselves. I followed Taghreed about as she chose a crate of bananas (from the Philippines); rice from India and Iran; crates of carrots, peas, onions (from Lebanon); a small crimson fruit with sharp thorns from Asia (this was called *najaran*, I was told later by Lucette). The United States was represented in this lush trade center by celery, some cereals, and a few deodorants and shampoos.

Wandering through the aisles of the two-story supermarket while Taghreed was choosing magazines and newspapers, I noted the china, from France, Italy, China, and Japan; the housewares, again from France; and the notions (coat and skirt hangers, in plastic) from Taiwan.

On the way home, I was given a lesson in Kuwait City geography, for I was totally confused. There appeared to be no street signs. The highways and overpasses all looked the same; the sandy lots along the highway all looked the same; the "landmarks" that I had struggled to note in my mind to make sense of the layout of the new city seemed to repeat themselves: the mosques and the water towers, blue-and-white striped, thrusting up into the sky like giant flowers; But, said Taghreed, look at the auto dealerships (Porsche, Jaguar, BMW); look at the large industrial companies, which are mostly trading companies; and look at the nurseries. These establishments were distinct and were found mostly in one place. They were like landmarks.

"And don't forget the roundabouts," added Taghreed. "Now we're coming to the huge one near our house, Sulaikhaat, renamed the UN roundabout, after the war, but everybody still calls it Bones."

"Bones?"

"Yes, because it's the turnoff to the orthopedic hospital."

Six lanes of cars were circling Bones, and dispersing in various directions at what seemed an incredible rate of speed. Yet Taghreed was unruffled. To keep myself from backseat driving, I stared at the roundabout, where new grass was sprouting and where an enormous truck with a crane attached was unloading piles of half-grown palm trees.

Half a dozen men in the orange vests of the Kuwaiti government were trying and failing with the crane, and while I watched, they had begun lifting the trees out of the truck by hand, three men to a tree.

"They'd better hurry," said Taghreed, who seemed to have registered the tree planting at the same time that she was negotiating the turnoff. "It's almost dark and the wind is coming up. Time for the *asr* prayer."

The palm trees already planted were moving in the wind and their fronds were splayed out against the sky like pleading hands.

While we turned into the road to Andalous, darkness fell, and the modern streetlights came on, as did the lights in the houses. They all emitted a murky yellow glow, shining through the fine veil of sand lifted by the wind, providing a visual backdrop to the sound of the call to prayer.

"The elements," remarked Taghreed, "are not always kind to Kuwait."

But the muezzin's call cut through the wind and even reached us inside the car, strong and resonant. No cracked speakers were allowed here; the deep voice of the muezzin repeated those words heard all across the Muslim world five times daily. "God is great! God is great!" Only faintly did that voice quiver. It must have been the force of the wind and sand against the loudspeakers.

The history of Kuwait is the stuff of fairy tales. Once upon a time there was a poor country with no farmland and no water. But the people were resourceful, and they looked to both the sea and the sand for sustenance. They grazed a few goats and sheep and camels from one small oasis to another; they mixed sand with water and dried palm fronds and built houses of mud brick; and they combed the bottom of the sea, and found pearls. But even the pearls and the animals could not feed many people, and water had to be brought by boat all the way from a neighboring country, Iraq. The people of Kuwait worked and worked, but life was hard. One day a visiting stranger suggested that the sand and the sea might hold a treasure greater than pearls, a treasure called oil.

Many Kuwaitis laughed and said this was not possible. How could black oil be worth more than white pearls? But the Prince of the nation said it was worth looking at. And that is how the poor country of Kuwait, composed almost entirely of sand, became a rich and prosperous fairy-tale kingdom overnight. Oil provided chests of gold and silver and precious stones, and people did not have to work so hard anymore. In fact, they hardly had to work at all. The ruler of the kingdom thanked God for these gifts and he shared them with his people, so by the 1980s the people of Kuwait lived a life of ease in beautiful houses. Their health care, their education, and even their income were provided for them. And the ruler built a fine tower in the sand, for all to see, a tower reaching up into the air, as a symbol of the country's good fortune. Every child in Kuwait knew that this tower was Kuwait Tower, a sign of prosperity and good luck, of a golden future.

By 1995, however, the luster of the kingdom had dimmed. The Gulf War of 1991 had jarred and shaken many people, not only those who stayed and endured during the months of Iraqi occupation but those, like the ruler, who fled to safety and asylum in Europe, America, and elsewhere in the Arab world. Despite the fact that the United States, Saudi Arabia, and other countries of the United Nations contributed to the cost of the war to stem the Iraqi invasion and free Kuwait, a great deal of money was expended on arms—and on the cleanup that followed liberation in March 1991.

"When we came back," said Taghreed, "the houses were black from smoke. The oil fires were still burning and the air was so heavy that the children wore masks to school."

Many people sustained losses. The Kuwait Society for the Advancement of Arab Children, directed by Dr. Hassan al-Ebraheem, was emptied of furniture, shelves, chairs, computers. Destitute and hungry Iraqi soldiers burned the society's books to make cooking fires, since there was no natural fuel lying on top of the magic carpet on the sand. But when I visited the society in April 1995, the building had been refurbished and refurnished. The only memento of the Iraqi soldiers' presence was an enormous iron cooking pot in the garden. "We found traces of rice in the bottom," said Taghreed, who directed the society's program of publishing new Arabic children's books. "And we decided to plant flowers in the pot—impatiens—it's flourishing, as you can see, B.J." She smiled. "A sign of peace?"

By 1995, almost no traces whatsoever of the 1991 conflict were evident. The bomb craters in the roads had been filled and paved over, the stone houses scrubbed and washed, sometimes by hand, and the gardens replanted. Sheikh Zayed, ruler of the nearby United Arab Emirates and a noted ecology buff, sent Kuwait seventy-five thousand palm trees as a get-well present.

A few traces of residue from the oil fires could still be seen on the walls of some houses, but only, I was told, on stone which absorbed rather than resisted the thick black soot of the clouds rising from the burning oil fields.

But people were chastened by the attack on their prosperous kingdom, and serious discussions of Kuwait's future path took place in the media, in Parliament, in family circles.

"For the first time in its charmed modern history, Kuwait is in debt," I was told by a portly banker. "The next generation fund has been borrowed against. But that is not the most worrisome issue."

I looked up from my notebook, surprised. "What is, then?"

"The next generation itself," replied the banker. "When I was a child, my father worked hard, and he instilled that work ethic in me. My children don't have it, no matter how hard I try. We have guest workers to do everything we can't or won't do. Do we want to live that way forever? I don't think so."

"And women's participation?"

"That is on hold for the moment, as I'm sure you know," replied the banker. "But women's position is related to children's position. They are a symbol of the family, the bedrock of our society, so to speak. So we have to deal with it." He sighed. "But I'm not sure how."

"Feminism?" I ventured. "Islamic feminism, maybe?"

He laughed. "Is there a special brand that would be acceptable to us here? I don't think the Western brand would export very well."

"Different feminisms for different groups," I suggested. "One for Kuwaiti citizens, one for the expatriates, and one for the lower level of guest workers?"

He did not smile. "It's not a good idea, to ask those kinds of questions. These are sensitive issues."

I knew these were sensitive issues, but I also knew I could not expect to deal with the woman question in Kuwait without asking prickly questions. Perhaps the way to do it was to think about the three groups as three separate societies and begin to ask questions based on that assumption. For they *were* three separate societies. The native Kuwaitis were descendants of the eighty thousand or so people living on the sandy wastes before oil transformed those wastes into a prosperous land. This group still remained more or less separate socially and culturally as well as economically. They constituted about 40 percent of the nation's population of nearly two million. The second group, professional expatriates, were mostly Arabs from Palestine, Syria, Egypt, Lebanon, and even Iraq, who had lived in Kuwait for years, managing, directing, teaching, consulting. They constituted perhaps 20 percent of the population, and they were Muslims like the Kuwaitis, but that tie was not enough to unite them. They were very rich, sometimes, and performed important tasks for the government, but they were not citizens and they did not vote. The third group, nearly a million, was the "guest worker" group. They were not rich, they were not citizens, and they had no rights whatsoever.

I thought I might start at the top, for the least affluent Kuwaiti *female* citizen was better off than the guest worker male. Kuwaiti citizens were essentially the ruling class. What did women of the ruling class want? Clearly the debate on divorce which Taghreed and I attended at the Meridien indicated that divorce was a big problem. As I visited men and women, in their offices and in their homes, the same answers were given to my questions about problems: divorce, marriage, children. Kuwaiti citizens, I sensed, were worried about keeping their own comfortable position as elites, which meant maintaining the status quo. This translated into discouraging one's children from marrying non-Kuwaiti citizens, men or women. Kuwaitis were also worried about the next generation; like the banker, they said that young people had no purpose, no work ethic.

Drugs and alcohol were forbidden, but these substances turned up on the black market. And hundreds of young men, not needing gainful employment, cruised the shopping malls and raced up the fine highways in their luxury cars.

"Aren't there many accidents?" I asked.

People nodded yes in reply, but statistics were supposedly "not available." I felt it significant, however, that during my short visit to Kuwait, just among the relatively small group of people Taghreed and Shafeeq knew, three young men were killed in high-speed auto accidents. Women were often blamed for the irresponsibility of the youth since they had ceded major child care responsibilities to nannies.

"But you must understand, B.J., that not all young people are purposeless here." This was the sentiment expressed by Dr. Saif Abbas, by Dr. Hassan al-Ebraheem, and by many other men and women who pointed to the dedicated lawyers, doctors, media technicians, economists, and engineers who had come back from overseas study to contribute their skills to the new Kuwait. "Yet I admit," added Dr. Saif, "it is a problem. But you have problems with young people in America, B.J., right? And don't they blame the women there, too?"

"Yes," I admitted. "But at least there is discussion pro and con about it."

I was also told that the renewed interest in Islamic faith and practice grew out of the nagging worry that Kuwaitis had been blessed by God, but needed to abide more strictly by the tenets of their faith, as a kind of thanks for their good fortune, and a recognition that the luxury might not last forever. Islam was also seen as a stabilizing force, in families and in society generally. What did this mean for women? That they take responsibility for husbands and children, and for those less fortunate than themselves? If Sister Shareefa's center was any example, they were already taking on such responsibility, not individually, but cooperatively—all Muslim women working together.

The second social group in Kuwait, which might be called the professional expatriate community, was less clearly defined. Few members of this group were born in Kuwait, and only a small percentage, including Shafeeq and Taghreed, held Kuwaiti citizenship. This group consisted of the people—petroleum engineers, teachers, doctors—invited to Kuwait by the Emir in the fifties and sixties to help in the planning and implementation of the ambitious development plans launched with the onset of oil wealth. Egyptians, Palestinians, Lebanese, Syrians, they found homes and stayed on to raise their families in Kuwait. In the workplace, the professional expatriates operated more or less as equals with Kuwaiti citizens, but their family social life tended to be separate. And they regularly gathered in private establishments, like the SAS Radisson, a kind of Club Med on the shores of the Gulf.

We sat in the club one Friday—Taghreed, Shafeeq, and I—in white lawn chairs padded with turquoise cushions, sipping fresh lemonade proffered by quick, slim dark Indian waiters in white coats. Baby Yazen was at home with Lucette; Zaina had gone off to the wading pool and the sandpile. Haneen was practicing her diving at the Olympic-sized swimming pool.

Far out on the blue sea, tiny boats tacked their white sails against the breeze, and young women and men in bikinis surfed closer to shore, near the last *boum* or pearling dhow, the symbol of Kuwait's past, which had been moored near the club and restored as a restaurant.

In the days of the dhows, the sea was an enemy, an adversary to be fought for a share of its wealth—pearls. From this same beach, the fleet set out, financed by merchants and staffed by athletic young men hired as pearl divers. No fancy diving equipment, no oxygen masks, just a deep breath and down, down, down. The life spans of the pearl divers were short and the merchants' profits irregular. The sea took its toll.

But in 1995, as we stared across that wide expanse of lightly ruffled blue water, the tales of the pearlers' tribulations seemed like ancient history, which of course they were. The sea had been tamed, even appropriated. Expensive desalination plants worked day and night to provide water for drinking, bathing, gardening, industry. There were no more daily treks by boat to Basra to bring back precious water to Kuwait in water bags made of animal skins. Expensive water was shipped in and stored in the city's water towers, those great striped blue-and-white cement structures that I had noted on my tours of Kuwait City. Built from a prize design for the Aga Khan Foundation, they resembled giant surreal flowers, beautifying the roadsides, reminding the drivers and passengers in the thousands of cars that roared along the highways that water was not to be taken for granted. Every house had on its rooftop one or two silver fiberglass barrels, hoisted high above the sand and dirt so their precious contents could be pressured efficiently into the family's sinks and showers and toilets.

The professional expatriate group lived, like Kuwaiti citizens, in such houses, and enjoyed most of the same benefits. But a quick glance around the SAS Radisson Club suggested some reasons why they spent their leisure time together. This merry group of men and women, in their short shorts, bathing suits, designer tee shirts (Club Marbella), and cork-soled beach sandals was clearly in a different world from the abbayah-clad women and the dishdash-wearing men whom we sat among at the Meridien Hotel lecture. Different worlds. But nearly equal in benefits in the prosperous kingdom. What did the expatriate women want? They had all read feminist texts, some even taught those texts in sociology and anthropology classes at Kuwait University, where many of them had served with distinction for years.

"Not feminism Western style, that wouldn't work here," a woman professor of English, an expatriate, told me when I visited her in her office. "But we are comfortable with ourselves, *except* we need access to equal divorce laws, better provisions for child custody and inheritance. Same as everybody here." She smiled. "You may have heard this before."

"What about political participation?" I asked.

She pursed her lips. "It would be nice, but what's the point? This is not a democracy, which you must have figured out by now. The ruling family is it."

"Parliament?"

"Trying." She smiled. "Sounds good anyway. Might get more democratic. Then we would like political rights. Now it doesn't much matter."

"What about the kids? Everyone says they're spoiled, no work ethic."

The middle-aged professor of English put her face closer to mine. "Not my children," she said firmly. "Most of us expatriates bring up our children to *work*. We send them away to college, and even away to private schools, in England, and America."

"Private school like the English colonialists used to do?"

She laughed a little. "You could say that, I suppose. But we're not the colonialists here, we're the paid help. Of course we miss our kids, but we see them regularly, on holidays."

The third group in Kuwait, the guest workers, didn't worry about their children having a purpose in Kuwaiti life. This group did not even see their children, who were often being raised in distant lands by grandparents, and supported by the wages sent home by fathers—or mothers. Lucette, Taghreed's nanny and cook, had two boys, aged four and six, living with her mother in the Philippines. She was separated from her husband, a guest worker in Saudi Arabia, but I had noticed in the few days I'd been a guest in this pleasant house that her husband had called her more than once.

"Getting together again?" I said, half-jokingly. Lucette bobbed her head, looked embarrassed, then turned serious.

"We must both work, madame," she said. "There is no work for poor people like us in Philippine Islands. I am lucky—to have good job, good person to work for."

What did workers like Lucette want? To keep her job, first; that God would keep her boys safe and well; that her mother's health would be good. That's all, she said. Taghreed was hoping Lucette and her friend, the cleaner Rozaleen, would sign another two-year contract.

Feminism among guest workers? Lucette laughed when I mentioned the word; she was not certain what it meant, but it didn't have anything to do with her, she was sure about that. What guest workers needed, of course, and what they could not say officially for fear of losing their position, was fair wages, good employers. This was clearly what that those anxious waiting women at the airport were hoping for.

It seemed there were problems on both sides. The word-of-mouth stories Kuwaitis told about the foreign help were legion: women as well as men stole; women were known to sneak out at night to have sex with the drivers; the help generally took advantage of good-natured, well-meaning Kuwaitis. On the other hand, local and foreign media, just as Shafeeq said, had begun publishing stories of abuse of the help: the master taking the maid to bed, in classic European upper-class fashion; the wife retaliating by forbidding the maid food and sleep; employers refusing to pay their employees according to the contracts they had both signed.

"The guest workers have no rights under the law," a Kuwaiti professor of sociology told me. "That must be addressed."

On April 3, 1995, *The Arab Times* reported the strike of seventy-nine male Bangladeshi workers of the Al-Raghad Trading and Contracting Company. The newspaper published a photo of the men, gathered in front of the Bangladesh embassy to protest living conditions, nonpayment of salaries, physical abuse, and the threat of deportation.

"These men are skilled," said Shafeeq, when I showed him the article. "Welders, electricians, cable joiners. The country needs their services. I would predict that something will be done."

Shafeeq was right. Two days later the Kuwaiti Labor Board announced the appointment of new staff to deal with the problems "of guest workers who are not being treated in proper fashion." An editorial urged officials to take action and establish a grievance board with discretionary powers.

Three societies then, in Kuwait. Three groups of women. Different histories, different needs. And Islam figured prominently in the lives of the majority of people in all groups; only 15 percent of guest workers were non-Muslims, but that was still over one hundred thousand people. Lucette told me that she and Rozaleen, both Christians, sometimes went to church on Sunday, as was their right. But Sister Shareefa had told me that the center was open to all, Muslims and non-Muslims. A kind of Islamic feminism? Perhaps. I needed to know more about all of the groups. Taghreed promised to help.

Though the physical evidence of destruction had disappeared, the Gulf War had changed many things, Kuwaiti friends and acquaintances told me. The experience of the conflict had cast into doubt what many Kuwaitis took for granted after forty years of good living: a guaranteed, stable, luxurious environment for all Kuwaiti citizens for many years to come. The new postwar anxiety was cited as a reason for the increased public support for the Committee for the Implementation of Sharia Law in Kuwait, the group that had sponsored the Meridien Hotel debate on divorce. Was this new declaration of Islamic identity a successful way to counteract that nagging worry about the future expressed by all Kuwaitis with whom I spoke? Yes and no, said women and men. At least there was now public debate of the issue, a professor of political science said.

"I think this is what happens in all countries after crises, B.J.," said Taghreed. "You try to reestablish the old traditions. You want to restore what has been lost."

What had been lost? This puzzled me, since for two of the groups at least, the Kuwaiti citizens and the professional expatriates, economic security did not seem to be in much danger.

Taghreed and I traveled along the six-lane highways around Kuwait City and Safat, its principal suburb, and trade seemed to be brisk in the luxury car dealerships, in the expensive shopping malls. The 1995 per capita income of most Kuwaitis was eleven thousand dollars, far beyond the expectations of most of the world's people. Only the guest workers, glimpsed occasionally by the sides of the highways as they waited for buses, purveyed a less-than-perfect economic condition.

What then was the problem? It was social and religious tradition, apparently, that was felt to be in danger. Certainly the demise of the women's suffrage movement and the renewed interest in Islamic practice seemed to indicate that prewar approaches to life in Kuwait were being reassessed. Was it tradition, though, or the past sense of security that had disappeared in postwar Kuwait? The Kuwaiti idea of "getting back to basics" reminded me of the United States after World War II, when women working in defense plants were encouraged to leave their jobs and go home to mind their husbands and children, to help restore the family traditions upset by war.

Americans, however, seemed to have a love-hate relationship with tradition; they were against "bad" traditions, but supported "good" traditions. Kuwaitis with whom I talked expressed the same sentiments.

But what was a good tradition and what was a bad tradition?

"A very difficult question," Taghreed answered. "People have different ideas. But everybody here in Kuwait agrees that some traditions are necessary and important!"

"Such as?"

"Weddings, of course, and condolence visits to those who have lost loved ones, and I particularly like the receptions celebrating the birth of a baby!"

The high points in everyday life: births, weddings, funerals, all surrounded by ceremonies and rituals. Anthropologists describe the events around which any ritual is organized, and the form of the ritual itself, as statements about what that particular culture believes is valuable.

"It's all about the importance of family ties?" I queried.

Taghreed agreed. "Marriage and reproduction, yes that's what it's all about, all the parties, the teas, who to marry, how to marry, what are the benefits or disadvantages of this or that alliance."

"But the parties and teas are only for women."

Taghreed smiled. "It's the mothers and grandmothers that look over the girls first. Think about it! Mothers want their children to marry people they know and trust, and that's usually within the same group. Kuwaiti citizens want their kids to marry Kuwaiti citizens and then there's no fuss about money. Expatriates want their kids to marry in the group, too. Custom and tradition have a lot to do with making this happen."

"I thought things were changing here in Kuwait."

"We need our families even more in times of change. Who else can we turn to?"

"What about women who don't marry?"

Taghreed shook her head. "Very few women—or men—don't marry. The ones who don't need their families even more. But society still doesn't accept it here. Marriage is a goal. My mother says it's our duty to our family and to Islam."

"Do you believe that?"

Taghreed considered. "In a way yes, I do. Who wants to live alone? Not me."

In some way, the Western feminist movement seemed to require a single movement, a single definition, the same life for all women. A universalistic ideology. This couldn't be applied to Kuwait at all. Most people might agree that feminist ideologies varied, in different cultural settings, but most would insist that the ideals of freedom of choice and equality between men and women were a given that should stand above environment and history. In Kuwait today, though economic prosperity had increased the number of personal choices for women and men, old traditions and histories limited those choices.

But sometimes traditions could be adapted to surprising new ends, as I was soon to find out when we were invited to the weekly diwaniyah of Dr. Rasha al-Sabah, a member of the ruling family.

A diwaniyah? The word was not unfamiliar to me but I knew it as Diwaniyah with a capital D, the provincial capital city of southern Iraq, where we lived long ago. But I realize now that Diwaniyah was actually named as the meeting place, or *divan,* of the Ottoman ruling council, which once met there. For the *divan* is defined as "a long, low, back-less sofa; or a counting house, tribunal or public audience room in Muslim countries; or a place of assembly."

In the village of southern Iraq where we lived, tribesmen gathered in the sheikh's mudhif or guest house to conduct the business of the assembly, or diwaniyah. At that time, in this rural mudhif setting, feuds were negotiated, guests were welcomed, and tribesmen gathered to celebrate on feast days. This assembly was for men only, although one might say that women conducted their own diwaniyahs at home and in the women-only *kabuls,* weekly at-homes or tea parties. The concept of the diwaniyah can be seen in England and America in men's clubs (which have only recently begun to admit women), and the idea of the kabul can be seen in women's clubs.

In Kuwait, the diwaniyah is also a men-only institution. Shafeeq had told me that now, since the war, urban men of the same kin group have built new community centers for themselves, where they hold diwaniyahs or family-based councils once a week. When Taghreed and I walked out at night for our after-dinner stroll, some local neighborhood diwaniyah was usually in session, if one could judge by the bright lights filtering onto the street, and the number of chauffeured limousines parked nearby.

"People come to the diwaniyahs when they need help or have problems to solve," said Taghreed. "When my brother-in-law died, we could not find out what had happened to his papers because he was divorced from my sister. But the papers were needed so the children could benefit from his estate. Shafeeq met somebody from the Ministry of Health at one diwaniyah, and somebody from the Public Records Office at another, and that was how we helped work it out so my sister could file claims for her kids."

The diwaniyah was clearly an institution of political as well as social importance, but many Kuwaitis were not happy about the proliferation of these private men's institutions.

"They only serve to keep people apart in their own little groups," said one.

"It just reinforces sexual segregation," said another.

"It works against national unity," said a third.

For reasons known only to herself, Dr. Rasha had decided to open her own diwaniyah, but one which departed in important ways from the traditional form. Dr. Rasha's diwaniyah was held in a public setting and was expressly designed for both men and women, mainly people associated with Kuwait University. This was a radical political act in a society where men and women still did not mix freely in public. And the diwaniyah, she announced, would focus, not on private social issues, but on political topics of interest to all Kuwaiti citizens.

"You must go, B.J.," Shafeeq urged. "It's an important diwaniyah, I think, both politically for men, and for women, too."

"Will it be in Arabic?"

"Oh yes, but Dr. Rasha is multilingual, so she welcomes diplomats and scholars and moves well among different groups."

What did I expect? A little knot of well-dressed women and a circle of men in business suits, a large lecture-style gathering, with Dr. Rasha as lecturer? I was not sure.

What greeted Taghreed and me, after we had climbed a flight of stairs in a spacious new stone building, was a large room, furnished on three sides with upholstered sectional sofas (the divans). These divans were almost filled with men and women, mixed together rather than separated by sex. We were late, and conversation was already in progress, but Taghreed set off across what seemed a quarter of an acre of soft silent Persian carpet to greet Dr. Rasha formally and introduce me as her guest.

Dr. Rasha, a plain woman in a dark brown pants suit, her hair cut short, extended her hand, and her eyes flashed welcome. It was the eyes that held you for a moment, then dropped you.

"Please be seated," she said in formal English. "You are most welcome." We trekked back across the carpet to the end of the third divan, where, below carved mushrabiyah panels of dark wood, a few men and women glanced at us perfunctorily and then turned back to the conversation, which Dr. Rasha had resumed.

Seated next to me was a gentleman in a tweed suit, sandy-haired and bespectacled. British, I thought. But all around the room, on the divans, sat gentlemen in traditional Kuwaiti garb, snowy white dishdasha, white kaffiyeh, and black agal holding the kaffiyeh in place. A few men in Western suits. A dozen women, none in abbayah, but one wearing a scarf wrapped around her head, *hijab* fashion.

Orange juice and coffee were proffered as the conversation swirled up and became louder as people on all sides of the room joined in. A man raised a question and another man shouted, "No! No!" Dr. Rasha said something sounding conciliatory.

While I struggled to understand, Taghreed whispered, "They're talking about the Gulf, the current argument about who has authority to control the little islands between the United Arab Emirates and Iran." The subject of discussion turned to communications, to the rumor that strict censorship rules would soon be lifted by the government. At least that was what I thought was said, and Taghreed confirmed it. Education was then taken up, particularly the issue of language learning, and what languages should be required in the public schools of Kuwait. Dr. Rasha spoke up, at some length. She was a professor of English at Kuwait University and had won several international awards for her work on language learning.

She was also the first woman undersecretary of state for higher education. Several people were now standing up, crowding closer to her.

"Come, B.J., she wants to talk to you."

I followed Taghreed, sat down next to Dr. Rasha, and she listened while I outlined my project and the part of that project I was pursuing in Kuwait. She looked at me hard, and listened carefully, but said only,

"You are welcome. Send us what you write, please. And now let me invite you to have dinner with our other guests. Please . . ."

She had a brisk, no-nonsense manner and she led Taghreed and me into the dining room, where a feast had been laid out for the evening's guests. This buffet was the product of multiple cooking traditions, from the far reaches of the Muslim world, gathered here at the benevolent ruler's family table. Indonesia. Pakistan. Philippines. Bangladesh.

Dr. Rasha spoke to all the guests, including my British neighbor, who turned out to be an Australian writer. Then she excused herself, to signal that the diwaniyah was over.

Widely regarded as a forceful figure in the social, educational, and political power scene in Kuwait, Dr. Rasha had been interviewed and quoted numerous times. She had said that if women were offered equal rights, they could contribute as much as men. "But," she had added, "when they are kept aside and the doors are closed to them the myth of male superiority is perpetuated."

As critics of the old diwaniyah system had argued, the men-only gatherings served to perpetuate the sexual segregation of the sexes and continued to divide Kuwaiti society. But Dr. Rasha had taken this established form of gathering and was using it to promote nontraditional ends.

Just so have women in other Muslim societies taken traditional customary practices and transformed them to fit changed needs. The *kabul* or at-home day for women was now used in Turkey, for example, as a basis for political campaigning and for attracting voters to women's causes. In Algeria, in the fifties' revolution against the French, the traditional conservative family unit served as a political cadre to support the indigenous opposition. Such grass-roots networking among women was not unknown in Western society. Church groups, women's clubs, and sewing circles were all efforts to network, to cooperate for mutual ends.

But Taghreed reminded me once more about differences between West and East. "You have to remember, B.J., that everything is personal here. Not like the West, where you deal with impersonal bureaus and lots of paper. If it's not personal here, people make it so."

Dr. Rasha clearly had the personal connections to make the coeducational diwaniyah a going concern. Although she said she was not a feminist, she was using the old diwaniyah framework to expand the network of respectable friendly contacts for men and women and between men and women. This meant women might, in the diwaniyah, deal with legal rights and other business with officials without ever having to go to an office themselves. It also meant that couples would begin to share friends as well as kinfolk.

Suad al-Sabah, Dr. Rasha's cousin, was also utilizing an old tradition in a new way. That tradition was poetry, admired and respected in Arab society for as long as we had written and oral history. The Prophet Muhammad himself is reported to have attended poetry contests, and a well-turned poem brought acclaim to all, men and women alike, who mastered the craft and moved the audience.

The power of the word was recognized early on by some Muslim religious leaders, who tried to ban poetry for its possible seditious or antireligious effects. But poetry survived those censors, to remain a highly honored art; even now, it was said, the only person who was allowed to break into the speech of a head of state was a poet. But of course that bold poet had better have a great poem to deliver, to justify his interruption.

Suad al-Sabah had been a great supporter of the arts, but she also wrote and published poetry herself. These poems, like Dr. Rasha's diwaniyah, challenged tradition, both in form and content. She wrote about the innermost thoughts and desires of women, about love and romance—issues considered inappropriate for public airing by men or women except in poetic form. The poetic metaphors were useful veils to mark what might be offensive to the public; a metaphor, said stern critics, might even cover political revolutionary ideals, for recognizing and understanding the meaning of the metaphor was the responsibility of the listener and the reader as well as of the poet.

Suad al-Sabah did not advocate political rebellion in her work. But she used the poetic tradition as a vehicle for discussing how to balance women's present needs for more openness and more public status against the more restrictive traditions of older established Kuwaiti society.

Hussa al-Sabah, the daughter of Kuwait's former Emir, also worked with tradition—the tradition of Arab civilization, of Muslim art. She directed and was the founder of Dar al-Athar al-Islamiyah, the foundation which supported the Islamic Museum and the library which is part of that museum. Hussa was currently engaged in rebuilding and reorganizing the museum, which was looted and almost completely destroyed during the Iraqi invasion.

"We were all very upset by that act," said Hussa, at Taghreed's and Shafeeq's dinner party for me. "What we had in the museum is, after all, not only our own Kuwaiti national heritage but the Arab Muslim heritage."

I told her that I had heard about her in New York, London, and Cairo. "You are a myth," I said, smiling.

Shaykha Hussa, slim, lively, in an understated elegant beige dress, looked surprised. "What have you heard?"

"That you personally went to Baghdad and asked for the return of the museum objects."

"What nonsense!" Hussa expostulated. "How could I? You know as well as I do that kind of thing would not be possible *anywhere*. Put an end to that myth whenever you hear it, B.J. Really. It was the UN team that brought everything back."

Over *musakhan,* the Palestinian chicken dish cooked with sumac and onions, which Taghreed made better than anyone I knew, Shaykha Hussa spoke eloquently about her work in restoring and maintaining the "national heritage we have," through the museum, through a quarterly magazine published in English and Arabic, through a lecture series by Islamic scholars from all the world. "It becomes more important every day," she said, "for us, but also for the generations to come after us."

The more than one hundred women who marched to the Kuwaiti Parliament in 1985, asking for the vote, were all members of the Women's Cultural and Social Society, the first formal women's organization in Kuwait, established in 1964, just over thirty years ago. Members were all Kuwaiti citizens, and the history of the organization went back to the days when women wrote to newspapers, citing the need to form "women's societies and charitable organizations through which we can get in touch with poor women and try to help them." This was in 1950, before the big oil boom began to take effect throughout the country. The letters to the press, and the pamphlets published by women activists, spoke with greater urgency in the sixties, when the women stated their general purpose in the following terms: "Let us establish a woman's society to take part in the awakening of women and to supervise and guide young people from well-established families and those from poorer families who lack education and knowledge."

Feminist scholar Haya al-Mughni, in her 1994 book on Kuwaiti women, states that the establishment of this group and its acceptance by the men of this patriarchal society were not due to male desire to emancipate women but to give them something useful to do, to keep them busy. This argument makes considerable sense, given women's increased leisure time, as the oil wealth brought servants and nannies to care for the children and do the housework.

Dr. Haya argues further that the organization served as a consolidating force for the old Kuwaiti merchant class, who wished to keep oil riches in the family, so to speak. For in this particular "women's union," women would in fact be meeting other women of their own background and class, and this would encourage them to arrange marriages within the group.

But this was only one side effect. Ms. Lulwa al-Qattami, the first president of the women's organization, guided its members to lectures and symposia on the affairs of women and the family, and second, to a realization of its duties toward those less fortunate, just as the earlier declaration had suggested. In an interview in 1988, Ms. Lulwa had explained to me that everyone knew Kuwait had been blessed by God with unexpected resources, making Kuwaitis rich beyond their wildest dreams. These resources, she said, had to be shared with those who had not been so lucky.

"This is what we must do," she had explained, "if we are to fulfill the tenets of Islam."

Thus, from almost the moment of its inception, the society had taken on charitable projects. Members had personally donated nine million dollars and raised another fifty-one million. In Lebanon, they had supported a village community, a kind of family-style orphanage for children who had lost one or both parents. In the Sudan, their ambitions had been greater.

"When I took some of my friends from the society to the Sudan, so they could see the desperate situation of many women and children, they were eager to give money," Ms. Lulwa said. "We started with one village, where we've built a medical dispensary, a mosque, a training center for women, and installed basic utilities—water, electricity." She had added, almost as an afterthought, "We know what it is not to have a regular supply of clean water. I'm sure you know our history before oil."

"Yes," I said. "And I've seen Khalid Siddiq's film about that period, *Bass Ya Bahar ['That's Enough, Ocean']*."

"Life was hard," continued Ms. Lulwa. "We have to pass on our good fortune to others."

In Kuwait itself, the society established and continues to maintain child care centers based on the Montessori model for 250 children of working women, "who feel their children need more than the basics provided by nannies."

Since the Gulf War, the society has been active in providing support for people whose houses and livelihoods were wiped away by the conflict. It is Ms. Lulwa along with the current officers of the society who represented Kuwait in the General Arab Female Union, and who attended the 1995 meeting of the International NGO organizations, held at the United Nations in New York.

Despite this record of accomplishment, feminist scholar Dr. Haya would level the same charge today against the society as she has in the past. This is a narrow, elitist organization, she implies, "which has not improved the position of women, but has served to maintain the patriarchal class structure." What is needed, Dr. Haya argues, is more attention to political participation and to the different strata of women within Kuwait.

When the society invited me to a meeting to see their members in action, after which I was free to ask questions, I accepted with alacrity. Taghreed was also invited, though she was not a member of the society.

"Why not?"

"I'm really too busy, B.J., my work, the children, so many other things . . ."

"Come on, Taghreed."

"It's true, B.J. And besides, they are mainly women from the old closely knit Kuwaiti families. And . . ."

"And . . . ?"

"The fees for joining are very high. Most young people can't afford it. It's a control mechanism, I think, to keep the group the same. Besides, why should I pay to do volunteer work?"

The wind was rising as we left Taghreed's and Shafeeq's house and headed for the six-lane highway again, circling the Bones roundabout, where some of the date palm trees sent by Sheikh Zayed had finally been planted in a circle. They were held upright like pole beans, with supporting stakes and wires, against the wind and sand that were now pushing more strongly against their slender trunks.

"A sandstorm is coming," Taghreed said, "but it's not too bad yet." It was strong enough to push against our car, however, sweeping dust into the air, and dimming those driver friendly green signs. The sky had turned from blue to a dull dun color and the dust came down, brown and gritty, as we maneuvered a second overpass and headed into the side street where the society owned an entire building.

A meeting of the officers of the society was just ending. The ladies were standing up, collecting their papers, pushing the armchairs back to the long conference-style table.

"I think we'll be more comfortable in the lounge," said the current president, Ms. Adla al-Sayer, welcoming Taghreed and me, and guid-

ing us to comfortable chairs while the requisite coffee was being ordered.

"You have to excuse us," she said, a thin, dark intense woman in a
yellow silk suit. She smiled. A good smile. "We are very excited, you
see. We have just returned from the New York NGO conference and
are preparing for the Beijing Women's Conference. The big news is
that our association has qualified as a *legitimate* NGO organization. So
it is all set. What a lot of time and money and forms it took."

Four or five other women moved their chairs close to the small
flower-upholstered sofa where Taghreed and Ms. Adla and I were
seated. One young woman, with long brown hair and glasses, sat with
pencil poised over her notebook. She was a reporter for *al-Qabus*
newspaper, covering the society's activities. They had told her about
me and my project. Would I mind if she interviewed me?

"Of course not."

I explained my project again. The young reporter wrote busily, then
looked up and said, "Which is the Arab country you've visited where
women are most advanced?"

"How would you define advanced?" I asked.

The young reporter, Hanan al-Zayt, pursed her lips, a bit annoyed.
"Well, you know . . ."

"Okay," I said, "let's start. Economically advanced?"

She nodded.

"Economically," I returned, "Kuwait is the most advanced."

The ladies were delighted. They laughed. "Of course." "She's
right."

Dr. Ferial Othman, a tall woman in a subtle beige print dress, identified herself as the head of the National Institute for Scientific Research,
and now spoke for the first time. "Yes, we do have that to our credit.
And women here have had a jolt recently, the war. Many became more
active, they went out, many were very courageous, they were surprised
at what they could do. But we have to keep going and not stop now."

The reporter said to me, "What else?"

"Well, education is another sign, they say, of advancement."

This was met with silence.

I tried again, "For example, what is the literacy rate for women
here?"

Still no answer. The women were talking among themselves in low
tones. Taghreed finally broke in to explain to me that the compulsory
education laws had only been passed since independence.

"It is our society," said Madame President earnestly, "which
launched the first successful literacy classes for women. The Ministry of

Education offered evening classes, I suppose modeled on the United States, but they were total failures."

"Failures?"

"Yes, failures. Because of course women couldn't go out in the evenings, they had to stay home with their husbands and children. We offered them in the mornings, and these classes were a success. We changed the policy of the ministry. Now all literacy classes are held in the mornings.

"Yes," continued Madame President, "it may look to you that we are advanced, and we are, economically, but women are still under great pressure here in Kuwait." Pressure? What pressure? In my travels through Kuwait, the only women who seemed to be under pressure, at least outwardly, were the guest workers, the nannies and cooks.

"Pressure, yes," repeated the president. "Pressure to have many children. To care for children. To stay home with children."

"What about family planning?"

"Oh," said Madame President, smiling a bit. "There isn't any family planning. No need. The government is trying to encourage a higher birth rate. With every baby that's born, the father gets a raise in pay, so does the mother. And there's good maternity leave. There should be a longer leave, I think."

Dr. Ferial said, a bit sharply, "Women give their children as an excuse to stay home and not work and be lazy. We all know that servants do the real work."

"Ferial . . ."

Dr. Ferial held up her hand. "I'm not saying that it's not important to raise children, it is very important, but that is not all that women have to offer."

The future? What about non-Kuwaitis? The president told me about the society's new efforts to help Kuwaiti women who are married to non-Kuwaitis, about how the society submitted a study to the National Assembly on these issues. It had also funded a study on the effects of the invasion on Kuwaiti women; had sponsored workshops and debates on women's legal rights, women's health, and the role of Kuwaiti women in scientific research.

Had they read Haya al-Mughni's book? Yes. The women exchanged glances. There was a pause. I waited.

"She makes some good points," said Dr. Ferial. "Don't you think so, Adla?"

Ms. Adla nodded vigorously. "Especially about political rights," she said to me.

"What is the most important issue facing Kuwaiti women today?" I asked finally.

"Political rights. Once we get political rights, we will get others more easily." This was Madame President talking. Dr. Ferial nodded in agreement.

"But," I offered, "people have told me that women in the religious revival movement are against women having political rights."

"No, no, no." Even the reporter had stopped writing and joined the negative chorus.

"Only the religious *men* are against political rights," asserted the president.

"So women don't always go along with their husbands?" I returned.

Madame President leaned forward earnestly. "Right," she said. "Absolutely. I think every woman in Kuwait should take her own part in this society. We all have very clear rights, but not everybody realizes that."

"Dr. Bedriya said the same thing," I interposed.

Madame President nodded. "Yes, she knows." I waited for further comment, but none came.

"So individual legal education for women is important?" I ventured.

She misinterpreted my question. "You can't do anything alone," she answered. "This is what you do not understand in the West, with your emphasis on individualism."

"Yes, but . . ."

She continued. "You need a group, a community, a committee, to raise a *group* voice, a loud voice, so that voice can be heard, so that people will listen. Do you see?"

"Yes," I answered. "I see."

I was sitting in a dusty pink upholstered chair, waiting to have my hair cut. Taghreed was sitting next to me. Our appointments in this small, well-appointed beauty salon, owned by Taghreed's sister Rajaq, were the last of the day. We were both exhausted by the Thursday shopping, ostensibly to buy Haneen some new running shoes and Zaina a bathing suit. Haneen actually sulked in a corner, leafing through the new *Harper's Bazaar,* direct from New York. Zaina, only eight, was interested in the workings of the salon, and strolled from one client to another. In the back room, stainless-steel sinks received the heads of young and old who were being shampooed, and rinsed, and then prepared, with pink towels around their shoulders, for the curlers, the dryers, the comb-outs. Zaina smiled at Susu, the good-looking Lebanese girl who actually ran the shop, and was, Taghreed said, "one of the best stylists in Kuwait."

The beauty salon was set opposite an educational bookstore in one of the shopping malls that dotted the city. This one was Salmiyah, the biggest. Since it was Thursday, the night before the Friday day of prayer, Salmiyah was the hot spot, crowded and noisy. We had literally been buffeted by people since we arrived, just after lunch. Salmiyah boasted videocassette shops, a Fashion Way Department Store with American (Esprit), French (Cacharel), and a lot of Indian dresses, skirts, and pants. No silk suits. The elite ladies bought their elegant togs elsewhere, in small boutiques, or, more likely, abroad. Taco Bell, Kentucky Fried Chicken, McDonald's, and Baskin-Robbins were all filled with teenagers, mostly boys, chomping on french fries, staring out the windows at passersby, adjusting their jeans, shuffling out onto the broad lighted pavement in new and fantastic sports shoes. They smoked, they gestured, they talked constantly and loudly.

"They need something to do," said Taghreed firmly. "If not work, then sports clubs, *something.*"

We had not found the right shoes for Haneen, but that was not why she was sulking. She was scolded, in public, by her mother, for running out to one of the groups of cruising teenage boys and greeting them all enthusiastically.

"You don't do that, Haneen," said her mother firmly.

"But they're from my *school,*" returned Haneen, casting one last glance at the boys watching us from a safe distance.

"I don't care. You don't run up to boys like that. Do you see anyone else doing it?"

Haneen subsided, but was not placated. She was also not yet quite aware of the power of her come-hither eyes, I think—the hard stare followed by a half-smile and a slight wrinkling of her nose as if to say, "I know something you don't know!" She carried herself with an air, and her parents clearly were worried about how to deal with the coming of age of their beautiful older daughter—raised in America, living now in a different and more restricted environment.

"It is hard raising kids in Kuwait these days," said Taghreed, in the silence. "But then, it was hard in America too." She sighed.

While Susu cut my hair, she told me her life story, in French. Young, pretty, in tight jeans and multicolored, low-cut blouse, Susu was blond, assured, and was indeed, she explained, "a guest worker. I had my own salon in Beirut, held on during the war, then prices went up. People in Kuwait offered me housing, paid airfare, a good salary, I thought why not try?"

Susu was not your ordinary guest worker, and neither were Soad and Amna, two other young women imported to work in the salon. They were cleaning up now; it was the end of the workday, but even as I noted this, other young women were drifting in, all casually attired. No head scarfs. They sat down, chatted, ordered coffee, lit cigarettes.

"I thought we were the last clients," I said.

"These aren't clients, just friends of Susu and Rajaq. They come in and talk and smoke and hang out. They call themselves pals, the American word."

"They all work?"

Taghreed nodded. "But as secretaries, accountants. They're what you might call middle-class Kuwaitis or rather middle-class non-Kuwaitis, whose parents have been here forever."

In the mirror, while Susu was clipping the last strands of my bangs, I could see the pals moving around, flipping through the fashion magazines, joking.

I wondered what their perspectives might be on the questions I'd been asking.

"Do you think they'd talk with me?" I said to Taghreed.

"Let's ask them," she answered.

The pals looked mildly interested, agreed, sat down in a semicircle of white wicker chairs around me. Susu pulled the heavy floral drapes to block public view, pinned the CLOSED sign on the front door.

"But don't use their real names, okay?" translated Taghreed. "That's the condition." I promised not to.

Taghreed proceeded to tell a joke, to lighten the atmosphere, I thought, but no one laughed. The seven young women stared at me silently; they wore jeans and classy boots and short fashionable printed tops, or tunics cinched in by silver Santa Fe-style belts.

I cleared my throat. "Well," I began brightly, "if you were the Emir of Kuwait, what would you do for women?"

Silence. Finally, Jamileh (black jeans, plaid tunic) said, "The Emir! I can't imagine being the Emir!"

To my left, Dalal added, "You see, madame, it's a strange question for us. I mean, being a man. No one could possibly imagine it."

I switched gears. "Okay then, what would you like the Emir to do for you?"

That brought quick responses. "Admit us to the university so we can get better jobs. Let us go on with our studies."

"But I thought all education here was free!"

"Yes, but standards are different for Kuwaitis than for us . . . we're born here, lived here all our lives, but we're not Kuwaiti citizens."

I said quickly, "So all you want from life is a better education? Better jobs?"

Laughter broke the tension that had accumulated in the pink-and-white room.

Najat, who wore a leopard-print top over her dark pants, summarized the comments. "Yes, that's true, but in our hearts, each one of us wants to marry and have children. We're all singles. We've all had relationships that went nowhere."

Blond Alix said, "Men give you a lot of talk, they'll do this, they'll do that. It's all bullshit—they go off and marry eighteen-year-old girls because their mothers tell them to."

"You should know, Alix."

"He really gave you a bad time."

"What a jerk!"

"Yeah, yeah, easy for you to say," said Alix. Then, turning to me, she added, "That's how girls have it better in America. They can forget the guy and move on to someone else. Not here."

I said, "But sometimes it's hard to find someone else."

The group fell silent once more.

Najat finally said, "Yes, but no one criticizes you or thinks you've ruined your reputation when the guy leaves. And how do we find someone else? We don't date, you know, we move in groups together, but the guys have all gone."

"What about feminism?" I asked.

"Feminism?" The pals were standing up now, stretching, reaching for bags, touching up their makeup, combing their hair. "Feminism?"

Then followed a long and to me incomprehensible comment from Dalal. Everyone burst into laughter. Even Taghreed giggled.

"It's hard to translate, B.J.," said Taghreed, still smiling, "but I think they mean that feminism is like an American export, sort of like McDonald's and Kentucky Fried Chicken, lots of flash . . ."

"But it doesn't do anything for you—or at least for me," said Jamileh.

"Like fast food." They were out of the salon, still laughing.

"So what did you think of that, B.J.?" Taghreed asked as we headed out into the six-lane highway, up the overpass, down onto the freeway, and to the Bones roundabout where the newly planted palm trees formed shadowed tiny silhouettes against the yellow streetlights.

"A different view."

"Yes," said Taghreed. "The war was hard on them. They lost a year of their youth. They're not married. And they're not in the university. They're in between. What can they do when the guys marry someone else because a woman tells them to—their mothers, that is. What would American feminists say about that?"

"I'm not sure," I answered. "Probably that the men's fathers put the men's mothers up to it."

"Not true."

Dinner was ready. Shafeeq, Zaina, Haneen, and Taghreed and I sat down around Chinese chicken with cabbage, carrots, and cashew nuts, and a vegetarian kibbe which Shafeeq liked.

"Lucette," said Taghreed, "the chicken is excellent."

Satellite dishes sprout like enormous white-and-silver blossoms on the roofs of almost every Kuwaiti house, sharing the space with television aerials of various sizes and complexity and with the water tanks, silver fiberglass barrels, held upright on shiny steel legs. Two great gifts of the oil revenues to the Kuwaiti people: readily available clean running water, and access to information worldwide.

The two channels, one in English, one in Arabic, of Kuwaiti National Television contribute to the daily flow of information throughout the nation, and I was delighted to be invited to visit the television building by Lubna Abbas Muhammad.

Lubna was a director for Channel 2, the English channel. She showed me around the offices, which looked brand-new, and introduced me to her colleague, Ali Dashti, who reported proudly that they had just received funding for their research project.

"We're going to test men and women viewers on their perceptions of women in the media," Ali explained, an earnest young man with a degree in communication theory from an American university. He also taught in the new mass communications program at Kuwait University, which was now in its second year.

Lubna was obviously pleased at the awarding of the research grant.

"You know, B.J.," she said, "it's really time for us here in Kuwait to rethink our views on men and women."

She was wearing black and white, a tall, stately young woman, her black hair carefully in place, and she suggested we go to the conference room, where another colleague would join us, a young woman documentary filmmaker who had just returned from film school in England and was launching a series of documentary films on Kuwaiti history.

The television building was three times larger than any television headquarters I had ever visited, in either America or Britain, but it seemed oddly empty, and our footsteps echoed along the hallways, white squares on white squares, white walls, glass doors. After a few minutes of chat over Turkish coffee, I realized that Lubna and Ali had both seen some of the documentary films I had made over the years, films about Middle Eastern women. They knew my interest, therefore, but they wanted to talk to me about technical matters. So I asked about funding, and staff and editing processes. The three exchanged looks.

"You can see we have the finest facilities in the world but no trained Kuwaitis to run them. We have to import help," said Lubna. "But people here think they know it all. This fall, we bought a special 3-D generating system, and engineering gave us all strict instructions not to use it until the thirty-day test period was up. But a couple of people didn't listen and they ruined the circuitry . . ."

"Twice!" said Ali indignantly. "This must stop."

"We have problems in other areas, too," began Lubna.

"Is money really a problem?" I asked, a trifle facetiously, remembering only too well the difficulty of raising funds for any films.

"No, not exactly," temporized Ali.

"Not exactly?"

Lubna and Ali began to talk at the same time. The newly graduated filmmaker, who had been working for the station for only a month, watched them, but did not speak.

"No training center on our premises."

"We need to retrain and upgrade."

"We're generating revenue from our ads, so we should get more money from the ministry. Now it all goes to the Ministry of Finance, no ifs, ands, or buts."

"We need to lobby for our position . . ."

"Which is?"

Lubna took over at a nod from Ali. "Quality programming done by Kuwaitis themselves. It's ridiculous that all our production is done by others, outside the studio. But some of these are problems that can't be fixed by money."

I waited.

Ali said, "The idea of working with the hands as low status. The idea that women can't do these jobs. That's nonsense. We have to change that."

"You know, B.J.," Lubna said, "because you've been writing about the Arab world for years. In the past here people who work with their hands—plumbers, carpenters, mechanics—had and continue to have inferior status."

"So you have other people do it, like guest workers."

There is a small pause. "Yes, that's absolutely right," said Lubna, a bit belligerently. "But we have to change that, to persuade people that manual labor is exciting, interesting, just like filmmakers in America. We need to learn to do these things ourselves."

"And how do women figure in this?" I asked.

"They must participate equally with men," said Ali. "Come to the university, Professor Fernea," he urged, "and see the mass communications program. Over half the students are women and they'll come to work for us here when they're done."

"And they will have a different sense of women's role and women's place, especially because by that time our project on attitudes toward women in the media will be finished," put in Lubna.

"What about Islam in all this?"

"Islam?"

The three young people looked at each other.

The quiet new filmmaker said, "We are all Muslims, of course. But that should not be an obstacle."

"On the contrary," agreed Ali. "Islam respects women, and they are supposed to participate in the life of the family and the life of the Muslim community. And I say, life in Kuwait is television these days. Everyone watches it."

Lubna interrupted. "We have to make it a *community* enterprise, one with high standards, that reflects our own values. Of course women have to be part of it."

"And none of the religious leaders would object?"

Lubna said, after a moment, "Well, if they want women to cover their heads while they're sitting in the editing room, who cares? They're doing the creative work, aren't they? Participating, aren't they? Why should that make a difference?"

Lubna was one of eight Kuwaiti women who fought in the Gulf War. I don't remember reading anything at all about Kuwaiti women's participation, although American female soldiers were a regular feature on the news broadcasts and reports in the United States. I said as much.

Lubna said, "Well, B.J., don't you think that's part of America's problem with the issue of Muslim women?"

"Yes, but there you were, in uniform, in combat. There. How could they miss your presence?"

"They didn't. But they chose not to mention us."

It was Lubna and an American woman sergeant who discovered the forty wailing babies, unharmed but starvingly hungry, left behind in an orphanage as the Iraqi army retreated. It was Lubna and her American friend who rescued the babies, found them all temporary homes, and cadged dried milk from American army rations to feed them.

And then Lubna told me a story about an American reporter who was covering the liberation of Kuwait, and was passing along the lines of American soldiers entering Kuwait City. He paused before the two women, dark-haired Lubna and the blond young American sergeant. The reporter began asking questions of the American sergeant, "So my friend said, 'You should interview Lubna, she was in my company.'

" 'This Arab girl here?' "

" 'Yes, this Arab girl here. We fought side by side.'

"The reporter had looked startled. 'You're telling me Kuwaiti women were actually in combat? I don't think so somehow.'

"Then my American friend got really annoyed. 'Look,' she said, "I don't know who you are, but I'm telling you I served with Lubna and she was damn good. She knows as much about weapons as I do.'

"The reporter folded up his notebook, put his pen behind his ear, and prepared to move down the line.

"My friend grabbed his arm and said, 'Why won't you write down what Lubna did? It's part of the story. It's a good story.'

"But the reporter said, 'Sorry, lady. Our view in America is that Arab women are behind our women, and they wear veils. That's what makes news, not what your Arab lady friend supposedly did. Negative sells in this area and I'm a stringer and need to make money.' "

I said, "So that must make you really angry!"

Lubna shrugged. "I went to school in the United States, I got used to it. But now I'm back home, in Kuwait. We've been waiting and waiting for all the rights that were promised us when the oil money came in the sixties. We got education, that's fine, jobs with equal pay, okay, but now we need more equality in our personal lives. Marriage and divorce laws."

"Do you consider yourself a feminist?"

Lubna answered, "What is a feminist? Someone who believes men and women should share the goods of this world equally? Then I'm a feminist."

"Maybe a more accurate term might be Islamic feminist?" I asked.

Lubna frowned. "What does that mean? I'm a Muslim. But I'm a feminist. Islamic feminist sounds like a made-up name, to pin labels on us again in the West. Why not just say I'm a feminist and I'm a Muslim. Is there some special brand of feminism that we're supposed to have, according to Muslim rules, or something?"

"That's what I'm interested in discovering," I answered.

Lubna was quiet, and then said, "When I was in school, I learned in America not to label things for other people, but to let them label themselves, not niggers, but African-Americans, not wetbacks, but Mexican-Americans. So why don't you let us do the same?"

Dr. Bedriya Awadhi, the lawyer whose divorce statistics so mesmerized the audience in the Meridien Hotel debate, does not call herself a feminist. She calls herself an international lawyer. We had waited about an hour and a half to speak to her, since she had just returned from an International Labor Organization conference in Geneva and her clients had been waiting for days to get her attention. We were finally admitted to her office, where she apologized and explained.

"I've been involved in the ILO for over ten years, the section related to international labor standards, especially those related to women— health, maternity leaves, wages."

Kuwait had a good record in terms of wages and maternity leave, Dr. Bedriya pointed out. "We do pay women and men equally for equal work. And our maternity leave is pretty good—two months full pay and six months half pay—in the public sector. The private sector is something else—only seventy days altogether."

But she believed that policy makers needed to pay more attention to women who worked and had families, because "this is the area where the future conditions of Kuwaiti society are now being formed.

"The West is fond of touting itself for improving women's roles," she said, in answer to a question. "They have done that, more or less, but they have neglected the family. It's interesting that only 32 out of 188 countries have ratified the international ILO convention on equality *within* the family. And the United States is not one of them."

Kuwait hasn't ratified it either, she added, though Libya, Iraq, Morocco, and Tunisia in the Arab world and all the Scandinavian countries have done so. The Scandinavians were doing the best in terms of male and female participation, she believed, pointing out that in Finland, fifteen women served as ministers in the government. Egypt, which was supposed to be way ahead, was still behind internationally, though it compared favorably with the United States (5 percent of the Egyptian cabinet members were women; in the United States it was 5 or 6 percent).

"You can tell, madame, since you were present at that Meridien debate, that divorce is one of women's greatest problems here. Plus increasing polygamy. Everyone has too much money," she said sarcastically. "Also, though women are receiving equal pay for equal work, in terms of promotion and opportunities for promotion, they're not doing too well."

"The glass ceiling," I replied.

Dr. Bedriya looked up, and I explained the term. She smiled. "That's a good one. I will use it."

She wrote it on a pad before her on a desk which was covered with books and papers, but still seemed uncluttered.

Dr. Bedriya was the first dean of the Kuwaiti law school, Taghreed said.

"Including sharia law?"

"Including sharia law."

"But how did you get into law at all? How did your father allow it?"

Dr. Bedriya leaned back in her dark blue chair and smiled. She had a wide-open smile that illuminated her face and lit up her eyes.

"Oh well, my father didn't want me to work, not proper for ladies, he said, but he did believe in education, so he said yes, I could go to college. But we didn't have a university in Kuwait then, so I went to Cairo. When I announced I wanted to study law, the Kuwaiti cultural attaché in Egypt refused to allow me to even apply!"

"I don't understand," put in Taghreed. "Once you were there, why didn't they let you study what you wanted?"

"You know what the Kuwaiti attaché said to me and my father, who had come with me to get me settled? He said, 'She can't go to law school, she's a girl and even *boys* fail the faculty of law. Do you want your precious daughter to *fail?*' My father said no, of course not, and he registered me in the faculty of arts."

Her phone kept lighting up—call after call after call, but Dr. Bedriya paid no attention. Finally, a knock on the door was answered, and a slight young man in a white suit entered. He put a sheet of paper before Dr. Bedriya and whispered to her. She looked surprised, asked him something which was unintelligible to us, then signed the paper, and he left.

Without explanation, Dr. Bedriya turned back to us and said heatedly, "I don't like injustice. Period. Government employees, foreigners, guest workers, women, anyone. I defend those who've been treated unjustly. I have to."

"Law school," I prompted. "How did you get in?"

"Well . . ." said Dr. Bedriya, leaning back in her chair and smiling a little again.

Taghreed and I waited.

"You see, I knew it was a lost cause. They would never have let me go. So I went to the classes in the faculty of arts, but I studied all the law books and went to those classes too. One month before graduation I asked to be transferred. They laughed at me. Just let me take the law school exams, I begged. They laughed again. Okay, they said. They were sure I would fail. But I didn't. All the other Kuwaitis failed."

She turned in her chair and pointed to the paneled wall, where various certificates, plaques, and scrolls hung in decorous black frames. "See that medal high up?"

We nodded.

"I got that medal from President Gamal Abdel Nasser, because I was one of the top ten in the law school exams." She laughed. "He thought I was an Egyptian!"

"Why did you decide to study law?" I asked.

"Why did I choose law?" She repeated my question, thought for a moment. "I guess because it was a challenge, that's why. And what I learned from those hard years was to prepare yourself, do your homework, know what you're talking about. The trouble with a lot of women's groups, even in America, madame, if you will pardon my saying so . . ."

I waved my pencil politely, indicating that I would not be insulted.

"The trouble with a lot of women's groups is that they don't do their homework. In the legal profession, if you don't do your homework, you lose the case, it's as simple as that."

I was writing busily.

"About women in your country, America, for example . . ."

"Yes?"

"They talk a lot of nonsense about Arab women because they haven't done their homework. They criticize their media's presentation of themselves, but they don't criticize the media when it's going after Arab women. That shows they are not doing their homework and looking at the picture behind the media presentation. For people who are supposed to be educated in terms of international feminism, it is shocking!"

"B.J. writes about Arab women, she knows that," put in Taghreed in my defense.

"I know you may do so, madame, but look at the general stuff that is written about us."

"Your point is well taken," I said, then asked, "What was your principal goal in the Meridien Hotel debate? With those impressive statistics about divorce?"

"I wanted to reach that audience of women. I knew they would mostly be conservative women in Islamic dress, because Dr. Muhammad, the sharia professor, was speaking. I wanted them to know what was happening, as was reported by their own government ministries. And I did a pamphlet that we handed out to everyone." She searched on her desk and found a copy for us, a small booklet titled *Women's Rights Under Islamic Law*. "I wanted them to realize that first you have to teach yourself about your rights, and then ask for further help. I mean, you must fight for your rights, no one is going to give them to you."

"How do the promoters of sharia law, the sponsors of the debate, feel about you and your work?"

Dr. Bedriya said, rather slowly and forcefully, "I don't care what they think. I am a good Muslim. They know that. I'm independently wealthy enough to survive. I love what I do. And that's all that matters."

"You're not married? No children?"

"No, I'm free to do what I want."

"Do you think your father would have been proud of you?"

Dr. Bedriya fixed me with an eye and considered. She nodded, finally.

"Yes, I think he would be proud. Of course it would have been better if I'd been a son."

"A son?"

"Yes, you know your feminist writers go on and on about the Arab family preference for sons. It's only partly true. They want daughters always. But they need sons."

"Need them? Why?"

"Because according to our present laws, only a son can protect his mother and her property. Only a son has that legal standing. And I don't think the laws are going to be revolutionized very soon."

Shafeeq, I remember, had said that to me when his son was born, less than a year ago. "When there's a son, everything stays in the family, B.J. But with only daughters, the father's family inherits a good portion of the estate."

The uses and abuses of tradition. Dr. Bedriya had given me a valuable reminder about the force of tradition. But she had also in her own life demonstrated that, at times, tradition could be circumvented.

Muhammad, Shafeeq's and Taghreed's driver, took me to the airport. I was going to fly to Abu Dhabi to visit friends, and then go on to Turkey, to continue my research. Muhammad and I had been talking back and forth during my numerous perambulations around Kuwait

City, in Arabic, of course. We had discussed Social Security in the United States, the laws in Egypt concerning inheritance if the husband dies, the new possibility being raised by the Kuwaiti Labor Board, for guest workers to bring their families to join them. Muhammad had wanted to do this for some time, he said. He missed his children and his wife.

At the airport, Muhammad did not stand back and smile good-bye, as I had expected. He took my arm and guided me into the waiting room and then in forceful language instructed a porter to find a chair for me to sit on. I was surprised at this new aggressiveness, for up to now it was his meekness that I had noticed.

But here Muhammad was the only man present to take responsibility for my welfare. No doubt Shafeeq had asked him to take good care of me. He had always taken good care of me in a deferential way, but now he was more assertive. When the Gulf Air personnel saw that my visa to Abu Dhabi was not stamped into my passport, Muhammad became my legal advocate, quietly but forcefully explaining who my host was in Kuwait, who my host was to be in Abu Dhabi (the American ambassador), who *I* was.

"Madame, would you allow them to telephone the ambassador to check?" he asked.

"Of course," and I proffered my address book with Andrea and Bill Rugh's phone and fax numbers. The tattered purple book went up and down the check-in counter, and finally they relented.

"All will now be well, madame," intoned Muhammad in his best Arabic, as he took my passport from the clerk and handed it to me. "Now take good care."

And he moved my chair close to the passport control booth and explained that the line would open "in one half hour. Stay here and rest, madame."

"Thank you, Muhammad."

"And to your husband and children, greetings," he said formally. "God be with you."

"And with you."

With a bow to the check-in counter clerks, Muhammad was gone.

I sat in the plastic chair by the empty passport control booth, reflecting on this sudden change in Muhammad's public persona. True, I was an older lady, and the guest of his employer. Was it my age and position that had prompted his new solicitude for my welfare, or was it just the simple fact that he was a man, and therefore automatically took charge of me, a woman, whether I wanted to be taken charge of or not? This was what a man was supposed to do in Muslim society. And

Muhammad didn't have too many opportunities to exercise his duties these days, as his own family was far away. I found I could not fault him for that. After my first surprise I had been happy to accept his help.

The plane was delayed, so I had time to muse, not only on Muhammad's new behavior, but on my visit to Kuwait. Feminism. "Feminism is not a word in my vocabulary," one of the ladies of the cultural society had said. "But women's rights and freedoms are in my vocabulary. Aren't they the same?"

Are they the same? My Kuwaiti friends, like my Moroccan friends, did not take seriously the idea of gender, the idea that femininity and masculinity are not biological, but are socially constructed roles for men and women that can and often do change, in response to changed social and economic circumstances. Economic change is usually cited as the spur to social change, economic shifts, or even deprivation. But these theories do not take into account the kind of sudden luxury without labor that Kuwait enjoys. But they also do not take into account Kuwaiti women's own experiences with what they see as unequality.

I remembered Mae, a former student of mine, now married in Kuwait, and her attempt to explain to her ten-year-old daughter about politics, and the issue of universal suffrage.

"What did you say?"

"I told her that long ago the Emir of Kuwait sat with other sheikhs and they decided together that the Emir was the best man to rule. When she asked me what was happening now, I told her that we elect some people, and those people decide who should consult with the ruler about what is best for the people of Kuwait."

" 'Can I go, too?' she asked.

" 'You're not grown up yet.'

" 'But when I'm grown up, I can, right, Mama?'

" 'No.'

" 'Why?'

" 'Because you're a girl.'

" 'Why does that matter, that I'm a girl?'

" 'Girls and women can't vote.'

"My daughter stood up," said Mae, and announced, 'Well, Mama, that's not fair. When I grow up, I'll take care of that.' "

Mae's daughter was right. It was not fair. If it was true that attitudes toward women were changing, as so many Kuwaiti women asserted, then Mae's daughter might be part of a majority by the time she was an adult. That might mean she would indeed vote. But in the meantime Kuwaiti women had much work to do, as they themselves were the first to tell me.

When I returned to Texas I found they had already begun, with a 1996 sit-in protest "for the vote" before the House of Parliament. Three hundred professional women. Lubna Muhammad, one of the organizers of the protest, had said to me in the television studio, "This generation is not as patient as our mothers' generation." The next one may be even less patient.

FOUR

¤ ¤

Turkey

THE NEW WOMEN'S LIBRARY of the Turkish Republic stands on the far northern shore of the Golden Horn, that shimmering finger of sea that formed the great harbor of Istanbul. So I had been told by my hostess Akile Gursoy, when she sent me off, my second day in Istanbul, with her parents' driver, Sedat. I had been invited to lecture at the women's library.

"I'm sorry I can't come with you now," said Akile, "but I have to speak myself at a public health conference. It's part of my teaching duties at Marmara University."

"Don't worry, I'm sure it'll be fine," I reassured her, then ventured, "Are these programs a regular thing at the library?"

"Yes," answered Akile, "but this one is rather special. The theme is *Woman and Earth*. They have a Russian eco-feminist, and two Turkish scholars . . . and you."

"But . . ."

"Yes?"

"My topic, 'Cross-Cultural Research on Women,' isn't exactly to the point."

"Oh yes it is, B.J.," said Akile. "They want to talk across cultures. And they were most pleased you agreed to come, so soon after your arrival, that is. Sedat will drop you there, then I'll come for the social hour and we can come home together."

That had been nearly an hour ago. Sedat and I had gotten off to a bad beginning. A small, dark-haired young man with an intense gaze and a nervous habit of chewing on his lower lip, he had started talking to me almost as soon as I had gotten into the car, saying something over and over again, which I did not understand, since I had no Turkish whatsoever, beyond "thank you," "please," and "hello." But he kept on talking louder and louder until finally, in desperation, he banged on the dashboard. We needed gas! Back to Akile's house we went, and fortunately, her teenage son Ali was just emerging from the front door in time to help us.

Now Sedat and I were alone, forced to drive so slowly through the district of Kadikoy toward the bridge, arching across the water from the Asian to the European side of the city, that I had plenty of time to admire the scenery. The bumper-to-bumper traffic on the Asian side was a clear indication of Istanbul's growth, from eight million on my last visit in 1988 to ten million people today. Apartment houses of dun-colored cement, some still under construction, climbed up the terraced green hills, which looked like the hills of San Francisco. These sloped down, however, not into San Francisco Bay but into the Strait of Bosporus, flowing in from the Golden Horn. The new high-rises dwarfed the older houses, and vied in height with the many mosques that dotted the hills. The mosques seemed to come in different sizes, small, medium, and grand, but the minarets, whether built of brick or stone or even cement, looked remarkably the same in that style distinctive to Ottoman Turkish architecture, the tall, slender towers tapering to a fine point, as if to draw the observer's gaze up, up into the sky, far from human habitations and concerns. Cypresses stood dark on the green hills, between the houses and mosques, and occasional splashes of pink and crimson and white signaled that spring was on its way to Istanbul, for the almond and apple and Judas trees were coming into bloom.

It was a silent ride, neither Sedat nor I uttering a word. I had no idea where we were going, though I did recognize the great historic boulevard shaded with sycamore trees that we followed along the European side of the Bosporus after we had crossed the bridge. Where could we be headed now?

I tried to quell my disquiet by staring hard at the gleaming water, which I presumed to be the Golden Horn, where small boats were bobbing on the sparkling foam-tapped waves, and where a white ferry, loaded with passengers, moved low in the water. I was, it appeared, probably going to be late for the lecture. I thought Sedat was worried as well, for he slowed down and sped up rather erratically. Twice he had even stopped and asked directions, to no avail.

But Akile had assured me of Sedat's reliability. After all, I told myself, he would have to be reliable to work for her parents, who were elderly and retired but still maintained a certain distinguished status as descendants of Celal Bayar, last prime minister under Atatürk and later the first civil president of Turkey until he was deposed in the coup of 1960. In fact, the apartment building where I was staying with Akile was called Bayar House, after her distinguished grandfather.

Sedat ground to a sudden jolting stop, leaped out, and left me in the car, its motor going, its driver's door standing open. I saw him running past a domed building standing in a grassy hollow, and up the hollow toward a children's playground where men and boys were kicking a soccer ball around the turf.

Should I too leap out and leave the engine running? Why was I so timid? Well, I rationalized, this was Akile's parents' car, and I was a guest in her house. I couldn't just abandon the car. Now Sedat was gesturing wildly.

The gesture was clear. I was to come. But I waited, and he ran back to the car, seeming to realize that the motor was still running. He nodded in my general direction a "yes, I can see, I forgot" nod, turned off the motor, shut the driver's door, and opened the back door for me. He was chewing nervously on his lower lip again as he ushered me out, across the playground near the men and boys, who had left their game and gathered round, presumably to see what Sedat and I were planning to do. A torrent of Turkish on both sides meant nothing to me.

"Where is the women's library?" I found myself speaking in English, much too loudly, and I paused, ashamed to find myself imitating poor Sedat. We were, it seemed, Sedat and I, in the same position as all speakers of foreign languages who seem to believe that if they can just speak louder, and *louder,* the import of their words will sink into the listener's uncomprehending brain. One of the older men pointed behind us to where, at the bottom of the grassy hollow Sedat had climbed, that domed structure of stone stood.

"Yes, yes," he said, and with Sedat, led the way down the grassy slope, past indentations set at regular intervals like tiers in an amphitheater of some long past era. Sedat skipped cheerfully, I followed more slowly, the older man behind me as we climbed out on the grassy proscenium and marched up to an arched door of what I realized with relief was the women's library. There was a sign that said so. Sedat banged, but no one answered. Oh dear. But before I could speak, two women, one young, in denim dress and tweed jacket, the other older, in a black pants suit, rounded the corner.

"Ah! You must be Akile's American feminist friend," said the older woman, holding out a welcoming hand. "So happy to meet you. I am Sirin Tekeli and this is Ceylan Orhun."

Sedat ducked toward me, smiling, no longer chewing his lip, but brandishing the car keys in his hand, indicating he was leaving (delighted, I thought, to be rid of me).

I stammered out, "Thank you," in Turkish to him and to the helpful soccer-playing father.

"Welcome," said Madame Tekeli, as she pushed open the heavy wooden door.

"Was this a theater once, long ago? An amphitheater?" I asked. "Before it was the women's library, I mean?"

The two women were switching on lights, pushing open the new wooden doors which had been fitted into partitions, dividing the old domed structure into rooms.

"A theater?" Madame Tekeli echoed. "I really don't know. It was a gift to us from the municipality of Istanbul, five years ago. They described it as 'an eighteenth-century historical structure,' isn't that your understanding, Ceylan?"

"Yes, yes." Ceylan stopped. "Oh dear, no one has set up the chairs, Sirin, and where's the woman who was supposed to do the refreshments? Is Fusun bringing her own projector?"

I wandered about, trying to be inconspicuous while the ladies set about their task. After all my worrying about the trip, I was nearly an hour early! It was the language barrier, I thought. I was so used to being able to get by in Arabic and French, it was worrisome not to be able to communicate at all. Poor Sedat was in the same position as I was. But he had gotten me here! Other women were coming in, greeting each other, beginning to set up chairs.

"Would you like to see our wonderful archives?" Madame Tekeli called.

"Yes, of course, but I know you've got many things to do for the afternoon."

"No, no, others are working now, it's fine."

"We feel very lucky to have the library," said Ceylan, joining us, and, I noticed, keeping her tweed jacket on. It was cold in the library, despite the signs of blossoms on the hills and the new green on the sycamores along the boulevard beside the Golden Horn.

Ceylan moved quickly through the dim library, and the light slanting through the narrow windows in the old stone walls flashed on her silver bracelets and rings, on her zircon earrings. The zircons seemed to fit surprisingly well with her tweed jacket and denim dress, brown straight hair, the high cheekbones of her wide, interested face. "We've done it, haven't we, Sirin? With the Women's Board we've started the first ever women's library in Turkey!"

"And a women's center, too, if you like," nodded Madame Tekeli, taller, slim in her black pants suit and silk blouse of muted print, her pepper and salt bobbed hair swishing and shining as she turned back and forth between Ceylan and me.

"You do counseling?" I asked, remembering women's centers in universities across the U.S.

"No, no, not yet, we may in time," answered Madame Tekeli. "But now the library is the main thing. We arrange lectures like today's, and exhibits, but the library is most important. Research. Documentation of women's condition in Turkey. How can we expect to influence public policy if we don't have proper documentation?"

Ceylan looked at me. "And," she said, with a sidelong glance at Madame Tekeli, clearly the moving force behind this activity, "now that the Islamists have won the municipality elections, we hope they won't take the building away from us."

"Ceylan!" Madame Tekeli spoke rather loudly, and her words bounced off the old walls, echoed from the overarching dome. The women setting up chairs for the lectures paused, and a young man arranging glasses and cups for the social hour, asked whether something was wrong.

"No, no." Then she turned to us. "We don't even think such things," she said.

Ceylan moved off to help set up the chairs.

"So Islamism is not a problem for women in Turkey, as it is supposed to be everywhere else these days?" I tried to keep my tone light.

Madame Tekeli paused. I wondered whether she was considering the problem itself or me, the American interloper and questioner. "We thought it might be," she said slowly, "but I think we are working things out. Come!"

She led me to a wrought-iron staircase, which spiraled up into the dome, a modern note in the otherwise lovingly restored building. She explained that the building had been empty for years, and had been restored to its eighteenth-century splendor just in time for the library's 1991 international gala opening. I asked whether Islamist women used the library. Did they feel welcome?

Madame Tekeli smiled a big happy smile. "Yes, they use the library. In the beginning we were worried. There was some comment about this stairway, for instance, improperly cutting into and erasing a former 'sacred space.'"

"This building was sacred space?"

"Anyone can make the claim, I guess, we are not sure ourselves. But it's much better now."

"How?"

"The Islamist women said first they needed to pray and the library was not an appropriate place to pray, and there were too many pictures on the walls, which is against the teaching of Islam."

"And then?"

"We have young women as interns and one who applied was wearing the full cover [black sharshaf—the dress that covers a woman's body from head to toe]. We hired her and she did well."

"That changed things?"

Madame Tekeli considered. "Well, that helped but then we had a visit from a very militant and yes, I will say it, very belligerent woman—an Islamic fundamentalist. I won't name her. Let's call her Nermine. Well, she came storming into the library one day and said, 'You don't have my books. They are very important books on women in Islam. How can this be a women's library without my books?'"

"And . . . ?"

"I came down and greeted her and said, but we do have your books, and showed her where they stood on the shelves. They were old editions, much used. The following week she brought us a big box of her books, all new editions, all beautifully bound, and presented them to the library. Since then, there's been no trouble—actually, lots of young women wearing *tesettür,* or modest dress, come in. They work with other young women wearing Western dress. We are very happy about that.

"We have records going back a hundred years," Madame Tekeli continued, leading me along the neat functional open-backed shelves, row after row, until I saw where she was headed. There on a shelf were several dog-eared copies of my own books! I was thrilled, for the books were not only sitting here in Istanbul, on the beautiful Golden Horn, but they were clearly being used.

I murmured something about sending new copies. "We would be *most* pleased to receive them," said Madame Tekeli. "Your films, too! We have quite a collection, as you can see, going back to the beginning of the women's movement here in Turkey."

"From the twenties, the time of Atatürk?"

Madame Tekeli shook her head vigorously, her short hair moving around her face as she did so.

"Long before Atatürk. *Long* before!"

"Really?" My tone must have indicated my doubt, for she turned and looked at me quite seriously.

"I know this is what many people, even some Turks, believe," she said, "and of course, the Kemalists [Atatürk's followers] are happy to promote this theme. 'Our leader emancipated women just as he reorganized the Turkish feudal society into one of modernism,' and so on. But it's not true."

She paused. I waited. I, too, had always believed that Atatürk had liberated Turkish women. This was certainly the story in the standard history books.

"Our women's movement, even what we might call today a *feminist* movement, goes back to 1869," she announced. "It is the oldest in the area."

"Older than Egypt?"

Madame Tekeli pursed her lips, and nodded. "You must realize," she said in the tone I had often used myself with ignorant students, "when the women's movement began here, Egypt was still a colony of the Ottoman Empire!"

I nodded. "Of course. What a stupid question. But . . . a women's movement as early as 1869? Things were just beginning then in Europe."

"Yes, you are right." Madame Tekeli smiled. "And since the Ottoman Empire extended into Eastern Europe at that time, we were part of those developments—intellectual, social, whatever."

"How do you chart it, though?" I asked, still not convinced. A Turkish women's movement from 1869? Could that be true?

"Through the tracts, the women's stories, the letters we have been able to amass here in the library," said Madame Tekeli, smiling. "It's all here," and she dramatically flung out her arm toward the shelves of folios, books, newspapers, films in cans and cases. "History! From 1869 the first glimmerings and then of course in the Tanzimat period it really took off. Those ladies were more serious feminists than many of our activists today!"

We were interrupted by a shout from below. "She's here, she's here," called Ceylan. "Tatyana and her friend Mildred, and the others."

"We must talk again," I said, and Madame Tekeli agreed.

"Yes, yes, we're coming."

We clumped down the steep curving iron stairway to the small lecture room below, where an audience was gathering for the lectures on *Woman and Earth*.

Tatyana Mamanova, a radical Russian feminist deported from the U.S.S.R. for dissident activities, was the principal featured speaker, followed by Füsün Ertug, Turkish anthropologist, Reset Erdener, author, and me.

"We have allowed thirty minutes for Tatyana and her American

Uzbek women selling bread in Samarkand. *Photo by Ergun Çagatay*

Two women wearing traditional costume at a folklore festival in Marrakech. *Photo by Thomas Hartwell*

Two women riding a motorcycle in the streets of Marrakech. *Photo by Thomas Hartwell*

Family walking down a Marrakech street. *Photo by Thomas Hartwell*

Sara Akbar, Kuwaiti woman petroleum engineer and firefighter, who took part in the international effort to quench the oil fires of the Gulf War, is shown with other members of Kuwait's team. The then Minister of Oil is shown in the center. *Photo by Claudia Farkas al-Rashoud*

Kuwaiti girls in traditional dress. *Photo by Claudia Farkas al-Rashoud*

Kuwaiti women students at the university. *Photo by Claudia Farkas al-Rashoud*

Turkish woman from the city (back) and the country (front), *Photo by Ergun Çagatay*

Women in Cappadocia, central Turkey, selling lace and scarves.
Photo by Ergun Çagatay

Members of a wedding party paying traditional respects at the mosque,
Istanbul. *Photo by Ergun Çagatay*

Crowd of young people, Cairo. *Photo by Thomas Hartwell*

A coeducational secondary school classroom, Cairo. *Photo by Thomas Hartwell*

Dr. Salma Khadra Jayyusi, Palestinian poet and critic, opening the first Arab Women's Book Fair, Cairo, November 1995. *Photo by Thomas Hartwell*

Landowner Samia celebrates her first wheat crop. Samia is a participant in Egypt's New Lands program offering women as well as men the chance to own and farm land. *Photo by Thomas Hartwell*

Iraqi women poll-watchers during the 1996 parliamentary elections, Baghdad. *Photo by Thomas Hartwell*

Reunion in the village of Al-Nahra, southern Iraq. Left to right, Muhammed (old friend and retainer), Robert Fernea, Elizabeth Fernea, and Selma, the late Sheik Hamid's youngest wife. *Photo by Thomas Hartwell*

...dy Blanc, Israeli feminist and peace activist, Jerusalem. *Photo by Thomas Hartwell*

Palestinian family returning from working in the fields, Gaza, Der el Balah. *Photo by Randa Sha'ath*

Kamilya Jubran,
Palestinian musician
and singer, tuning the
qanoon, Jerusalem.
Photo by Randa Sha'ath

Women in Black, Tel
Aviv intersection,
1994. *Photo by
Heather Logan Taylor*

research assistant, who will help translate," explained Madame Tekeli. "We are delighted to have you," she said to Tatyana, gripping her hand. She turned to Füsün, Reset, and me. "She is very famous in New York, they say. We are lucky to have her. And you, of course, my friends. Twenty minutes each!"

I was the final speaker on this rather eclectic program to which my friend and colleague Akile Gursoy had attached me. I had chosen the topic "Cross-Cultural Research on Women," hoping to encourage reactions from Turkish feminists in the audience about the uneasy relationship between feminism East and West. What were the stumbling blocks that kept Western women and Middle Eastern women apart, suspicious, and wary of each other? What did we share?

But alas, my hopes for a dialogue with Turkish feminists were soon dashed. Tatyana and Mildred spoke for more than an hour, Reset Erdener's lecture on goddesses in Turkey was informative but long, and the young anthropologist Füsün Ertug's presentation was so good that the question period went on and on. I begrudged none of it—but when I looked at my watch, we had already run into the promised social hour. Clearly it would be better if I didn't speak at all—the caterers were clattering glasses in the lobby—but there I was, on the program. A brief ten-minute summary was then quite enough; afterward several young women came up to me, including Füsün. They had all read my books! This was very head-turning, especially when the newspaper reporter asked for an interview. But what did he want to know? More about Tatyana. Was it true, as she had told him, that the eco-feminists in America were so powerful that they would eventually save the world from death by pollution and overuse of resources? Was this really what she had said, or was it just the translation of her words from Russian to Turkish?

I cast about in my mind for an answer. The young Turkish girl who was interpreting for me said earnestly, "You should say what you believe."

A rephrasing of the question was going on, in a coquettish exchange between my young interpreter (jeans, leather jacket, dark hair flying, dark eyes flashing) and the young reporter (leather jacket, mustache, dark eyes flashing back).

"Is the eco-feminist movement a serious threat to the establishment in America?" he asked, and the young woman repeated the question quickly, looking back and forth, at him, at me, at Tatyana and Mildred in the corner with Madame Tekeli and a news photographer.

"No," I said truthfully, with a small touch of regret.

The reporter laughed and smiled once more when my flashing-eyed young interpreter brought him a glass of wine, actually two glasses of wine, one for him, and one for me. We headed toward the back of the room, where I could see Akile coming in, smiling and waving at me. Cookies were being passed, flashbulbs were popping, and the audience had gathered around to grill the lecturers. The reporter, wine in hand, drew closer to the knot of intense young women arguing about goddesses with Reset Erdener. It appeared that in Turkey feminism was news!

"What do you think now about Turkish feminism?" Akile asked at breakfast.

I had been in Istanbul a week, had lectured at Marmara University, showed my films in two public settings, talked with students and faculty, interviewed Sirin Tekeli. With Akile and a friend, I had driven up the coast to the end of the Bosporus, where the strait opens out into the Black Sea; here the path to the family restaurants serving fresh fish and fresh *arugula* was lined with wandering cows from nearby fields, and also patrolled by armed guards. ("We're close to Bulgaria and not far from Russia," explained Akile.) Wherever I went, the people I met spoke about women, women's dress, women's place in modern Turkey.

I cut another small piece of feta cheese and nibbled an olive, luxuriating in the breakfast choices that Akile and her part-time maid, Ayten, managed to lay out each morning on the dining room table. Today, on the bright yellow tablecloth were blue bowls of apricots, olives, walnuts, yellow raisins, cucumbers, tomatoes. A loaf of fresh bread almost the same straw color as the oak cutting board. A tall box of cereal, cornflakes in a Turkish-labeled box. Milk in a blue pitcher. A glass bowl of yogurt, clearly made at home, for the skin still lay over the top until my harsh silver spoon dipped into it.

"Everybody seems to talk about women," I said slowly, "but maybe it's just because they know I'm interested in the topic, and that's what I came here to find out about."

"No, no," said Akile. "Not just that. Woman's place is an important issue to everyone these days."

I sipped my coffee.

Akile went on: "Women, you see, B.J., are an index of our so-called modernization, that face we present to the world, that process that Atatürk advocated and worked for so hard. A secular, not a religious Turkey, he said. He got rid of religious family law, after all, and abolished polygamy. And he banned the veil for women, the fez for men. He thought they were backward pieces of clothing."

"And now the Islamists are challenging the hallowed Atatürk secular tradition? And maybe bringing back religious law?"

"Exactly."

From my guest place at Akile's table, I looked out across the Sea of Marmara, a view I had enjoyed every morning since my arrival, when the smog from the day's motor traffic had not yet risen to blur the bright blue of the sky and the darker blue of the water; I watched the fishing boats and tugboats and ferries plying their way from shore to shore, from Asia to Europe and back again. Today the sea was the same color as the sky, the northern horizon a dark smudged line. Turkish flags, bright red, each bearing a star and a crescent, fluttered from many of the balconies on the apartment houses below and around us, tall, brick-colored, brown. For this was National Sovereignty Day, April 23, and in case we had forgotten, there came a loud rapping on the front door. Ali's little black terrier, Shorsha, went wild, yipping furiously. What did he know that we didn't know?

Akile opened the door to two smiling little girls, who stood up straight in proper white blouses, blue vests, and matching blue pants.

"Oh ho!" she said. "You've been to the children's parade!"

The little girls nodded and smiled politely, but they were much more interested in Shorsha, who knew they had come to take him for a walk around the gardens of Bayar House, where Akile and Ali lived in their own four-room place; where her parents occupied the penthouse apartment; and where her sister Emine and her husband and children lived two floors below. The family group had extended itself vertically rather than horizontally.

Akile was explaining that Turkey's National Sovereignty Day was a real children's holiday, for schools were closed, and in the nation's capital of Ankara, children actually took over parliament for the day.

"And we have fireworks," put in one of the little girls, who was introduced as Akile's niece. The other girl, in pigtails, had already, with a self-important gesture, taken the dog's leash down from its hook and was ready to go. So was Shorsha, barking joyfully.

We sat back down at the table, and Akile poured more coffee. She had patiently answered my continual questions, suggested future reading, brought me clippings from the English newspapers.

"I always thought it was Atatürk who got the women's movement going," I said, "but Sirin Tekeli insists that the women's movement here is much older, mid-nineteenth century actually. What do you think?"

Akile's fine brown eyes were intent. "Sirin should know, B.J. She's done all this research. And she's a real feminist. She even calls herself that."

Yes, I thought. I had actually asked Sirin, in our later interview, when exactly she had become a feminist. And she had replied that she had become one without realizing it. "I had the thoughts but not the label," she told me. She had discovered that her own views were those called "feminist" in some of her readings.

"Are people really worried about the Islamists?" I asked. "I mean, I haven't seen many veils on the streets of Istanbul."

"But at the university," put in Akile. "Yesterday . . ."

I shook my head. "Five or six women wearing white head scarfs and dark long coats. Out of how many students? Sixteen thousand? That hardly seems to be a threat to me."

"Well, for many Turks, the sight of one woman dressed like that is enough to upset people. It's not usual. Remember we have this national heritage—we're supposed to be a secular country."

I couldn't tell from Akile's tone whether she was being ironic or not. But I knew that Atatürk had literally put religion on the back burner. Mosques, churches, and synagogues were not razed, as they had been in Central Asia by the Russians, but lands belonging to the religious establishment were seized (as was true in Nasser's Egypt) and the Sufi organizations were declared illegal, their *tekkes,* or lodges, closed. Atatürk had definitely promoted women's rights. Equality of men and women, he said, was a sign of an advanced modern society. I thought back to Cairo, and the hundreds of women on the streets of Cairo wearing what they called Islamic dress. Was the Turkish new costume based on the same belief, I asked.

"Well." Akile paused. She had seen my film on the subject, *A Veiled Revolution,* which I had produced for Channel 4 Television, London, in 1982.

"Yes and no. It's the same idea perhaps, but expressed differently. Turkey is not Egypt," she added gently.

Don't generalize, in other words. "Yes, Akile. I'm just trying to find my bearing in a new place, a new Muslim place."

"Remember that Turkey is not Muslim the same way that Egypt is Muslim," she cautioned.

We were interrupted again by the arrival of Ayten, Akile's cheerful young maid, who banged in, bearing shopping bags full of groceries. She greeted us with a smile and a bob of her scarf-covered head, and Akile translated her enthusiastic announcement:

"Some good lamb today, madame. We'll have it with lentils, okay?"

"Okay," Akile agreed.

"Now, Akile," I said, "what about her? She wears a scarf and loose clothing. Is she part of the new Islamic movement, women covering up?"

"No, no, no," answered Akile. "She's wearing the traditional scarf of rural Turkish women. What's going on today is quite different. The modern new dress is called *tesettür,* or the modest dress code. Women are wearing different clothes, tying scarves differently. There are many practices, you'll see."

I had watched Ayten when she came to clean Akile's spacious apartment with its windows facing the sea; to iron Ali's shirts on the screened-in porch that looked over the garden; to cook vegetables and meat with spices I had never used. Her head scarves were, as they say, a treat. A different one every day. Flowered scarves in greens and pinks, golden paisley on black scarves painted in abstract designs, crimson and navy blue. But all the scarves had hand-tatted borders, crocheted edging in a dizzying variety of patterns, tiny circles and squares, flower petals, and once, a border of small orange carrots!

"Ayten's scarves carry messages," said Akile, smiling. "She would probably laugh if I told her that, but that's what it is. Those borders told people in the old villages whether a woman was married or single. They still do, I guess."

"Palestinian embroidery on women's dress does the same," I said.

"The language of clothing," suggested Akile.

"The language of the scarf is not the language of the veil," I offered, and we both laughed.

Ayten interrupted to ask where Shorsha was.

"I'm surprised she cares," Akile confided, "because most Turks are not exactly dog lovers. But when we took in the puppy, and I expected hostility from Ayten, she lectured me on our responsibility, since the dog was a living thing God had made!"

I glanced at Ayten, who was smiling indulgently at us. Could I interview her some time? When Akile asked her, she laughed out loud. Her reply, roughly translated, went something like this: "What would I have to say that would be important or interesting, but sure, I'd be happy to talk to your friend if she wants. Maybe day after tomorrow, when lunch is finished?"

The more I talked with Akile and other Turkish women, the more I realized that *tesettür,* the new modest dress, was a complex symbol of many other things going on in Turkish society: the move from country to city, the weakening of family ties, the need for women to work, the old battle between secular and religious ideas about nationalism. With its history of women's concerns, women's rights, early feminist thought, Turkey posed a much more complex mix of attitudes and developments than was the case in other countries. The veil itself, unlike the rural colorful scarves, was a blind spot with Turkish intellectuals, men as well as women, just as it was a blind spot with Western intellectuals, especially feminist intellectuals, for whom "no veil" equaled progress, whereas veils or even modest dress equaled backwardness.

Akile was right to remind me that the situation of women in Istanbul, the great cosmopolitan capital that spanned two continents and many civilizations, was different from that which obtained in rural Turkey, where women's lives had changed little from past ways, despite Atatürk's reforms. Ayten's language of scarves was still used among men and women of Anatolia, but that language was very different from the verbal battles over *tesettür* currently being waged in Istanbul, in Ankara, and, to a lesser degree, in some of the larger cities like Izmir and Bursa.

But as I watched Ayten and noted the scarves on the heads of women on the streets, I wondered why anyone would give up such an attractive and meaningful head covering for the plain white scarf and long drab overcoat of the Islamist women. Were those plain garments a loud statement of Islamic identity? Or something more? A reaction against the rural norms? Because Ayten, when I did interview her, insisted that she covered her head because of Muslim custom.

"My scarf?" she echoed, in Akile's translation. We sat at the dining room table together and Ayten answered my questions quickly, easily. She seemed to be enjoying herself.

"Yes, well in the holy book it says to cover your head. It has to do with belief in God. We all know it. It's sinful to go around uncovered."

Akile and I, both with our heads uncovered, looked at each other, and Ayten, seeing us, blushed in embarrassment, the rosy color in her cheeks sweeping upward, past those straight black brows above dark eyes, to be buried in the scarf edging her forehead.

"Oh," she said. "I didn't mean to insult. We're used to it. You're not," she said to Akile, "and as for Madame . . ."

"I'm a Christian, not a Muslim. . . ."

She nodded vigorously. "That's it. Yes."

Here was Ayten, a girl from the village now living in Istanbul, traveling one and a half hours by bus each day to Akile's house, and the same time back. She was representative, Akile said, of the majority of Turkish women, even those living in the city. But Ayten kept her ties to the village—going back twice a year for the chestnut harvest, the

Islamic feasts. She was religious, but an independent woman. Could she be considered an Islamic feminist?

When I asked, she looked puzzled. "I don't know what you mean, madame."

"But you wear the scarf to cover your head, and yet you're working hard outside the house, and . . ."

"So I follow the Qur'an. I cover my head." She smiled. "So what does that have to do with what else I do?"

Akile and I looked at each other. I tried once more.

"What about your daughters?"

"Oh well," she said airily. "I want them to study and get clever and maybe then they won't want to wear the scarf. The more educated and cultured women are, the less they cover up it seems."

I opened my mouth. "Even today?"

"Oh, you mean very religious women. Okay. I see. Well, I believe in God, and I try to follow the holy book, but I'm not that religious. My daughters will do what they want. Maybe they will wear the scarf, maybe they won't. They'll still practice their religion, though. Now I have to get back to the vegetables or you ladies won't have much dinner tonight!"

She got up, and retied her scarf, so the little tatted flowers formed a pleasing border along her face. Quite fetching. I did not have the heart to point out the contradiction in her statement . . . she had to wear it, according to Qur'anic admonition, yet her daughters didn't? But I couldn't resist one last question.

"What would you tell American women?" I called out, following her into the kitchen, where she was chopping spinach.

She laughed hilariously. "I have trouble thinking of such matters," she said. "What could I possibly say that would mean anything to them, so rich and far away."

"No, seriously, Ayten," put in Akile.

She set down her knife, raised one finger to scratch her head under that flower-bedecked scarf, and looked out at the shimmering sea.

"I want to say that many people are happy here," she told me. "They shouldn't think we are unhappy. Look at me. I didn't want to get married, but my parents said I must and that my husband was a good man. So I did. And now I have two daughters and live in Istanbul and my husband *is* a good man. And I am happy."

Feminism or at least efforts to improve women's lives seemed alive and well in Turkey. The women's library had already become a landmark in the city, though some women I met accused it of elitism. And I was meeting many women—and men—who were involved in a multitude of what might be termed feminist activities.

"We need both intellectual feminism and activism," said Akile, who took me for long walks each evening along the Bosporus. While we strolled in those early spring evenings, she was kind enough to listen to my adventures of the day, such as an interview with Laila D., who worked for the newly founded women's secretariat of the Turkish government.

"We are underfunded, but we're working hard," Laila D. had said. "I suppose it's the same in America?"

I agreed.

What was the goal of the secretariat, I asked her. "To document women's experience in employment, salary, promotion, sexual harassment, health. To create the data base on which policy may be enacted," she replied.

One day I had coffee with Alev Alatli, a popular and avant-garde Turkish novelist, whose work among the poor women of the squatter settlements was well known, but who insisted she was not a feminist. "Let's not waste our time on labels," she said tartly.

"Oh, but what she does is very important," several women said when I described that meeting. One added, "And her novels are groundbreaking, looking at relations between East and West—that's a kind of feminist statement, too. She even had you as a character in one, B.J. You were a Western feminist come to ask questions of Turkish feminists; did you meet her when you were here before?"

I confessed that I had.

And I listened while Akile commented and cautioned and told me about other groups, new and old, dealing with women's issues, which she termed "central political issues." There was a feminist legal aid committee, a group which worked with battered women; there were many study groups, including Hand in Hand (Women and Goddesses), and there was the Foundation for the Support of Women's Work, begun by Sengül Akcur, about which everyone spoke warmly, and which Ceylan Orhun had arranged for me to visit.

"You'll go to the *gecikondus* [the squatter settlements]?" Akile asked. "The foundation works with women in these settlements, and it's very important to actually see the places."

"Ceylan promised."

Ceylan was waiting for me at the Hilton Hotel on Taksim Square, the center of Istanbul's business and tourist district. Over lunch (grilled chicken, fresh arugula salad, apple tea), she filled me in on the history of the foundation we were about to visit and her own beliefs about what feminism should be.

"We are practical—helping women to earn money—but also spiritual in our outlook," she began.

"Spiritual?"

Ceylan nodded. She wore wonderful turquoise earrings, the same silver bracelets she'd worn at the women's library, and a fashionable flowery print dress under the tweed jacket.

"Yes, spirituality. I have been given the time and the means to do what I want in this world. I want to give it back."

"How do you see yourself doing that?"

"Well," said Ceylan, "I write about women of course, short stories and articles in the media; and I've gotten into what you would call a New Age project, writing about goddesses and food."

The restaurant was full. Young men and older men, mostly businessmen by the look of their crisp suits and silk ties, sat with their laptop computers, their leather briefcases with brass edges and handles beside them. A young woman sitting alone was talking on her cellular phone while gazing out the window; she started when a smiling young man in one of those crisp suits came up behind her. She smiled and hung up the phone.

"Food, textiles, these are women's work, yes?" Ceylan asked me.

"They've always been described that way."

"And they are part of women's spirituality, part of our relationship to the earth. Spirituality, I honestly believe, must be part of all feminist movements. Isn't it so in America?"

"Well," I temporized. "Yes, there are groups interested in women's spirituality, in the goddess theories, all that."

Ceylan looked at me reproachfully. "You sound like you don't take it very seriously."

"No, no," I said, and then stopped. "Well, to be honest, I don't. I think a lot of not-so-great theories have been propounded, supported by no data at all."

"On goddesses, female goddesses?" Ceylan laughed. "Turkey is full of them. Don't you remember the lecture at the women's library by Professor Erdener?"

I did remember it. I also remembered my uneasiness with the wing of the American intellectual feminist movement that tried to posit a matriarchy, a rule by women in some shadowy past. The proof that matriarchy existed? Goddesses, in ancient Sumer and Babylon and Greece and Rome. I had been always careful to tell my women's studies' classes that such data was interesting, but purely speculative. Reverence for a powerful saintly woman did not translate necessarily into political power for nonsaintly women, I said, and would cite my own experience as a teenage member of the all-female Sodality of the Blessed Virgin Mary. Though we revered the Virgin, membership in her sodality did not mean that I, or any other woman for that matter, had any power in the hierarchy of the Roman Catholic Church.

"You don't think there was ever a matriarchy in the world, do you, Ceylan?"

"Of course not. But I think there was a different scene than what we have in the patriarchy of today. More egalitarian relations between men and women. Look at the Turkish experience! Look at Çatal Höyük!"

Çatal Höyük. The Neolithic site in central Turkey. Well, she was right there. Only in the last generation had the historical picture of male/female relations begun to change with the discovery of not just Çatal Höyük, but many Neolithic towns and villages on the central Anatolian plateau, including Asikli Hüyük, near where Füsün Ertug was working.

"Yes, Ceylan." I paused. "We have much to learn from Turkey."

"Our foundation's project for the Beijing conference is called Project Çatal Höyük, in honor of those discoveries, which are changing the way the sexes think about each other."

I waited. "How's that?" I asked finally.

"We need a new goal for feminism," she said. "We need to unite the masculine and feminine aspects in women and in men, so the new generation will be better, happier, more adapted to our beautiful earth."

I said nothing.

"Don't you agree, B.J.?"

"Oh yes, but how?"

"First get real with history, right? Women were important, right?"

"Why do we need a precedent?"

"So we can get the power to change things. There are lots of feminists here in Turkey, but we still aren't very powerful politically. We have to show we were strong in the past to get strong now."

Ceylan took my silence for assent, and stood up.

"So, then, we are agreed, American feminists and Turkish feminists."

"Yes." I stood up too. "But, Ceylan, what about Islamic feminists? Are their goals the same as ours?"

We walked through the crowds of businessmen and businesswomen assembled in the Hilton Hotel lobby: Japanese, German, and Spanish were languages I recognized. We swung through the revolving doors and onto Taksim Square, the top of the hill, noisy with cars and buses; no white scarves and dark coats visible. We were heading for the street-car, which would take us to the Foundation for the Support of Women's Work.

"B.J., my friend, some of the religious intellectual women are stronger feminists than I am, at least in their writings. They're examining the roots of our traditions. Good for them!"

"I think I've heard that before," I murmured.

"You have. From Sirin. And you will hear it again. What secular and religious women need to do is stand together. We'll all be stronger for learning about each other. But cutting each other down weakens us all." She paused, smiling. "Now let's get to the foundation. They're waiting for us."

Istanbul's streetcars, binging along on the shining rails fixed into the ancient cobblestones of the old central city, reminded me of the cable cars in San Francisco. Many were clearly designed for the same land-scape, steep hills, damp streets, often slippery with rain. They were old, painted bright red and green, and always crowded as they maneuvered through the hills of the city by the sea.

As the Galata Tower loomed ahead, we jumped down and cut into a dark doorway between rows of electrical parts shops and a pushcart full of bright red tomatoes and purple and white turnips, glistening with water that the vendor was sprinkling over them from a small saucer in his grubby hand.

"This is the foundation," said Ceylan. She greeted the doorman, who sat in a rickety bentwood chair at the entrance. He nodded and gave us a toothless grin.

"The people of the neighborhood have been really wonderful, B.J. And you know what, I've bought an apartment in this building, at the very top, with a great view of the Golden Horn. An artist has bought the one next to me."

The entry was dark and obviously there was no elevator. We started up, and I found I was quickly out of breath, climbing the very steep, narrow, and shaky iron stairs that wound up and up and up . . . to a landing where, through a half-open door, women's voices reached us, raised in strong disagreement.

"Come!" called Ceylan. "Greet our visitor. She's an American who's writing about feminism in Muslim countries."

Several women were seated in the dim room, around a large table covered with jars. Jars of jam? Food? They seemed to be pasting labels on the jars, arguing fiercely as they did so. Could this really be the staff of the famed Foundation for the Support of Women's Work, spending their time pasting labels on jars of canned food? I used to do this myself as a child with my mother, when she had finished the fall canning.

As if to answer my unspoken question, Ceylan announced that these jars were part of the Turkish women's food project for Beijing: quince jam, eggplant preserves, tomatoes, turnip pickles, all products of local women. And they were also being marketed in the health food stores of Istanbul and Ankara, and earning money for these women.

One of the seated helpers looked up. She was wearing two ancient sweaters, one gray, one brown, and her gray hair was pulled back into a bun, grandmother style.

She said to me, "I'm surprised you've come to see us. American women have never seemed interested in anybody but themselves."

"Oh, Auntie, please!" Ceylan raised her voice. "She's our guest!"

But the older woman would not be silenced. She smiled at me pleasantly enough and added, "I am sorry, I should have said that American women do seem to be interested in Muslim women who wear *veils*. We don't, so who cares about us?"

I murmured something to the effect that everyone in Istanbul spoke about the foundation in glowing terms and I had come to see for myself.

The old lady looked up at me intently, nodded, and went back to her labeling. Through the glass jars with their brass lids, the eggplant preserves gleamed purple in their glistening oil.

In a gentler tone, she said, "We're active feminists here. We are more concerned with women less fortunate than with our own *selves.*"

Ceylan tugged me gently on the arm. "B.J., this is Sengül Akcur, she's the founder, the president, whatever."

She was a tall woman, dark hair pulled away from her face, simply dressed in slacks and a heavy brown turtleneck, which was softened by a filmy scarf and a string of black beads. She shook my hand, a strong grip. Her black beads clinked. She led me to another corner of the foundation headquarters and sat us down on a brown corduroy settee, not new, but neat and clean. Ceylan brought us cups of Nescafé.

"The food project is a good one for poor women?" I inquired.

"Yes, I think so." Madame Akcur looked at Ceylan. "Catering, canning, preserving. We have some marketing problems with the preserved foods, but the catering is going well—they're making money cooking for parties, large groups. Yes."

Ceylan smiled. "Go on, Sengül. Tell her."

"Okay, I will. B.J., even in our activist feminist group, we have ideological differences."

"Like what?"

"Whether the menus of the catering ladies and the preserved foods we are trying to market represent 'authentic' Turkish cuisine or not."

Without thinking, I said, "Why does it matter?"

"Why indeed?" said Madame Akcur in a low voice. Then, clearing her throat, she spoke up firmly. "Let me tell you about this foundation. It's different, I think, from similar foundations you may have encountered during your travels in Muslim lands. And it may help to have some background before you set out to visit one of our projects today."

I took out my notebook.

"Maybe I should start by explaining that historically in Turkey, all services come from the top, and we think that's why they fail. Atatürk, you know, *decreed* that women should no longer wear the veil. Women themselves had nothing to say about it. They were not consulted, of course. We're trying a new way."

"Which is?"

"First, getting to know the women we are trying to help, the women in the *gecikondus,* the squatter settlements. Getting them to trust us. Getting to know their needs. Then creating a project with the women themselves."

"What are their main problems?"

Ceylan and Sengül both began talking at once, stopped, deferred to each other. Ceylan rose. "I have to go," she said. "B.J., you are in good hands. Sengül is the mother of us all!"

"Problems! Do these women have problems! First, they are very poor."

"But many people are poor in Turkey!"

"Yes! Yes!" Madame Akcur's eyes flashed. "But these women in the *gecikondus* have come from the country—they have no support systems. In the newest settlements, they live in shacks with the animals, worse conditions than in the village! They need work, but they also need health clinics, and day care, and people to talk to. How can they work if they don't have child care?"

"And the government ministries don't encourage things like this? I know Egypt tries."

Madame Akcur looked at me, turned away, made a face.

"Yes, the government does try. I say that charitably. Because what they do is ridiculous—they teach women to paint Mickey Mouse on glasses. It's junk. Who will buy it? Women can't make money this way.

And that's the point, to help women make money and ease their lives."

"Even if what they are selling is not authentic."

Madame Akcur inclined her head. "I take your point. Yes." She paused. "Now you should go and see for yourself, as you said earlier. Pinar will take you."

Squatter settlements are scarcely a new phenomenon. Historically, all peoples left homeless by disasters such as flood, fire, earthquake, tornado, and war have tried to shelter themselves afterward. When the natural disaster has passed, new homes may be built, and life may return to some kind of normal routine. But since the end of World War II, the development of industrialization and the rise in population, different housing pressures have been building in countries all over the world, as millions of rural peoples have migrated to the cities in search of employment and better living conditions. What happened in America in the early part of the twentieth century, the move from farm to city, has been happening in the Third World for the past forty years, but much more swiftly and with far more severe consequences. A squatter settlement, called a favela in Rio or a bidonville in Casablanca is called a *gecikondu* in Turkey. *Gecikondu* means "settled at night," i.e., a house literally built overnight to take advantage of an old Turkish law that stayed the hand of an official demolisher if the house to be demolished was already in place and inhabited.

In 1987, one third of the ten million people in Istanbul lived in *gecikondus*. Three million officially. Probably many more. Half of them women. Working class. Poor. This was the focus group of the Foundation for the Support of Women's Work. The foundation has built and now runs three kindergartens, which double as community centers. These are the places where the women's food projects originate.

My visit was to a *gecikondu* settlement called Kocasinan. We drove for an hour through the heavy traffic of central Istanbul and headed north through nearly empty land, then spent another twenty minutes zooming along the highway. Pinar and her friend Can sat in front, talking animatedly together; my seatmate, Fügen, was silent.

"It seems very far," I ventured, in a pause in the conversation.

"That's part of the problem," said Pinar over her shoulder. "No one sees these communities. They are not in view, so we can forget about them."

I had prepared myself for a collection of sad huts with corrugated iron roofs, animals defecating in the muddy ruts, children running barefoot, crying. But we drove into what looked like a middle-class suburb. A main street was lined with shops; the fragrant smell of fresh bread drifted from a bakery. Three- or four-story apartment blocks stood along neat sidewalks fronting well-paved roads. The driver came to a stop outside a low building, and children burst out the door, holding fast to motherly adult hands. I had been brought to the child care center of Kocasinan, "one of the first projects of the foundation," said Pinar, and from surface appearances, clearly a successful one.

Pinar led the way into the center. For a facility caring for one hundred small children, it seemed very quiet.

"They're napping," explained the two young women who greeted us. "This is the second session. The first session just left."

I was given the tour: small shoes on shelves, small jackets neatly hung up. We were offered shower caps to cover our shoes, as was the custom here, but I took mine off instead and added them to the pile by the door. This, I was told, was the model, the pilot project for the foundation's two other centers; still another was under construction. Two more were on the drawing board but more funds must be raised.

"So?" Pinar turned to me.

I said that I had expected shacks and poverty.

"In the beginning, yes, it was like that," said Pinar. "It was awful. You have to realize that the people have literally created this place. First came the shacks, then small cabins, now the modern suburb you see. And since they built it all, they have forced the government to put in sewage and water and electricity."

I must have looked as doubtful as I felt.

"Hundreds of thousands of people—millions, actually is what we're talking about," Pinar explained. "And they vote."

"But there's still poverty? It doesn't look like it to me."

"Even here, the women need us. They need child care. In some of the new *gecikondus* the people have nothing—they live in huts and shacks like you expected. We want to move into those *gecikondus* when we have more money."

We walked around the nap rooms, which were simply the classrooms with pads laid on the floor, children resting, small chairs piled against the bright blue walls, where murals of paper cut-out animals were pinned. A row of puppets hung on hooks from a coat rack, and nearby were tables of glue, bundles of branches, piles of newspaper, cast-off plastic containers.

"Puppets?"

"Yes, a Turkish tradition, you know. At a parents' meeting, one of the fathers volunteered to make some puppets for us to use in the kindergarten. He works with a puppet theater. When we pointed out we had no funds for materials, he said he didn't need any: he could use junk, and he did. The branches and newspaper and plastic bottles."

I admired a puppet sheep with papier-mâché wool, a donkey, a bird, an old man with a beard and a purple papier-mâché turban.

"Yes," said Pinar. "They're good, aren't they? He's got some older children interested and they come and work with him after school. Now we have several orders from a small factory to make the puppets for sale." She smiled. "Everything helps."

"How did you all get into this project?" I asked the four workers as we sat around a wooden table in a sunny corner of the center. We could hear the children calling and chattering, up from naps for snacks, the same as ours: homemade cheese rolls, and *ayram* to drink, that delicious Turkish mix of yogurt and water.

The visit, surprisingly short, seemed over and I drove back to Istanbul with some of the young women staff members, whom I questioned about the relationship between their work and what we think of as feminism:

PINAR: None of us were active in the eighties, in the women's movement.

CAN: I was put off by the militant feminism.

FÜGEN: I wanted to work not for elite women, but for ordinary women, *real* women.

CAN: I heard you talked at the women's library. I think it's great but it's for a small rich group, not for us. Here we work *with* women, we don't impose our ideas from above.

FÜGEN: Did Sengül tell you? The food project was created by a woman from the *gecikondu*.

They talked about child care, kindergarten, puppetry, food preserving, and catering. About nutrition classes, health classes for women and babies, sewing classes, parents' meetings. These, they said, were all part of the *gecikondu* programs sponsored by the foundation, supported by donations from Turkish citizens. I looked at the bright faces of these young women who were working for minimum wages, who seemed to enjoy what they were doing. And I wondered privately what all these good works had to do with the ideological struggles over women's status currently in process in Turkey between secularly oriented groups and religiously oriented groups. Perhaps women were being used in larger political games, as they have been in many countries in the past, and continue to be used today. This had actually been suggested to me by several Turkish women:

"Sometimes I think the media is purposely setting us against each other, fundamentalist women and secular women. This is a mistake. We have many things in common. We're all Turks. We're all Muslims."

"Women don't have too many problems with each other. But men always try to manipulate us."

"After all, it's your *intent* that's important, as the Qur'an says, not whether you're a man or a woman. We have a woman prime minister and what good does it do? She has not a good intent. She's not interested in people's problems, men or women. She only wants to stay in power."

"And what is *tesettür* after all? A way of dressing. Women should have a choice, to wear what they want. The secular authorities are discriminating against women who wear this dress—suspending them from jobs, and so on. And then they criticize the religious officials *(ulema)* in Iran for doing the same thing if women don't dress the way *they* want."

Could feminism in Turkey be expressed in both secular and religious terms? I realized I had to interview some Islamist women before I could begin to understand.

Akile agreed, but she added, "Don't forget the issue of class, B.J. It's just as important as gender here. You need to interview an upper-class Islamist and a working-class one."

"Where does your maid, Ayten, figure in all this?"

"Ayten? A different point of view entirely." Akile smiled. "And maybe the most important. For the majority of Turkish women are just like Ayten, village women now living in the city. They've brought their values with them. That complicates things."

Resolving to interview Islamist women was one thing. Reaching them was another. But once more, friends came to my rescue. Halit Refiq, one of the most distinguished figures in Turkish cinema, invited Akile and me to dinner. When I told him what I hoped to do, he said almost immediately, "You must talk to Ayse Sasa."

Gulpër, his musician wife, agreed. "She is something else, B.J. We've known her for years, a real free spirit, and suddenly, whap! She's wearing a head scarf and covering up and taking us to the Sufi Center once a week for the musical ritual and the sermons. . . ."

Halit snorted. "We're reasonable Muslims," he said. "We don't need this . . ."

"But the music, Halit, and the whirling . . ." Gulpër's voice was throaty, enthusiastic. "I loved it. Come on, you did, too."

"Very good dessert, Gulpër," said Halit, changing the subject. "You like it, B.J.?"

"What is it?"

"A very famous Turkish dessert, made with breast of chicken pureed. Isn't that right, Gulpër? Then they whip it all up with cream and flour and put it in the oven."

Gulpër was not to be put off. "And you know, B.J., Ayse tells me there are centers like this for women only now—different rituals, different music. Let's go!"

"I'd love to."

"But first Ayse Sasa; I'll arrange it," said Halit, with an ambiguous glance at his beautiful wife.

Ayse Sasa was a well-known screenwriter and filmmaker who had recently made a public declaration that she was a born-again Muslim. A long interview with her, complete with portrait, appeared in 1995 in the most widely read of the new Turkish magazines directed to the religiously minded audience.

"I have been saved by Islam," she told me. "Literally it has saved my life. Believe me!"

We were seated in an office of the new Istanbul Film Center, an impressive teaching and production studio around which I had just been given the tour by Halit Refiq. Ayse was at home here; she had been greeted in the hall by the young administrators, for her work throughout the past twenty years had put her in touch with most of the figures in the Turkish film industry. It was close to four o'clock, but it had been raining, a cold bone-chilling rain, not at all spring-like, and the sky was already darkening, anticipating evening.

Halit had seated himself behind his desk, eyeing Ayse with an expression I could not identify. Finally he spoke:

"What kind of Islam are we talking about, Ayse? I'm a Muslim, the majority of people here in Turkey, ninety-nine percent, are Muslim. You yourself were born a Muslim . . ."

"Yes, in name only, in name *only*," said Ayse, emphasizing the last phrase. "Please, Halit, do give me a cigarette. I need one. And, my friend, try to understand what has happened to me to give my life meaning for the first time ever."

Halit did not smoke. But he went out, found someone in the hallway with cigarettes, and brought one back to Ayse. "Ayse, we've had this conversation before," he said shortly. "I'll leave you—I have some recordings to check—and let B.J. interview you by herself."

He paused by the door. "Will you need a ride home?" he asked. "I'm taking B.J. back."

"Thank you, thank you, my dear, but my car and driver are coming soon."

Ayse inhaled deeply, and then exhaled; the smoke hung between us in the cold, still air. A tall, slender woman, middle-aged, she was wearing beiges and blacks—beige cashmere sweaters, a black long skirt; a black abbayah of fine wool, which was draped around her when she swept into Halit's office and was now folded over the chair in which she sat. But her head was wrapped in black, framing a face not beautiful, but not plain either, a startling face with rather high cheekbones, deep dark eyes, and a full mouth, which she compressed into a thin line when she pulled on the obviously much-appreciated cigarette. Ayse, in her muted, well-cut Islamic-style garments, was a presence, clearly. Articulate. Proud. She sat slightly forward on the hard chair.

I cleared my throat. "Tell me about your family," I began.

"Family? Oh, please. My parents are dead, I have been married and divorced three times—*never* have I had the peace I have now."

She told me in some detail about her revelation, the way in which her rediscovery of the religious faith into which she was born had saved her from depression, "from madness," she insisted. "I have never been so calm and contented."

I asked how she practiced that new belief.

"Every day of my life. In prayer, yes, but also in my written work. I've incorporated my religious experience into my new collection of essays on film theory." She produced a paperback from a voluminous black leather bag and handed it to me. It was in Turkish. I apologized for not being able to read it.

"It's sold very well," she announced and took it back. "Third edition. Also I am now a Sufi practitioner. Every week. The music, the sermons, the prayers, and yes, the ecstasy!" Once more she exhaled smoke, which rose higher into the cold air like a great opaque bubble. She gestured toward it. "The unseen!" she said enigmatically. "The Sufis consider the unseen as part of life, they try to incorporate it into the seen, what we know, that is, the world of our everyday life. They try to see the *other* unseen dimension. I, too, now try."

I was sympathetic to her enthusiasm, for I, too, had seen and admired the Sufi rituals in North Africa. But I said that I thought Atatürk had shut down all the *tekkes,* the Sufi religious lodges, and banned Sufi practice by the *tariqas,* including the ritual whirling of the Mevlevi dervishes of Konya.

"Yes, you are right. Now they are open again. But they are not *tekkes* these days but cultural centers or folklore centers. And people flock to them. A very wonderful experience, you must come. Many tourists and non-Muslims do. You are welcome. Please. As my guest."

"I would love to." I paused. She was peering out the window.

"So you think Islam is good for women?" I asked.

She stared at me. "What? Good for women? What does that mean? Islam has saved my life. I am a woman. So of course it's good for women."

She peered out the window again.

A black car was drawing up to the curb. "For me," she said, indicating it.

She stood up, ground out the last of that borrowed cigarette, rewrapped herself in her black robe, shook my hand, and, with much panache, moved out the door. The chauffeur, I noticed through the window, stood in the rain holding the passenger door open for her.

Halit drove me back to Akile's house through the rain, so grimy this evening from the smog that the streetlights were a dull yellow. Halit said, "I feel I am the best kind of Muslim, B.J. No fanaticism. Not like these new ones."

"Gulpër said the other night that you went to the Sufi meeting with Ayse."

"Yes. It was a very interesting spectacle. But it did not move me. I was an observer only."

"Ayse *is* moved, I think," I answered. "Her feelings are real, honest ones."

Before answering, Halit maneuvered around a bicycle which was sliding on the dark slippery street and honked at a motorist pulling out unexpectedly in front of him.

"Well, yes, I believe they are, you are right, B.J. I don't agree with her new understanding of Islamic belief, but it has helped her a lot. I don't knock it. She's had lots of emotional problems. Gulpër also thinks it's helped her. We've been friends for thirty-five years, after all. We've done a lot of films together. We respect each other."

I asked about Ayse's new book.

Halit was struggling with the horrendous traffic again, the lines of cars moving six inches at a time along the hills, the main streets leading to the bridges lit by smoky yellow lights under the smoggy dripping sky.

"I'll give her that," he said, nodding to himself. "She continues to work. She's trying to develop a new film theory based on Islamic metaphysics. She has disciples you know. She's highly respected in the Muslim community, her work *is* interesting. I call it dream cinema theory."

"She told me it was something like getting at the unseen through the seen," I said. "Would that be more like Sufi metaphysics?"

Halit nodded. He quoted the blurb on the back of her new book, a statement written by Ayse herself. " 'It is said that technology has separated reason from the senses of our life,' our being maybe. I'm not exactly sure of the translation, B.J., but that's the idea. And then she says, 'If it is possible to make this connection again, that is the Sufi goal.' "

Ayten. Ayse. Akile. Gulpër. Alev. Laila D. Sirin. Ceylan. Sengül. Impressive women: but all upper class, except for Ayten, who was working class. But she was from the country, and according to Akile, representative of the majority of Turkish women. For even though Turkey was now mostly urban, the new migrants brought village mores with them. What did I know about rural women? Based on my limited experience, it was difficult to judge whether Ayten's experience and outlook were typical, whether her Islam was more or less like that of the new religious groups and the secular Kemalists. Were there Sufi revivals in the countryside? Sharon Bastŭg, who taught at Ankara's Middle East Technical University, said by phone that there were indeed new groups, new garbs, new ways of wearing and tying scarves. I said I was hoping to get to Ankara, perhaps to go farther east and visit the village where Füsün Ertug was living, the anthropologist who had talked about women's work during our session at the women's library.

"Let's have Füsün to lunch," suggested Akile. "She's a friend, and she is still in town, I think. Ask her whether you could come visit. If it's not appropriate, she'll say so."

Kizilkaya. The village next to Asikli Hüyük. That was where Füsün was. On the map of Turkey, Kizilkaya lay south of Karaman but Füsün had said it was also near Aksaray, in south central Anatolia. Aksaray was a well-known site where Turkish archaeologists had been excavating ruins of ancient cities from the Akkadian, Roman, and Byzantine eras for many years. It was southeast of Ankara. Perhaps I could visit both village and city?

I remembered my earlier trip to Anatolia in 1987, when the wonderful air-conditioned Varan buses headed out of the magic city of Istanbul, over the hills and away from the sea and from the smog, and the crowds of people. I remembered the long, flat, seemingly empty plain on the other side of the hills, stretching as far as we could see, going on and on along the Black Sea coast. On Turkey's eastern border lay Russia to the north and in the south, Iran. Travelers had not been kind to Anatolia, describing it as barren and bleak. Gertrude Bell wrote, "It is the Ancient East, returned after so many millenniums of human endeavor to its natural desolation." That was 1909.

But somehow Gertrude Bell had not noticed the grazing lands, the lakes on the plateau, the mountains, extinct volcanoes whose soil, they say, is ideal for raising grapes—and horses. Those old mountains rose like far-distant smoke on the horizon, but we stopped at a lake or two and stayed the night in Ürgüp, center of Cappadocia, where the fantastic rock formations have provided cave shelter for political refugees and religious dissidents for centuries and now strange sights for the tourists to marvel at. We stayed in a hotel, the Evyan, which had been literally carved from the rock, and was lit by lanterns which cast shadows on the rough stone walls, on the patterned red-and-beige kilim rugs and the handmade wooden tables and chairs, reminiscent of European country furniture. And I remembered the women's scarves. Every woman we saw had her head wrapped in a colorful scarf like Ayten's and all seemed to have different hand-crocheted edging— daisies, carrots, grapes. A language of scarves. A different landscape. Different customs. And these were being added to the city tradition, which at first appeared more secular, more Western in outlook. Were the women who wore the white scarves and the dark coats generally rural migrants? "Some, maybe," agreed Akile. "But mostly they are the second generation of village women, those who have grown up and gone to school in the city."

On the 1987 trip, I had hoped to visit the ruins of Çatal Höyük, that ancient Neolithic town Ceylan had talked about, the town whose discovery in the 1960s opened up a whole new chapter in human history. Even before visiting Anatolia, I had talked about Çatal Höyük in my Middle East courses at the University of Texas, using the evidence from the excavations to suggest that patriarchy as we know it was not always present, that men and women may in the past have lived, not in hierarchical positions, but in a more complementary relationship to each other. For archaeologists at Çatal Höyük had discovered no palaces, but only houses, some larger, some smaller, each with its own religious shrine. No monarchs, no spiritual leaders, apparently, but more egalitarian groups. From the remarkable paintings on the excavated walls, one could see that women and men wore unisex clothing, including beads. Leopard skins were much in fashion. Men sported Mohawk haircuts. Women were buried with mirrors and beads and weaving tools, men with their tools and beads and weapons.

"Oh, Çatal Höyük is just a pile of stones and a few holes," the guide in Anatolia had said. "You can see it all in the museum. Much better."

So to the museum we had marched, and I stood for a very long time in front of the reconstructed room of a nine-thousand-year-old Çatal Höyük house, its walls decorated with paintings in patterns not unlike those of the kilim rugs in the hotel where we were staying. The head of a longhorn bull was mounted over the fireplace (signifying a man's power, said the printed label) and the full-breasted, large-hipped statue of mother-goddess sat by the hearth (signifying women's creative power, their fertility, said the printed label). I kept thinking of the adobe houses in Santa Fe, with their patterned Navaho rugs, their hearths, their mounted elk heads. The Navaho, too, preserved a kind of matri-focal society, as did many Native American Indian groups, like the Iroquois, where women sat on the high councils.

In 1995, Füsün was telling me that while the men of Çatal Höyük hunted, the women must have gathered plants and herbs, just like the women in Kizilkaya do today. Her eyes shining, Füsün was sitting at Akile's table and talking enthusiastically about her research.

"But I always thought you were a field archaeologist," said Akile, offering cheese and bread and lentil soup and fruit—and *pekmez,* that distinctive paste of grapes that doesn't taste like grapes at all.

"And they probably developed *pekmez,*" went on Füsün, as though Akile had not spoken, covering her slice of bread with that blackish grape spread. "Preserving. Women did that . . ."

"Field archaeologist?" I persisted. "How come you're into village women's work today?"

Füsün smiled. "I have a great adviser at Washington University, B.J., Professor Patty Jo Watson. You know her."

I nodded.

"While I was working with the archaeological team at Asikli Hüyük, I used to go to Kizilkaya, the nearby village, to talk with the women. The more I talked to them, the more interested I became, especially because it turned out that the plants they were gathering, using, cooking, and preserving were possibly the same plants as the seeds we were finding in the ancient sites. That meant these plants might have been eaten and presumably gathered by women for thousands of years!"

"Hunting and gathering societies," put in Akile, "like in the textbooks."

"But you can't find much in the anthropological literature about gathering today," said Füsün. "Nothing! They're always looking at what men do—farm, hunt, herd." She smiled. "But the women's activities, gathering food, spinning, weaving, preservation, and preparation seem just as important to me. Don't you agree?"

I nodded again.

"And," she added, "I know your work, B.J.; Dr. Watson gave it to me, but you don't have anything on this gathering process, either. So I changed . . ."

"And became a social cultural anthropologist like me," finished Akile.

I was thinking that I *must* try to go and visit her village, then shook myself as I realized that I had lost the train of the conversation. Füsün was saying that she thought at first that the women were only gathering herbs, to flavor their food.

"But when the plants were analyzed in the lab in Ankara, the scientists wouldn't believe what they'd found!"

"Yes?" It was Akile.

"Those so-called weeds and herbs were loaded with vitamins and proteins!"

She covered another slice of bread with *pekmez* and I followed suit. A strange taste, but pleasant. Not grapey, what?

"When I went back and told the women in the village, they just smiled and said, 'Well, we told you. Who are those scientists in Istanbul? Have they ever been here, to our village? No. Do they know how we live? No. We couldn't live without those plants. When the crops fail, or the locusts eat the grain or there's no rain, that's all we have to eat.' "

Akile said, "What a shame they lose all that knowledge when they leave the village and come to the city!"

"Not so fast, Akile. Have you ever looked down when you go over the bridge? Or watched women by the Bosporus? I've seen them, in their village scarves, cutting weeds. And we don't even know what they're doing!"

"Füsün."

"Yes, B.J.?"

"Could I ask a great favor? Could I come and visit? Of course," I added quickly, "if it would upset your work, I'd understand."

Füsün put down her bread and clapped her hands together. "I'd love to have you. I'm leaving tomorrow. Could you come two days later? I'd have asked before but I thought you wouldn't want to take so much time."

"How far is it?"

"Two days about, from here. I could meet you, you could spend a couple of days there, two days back, about a week altogether."

"Yes, thank you so much. I would love to come." And I'd stop in Ankara on the way back, I thought.

I was elated! I would soon be off to the village, to see what rural women were doing. For whatever scarves or *tesettür* meant, the bottom line for all women—and men—was survival—food. It was not by chance that one of the demonstrations Turkish women were preparing to take to the Beijing Women's Conference was called Project Çatal Höyük—the project documenting women's contribution to human survival—gathering, preparing, preserving food. Was this feminism? Some would argue that it lay at the base of any movement for change, for it was economic necessity.

And Asikli Hüyük, where Füsün was working, was even older, the grandparent of Çatal Höyük.

I could hardly wait. I had an interview the next day with a young working-class woman, Fatma, who had recently been expelled from nursing school for insisting on wearing the forbidden *tesettür,* the Turkish form of modest or Islamic dress. Dr. Aynur Ilyasoglu, who had recently finished a book about women who had chosen *tesettür,* had arranged the meeting at her house. I would go by taxi, do the interview and the day after, I would be off to Anatolia!

Next morning, I rose early, dressed, and sat down at the dining room table to make notes for my coming interview. Akile and Ali were still asleep, but Shorsha was barking, and barking. I had often taken him out to do his daily business—part of my responsibilities as a long-time guest. And he was a cheerful and lively little dog. Why not right now? A quick walk in the beautiful blossoming morning to collect my thoughts, I decided. Then back for coffee with Akile.

Shorsha, on the leash, went down with me in the elevator to the small back hall, where the doorman, still rubbing sleep from his eyes, greeted me. By this time, I had enough words of Turkish to greet him back. Shorsha pulled hard on the leash, barking joyfully as the garden grass and flowers came into view. I looked up, stumbled, and the next moment was flat on my face. I had tripped over a tiny step in the hall and crashed down so heavily on the hard, beautiful marble that for a moment I could not move or speak. As I lay there, trembling, Shorsha still yipping, the doorman running to help me up, three thoughts ran through my head: I'm alive, my arm is broken, and I can't go to Asikli Hüyük.

I was right on two counts. But I had not broken my arm, Akile's father's personal surgeon assured me after I had been rushed to the nearest hospital, helped past a long line of Turkish men and women waiting for doctors, and set down in the X-ray room.

"You can write about Turkish hospitals," said Akile lightly, "instead of the village." She knew how much I had looked forward to going.

"Village? What village?" returned the doctor, an elderly man, nearly bald, with stooped shoulders under his regulation white coat. "This lady must rest. She has not actually broken the bone, but muscles and tendons are torn, and the bone is bruised. Pain?"

"Yes," I said.

"Much pain." The doctor nodded. "Here is a prescription. It will ease after maybe ten days. Light exercise after two days. Meanwhile, rest. Rest! Why do you take dogs for walks, madame? I don't understand Americans at all. The dog is the task for a child or a servant, not a guest." He shook his head at my unaccountable behavior.

"I like to take dogs for walks," I muttered rebelliously.

He looked at me and raised a finger, just as my mother used to do when I had somehow erred.

"Rest!" he thundered.

Chastened, and feeling ridiculous ("would-be feminist falls flat," I joked to Akile), I postponed my interview with Fatma and lay down on my guest-room bed. Ayten brought me two pillows so I could prop up my arm. Well then. No village visit. No trip to Ankara. No trip at all. I felt like weeping, and found myself doing exactly that, the throbbing pain in my arm was so intense.

I told myself to be thankful I had not broken my arm, and that I was in such a hospitable Turkish household.

Akile's mother came down to sympathize and brought a selection of soothing herbal teas, all gathered in Turkey, she said. Akile's sister Emine invited us upstairs for dinner—a delicious manti with yogurt sauce, the ravioli of Turkey. The bright conversation of Emine's and her husband's guests, all professors at the university, circled around me, in English and French as well as Turkish, but my responses were minimal, given the effort needed to concentrate on feeding myself as an adult should! I clumsily made do with a soup spoon in my left hand. For after two days, my injured arm hurt even to move. Following doctor's orders, Akile took me for short walks once more along the shores of the Sea of Marmara; we strolled behind a father and son, who shooed the birds, gulls, and doves from the sea, calling and cooing as they waddled on the path in front of us. An old man fished from the pier; we bemoaned the demise of a fine old mansion of intricate carved wood that was falling apart, not far from the beach. A pair of young lovers sat on the new grass, below a stand of snowy-blossomed apple trees.

I told myself again how lucky I was to be in Istanbul in spring, even with an injured arm, the apple trees a froth of white, lilacs bordering the gardens, white and purple, their scent filling the streets. One day the wind blew so hard that the sycamore trees, shedding their pollen unexpectedly, covered the streets and taxis with a fine yellow dust.

"All Turks love flowers," Akile's mother said. Her parents had invited us to an elegant lunch in their penthouse apartment, where carnations and new purple tulips graced the table.

"They are all there, the flowers," said Akile's father, "in the ceramics and in the old paintings. The most famous portrait of Sultan Mehmed II shows him smelling a rose. Remember, Akile?"

"I have seen it, too," I answered.

"Turks believe," he said, "that the portrait indicates the Sultan's wisdom—a powerful man who recognizes the beauty of the nature he tries to control."

"Have more tea, my dear," said Akile's mother solicitously. "It will help you to get well."

Rows of white and pink roses blowing in the spring breeze lined the front windows of Aynur's tiny house, where the choppy blue sea was visible from every window and where Aynur herself sat in an easy chair with her leg propped up before her in a heavy cast. She had broken her leg two weeks earlier.

Fatma, the young Islamist woman I had come to interview, was making Turkish coffee, her small son hanging on to her knees as she did so, turning his dark head every so often to stare at me.

"We are the walking wounded," I said to lighten the atmosphere, trying and failing to lift my arm, which after a week was fairly comfortable in a sling. If I rested the sling on the arm of a chair, I could even write for a short while, which is what I was preparing to do.

"Doesn't one feel foolish?" Aynur returned. "I just tripped on my own stairs going down to water the roses. I was thinking about something else, not watching where I was going."

"Your roses are very beautiful," I said sincerely, and looked up to thank Fatma as she offered coffee, sat down beside me on the comfortable old sofa, and positioned her son under her arm.

"She says she's ready to answer your questions," Aynur said. "I'll translate as you go along."

Fatma was a slight young woman with a thin, angular face, and dark hair tucked behind her ears; she wore black, a longish skirt and a dark sweater over a yellowish blouse. She watched me intently from huge brown eyes while Aynur explained that she was a "remarkable girl, very strong and very intelligent," whom she, Aynur, had interviewed for her recent book, right after the girl was expelled from nursing school for wearing Islamic dress. Fatma had offered to help Aynur after her accident, and when Aynur could walk again, Fatma would return to her native village, near the Black Sea, and try to negotiate with her family so she could divorce her husband.

Before I could open my mouth for a question, however, Fatma began to talk. She talked. And talked. I was being lectured, it seemed, on the constitution of the perfidious male, her husband (unfaithful, a drunk, a jailbird), and on the requirements of the ideal *Muslim* male (charitable, religious, faithful to his wife and family). "I should have waited, and not married him, but I thought I could change him. I was so depressed after being thrown out of school."

The little boy snuggled up against her; she smiled down at him. "This child is the good that came from that awful marriage," Aynur translated. I interrupted to ask whether she would be able to keep her son in case of divorce.

Fatma did not answer, but turned to Aynur. "You know I worked all the years we were married. So I'm a person who can take care of myself and my son, right, Aynur?"

"You get to keep your son in case of divorce?" I repeated. "Is that Islamic law?"

Fatma looked annoyed, then troubled. "I will keep him," she said firmly. "Islam honors mothers!"

"But the law?" Aynur interposed.

Fatma set her mouth in a firm line and clutched the little boy, who, nearly asleep, blinked his eyes. "My family will help me," she said. "But I may have to stay and help on the farm. And I'd have to live the way village women do—it's hard. So many restrictions."

"But aren't they *Islamic* restrictions?"

"No, no," she burst out. *"Village* restrictions. Old norms, not Islamic principles. Islam is just and kind to women. People have just interpreted it wrongly—Islamism is new, what I believe in, it's not the old norms at all, but *good* norms, *living* Islam."

"What is living Islam?" I asked.

"All of one's life practices," she returned fervently. "Not just the forms, going on the pilgrimage to Mecca like some people who have an identity card that says *Muslim*. No, it's living it!"

"How?" I persisted.

"First one must love God. One must be kind to people, to those in need. It's from the heart. Not to be too harsh and stubborn to anyone. Marriage is part of it, of course, a very important part of it. Faith. Be faithful, too."

"To your husband or wife?"

"Yes, and that's not just in Islam. Any woman would react like I did to his betrayal, sleeping around, wouldn't they? But he said it's natural for a man to do that." She pursed her mouth, trying to contain herself. A tear rolled down her cheek, to be swooped up in a handkerchief with a loud blowing of her nose. The child looked up, troubled.

"Yes," I said, looking across to Aynur, who was silent, letting me run this interview by myself, and then translating for me. "Even in my society, what's okay for men is not okay for women."

Fatma seemed not to hear my words. "The Qur'an," she said fiercely, "makes it clear. If a man betrays his wife in this way, he goes to hell! So if he really believed in Islam, he wouldn't have done it!"

The child pushed out from his mother's arm and went to the window, where he stood quietly, looking out at the straight rows of pink and white rosebushes which framed the rippling blue water, the bridge arching from the European to the Asian side of the Bosporus. Even now, in the middle of the day, the bridge was clogged with slow-moving traffic, trucks, cars, motorbikes, and the smog rose in vaporous gray clouds from their endless exhaust. But against the rosebushes and the pale waving grass at the edge of Aynur's garden, the bridge over the sea and the distant traffic seemed set into a single video frame, a picture of something far away, distant, removed from us in this small, warm, now suddenly quiet room. Aynur, the intellectual, with her foot in a cast; troubled Fatma and her little boy; me, the outsider with the bad arm, questioning, searching.

Fatma turned to me and burst out: "What religion are you, or are you like many Westerners and have no religion?"

"I was brought up Roman Catholic, a Christian," I answered.

"And in your Book does it say that Muhammad will come as a later prophet?"

"No."

Fatma looked puzzled. "Then why are you interested in Muslim women?"

I explained about our years in the Middle East, my writing, my teaching.

Fatma said, "So, on the basis of all your studies, you tell me what *you* think. Does Islam help women or oppress them?"

I considered my answer. "If women are strong and know their rights . . ."

Fatma interrupted, laughing. "You're the one who's being interviewed now, madame, isn't that true, Aynur?"

Aynur smiled. Fatma's little boy had returned to her lap and was winding a strand of her dark wavy hair around his finger. She shook her head, tossing the hair back away from her face and those intense brown eyes.

"If women are strong enough and know their rights according to the Qur'an," I repeated, "then women in Islam should be reasonably well off. Except for polygamy, which is illegal here in Turkey. But the Qur'an allows it."

Fatma sat up straight, dislodging the little boy who rolled into the other corner of the sofa and proceeded to go to sleep.

"Well, that would be possible in my real living Islam only with my permission," she said, a bit too loudly.

"The Qur'an doesn't say that the first wife has to give permission," I pointed out, and noted that Aynur was nodding again, yes, yes, yes, almost to herself.

Fatma said, "I have studied these issues. I have looked carefully into the chapters of Islamic law, as outlined in the Qur'an. It is clear to me that polygamy is not a normal state in Islam. The Prophet does not *approve* of polygamy."

"But it's allowed." Aynur spoke for the first time in her own voice. "Definitely allowed."

Fatma said seriously, "I have thought about this. It seems that in time of war or crisis or something terrible in our country or the world, I would allow my husband to have another woman under his protection." She paused, looked up at me. "Yes. Under his protection only!"

I managed to get out, "I have heard others say that. But does it work out that way in real life?"

Aynur smiled at me. Fatma looked wounded.

"You are so cynical. You don't *believe!* I can deal with all these problems with the help of the Qur'an and my Muslim sisters. Islam is a *modern* religion. It is not passé. It can be applied today. We call it today Islamism. But one cannot be a partial believer. One must be wholehearted." She glared at me. "And I was expelled from nursing school because of my belief. Is that right? The people who did it call themselves Muslims! They are not!"

"What do your parents think of your Islamism?" I asked, hoping to change the direction of the conversation.

Fatma smiled, her mood changed. "They think I'm a bit extremist, but I don't care what they think!"

"Well, that's certainly a new development," said Aynur in English, then translated in response to the younger woman's puzzled look.

"Yes, it's new," Fatma said, "a new and useful old belief—Islamism! I have found it—I have found faith. No matter they expelled me from nursing school. It wasn't fair, but my faith will keep me. It will work out."

□   □   □   □

On a bright, shimmering day, I was taken up to Bogaziçi University, once Robert College, on the hills above Leander's tower, where I had agreed to conduct a workshop in cross-cultural women's studies. Cliff Andrus, Texas colleague and Fulbright professor of English at Bogaziçi, came to collect me afterward for coffee. He looked bemused.

"Your session was quite acrimonious, I gather," he said. "Everyone was talking about it. What did you say, B.J.?"

I thought back to the workshop. Twelve faculty members, all women, listened politely for the first ten minutes as I held forth about the need to consider what feminism meant in different cultural settings. Then pandemonium broke out as the Turkish women began to argue among themselves.

"It is the same everywhere!"

"Feminism is universal!"

"No, it is not. What about here in Turkey?"

"What you are saying is dangerous. You're suggesting we dilute our principles."

"What principles?" (An angry exchange followed in Turkish which I did not understand. The chair brought us all to order.)

"You know perfectly well what set of principles! Equality, the self. Don't backslide now. We must move against those who challenge us."

"Islamists, you mean?"

"Yes."

"The covering then?"

"No, that's not important."

"Yes, it is."

A young woman to my left looked extremely upset and began to talk about colonialism and post-colonial theory. An older woman dismissed her point peremptorily, interrupting once more and talking about "backsliding." The bell rang, and the chair brought the group to order and asked me to make a final comment. I suggested that it was important to consider women's own expressed needs before formulating any feminist agenda for reform in any country, including the United States. This was followed by grumbling and then a cry from the audience.

"Compromise!" shouted a dark-haired woman, middle-aged, in an elegant suit. "One must never compromise. We *know* what women's needs are."

"But you're not talking about reality!"

"All women deserve our respect!" said the young woman, who had come up to me, full of apologies as the group broke up, still arguing.

"You must understand, Professor Fernea," she said, "that some of my colleagues still hold rather old-fashioned, unenlightened views." She explained she had gotten her Ph.D. at Princeton a year ago. "I think the feminist climate all over the world is *quite* different now, in terms of ideology and practice. Don't you agree?"

I smiled noncommittally. We shook hands. The chair, a professor of English literature, said, "Well, that was bracing! Let's go to lunch."

What was one to gather from the lively exchanges? "People in Turkey are just as divided about feminist goals and definitions as some of us are in the United States," I told Cliff. "Human rights. Women's rights. Are they universal? Everything, everywhere? Or are there different cultural expressions of those rights?"

"Come teach my honors English class, B.J., and ask my students."

This was not planned at all, but why not? I found, in Cliff's text, Adrienne Rich's great poem, "Diving into the Wreck." Was this a feminist text? Why or why not? The students were articulate and enthusiastic. Their responses more complex than I had expected.

"What do *you* think is feminism?" asked one of the two males in the class.

I repeated my earlier statement about ideology needing to respond to women's own self-expressed needs.

"And what about religion?"

"Religion is one of those needs," I replied.

"So we can be Muslims and feminists too?" asked a young woman in jeans, her square face framed by a head scarf, the only "covered" girl in the room.

"How would you do that?" I asked.

"I would use my strong belief to work in my Islamic community with men and women to improve women's role."

"How?" I persisted.

"Make laws of divorce and marriage and inheritance equal."

"They are already, according to Atatürk's reforms."

One of the young men looked annoyed. "On paper yes. But families use their version of Islamic law as justification for going around the civil law."

"We need to reform the religious law and people's belief in it while still remaining devout and pious ourselves," said the young woman in the head scarf. "Women's rights are there in the Qur'an."

I bade good-bye to Akile and Ayten and Ali and Shorsha, the little black terrier who had unwittingly been the cause of my painful crash onto the marble terrace of the Bayar House. The big Bairam feast was approaching and Akile had asked Sedat, my driver of the first day, to take me to the airport early so as to avoid the crowds. We went around the city in a completely new way, Sedat and his young wife giggling in the front seat at this marvelous paid outing while I supported my still painful arm on one of the two pieces of luggage. As we passed at the usual snail's pace over the bridge from the Asian side to the European side of this great city on the water, divided between East and West, I leaned over and looked down. Could it be? Yes, it was. A group of women, in head scarfs like Ayten's, stood close to the Asian shore. One was bending over, cutting or pulling weeds near the water. A half-grown girl with her head uncovered looked up toward the bridge. And as we took the right exit, I looked down again. Three more women stood at the edge of the water. We whizzed by, but not before one of the women's knives flashed in the sun. Women gathering greens, as they had for ten thousand years.

FIVE

¤ ¤

Egypt

IN MY LONG SEARCH for Islamic feminism, I turned to Egypt, Bob's and my second home, where we had lived for many years, where our three children were born. This seemed an obvious move, given long personal associations and continuing friendships, but more important, perhaps, because of Egypt's position as the cultural center of the Arab world, and because of its political and religious leadership. Since medieval times, Sunni Muslims throughout the world have looked to Al-Azhar, the tenth-century mosque and university in Cairo, for spiritual and intellectual guidance. The Coptic Patriarch also lives in Egypt, ministering to his flock of six million Christians, who still constitute 10 percent of Egypt's current population of sixty million.

I thought I knew something about the situation, after years of residence, writing and translating, producing two films about Egyptian women. I knew that since Pharaonic times they have been considered, by historians East and West, as the most independent and feisty women in the area. Egypt is cited as the birthplace of the first Arab women's movement; today a woman leads the Cairo Stock Exchange and a woman was chosen as executive director of the prestigious Regional Economic Research Forum. More women engineers are found in Egypt than in Europe. A few women have served as cabinet ministers, as ambassadors abroad. Women have graduated from Egypt's universities by the thousands.

But there is another side to the picture. Western media have noted the recurrence of modest dress; after years without the veil, women seem to be covering themselves up again. And although thirty-four women served in Parliament in the 1980s, that number had dropped to eight in 1996. The overall literacy of women and men is still only 44 percent, despite forty years of free compulsory government-funded education. How could one explain such contradictions? I decided to begin my search with a consideration of the Egyptian feminist movement itself and its relationship to the religious revival, which is often called fundamentalism in the West.

The histories of international feminist movements give pride of place to Egypt, and point to the example of Huda Sharawi, founder of the first Egyptian Feminist Union, who in 1923 dramatically shed her face veil on return from an international women's conference in Rome. Sharawi's "unveiling" is the moment at which all Arab women's movements supposedly begin.

But that famed Feminist Union split in 1936. Huda Sharawi continued to lead the secular branch until her death in 1947, but Zaynab Ghazali, a member of Madame Sharawi's group, left to form her own, the Muslim Women's Organization. She was eighteen years old.

"I was working with Mrs. Huda Sharawi in the women's movement," said Zaynab Ghazali in a 1981 interview, "which calls for the liberation of women. But I, with my Islamic upbringing, found that this was not the right way for Muslim women. Women had to be called to Islam."

Zaynab Ghazali continues to write, lecture, and agitate for a nation that is designed around what she views as Islamic principles. Her refusal to compromise and her opposition to various Egyptian governments have led to imprisonment and even torture, but she remains convinced that she is only following the path which God has told her to follow.

In the same 1981 interview, Zaynab Ghazali said that a woman's "first, holy and most important mission is to be a mother and wife. She cannot ignore this priority. If she then finds she has free time, she may participate in public activities. Islam does not forbid her."

"So you see, B.J.," my Egyptian friends said to me, rather wryly, "we seem to be the birthplace not only of Huda Sharawi's secularist feminist movement, but of a fundamentalist women's movement as well."

What they were telling me of course was that, contrary to Western belief, the religious revival and women's participation in that revival are not new in Egypt, but an adaptation and perhaps even an elaboration of Madame Ghazali's strong views on the basic goal of Muslims everywhere: to establish a state based, as she said, "on the principles of the Qur'an and the Sunna, and ruled by the Qur'an, not by positivist constitutions."

For many Muslim women, however, Madame Ghazali's views are extremist, and not at all representative. Dr. Zahira Abdine, for example, who has for many years been part of the Muslim Women's Association, sees piety and service as first principles. "We believe, as Muslims, in service to God, and also to others," she said, also in 1981, and she puts her beliefs into action. She has served for many years as director of the Children's Hospital in Giza, as well as a professor in the medical school, and she is a tireless fund-raiser for the poor, especially women and children. She is also a leader, with her husband, in the practice of Sufism, the mystic branch of Islam.

But in 1995 and 1996, when I visited Egypt three times, things were somewhat different. Islamist groups continue to be charged with terrorist and fanatic acts, a rash of killings that have created great problems in Egypt. But their activities again are seen as extremist, and are not condoned by the majority of Egyptians, who have never been as interested in violence as they are in raising their families, and enjoying what life has to offer—food, jokes, music, socializing. The Islamist strike against the Nobel Prize–winning novelist Naguib Mahfouz was widely seen as a travesty and disgrace, which turned off many average Egyptians. These were the people who earlier tacitly approved Islamist moves against the government as a way to call attention to the country's problems—poverty, overcrowding, corruption in high places. As Karl Marx said long ago, "Religious distress is the sign of social distress," and this is certainly the case in modern Egypt.

In all the charges and counter-charges, pro and antigovernment, the position of women continues to be a major issue for debate. Although the West may see this as expressed in a simple "return to the veil movement," the issues are not quite so simple, explained Randa Sha'ath, prizewinning young photographer with *Al-Ahram* weekly, whom I interviewed at home.

"The veil? That's all Western feminists talk about," she said.

"Well, it's what they can see with their own eyes," I protested mildly. "They can't all speak Arabic and read the opposition newspapers."

Randa went on, "But they are obsessed with it, B.J. And besides, what Egyptians have put on these days is not the veil, it's a new kind of modest dress, Islamic dress, the long dress, the head scarf. They even have fashion shows which are actually called 'Islamic dress fashion shows.' "

In 1996, I saw very few Egyptian women, even those who have donned the *hijab,* or modest dress, who had covered their faces, and thus "returned to the veil." Generally, they looked more like Huda

Sharawi herself, that first Egyptian feminist whose 1923 photos show her in the garb she continued to wear during her lifetime, a long loose black dress and a tight black head scarf tied behind her head. Randa pointed out, as did many other women, that at the end of the twentieth century far more important issues were at stake for Egyptian women than the dress code: law, social freedom, political participation, work. "And besides," she added, "what does one really mean by *hijab*? I've seen girls in jeans and sneakers and Mickey Mouse sweatshirts, with scarves over their heads. Is that *hijab*? Is that oppression?"

"But why put that dress on at all?" I persisted.

"It's a small price to pay," said Randa, humoring me. "If you're a poor woman, say, and want to go out and work or to continue school, *hijab*'s a way of getting your own way in the family, which is still, of course, patriarchal."

I went to see Nawal Sirry, who in 1981 had first alerted me to the importance of the new dress. That was the year I returned to Egypt, armed with a grant from the National Endowment for the Humanities, to make an educational documentary film about the effects of change on Arab women.

"The new interest in Islam is *the* most important thing that is happening to women," said Nawal, who was then head of all news transmission for the Egyptian Television Corporation. "You can see it in our studios, on the streets, in the workplace. It has many meanings, B.J. You lived here before, haven't you noticed?"

It was true. The streets looked different from the 1960s, when we had lived in Egypt. In those days, our nanny, Farida, wore a loose cotton dress and covered her head with a *tarha*, a scarf, like all working-class women, whose street garb still has not changed. It was middle-class women, Nawal Sirry said, college-educated women, who were covering themselves up, in a new response to social changes.

"Here in Egypt," she said on camera, "all our fashion comes from the West. These girls are striking out on their own, finding their own mode of dress, against the flow, and I admire them very much."

Was *hijab* a protest against Western intrusion, I asked, even after the end of colonialism? A statement of identity? Religious reconversion, as born-again Muslims, similar to the born-again Christian movement in America?

"All of those things," replied Nawal Sirry. "Ask around and you will see."

My film *A Veiled Revolution* premiered in 1982 on Channel 4 London and at the Margaret Mead Film Festival in New York. That day at the American Museum of Natural History, a young woman stood up in the audience and asked, "Are these women saying they don't want to be seen as sex objects on the streets, so their cover is a feminist reaction?"

"Perhaps," I allowed, "but there are many reasons for the cover. Certainly a wish not to be seen as a sex object is one of them." And I cited for the audience some of the other responses from women interviewed.

"When I wear this dress, men don't pinch me on the bus."

"At work, it's easier when I wear this dress. Men don't harass me. It says I'm working for my family, I'm a respectable woman, I'm not playing around."

"I can go out when I like. My parents don't worry when I'm wearing *hijab*."

Of course, a small minority cover themselves completely, from head to toe, and retire from the world, staying at home and letting the men of their family deal with the public—doing the daily shopping, for example. That was true in 1982. But what about 1996?

"There are still a few women like that," allowed Nawal Sirry, when I accepted an invitation to tea at her modest apartment in Dokki. In the 1982 film, she had worn Western dress, but now greeted me in a midlength skirt and a loose flowered silk tunic of taupe, green, and apricot, plus a head scarf, which she took off when we sat down in her neat living room. She closed the window, muffling the cries of vendors and rumble of taxis which reached us from the street below.

"There are always some who feel they must withdraw from the world. But you know, B.J., Christian women did that too. Aren't there nuns in your country anymore?"

"Yes, there are," I acknowledged, "but most are involved in service, and the old silent reclusive orders like the Carmelites are dying out."

Nawal Sirry poured the tea. "You may not know, B.J., that I was attacked by Nawal al-Saadawi because of your film." (Dr. Saadawi is a well-known Egyptian radical feminist.)

"What?"

"Yes." She laughed a small laugh. "In *Musawwar,* no less, an important periodical."

"But why?"

"For suggesting there might be something good or practical about this dress, which, as you see, I now wear myself."

I apologized for any harm this might have caused her.

"Not at all, not at all," she said politely, and, sipping her tea, said diplomatically, "At the time it was helpful to me, not the opposite.

Nawal is a very important part of our women's history here in Egypt, but I fear that she is out of touch these days."

I had brought her a cassette of *A Veiled Revolution*. She looked at the title and smiled at me. "The revolution is over, I think," she said. "We've settled into a kind of balance, normalcy if you like, on this issue. It's been twenty years, maybe more, since this dress began to be worn. These days, well, what do you think?"

"Lots of women are wearing this dress, lots of women not."

"Nothing wrong with that. That is their choice. Everyone has to decide for herself. But, as you've been traveling around Cairo, what percentage do you think are wearing some form of the dress, like me, or the longer, fuller style?"

I said that my view was not exactly based on scientific evidence.

"But what is it?"

I explained that I had been standing on a street near Cairo's Bab al-Loukh Station two days before, waiting for a friend, who was very late. As the sun slowly set, and darkness descended, I began to count women who passed me, partly out of interest (who had their head covered, who did not) and partly out of anxiety that my friend would never come, and I might be in the wrong place, and would soon be mugged!

Nawal objected, "Not in Cairo, my friend. We have a very low crime rate here."

"Well, my ride did finally come. But by that time I had counted seventy-seven women. Thirty-eight or thirty-nine were wearing Islamic dress like yourself, or maybe close to it. A few of the rest wore turbans on their heads."

"About what I would expect," Nawal said. "Now have one of these delicious almond cakes—they're from a special bakery in Zamalek."

Over the cakes, which were indeed delicious, she told me she had decided to leave her longtime post at the Egyptian Television Corporation and accept an offer from ART, the new Arab media consortium, which was beginning to transmit, by satellite, all over the Middle East.

"Egypt refused to have the transmitter here," she said, "because the funds come from Saudi Arabian businessmen, but I have it in writing that I will have complete control over my area—developing social, economic, and public interest programs. I'm pleased. It's a new challenge!"

Islam, then, is a basic strand in the Egyptian social fabric, where 90 percent of the people are Muslims. Islam is a given in the lives of Egyptian women, but how it is expressed in response to the conditions of national life is currently being contested on all sides. The media reflect this contest, as do educational and religious spokeswomen.

Iqbal Baraka, editor of the women's magazine *Hawa*, agreed to an interview in her office at the Dar al-Hilal Publishing Company. The photographer Tom Hartwell had also come, and she fluffed up her brown-blond hair and adjusted her amber necklace over the long-sleeved ecru silk blouse before posing for her portrait, in front of a wall-to-wall bookcase jammed with periodicals, file folders, pamphlets, books large and small.

"I don't wear Islamic dress, as you see," she began, pushing back the chair across which her tweed jacket was haphazardly hung. "I don't need to prove anything. That seems clear to me. I'm a good Egyptian, too."

Iqbal, a well-known novelist and short-story writer and former editor of the avant-garde magazine *Sabah al-Khayr,* was brought into the company of Dar al-Hilal to rejuvenate the magazine *Hawa*.

"*Hawa* used to be a very popular women's magazine, but has lost readership in the past fifteen years. Public events, including the reaffirmation of Islam—what you in the West call fundamentalism, but wrongly, I think—passed it by. I'm trying to bring back the readers, and to do that, I take as my basic assumption that women are not simply the tools of fashion designers and manicurists, that women have real and serious interests and concerns we must deal with." She stood and called out for her assistant, "Manal! Manal!"

Manal did not come running, but she did saunter in, giving a side glance at me and a slightly more interested glance at Tom.

"Bring us a copy of the last few issues, please," said Iqbal.

Manal, except for her dyed red hair, was all in black from the tips of her fashionable boots to the top of her long-sleeved turtleneck, which was adorned with a jingling necklace of golden coins.

"Okay," she said, giving us another glance, and sauntering out.

"Manal is very smart and very arrogant," said Iqbal. "We should have asked her about your interest, feminism, but I think she would just have laughed."

Tom came to life. "Doesn't look like she ever laughs," he said laconically.

"What do you think about feminism, though?" I asked.

Iqbal smiled, answered the phone, hung up, answered the phone again, put it down without hanging up, carefully, "to give us a few minutes of peace," she explained. "Feminism. Oriental feminism is not like Western feminism, which I think is only interested in the individual woman."

I was nodding. "You've heard this before," she said. "What I should add then is that oriental feminism is certainly a movement, but our demands are different from yours in the West. We need more social freedom, more equality within our families. We don't need economic equality like you do—we've had that for a thousand years. Really." She smiled, but anxiously. "You see what I mean. And we need to reform the family laws, for the benefit of children as well as women."

We were interrupted by Manal, who placed a pile of *Hawa* issues on Iqbal's desk, gazed at us, and went out again, without a word. Her gold coins, jingling in the quiet office, spoke for her.

Iqbal came around her desk and opened up the magazines for us. "This is the kind of thing we're aiming for, you can see for yourself. And our readership has already increased!"

Here is a sample of headlines from recent issues of *Hawa:*

"NEWS OF LITERARY WOMEN: WHAT ARE THEY TELLING US?"

"PAINT YOUR APARTMENT YOURSELF."

"AN INTERVIEW WITH A TERRORIST."

"A DAY IN THE LIFE OF THE BALLET DANCER."

"FAMILY LAW: STORIES FROM THE COURTS."

"The headline we got the most comment from was the one I wrote," she said. "It went like this: 'WE ARE WAITING FOR PRESIDENT MUBARAK TO APPOINT A WOMAN JUDGE.' It is really too much," she added. "We have many women lawyers, but no judges. Why not? Tunisia has women judges, so does Jordan, so it is hardly against Islam."

"How," I asked, "does the government view your new initiatives for women readers? I have been told that the government monitors all media activity."

Iqbal Baraka allowed that was true, but since she was a member of the powerful Press Syndicate, she had some protection from government watchdogs. "And I'm hardly an Islamic fundamentalist," she added.

The phone still lay on her desk off the hook, but Manal was coming in and out with papers, and she finally spoke, but only to Iqbal herself. "He's on the phone again. He must talk to you," she said in Arabic.

We shook hands, and Tom shot one more informal picture while Manal watched expressionlessly. Down the echoing, crowded staircase of this nineteenth-century building we trudged, noting the plaque in French and Arabic—"Built in 1892"—and the walls covered with portraits of Egyptian journalists and writers of the past century. Dar al-Hilal Publishing Company, in its myriad activities of publishing books and magazines, was still a force in the world of media, and Iqbal Baraka a new part of their effort.

Safinaz Kassem is more confrontational than Iqbal, in her full-length Islamic dress, topped by the inevitable turtleneck (to cover the neck— that supposed beautiful and enchanting part of women's anatomy) and a head scarf. She is a respected literary and drama critic for the periodical *Al-Musawwar,* which seems to hit the middle ground between secular and religious concerns, publishing Nawal as-Saadawi as well as Safinaz Kassem. But Safinaz's past history as a member of the old cultural left is reflected in her chosen style of Islamic dress. At our first meeting, she was wearing not the two-piece silk ensemble with matching turban or swirling scarf that is almost a uniform these days for middle-class and upper-middle-class Egyptian women. No, she reflected her past allegiances to the working class in the peasant style of her dress: the long, simple flowered cotton like the housedresses my mother used to wear, adorned only with bias tape binding at neck and wrists. "Call me," she said, when I politely requested an interview.

But when I called, she begged off, saying she had been overwhelmed by requests for interviews from Western journalists and had decided not to do any more. "They talk and talk and then they twist my words and I'm sick of it."

I said I was trying to correct some of the misapprehensions and stereotypes about Islam that are found in the West.

"Forget it," she said shortly. "We don't need to correct your stereotypes. That's your problem. We know who we are. We've been here, Islam has been here for a thousand years. We don't need you."

Somewhat taken aback, I pulled myself together and said, "Well, maybe we need you. And you can read what I write before it's printed."

"Okay, no one has said that to me before," she returned and invited me to her twelfth-floor flat.

But I never got to interview Safinaz Kassem; on the set day she was in bed in terrible pain. "My back has gone out again," she said over the phone. "Please don't come. I feel awful. We can meet again—at the book fair. You're coming, I hear"—and we did meet then, but not for a lengthy interview.

Hesna Makdashi, the person behind the first Arab Women's Book Fair planned for November 1995, was the editor and publisher of *Nour,* the women's literary journal—a promising new entry into the field of women's writing and writing about women. "I saw a gap between what women were actually doing, and writing, and what was being made available to the public here in Egypt. And I thought, why limit this to Egypt? So I launched *Nour*. We have readers all across the area now."

Hesna is no novice to the publishing field; for ten years she was an editor for Dar al-Fatah, the house that created children's books under the auspices of the Palestinian Planning Center. "That was long before anyone ever thought of peace between Israelis and Palestinians," said Hesna, "though we always hoped against hope.

"But I'd been traveling around the area and everywhere I went there were women's book clubs and discussion groups and they wanted to read things by women writers as well as by major figures like Mahfouz and Idris and Saleh.

"Then," said Hesna, "I went to a feminist book fair in 1992 in Amsterdam, with Nadia Hijab who works for the UNDP and Leila Shaheed, the PLO ambassador in Paris. We asked ourselves why there weren't any book fairs like that in the Arab world? We have wonderful new writers, and a strong cultural life, and yes, a feminist movement, though it may not look the same as yours in America, B.J. But then why should it? We're Arabs, not Americans, and most of us, though not all, are Muslims. So it's bound to be different."

"Islamic feminism, perhaps?" I couldn't resist asking.

Hesna paused. "What does that mean exactly? Feminists who are also Muslims, or a special brand focused on Islamic revival? I'm not sure. Talk to some other women and then let's talk again—at the book fair."

I kept looking and asking and interviewing. And in my walks around the city, and my interviews with women and men, the name of Heba Raouf Ezzat was often mentioned. I had heard her name also in Kuwait and in Beirut. Who was Heba Raouf Ezzat? The principal intellectual force, it seemed, behind what is termed the liberal wing of the women's movement within the Islamist "back to fundamentals" movement in Egypt.

Heba Raouf was fourteen years old when I made my film *A Veiled Revolution* in Cairo. Those were early days, when women were beginning to form study groups, grass-roots Islamic consciousness-raising groups in which they met regularly in homes and mosques to discuss their faith. They read together the laws relating to women and the family and the wider Muslim community, they tried to question and analyze the history of the Muslim faith as well as the implementation of that faith throughout the fourteen hundred years of Islam. We were able to film one of those study groups, in a beautiful new mosque in north Cairo, thanks to the help of Dr. Zahira Abdine. When I looked at the footage later and was identifying, for editor Terry Twigg, the names and occupations of the women in the group, I realized with some excitement that I had happened on an important and seldom-mentioned characteristic of these new Muslim women's study groups. They cut across class lines in ways that Huda Sharawi's Feminist Union had never done. For Madame Sharawi's union was composed, like early women's movements in the United States and Europe, of rich, educated upper-class women. The study group pictured in *A Veiled Revolution* showed a different mix: an insurance secretary and a shop girl sitting in the same space and on the same level as two medical school students from poor families; a former party-giver in high society; and Dr. Abdine herself, the leader of the group, an official in the nation's Muslim Women's Association. Islam, following the example of the Prophet Muhammad, was embracing all classes, rich and poor, male and female.

The study groups, purposeful and serious, led women into community service, just like Dr. Abdine. The two medical students gave their time to a free clinic each week at the Mosque of Sayyidna Zeinab, which sits in a relatively poor quarter of Cairo. Other members offered free tutoring to children who needed to prepare for the all-important baccalaureate exam that would determine their future in the wider society.

Heba Raouf Ezzat's activities mirrored those of Dr. Abdine and her study group. She teaches political science at Cairo University, but also edits the women's page of *al-Sha'ab*, the principal opposition newspaper. But her women's page discusses, not necessarily specifically female issues, but problems of general concern to all Egyptians, male and female: corruption in high places, graft in the allotment of building contracts (to the point that buildings are so badly built they fall down, killing the inhabitants); pollution of the environment, which causes harm to children, the next generation of Egyptian citizens. Pollution is no joke, for recent studies show lead three times that of allowable levels, which endangers adults but particularly growing children.

Heba enjoys the support of her active Islamist husband. Their activities grow out of the young couple's firm faith in Islam. Heba has stated: "We need a new women's liberation movement—not feminism—but a new movement that is based on Islam."

"So," I asked, "the consciousness-raising groups and the study circles and the Sufi groups I have witnessed in Cairo are not like feminist groups in the West?"

Heba said, "No, not at all. Feminists," she stated, "are secularists who are fighting male domination. Many of them regard religion as an obstacle to women's rights and they concentrate on women's superior or special nature. Conflict is the main concept of their theory, a theory they even say they want to turn into a paradigm."

But what was the base for her proposed Islamic women's liberation movement?

"My effort is quite different. I am not an Islamic feminist. But I do believe in Islam as a worldview, and I think that women's liberation in our society should rely on our faith, on Islam. This necessitates," she added, "a revival of Islamic thought and a renewal within the whole field of Islamic jurisprudence."

Heba had articulated one of the important subtexts of the new Islamic movement: women should play a part in interpretation and implementation of the law, something they have never done before. Throughout Islamic history a few women have been educated in the theological schools of the great mosques—Karaween, Fez, al-Azhar, but seldom have they had the authority to issue fatwas (like papal edicts) or serve as judges in the religious courts. Women's names are often found in the *silsillas*, or chains of authorities, which give Islamic *hadiths*, or traditions, their validity, but women have almost never appeared in history as fulfilling public positions of religious responsibility, though they have always served as ritual specialists (*fqihas, mullahs*) within the women's community. It was the secularly based governments in Tunisia and Turkey that opened the door for women to serve as judges. Certainly, over the years, religious leadership has not been open to women, no more than within the papacy and, until recently, the hierarchies of Judaic and Protestant Christian denominations.

Thus Heba and Safinaz and other women like them represent not a return to the past, but an important challenge to the present. For Heba's suggestion about reevaluating previous interpretations is tantamount to asking for a basic change in the position of women.

"I declare myself an Islamist," said Heba. "But this doesn't mean that I accept the dominant discourse about women inside the Islamic movement. My studies focus on the need for a new interpretation of Qur'an and Sunna [the sacred laws]."

And the heritage of the past?

"We should benefit from *fiqh* [Islamic legal theory] and the contributions of previous generations of Islamic scholars. But this doesn't mean that we have to stick to their interpretations of Islamic sources while we ignore the sociology of knowledge."

Heba would like to abolish the public-private dichotomy of both Western and Islamic thought, a suggestion close to Western feminists' call for discarding the old binary opposition between reason (men) and emotion (women), which is used to rationalize a separation between male and female realms. But Islamic women scholars like Heba see it slightly differently. They do not appear to be interested in the idea of well-balanced individuals, but in the idea of well-balanced families and a well-balanced society. Family feminism, maybe?

My search went on. I sought out Hala Shakrallah, one of the founders of the New Woman Center for Research and Study, which was housed in a crumbling nineteenth-century building near Bab al-Loukh Station, set between a furniture repair shop and several fruit stands. The grand winding staircase to the third floor was barely passable, with its chipped marble steps and shaky brass-veined mahogany banisters, but at the top, the door opened on to a peaceful set of rooms, filled with remnants of a European past (carved étagères, marble hall tables, a great gold-framed mirror, shadowed by use) and with more functional equipment—metal desks, Formica tables, computer screens, a fax machine.

"One of my cousins gave us this flat to use, rent-free, so that's how we were able to get started," said Hala, coming, full of apologies, late, she said, "because I was raising money. We need it! We share our space with al-Nadim, a new center to aid women and men who are victims of violence—domestic violence—yes, but war as well."

"Your assistant was very helpful," I answered.

"Yes." Hala smiled, a small dark-haired young woman with the pleasant innocent air of a child. "She's one of our university interns, daughter of a Sudanese exile. She's working on our program to aid Sudanese exile women. There are three million Sudanese refugees in Cairo."

"That many?"

But Hala changed the subject abruptly. "Now tell me what you're doing, please. What is your project? What brings you here?"

I told her I'd read her very interesting piece in a local development journal about the need to match feminist reforms, not to Western patriarchy, but to the Egyptian patriarchal system. She nodded. "Yes," she said, "it is important to remember that not all patriarchies are exactly carbon copies of each other."

"So do you consider yourself an Islamic feminist?"

Hala's cheery expression faded, her mouth turned down in displeasure. "I object to the term," she said shortly.

"Why?"

"Because I'm a Christian, not a Muslim."

My face must have shown *my* concern, for she put a hand on my arm.

"Don't worry, people always forget that we have many kinds of people in Cairo, not just Muslims. But I'm a feminist, all right!"

Hala Shakrallah's group, she told me, was working to establish what they call the third way of feminism, not, she said "the Western dominant view of us as the other" nor "the Islamist view that all must proceed from Muslim religious doctrine" but one "which we forge ourselves from our own traditions, yes, and the demands of our new modern lives."

"Our group is part of the movement which refuses to recognize religious law as divine, and unchanging," she said. "That's why the current debate about the civil marriage contract is important to us. We can talk about it later, if you like."

Hala said she saw problems with some types of feminism found in Egypt and also in many other Third World countries. "The Western feminist formulation negates large parts of *our* heritage, and is racist in orientation. The type of feminism we often see in Egypt is a mirror image of that Western feminism, an internalization of this Western paradigm, and it makes us false to ourselves."

This was new to me, and I asked what difference it made.

Hala said sharply, "It makes a lot of difference to women, if they think that the West and only the West is the father and mother of secularism, liberalism, independence, equality. What nonsense!"

"Nonsense?"

"Absolutely. Many scholars in the Middle East historically and now have the same ideas. I see you don't agree with me, though."

"No, I just hadn't put it that way in my own mind, I guess," I confessed.

She smiled suddenly, that cheery smile that made her look again for a moment like a happy young girl. "Just remember, the drive to liberation is found everywhere. The West doesn't have a corner on liberation."

I wrote that down.

"So that's the background," she said, "of why we need a third way—and it is out of these concerns that our New Woman Center came into being. We're ten years old now, started as a study group, and now we publish a magazine, co-sponsor the center for victims of violence, hold workshops for women on issues of violence."

She got up, crossed to a shelf by the window, brought back some printed materials. "See," she said, "here are the results of our new study on domestic violence—a random sample of five hundred respondents, four hundred women and one hundred men. Because, you see, we don't have much data. Anecdotal evidence, yes, we all know the violence is there, but rhetoric doesn't really help much in the long term. We need to act—and think—and work."

I looked at the dramatic black-and-white poster on the wall behind her—a profile of a woman in a sheer black head scarf facing a man in a white turban. The Arabic read literally, "LIBERATING A WOMAN MEANS LIBERATING A MAN." But the English translation lettered across the bottom of the poster read, "WOMAN'S EMANCIPATION IS HUMAN EMANCIPA-TION." Was the subtle difference in the translation designed for the Western paradigms perhaps?

Hala looked at the poster. "I never thought about it. But maybe you're right."

"And circumcision?" I asked my last question.

"How do we deal with this, as feminists?" said Hala. "I am trou-bled. It seems so clear to us, but in the discussions we have been having with representatives from our organization and the Cairo Com-mittee on Human Rights and a few doctors, some of the women say that circumcision is a trade-off."

"A trade-off? What do they mean by that?"

"If we agree to be circumcised, they say, we are freer in other areas."

"People have said that to me, too," I put in.

Hala shook her head. She looked down at the Formica table and was silent.

"What do you say?" I got out finally. "In answer to that sort of statement, I mean."

"Only that we can't see circumcision in isolation, that it has to be looked at and dealt with in relation to other oppressive relationships within the family, or the society, too. Class must be involved. But . . ." she paused, "it's not just poverty you know."

"But it's a factor? With illiteracy?"

"One of many. The tradition is very old, it's a tradition of women, not men. And it's not Islamic."

"Yes, I realize that, but many of my feminist colleagues in America think it is."

"But don't they know that Christians do it, too, and women in Africa who are neither Muslim nor Christian? I thought Alice Walker made a film about it. I guess you could say it's special to the Nile."

Hala added, "I have a daughter. My generation is not performing such operations. The practice will come to an end."

"How does your husband feel about it?"

"He's a writer, a dramatist; he's against all that and as feminist as I am. He works with the al-Waisha Theater group; they perform at the Hanager Center. He and I think the same about many things."

"Let's go back," I said, "to law. The civil marriage contract. Is it a feminist issue?"

Hala nodded her head vigorously. "Absolutely a feminist issue. And you know it is an issue for all women because everyone seems so opposed to it. But it's perfectly legal and has been in Egypt for a long time. It's not new at all."

I had heard about the contract recently—advocated by women's groups. It had become the subject of a stormy Parliamentary debate. Many people thought it would pass; many people thought it would *not* pass. What was so special about a civil marriage contract? It gave women greater say in their marriage arrangements. Under the civil marriage contract, a woman can designate her wishes for the future (that her husband may not take a second wife, for example), ask for equal inheritance (in contradiction to Islamic family law), assure that she may ask for a divorce without checking with every member of her family and her proposed husband's family.

Several of the eighty-seven women who ran for Parliament in the 1995 elections supported the civil marriage contract, some said to their loss. For the civil marriage contract has been derided as a way for wealthy families to maintain their wealth, but the real issue seems to be an effort to make fathers responsible for the protection of their daughters' future. The civil marriage contract becomes the legal tool to help the father fulfill that task.

My last interview was with Nadia Atef, an old friend I encountered accidentally at the office of the American Research Center in Egypt.

"Nadia! I had no idea you were here."

"Yes, I'm usually abroad, working in Europe, but I broke my leg badly so I came home to recover."

The old, sprightly Nadia, who told jokes on every occasion, who had made a profession out of the folklore of telling jokes—for political, social, and cultural occasions, was not much in evidence. I asked her if there were jokes about the new Islamic movement.

She became serious. "Never," she said firmly. "One never jokes about Islam, about religion, about women's honor. Those are no-nos. Why," she burbled suddenly, "we can even joke about circumcision, but not about Islam."

"Not about Islamic dress either?"

"Come on, B.J., be sensible. That's not a joke subject, either. It's for survival. You've lived in Cairo, in other Arab countries. Women always figure out some way to get around the system, but they don't always *joke* about it. Covering is the newest and most efficient way to get around the system."

"And that's all it is?"

"I'm not at all belittling the religious belief that leads some women to choose Islamic dress," she asserted, "but if you look around you these days you see, that after twenty years, these covered girls get better jobs, get married more easily, have an easier time with the bureaucracy—"

"Bureaucracy?"

"Yes, yes, of course. Getting their electricity turned on, getting a train ticket, servicing their telephone. Covered girls can cross boundaries. They have power! And they have authority."

"Not everyone would agree with you," I temporized. "But are there new jokes about that?"

"Not yet," smiled Nadia. "But these covered girls are definitely a force to be reckoned with, whether or not you call them feminists."

Where had my journey led me? In terms of women's lives, women's demands, women's movements, Egypt was no longer the country I thought I had known in the past. In a generation women had emerged into professional and public life, not always in ways approved by men, who dominated the system. They had, with men, reembraced their religious heritage, mostly Muslim, but also Christian—creating new forms of dress, new methods of education and of political protest. The outward forms were symbols of a more complicated effort to deal with a new Egypt—an Egypt that was bigger, poorer, but in which both men and women were more active in trying to improve their own lives. This, in the words of my friend Nadia Atef, was no laughing matter.

A more positive sign for women's future is the New Lands program, an Egyptian government initiative to reclaim desert lands for cultivation, and thus help relieve unemployment and urban overcrowding. I had been told that under the program, women have been given title to land, provided they farm it themselves. Could this possibly be true? I headed north, to a village near Alexandria, to find out.

Salwa Yacout is thirty years old and unmarried. She is the eldest in a family of four boys and three girls, and was born in Moscow, where her father was a functionary in the Egyptian embassy. A slight, pretty girl with a heart-shaped face and a pleasant, forthright manner, Salwa is the proud owner of five acres of good fertile land in the Nile Delta, and is farming it herself. This is her second career. After graduating from the College of Agriculture in Alexandria in 1987, she worked as an engineer/inspector at the big Taverna food factory, safe-testing meat, bread, and chickens before they were released on the market. From her college friends, she heard about the New Lands program, whereby agricultural graduates are given land if they agree to farm it for ten years. The program has been recently extended to include women, both single and married.

"I took the exams to get my land," she told me, crossing one jean-encased leg over another and pulling down her long-sleeved black sweatshirt. "Everyone has to—to see what we know about soil, fertilizer, livestock breeding, things like that. We're in an area where people are already farming, and we're supposed to bring them new techniques, I guess. But they help us, too. I mean, I never farmed before in my whole life! They've been doing it for ages."

"And you're pleased?"

All the lines of her face tilted upward as she smiled. "Yes, it's really a good job. I love it! I feel really lucky!" She tossed her head, the black hair drawn back into a ponytail.

"What does your family think?"

Salwa looked out the window of the mini-van that was taking us all from the college, where the Rural Cottage Industries Development Group is headquartered, to the row of villages and the field training center: Salwa, myself, Hamid the driver, Ahmed, the accountant who was to teach the day's class on money management, and Anne Johnson, my former student at the University of Texas, who is the project adviser. The project, funded by USAID through the National Council of Negro Women in Washington, D.C., aims to increase women's participation in this agricultural development scheme by providing small loans and business training.

"There were big problems at first," answered Salwa finally. "Especially with my mother. She wanted me to get married right away when my father died. But I said, that's my decision, not hers. Then she came to my farmhouse, and stayed for a few days. Now she says she's proud of me."

Ahmed turned from the front seat. "And she is, Salwa. I met her, remember, and she told me the same thing."

The scenery outside our car window on this late spring morning had changed. We had turned off the main highway, its medians lined with well-pruned ficus trees and billowing bushes of pink oleanders, onto what in Texas would also be called a farm road—two lane, serviceable, but not elegant. Of course this was a farm road—to the row of villages, to the farmhouses and plots of land where several thousand new university graduates were working to make a living, alongside farmers who had been there for generations. We passed ditches, in which water flowed sluggishly, passed pumping stations, and a single cart piled high with white clover, drawn by two donkeys.

"Fodder!" pointed out Salwa. "At last it's coming. We need it."

"Can you really make a living on five acres of land?" I asked.

"Not really," answered Salwa slowly. She had taken a clipboard out of the worn leather folder on her lap, and was calculating, back and forth, between one column of figures to another, as we drove along. "Not really. Everyone needs a second income, right, Anne?"

Anne's eyes crinkled with amusement. *"Jamoosas,* Salwa! You need more *jamoosas!* Water buffalo, B.J., that is, in case you've forgotten your Arabic."

"Yes, yes, Anne. I have two already," she said to me, "but Anne thinks I could do with more. She's right. Or maybe some ducks?"

"Jamoosa," repeated Anne. "Adapted to the climate, right, resistant to pests, right? Lots of meat, butter, cheese, milk. Ah good *jamoosas!"*

Ahmed laughed from the front seat and Hamid joined in. This seemed like a private joke, and it turned out to be just that, related to Salwa's position in the project. For in addition to farming her own land, she served as coordinator for the animal healthcare program— and the jamoosas were part of it.

I said that it must be hard to be a single woman on the land.

"Of course. But everything in life is hard. You have to work."

Ahmed turned around again, "Especially on the irrigation system, right, Salwa?"

This was clearly an in-joke, for chuckles and glances were being exchanged across the front and backseat. Hamid, our driver, looked at us in his rearview mirror and waited for what would come next.

Salwa finally explained, "They're talking about this guy who stole one of my drip irrigation tubes last week. Two people saw him, so I went and asked him what he was doing. He apologized, but then a few days later he swiped another one. So I told him I was going to take him to court. He just laughed. People here think women are easy prey. But I did report him to court. I was really angry."

"And what happened?"

"They're coming from the court next weekend to talk to me and to him. So we'll see."

"Here we are, ladies and gentlemen! Money management morning!" cried Anne.

The driver pulled over onto the sandy shoulder of the central paved street to give passing room to an overloaded cart, piled high with dried palm stalks, the gray donkeys pulling hard against their blue-painted harnesses, the bells and charms on their beaded bridles jingle-jangling as they slithered past our van. We stepped down onto the walk leading to a large whitewashed building where women and children were passing in and out. Nadia Loutfi, a tall dark-haired young woman, stood at the door and greeted us, welcoming Ahmed effusively.

"We have a big crowd of ladies today," she said. "They've been waiting at least half an hour to hear your pitch, Ahmed."

"See you later," called Salwa. She was off on her own business.

We filed into the auditorium of the building, a community center set up by the Ministry of Social Affairs. Anne seated herself and me at the back, behind the rows of chairs where women, some holding children, sat in their purple-and-green-and-scarlet-flowered gullabiyas, the traditional Egyptian country dress, waiting for Ahmed. He set up his easel, moved a small desk closer so he could lay down books and papers and a packet of Magic Markers. The murmuring women slowly quieted, as Nadia called them to order.

"She's the MC today, handles questions, keeps order," whispered Anne. "She's a farmer, too."

Nadia looked trim and prim as she spoke, her hands clasped in front of her; she wore a white long-sleeved blouse over a white turtleneck, her brown skirt buttoned from waist to ankle-length hem. Her head was wrapped in a white head scarf, but the entire ensemble did not at all resemble the Islamic dress I had seen so often in Cairo. Why? The blouse was not loose, I realized, but rather form-fitting, her skirt was anchored by a wide brown belt, and the scarf was tied around her head in the way of the women in the village, though theirs were more colorful.

"How many of these village women can read?" I asked.

Anne shrugged her shoulders. "Probably none," she answered, "but they have to take this course and submit a plan before we give them loans for animals, poultry, other kinds of projects."

"So how can Ahmed teach a class in accounting when nobody can read?"

Anne smiled her crinkly smile again. "Listen and see," she suggested.

I subsided. Nadia introduced Ahmed and stood beside him as he pulled an egg out of his pocket. A giggle ran throughout the audience.

"I thought this was supposed to be about money, not eggs," said one woman pertly, "didn't you, Fawzia?" nudging her neighbor.

"Eggs *are* money," answered Ahmed loudly and began to draw eggs on the easel with his black Magic Marker—one, two, three, four, five. Yes, the women can count eggs, and shortly they were chorusing, four plus eight equals twelve eggs and that means sixty piastres at five piastres an egg. In the midst of the next, more complex chorus, twelve eggs per day for eight days, a small boy ran up on the stage behind Ahmed's easel, pulled up his shirt and— "Oh!" Nadia came to life, leaped up on the stage, calling out "Um Ali" in a piercing voice, whereupon Um Ali giggled, ran upon the stage, and scooped up the child just as he was about to pee on the platform.

Ahmed, Magic Marker in hand, waited until this small drama had unfolded, then made a joke I couldn't catch. But it seemed to be about eggs again and laughter rippled through the rows of women, some nursing babies now, some dandling toddlers, but all watching that man with the Magic Marker.

"Anne has told you about the women who want loans for food projects, or to invest in animals, right?" Nadia said to me later. "That they have to attend these classes and come up with an idea. We help them plan. You see, not only the graduates are eligible for loans. The New Lands program is for everyone."

We sat side by side in the project office, on straight chairs set against a whitewashed wall, bare except for a UNICEF poster, "All Children Are Valuable," and a gold-framed plaque on which had been stitched, like a sampler, the Shahada or Islamic profession of faith, "There is no God but God and Muhammad is His Prophet."

"So everybody's eligible, not just university graduates?" I said, remembering the gullabiya-clad women and the children who guzzled free "refreshments,"—soft drinks and cookies—one of the rewards for attending the two-hour management session.

"Right. Anne has probably told you that the idea behind this project is we learn from the peasant women and they learn from us. They have more practical experience, we've studied agriculture in books. A joint effort."

"And it's working?"

"Yes," said Nadia, "really quite well."

Nadia came to the project five years ago, after a stint at teaching history in secondary school. Her fiancé had land, "so I became eligible to apply," she explained. After their summer marriage, they will combine forces. "Ten feddans is a good piece," Nadia pointed out. "We're going to live in his house down the road, but I'll keep my house anyway. Do you want to come and see it?"

"Oh yes, I'd love to."

Like all government-issue residences, Nadia's house was a two-room brick structure with a small kitchen, bathroom, and a large courtyard, all surrounded by a high mud-brick wall.

She pointed to the wire chicken coops, which her fiancé had built all along the far wall of the courtyard. But the birds were not penned, for as we opened the door, chickens, ducks, and turkeys clucked, quacked, and gobbled toward their mistress, circling and ruffling feathers until she gave them what they expected, handfuls of corn from a shining metal basin which she brought from her tiny immaculate kitchen. A traditional *tanur,* or oven, sat in another corner of the court, but Nadia said quickly that she bought bread most of the time from her neighbors. "I'm just too busy with the birds. And running training sessions, like today." She paused, smiled. "But usually I don't have to run after little kids about to pee," she added.

I said something about Ahmed's impressive lesson.

Nadia put the feed basin back on the kitchen counter, locked her door, scattered the birds so we could get out to the courtyard. "Wasn't he great?" she agreed. "He really understands the women and how to get through to them. We all help each other out here."

"And it's hard work," I offered, remembering my own aunt Mary, the only one of my mother's siblings to stay on the Wisconsin farm, and how hard she and her husband had worked—from dawn to dusk, literally, and sometimes after dark. Nadia padlocked her outside door and nodded to her neighbor, a woman in a purple gullabiya who stood outside, watching us as we headed up the road.

"You caught Ali before he peed," the neighbor laughed. "That kid!"

"But he's just a baby, really," allowed Nadia.

The neighbor bobbed her head at us, smiled, went back into her house.

To me, Nadia said, "Yes, I do work hard. But I love it. So does my fiancé. My parents like it, too. They were not pleased in the beginning, but that's changed. They believe in hard work." She paused and looked sidewise at me. "Most Egyptians do work hard, you know, though we hear that's not what Americans think—they think we're lazy."

I protested mildly.

"That's what they say on the TV," she asserted. "Arabs are lazy. But we're not. Look at the folks on this project."

I said that it looked as if everyone was working.

We had come full circle back to the community center, where Nadia announced, "Okay, here's Kawthar. Anne says she's going to take you around, because today is collection day, so you'll get to meet the women who have loans. See for yourself what they're doing. One hundred percent payback is what Kawthar claims."

Kawthar, a solid young woman, stood waiting for me at the center's entrance, official collection book on a clipboard under one arm, her white head covering and the black-and-white gullabiya giving her dignity and respectability. But her huge black sunglasses and the white baseball cap she wore over her Islamic headgarb combined to give her a faintly rakish air, as she marched purposefully ahead leading me down one sandy lane after another, narrow lanes which divided the homesteads from each other, identical homes distinguishable only by the different kinds of laundry hung out to dry—jeans, men's white underwear, children's gowns, socks, long gullabiyas, printed baby blankets.

"Hey, Kawthar! Hi!" Small children ran beside us, jumping up and down, tumbling down laughing over the sandy roadside. "Who's the Americani? Your boss?"

"Mind your manners!" Kawthar shook the collection book at them, which led to another round of mirth. Someone pulled my skirt, ever so gently, then ran away giggling.

"Stop it! Behave!" But Kawthar could not help herself, and burst out laughing too. "Isn't it a beautiful day?" she said.

We passed the mosque, its white-and-yellow-painted arches shading an open terrace. In the distance I could see a steeple. "Church of Saint Mena," said Kawthar. "They have five hundred acres of land, madame, they are damned rich."

Further along, an outside garage stood open at one end; two tractors were visible inside, resting since plowing season was over. We detoured around a large combine which had been pulled out onto the road and was being serviced by two men, one on his back under the machine, a second, younger one, holding tools.

"Hey, Kawthar? How're you?" The young man waved a tool in our direction. Kawthar hollered back.

"The machine belongs to the project," she said shortly. "You contract out for it when you need it for the harvest." Then, as we ambled along, she proceeded to give me a lesson in cost accounting. "My fiancé and I have figured it all out," she said. "One man with the combine can harvest my land in one day, the wheat and barley, but if the combine is already in use, we can hire eight men, who can do it by hand in four days. Costs about the same," she concluded, "but you have to feed the men."

"My aunt Mary used to cook for about eight men," I said, "during harvest." But Kawthar wasn't really listening.

"You have to feed the combine, too," she smiled, "and gas isn't cheap these days."

I followed Kawthar as she visited two houses and pocketed two envelopes containing money, the banknotes in full view of the woman paying on her loan, while Kawthar thumbed through them carefully, and checked off names in her trusty loan book.

At our third stop, we were invited in for tea. "Okay, let's do it," said Kawthar. "Abla said she'd like to look at you a bit. Not every day does she get to see little me"—she laughed at herself, tall and solid—"pay on her loan, and at the same time stare at a real American woman up close who can actually speak Arabic."

"Hello, hello, hello, lovely morning this," began Kawthar, but the woman interrupted with a smile.

"Yah, yah, you want your money, Kawthar, okay, here it is, come in, the house is a mess, but come in anyway." We were ushered into a small courtyard where every free space was covered with gleaming tin trays of charcoal and beans drying in the spring sunshine. The voices of doves cooed softly above us, Kawthar in her baseball cap, me with my notebook, Abla with a baby on one arm and a toddler by the hand. She opened the door to the guest parlor, neat and clearly seldom-used.

"I came here without anything," said Abla over glasses of tea. "I left my family's apartment in the old city of Cairo and followed my husband. He got land when he graduated from the agricultural college, then I stayed on and now I have land of my own."

Kawthar said, "Have you thought about what I said, Abla? Coming to help us teach? You've done well with your *jamoosa*—you could show other women."

"Mmm, I'm thinking," answered Abla. "But not quite yet. I don't want to leave my *jamoosa* until she calves . . . she is a real treasure. She produces milk that I sell to the guy who comes by every day. I love her dearly. So we're making it, Kawthar. Making it, thanks be to God."

"What do you grow?" I asked politely.

Abla looked at Kawthar. "She's writing this down, why?" Kawthar explained that I was writing a book to tell American women about Egyptian women.

"So I'll be in your book?"

I nodded.

"Say I'm good-looking, okay?" She cackled delightedly when I nodded again in assent.

"What you grow—" prompted Kawthar.

"Oh yes, we get more per acre for vegetables, but we grow some grain too. So we make about fifteen thousand Egyptian pounds a year [about five thousand dollars]. Probably doesn't seem like much to a rich American like you, but the land and house are ours, we don't have to pay rent."

"And you have pigeons," I added, for the soft cooing continued to thrum over our conversation, a kind of accompaniment to the shouts of children outside and the rumble of donkey carts on the nearby road.

"Yes, we're lucky," she agreed, shifting her baby to the other arm and embracing Kawthar as she saw us to the door, and stood, waving us off. When I looked back, Abla stood there, the baby clothes and men's white gullabiyas on the laundry line blowing out in the warm breeze. The top of the house was stacked high with fodder, for the *"jamoosa*—the treasure" and dung cakes were carefully laid out in a row to dry for future fuel, like a border of dark sculptured petals along the edges of her roof.

"Hey, Kawthar!" The woman passing us going the other way was balancing a huge tray of cooking pots on her head, gleaming from recent washing, her pink gullabiya swishing around her ankles as she strode on, moving like a dancer.

"No piped water in the houses?" I asked.

"Not everybody," replied Kawthar shortly. "Not yet." She did not elaborate, but adjusted her baseball cap. "These hats are great against the sun, aren't they?"

We walked along, and I asked her how she had ended up in the New Lands.

"I heard about it in college, and I couldn't believe it at first, land for women all by themselves? I thought why not try? I always wanted to farm, but my folks are city folks and didn't know anything about the land. When I got this chance, I jumped at it."

"Your family agreed?"

Kawthar shook her head vigorously, and the baseball cap tipped over one eye.

"Oh, gracious no, they were mad, were they ever mad! I thought they'd never shut up. But I've been here seven years now, so they've come around. They're pleased I'm making it by myself, but they still won't come out here, they think it's too backward!"

I considered. "Don't you have any problems at all out here?"

"Oh yeah. Always. But women work better than men, I think, to solve problems. I think this project is helping everybody."

"All the women in the villages, too?"

Kawthar stopped in the road and looked at me. "Well, not all. But the number of women who apply and get loans is growing, and more and more of the little projects make money. And when the women see they can make money, everyone wants to get in on the act."

"No problems at all?" I persisted.

Kawthar looked around us on the road, as though she thought we might be being followed.

"Water," she said. "There's never enough water. How can there be, though? The Nile's not wide enough for every single Egyptian person's farm. It never will be."

"So Salwa having her irrigation pipe stolen is not unusual?"

Kawthar paused before answering. "Well, most people ask before they take it. But it *is* hard for a woman alone." Pause. "Me, I'm ready to get married. I found a guy, he's from Cairo, too, seems okay. We're engaged now, our land is in the same village, and we're thinking of getting married in the summer, after the harvest." She pulled down her baseball cap once more and peered up at me from under its bill. "Our families gave up on us long ago," she said. "I'm almost thirty and so is he!" She laughed. "We'll show them!"

We had reached the door of the center, where Anne was waiting, and Hamid the driver, and Ahmed the training instructor, ready to take us back to Alexandria. Salwa had decided to stay over.

"Thank you, Kawthar." I shook her warm, firm hand.

Kawthar said, "Hey, I thought Anne said you were going to ask me about what women are supposed to do, and all that."

"I thought I had."

"No, you haven't. And I want to say something for you to write in your book. I think in any country that a woman is not just one person, she is four persons."

Anne said, "Oh come on, Kawthar, four people! That just makes things more difficult."

Kawthar put a hand on Anne's arm. "That's what you say, but I think you're wrong. Being several different people—a daughter, a sister, a mother, a wife, means a woman is stronger; she can operate on all burners!" She grinned at Anne, a big wide grin. "You can say in your report, Anne, that farming lets a woman do it all. It's a good life." She produced her loan book. "And I got all the payments today. Still one hundred percent payback. A good record."

And that was the message I conveyed to the women professors of Alexandria University's Department of Home Economics in the Faculty of Agriculture, the women who were and continue to be the driving force behind this new program for women farmers and the training and loan program that allows both the graduates and the village women to improve their earning power, and hence, they say, their lives. Dr. Soheir Nour, Dr. Madiha El Taliawy, Dr. Mawaheb Ebrahim Ayad, Dr. Samiha Nassib agreed to talk with me.

"If you want to raise the standard of living in any country, you have to work on agriculture, on home economics, which is really the food and care in the home," said Dr. Nour. "The future of any society is tied to the welfare of mothers and children." Dr. Nassib and Dr. El Taliawy as well as Dr. Ayad all told me, in different ways, that "it was not women alone, as individuals" they were concerned about, and helping, but "the group of which women are the crucial part—the family."

I told them how impressed I was with what I had seen; they seemed pleased, but allowed that there were still problems of illiteracy and poverty, "and we need more transport between villages—maybe we can get a bicycle project going, they're good for the environment, too."

"Think how much faster we could move, madame, if the women could read and Ahmed didn't have to do his money management bit with the eggs!"

How were they able to persuade President Mubarak to grant women equal rights with men in the land grant program?

The four ladies, all fashionably dressed, all educated, all concerned about their fellow Egyptians, looked at each other, and turned back to me.

First, it seemed I was under some misapprehension. The Mubarak program for agricultural college graduates had awarded land to women long before they got involved.

"Really?" I was honestly amazed. I thought I followed women's activities in Egypt and I had never even heard of this program. Or perhaps I wasn't looking for it?

"Then you see," said one of the professorial ladies, "We thought we could help women maximize this opportunity, so we started different programs for them."

I nodded. "Business training. Loans. Yes, I saw that."

"But others, too," put in Dr. Soheir. "Pesticide education. Animal health care. Maternal and child health classes. All of these things help women to succeed in their new efforts."

I remembered that one of Kawthar's loan clients had asked me if there were projects like this one for American farm women. I had to confess that I didn't know. I did say that in America anyone with money, male or female, could purchase land, hire a manager, and farm. "The same here," said the Egyptian woman. "But you have to have money first."

Money. That was it. The New Lands program was reminiscent of the Homestead Act passed by the United States Congress in 1862, which provided that "any person over 21 who was the head of a family, who was a citizen or an alien who intended to become a citizen could obtain the title to 160 acres of public land if he or she lived on the land for five years and improved it, or was willing to purchase it for $1.75 per acre rather than fulfill the residence requirement." Technically, then, women were eligible, but only those who were heads of households—not unmarried women, as in Egypt today. And of course the laws regarding land ownership varied. Some states did not allow for women's rights to land; interestingly enough, those which did were those where earlier Spanish laws prevailed, as in Texas. These were the laws, from the Moors, that granted women such rights in the seventh century. Early Islamic feminism in America.

But Egyptian friends pointed out that awarding land to men, and also to some women, is common in the Middle East—for service to a sovereign, for bravery in battle, or even for special continuing services (like the Sayyids in Iraq who were given land in exchange for their mediation during feuds and conflicts). Land is the best gift, people said. Land remains forever. And land in Egypt is unusually valuable, since only a small portion of the nation's physical area is fit for cultivation.

The New Lands project east of Alexandria, one of many throughout Egypt, constitutes about one hundred thousand feddans, a small percentage of the total cultivatable land in Egypt. About nine thousand settlers have taken on small parcels of land, including nearly a thousand women, again a tiny portion of Egypt's sixty million population. But the grains and vegetables and livestock they produce also help to feed other people in Egypt. For Salwa, Nadia, and Kawthar, the project has provided a new life, an independent life. Is this what we mean by feminism?

I went on, to try to find out more about the issue which, said my friends in Egypt, had replaced Islamism as the major political focus in the country today—female circumcision.

The Ibn Tulun mosque, built in A.D. 876, is the most ancient Arab monument in Cairo, a classic example of early mosque architecture that is on the itinerary of every art history tour of the city. With its harmonious proportions, severe, yet spacious cloisters, its pointed arches, and its minaret of simple brick, Ibn Tulun is a tribute to the architect, supposedly a Christian prisoner who earned his freedom with this noble design. The mosque is also a tribute to the vision of Ahmed Ibn Tulun himself, founder of the Tulunid dynasty. He proclaimed Egypt an independent country in 868 and ruled until 905, only to be overcome by Baghdad's Abbasid dynasty, the line of Haroun al-Rashid. Saliba Street, which winds in front of Ibn Tulun, was once one of the great cosmopolitan streets of Cairo, a kind of medieval Fifth Avenue, where merchants from the then known world strolled with writers, scholars, physicians, and Quranic sheikhs. They sat in the Saliba Street cafés, browsed in its bookshops and prayed in its mosques—Ibn Tulun, but also Sultan Hassan, at the foot of the mighty Citadel.

Today, appropriately enough, given its history, the working-class area around Ibn Tulun boasted a hospital and a relatively new clinic for mothers and children. It was in this clinic that I sat one morning in the spring of 1996, waiting to interview the director of the Egyptian Society for Prevention of Harmful Practices to Woman and Child, i.e., female circumcision. I had been brought to the clinic by my friend Nadia Atef, an Egyptian anthropologist who sat on the board of the society.

"Please come in." Aziza Kamel, the gentle gray-haired lady who runs the low-key educational program, greeted us and ordered coffee. "We feel lucky to be here," she said, in answer to my comment about the spacious office and the convenient location of the society—right down the hall from the mother and child clinic, with its sunny court shaded by an enormous jacaranda tree, now in full purple bloom.

"My husband found this space for us in 1991," she explained. "He works for the Cairo Child Welfare Society. But we've been working on the problem since 1979, when circumcision was declared illegal by the Egyptian government."

She introduced me to the staff of five young women, two of them interns from Cairo University where they were studying social work and journalism respectively. "They help with the workshops," she went on. "We do lots of workshops throughout Egypt, but we go in groups. I always take a doctor, a lawyer, a religious official, as well as a woman who has been circumcised and one who hasn't. The workshops are usually quite successful, we have good discussions and the local people follow up—in the clinics, house-to-house medical teams, and so on." She took off her glasses, wiped her eyes, sighed. "But you know, madame, it goes on—and it's getting worse."

The society is only one of dozens of groups (the Cairo Committee on Human Rights is another) that are involved in Egypt's long-standing campaign against FGM (female genital mutilation), a campaign which began nearly forty years ago, when the Minister of Health for-bade its practice in public hospitals or by any licensed health profes-sional—doctor, nurse, midwife.

"We were pleased with ourselves at the time," said Aziza Hussein, then president of the Cairo Family Planning Association, which had been involved in the drafting of the decree. "Then, twenty years later, when we did a follow-up study, we discovered, to our surprise and consternation, that the practice of circumcision had not slowed, but continued, especially in rural areas. So we decided we had to work harder."

Egyptian doctors, nurses, religious specialists, lawyers, journalists, and representatives of women's organizations gathered in 1979 for a conference on female circumcision. They concluded that it was "harmful" and "a kind of mutilation and distortion of bodily organs having a special function. . . . The absence of any health benefit oc-curring from this operation," they wrote in the final report, means that "female circumcision is harmful and therefore its confrontation and opposition become imperative."

However, despite the stepped-up eradication campaign and the legal ban, recent data indicate that the incidence of female circumcision continues to rise in Egypt, particularly the practice of clitorodectomy, the removal of a small segment of a woman's clitoris. A few communi-ties have worked together to stamp out the practice, but overall, the operation, which predates Islam and Christianity, is still common among both Christians and Muslims in Egypt, and found all along the Nile, deep into Africa. Since the practice is illegal, has no religious sanction, and is seen by specialists as harmful to women, both physi-cally, socially, and psychologically, I asked Madame Kamel why it con-tinues to flourish.

Madame Kamel shook her head in its flowered scarf and old-fash-ioned black snood. For a moment I thought she might weep, for her brown eyes filled with tears behind her pale-framed glasses.

"CNN was an incredible setback," she said finally, after clearing her throat several times.

"CNN?"

Nadia interrupted. "Yes, B.J., you remember the documentary film on circumcision that CNN showed during the nineteen ninety-four Population Conference? That's what Madame Kamel is talking about."

I had not seen the film but recalled reading that it had created an uproar; the filmmaker and the circumciser were jailed, and it wiped out all the hopeful results of the 1994 Population Conference related to

FGM, with its final program of action containing five passages condemning the practice and outlining measures to eradicate it. Egypt had officially endorsed the program, as had the majority of governments in attendance.

I brought my thoughts back to the society's office near Ibn Tulun, to hear Aziza Kamel saying sadly, "As long as we worked quietly with families, we were going on very well, but now no. That film forced everybody to take a stand. We were having some success, we thought. Now we have to start all over again. And the press!"

"Aziza, don't forget, the Board is behind you," said Nadia soothingly.

But Aziza Kamel was right to be sorrowful. After the CNN film, charges flew back and forth in local and international media. The film was "a new form of Western imperialism," according to some members of the religious community; *al-Sha'ab,* one of the opposition newspapers, cited a Western doctor, one J. E. Lorry, who purportedly had written a medical article in favor of female circumcision. The minister of health issued a new decree, stating that all circumcisions of males and females had to be performed in hospitals, with medical personnel (not local barbers) in attendance. This, he said, was to "clarify" the situation, but it only served to widen the confrontation, for the decree was seen by many to sanction a formerly banned operation. Then the rector of al-Azhar University, the religious center of Egypt, issued a fatwa to the effect that female circumcision, like male circumcision, was part of one's adherence to Islam. This marked a radical change in the official position of al-Azhar, which had previously either condemned the practice as "not sanctioned by Islam" or maintained a carefully neutral stance. Following the publication of the fatwa, Egyptian women's groups and human rights groups went into action. They began by taking the minister of health to court in spring 1995, in an effort to have his decree rescinded. Their grounds for argument: the Egyptian penal code forbids permanent mutilation of any citizen. The court denied the plaintiffs' request to suspend implementation of the decree; the case has been referred to the State Council Judiciary Commission for legal opinion. At the same time, nine members of the Egyptian Organization for Human Rights announced they were taking to court the sheikh of Al-Azhar University himself! This was the first time in recent history that a senior Islamic religious leader had been charged in this way. As of 1997, both cases were awaiting adjudication.

By the spring of 1996, a new task force of fifty nongovernmental organizations had been put together to fight what was now defined as a political battle as well as one about religion and health. Aziza Hussein, who was past seventy, came out of retirement to organize the task force, which was headed by the social scientist Marie Asaad, also a longtime worker on the problem. "FGM," wrote the spokespeople for the New Woman Center for Research and Study near Bab al-Loukh in Cairo, "is a political issue which extends to larger issues concerning the status of women in Egypt and their efforts to struggle against the various forms of violence practiced against them." The New Woman Center, a ten-year-old feminist group, was articulating a sentiment I heard from many different sources as I traveled across the city, visiting and talking with women and men in the offices of institutions where the issue of FGM was now a major focus of action, close to family planning, legal aid, and political rights.

I began to try to identify the major players in this battle over women's bodies, which, in its passion and fury, reminded me of nothing so much as the struggle for and against abortion in American society. Politicians were asked for their opinions on the subject; protest groups marched both for and against the practice.

The major players in Egypt were, not surprisingly, representatives of major government institutions: Dr. Ali Abdel Fattah, minister of health, whose decree restricting circumcision to hospitals was seen as giving approval to the practice; the rector of Al-Azhar University, whose new fatwa had given religious sanction to FGM. On the other side was the minister of population and family welfare, Maher Mahran, who had come out against the practice and vowed that "Egypt is going to work on the elimination of female circumcision." Aziza Hussein wrote a formal letter to the minister of health, requesting that he rescind his decree (he refused). The distinguished journalist and long-time activist for women's rights Amina Said penned a piece, "The Disgraceful Decree," which appeared on December 16, 1994, in *Al-Musawwar* magazine, only a few weeks before her death. Aida Seif El-Dawla, who worked with the Cairo Committee on Human Rights, wrote "A Feminist Perspective on the Debate on Female Genital Mutilation." She concluded that the FGM battle had been transformed from a discussion of "an abstraction known as tradition to the arena of concrete political power struggles." Ms. Seif El-Dawla saw the circumcision struggle as a new move against Egyptian women's growing political and social independence.

Thus, rather to the surprise of some outside observers, the major political issue of modern Egypt in both rural and urban areas, is now no longer Islam, but female circumcision.

To observers like myself, the battle lines seemed clear. On one side, feminists, women's advocates, far-seeing officials like Dr. Mahran, the

International Population Council, helpful NGO's, nongovernmental organizations both inside and outside Egypt—all appearing, to me at least, as proponents of right and progress. For who can condone this practice, ancient and customary though it may be; it is clearly an assault on women's human rights, and acts as a detriment to women's sexual, maternal, and general health. On the other side, the forces of tradition seem to be massed: religion, local political hierarchies, and advocates of custom, mostly female. These latter groups appear to be taking a stand against the increased participation of women in Egyptian public life, their entry into the workforce, and into politics (after all, eighty-seven women ran for Parliament in 1995).

All very obvious, I thought. But I discovered, during my three trips to Cairo in 1995 and 1996, that the view espoused by most Westerners, including myself, was an oversimplification of a complex reality, which had religious, social, political, and often very personal ramifications for many Egyptian women. Dr. Nawal al-Saadawi raised local and international consciousness on the subject years ago, with her powerful essays and short stories, and her account of her own circumcision. Why then, I asked, did we see an increase, rather than a decrease in the number of female circumcisions being performed in Egypt today?

Here is a sample of comments made to me.

"It's partly reaction to the West," was the general consensus of several women who called themselves feminists, and who were opposed to and working against the practice. "The pushy attitude of some Western feminists has put many Egyptians' backs up. We, as Egyptians, are the ones to choose whether or not to eliminate this harmful practice."

"American feminists focus on this one issue, to the exclusion of all the other problems of Egyptian women. Why? Is it jazzier? More exotic?"

"Do we in Egypt give you in America advice on how to deal with your own problems like abortion and racism? We may criticize you in our own press, but we don't come to America and tell you what to do."

"If the West hadn't poked their fingers in, we would have had an easier time getting rid of this practice."

I asked whether this was really true. Several women and men pointed to the experience of the Sudan, where a more radical female circumcision is customary. British colonial administrators banned it in the 1940s, as "barbaric." In response, thousands of Sudanese men and women took to the streets, protesting the new British law as "destroying local culture and not to be obeyed." Was this, however, I asked, the same situation? Not quite, people admitted, but there were some similarities. "It's the women in both places who perform the operation, after all," said a woman anthropologist. "It's a women's ritual, so the fight has to do with women's power against men, old women's power over young women, and with who owns tradition."

But, I asked, how can this practice be justified on traditional religious grounds, when it is not found in other Muslim lands, and historically appears to be a Nilotic phenomenon, found among Christians, Muslims, and what used to be called pagans in countries all along the river into Africa—Kenya, Somalia, Burkina Faso.

"Well, because it is specifically Egyptian, not Syrian or Iraqi or Moroccan, or even Saudi Arabian. It's our own. It shows our differences from other Arab Muslim countries."

And so on.

What was I to think? How could I write about it? I turned to an old friend, the distinguished anthropologist Laila Shoukri al-Hamamsy, who was a former director of the Social Research Center at the American University in Cairo, held a Ph.D. in anthropology from Cornell University, and served on the staff of the International Labor Organization, in Geneva, a branch of the United Nations. She took me to lunch at the Automobile Club, once the old Muhammad Ali Club, in downtown Cairo.

"We all need to know a little more about the origins and functions of this practice," Laila began by saying.

"Doesn't everyone know enough about it already?"

"What exactly do we know?" returned Laila. "Is it sub-Saharan African in origin? Is it a rite de passage like boys' circumcision?"

"You surely don't equate the removal of a boy's foreskin with the removal of a woman's clitoris, which is supposed to be the site of generalized sexual pleasure? Come on, Laila."

"Oh come on yourself, B.J., do we really know that? Are there no other erogenous zones in a woman's body? What about a man? Do we know whether circumcision is positive or negative as far as his sexual pleasure is concerned?"

I was silent, staring at Laila. She must recognize, I thought, the harmful effects of this practice. But Laila was ordering coffee, signaling to the elderly waiter in the rather hushed and discreet paneled dining room of the club.

"You know I'm against this practice," she finally said. "But I am asking here another kind of question. Why this uproar now? After years of consistent efforts to eradicate it? I think feminists and the dedicated people of the human rights center are being set up for a no-win confrontation with government and religious forces who are against any kind of women's autonomy and particularly any kind of women's autonomy that looks as though it's related to the West."

This run-on-sentence answer was typically Laila, whose mind had always worked quickly, one idea after another tumbling out onto the conversational table!

I replied mildly that I thought the confrontation was already in progress.

"Yes. But why?"

"What are you trying to tell me, Laila, that the practice is illegal, but now the question is how to get rid of it?"

"Yes, B.J., exactly. It's a horrid and useless practice. But how to get rid of it? We need to do more research!"

"There must be plenty of research," I insisted.

Laila shook her head. "No, there's not. There's lots of indignation and rhetoric, lots of conferences and platforms of action and hand-wringing and promises. Very little actual data."

I ran down the list of the justifications for the practice I had read. Circumcision "controls the sexuality of women who are more highly-sexed than men." "Women need this natural curb. Left to their own uncircumcised devices, they would run wild, become promiscuous, and thus ruin the blood lines, the family structure that keeps society together." "Circumcision makes women more attractive to men." I cited them all to Laila.

"That leaves out the women themselves, doesn't it?" Laila pointed out.

I thought she hadn't really been listening to me, as she was nodding to friends at the next table, and signaling once more to the waiter, who had still not brought us coffee. But I underestimated Laila. She was listening, all right.

"Women," she said, "use circumcision, the act to do or not to do, as a negotiating position."

"Negotiating what?" I asked.

"Education, marriage, whatever their parents want or don't want them to do. Like, they say, if I agree to be circumcised so I won't shame you, then you have to let me a) go on with my studies; b) marry Ahmed, not Ali; and c) work at my job after marriage."

The coffee came. I looked at the tiny white cup, its foam or "face" slowly receding toward the rim of the cup, a sign that the coffee had boiled up just exactly the right amount of time.

"Always good Turkish coffee here," said Laila, laughing a little. "But you have to wait for it these days."

I nodded.

"You're having trouble with my argument, B.J."

She was right. I was. "Negotiation?" I burst out. "What do you mean? I agree to be cut up in my most private parts, and in exchange I can marry whom I like? It doesn't make sense."

Laila was not paying attention again. She had put on her glasses to get a better view of someone at the far end of the paneled dining room.

"We're talking about poor rural women, I presume," I offered, being unable to think of anything else to say. I cleared my throat to get her attention.

"Yes and no." Laila cocked her head, peered across the room, then took off her glasses. "That is Ashraf," she said. "I thought he was back from America, but wasn't sure." She turned back to me.

"Naturally," Laila replied. "Poor rural women, you say. Well, of course they're always brought into the picture, aren't they, maintainers of tradition, poor, illiterate, victims of men. But I think we're dealing here with a much more complex situation. We can't just say it's because the circumcised women are uneducated or from a lower class. The figures are close to ninety percent . . ."

I put in hastily, "I *am* asking myself, Laila . . ."

"No, you are just interrupting. Wait a minute. I meant ask yourself comparable things from your own society. Like why the chastity belt was a custom in Western Europe in the Middle Ages and why it disappeared? Ask yourself about clitorodectomy in Europe, my friend, used in the nineteenth century and well into the twentieth as a surgical "cure" for women's hysteria. Ask yourself about male circumcision. American men I know call it a mark of culture. That's what they're saying today about female circumcision."

"Okay, okay." I tried to smile, but the situation was not amusing.

Laila was not laughing, either.

Suddenly she said, "And what about men? Does anyone believe they want to sleep with women who are in pain? I doubt it. So is it the men making the women do it, or women making women do it because they think men want it? Or what?"

The Automobile Club was almost empty of the lunch crowd now, and the elderly waiter came, smiling, to ask if we wished something more. Laila shook her head.

"B.J., I don't know what to say exactly. This is not a confrontational kind of country, like you have in the United States. It is very worrying."

□ □ □ □

As I write in the spring of 1997, efforts to eradicate female circumcision continue. Aziza Kamel still works in the clinic near the Ibn Tulun mosque, Amal Abu Hadi in the Cairo Committee on Human Rights holds workshops across the country, in the Fayum, in Assiut, in Tanta. Marie Asaad has raised more money for the task force. A small community in central Egypt has banned the practice. One hopeful sign is that a new leader has been appointed rector of al-Azhar. How he will respond to the situation and to the court cases remains to be seen.

Is it true that women are breaking through into public space in Egypt more than ever before? Certainly, women have been forced to enter the workforce in great numbers, particularly since men have had to migrate in search of work, leaving thousands of households headed by women. Since 1973, when the Middle East had the lowest percentage of women in the workforce outside the home, the economic situation of high inflation, the increase in men's migrant labor, and the increasing educational opportunities have pushed women out of the home. They work today in factories, shops, offices, airline offices, as well as on the farms and in professional positions in places like Egypt's Television Corporation, where 50 percent of the employees are women. Women constituted 15 percent of the 1996 workforce, according to official statistics. But the total is far higher, economists believe, because of the large number of unreported part-time workers. Domestic service, one of the oldest wage-earning spheres for women, is not monitored or controlled by Egypt's labor laws, and thus the numbers are not clocked into the official surveys undertaken by government statisticians.

Amina, for example, works for two families, on alternate days, and has done this for the past fifteen years. She was making *molokhiyah* when I interviewed her, picking through a mound of the bright green spinach-like leaves, about which exiled Egyptians dream. With a crescent-shaped, two-handed chopper, she began to chop the *molokhiyah* on the marble counter of her employer's kitchen, deftly, quickly, until the green leaves were reduced to a thick runny paste.

"Oh yes, I got my high school certificate," she said, "and I had a good job in Ataba, working as a cashier in a cloth store."

"You quit to become a maid?"

Amina nodded. "Much better." She paused to heat butter in a skillet where she proceeded to brown finely chopped garlic and coriander. She held her neat head, wrapped in a tight navy blue head scarf, straight and high above her slim body, clad today in a flowered skirt and an olive-colored long-sleeved turtleneck.

Amina had explained earlier that she didn't have time to sit down and "be interviewed," but she'd be happy to talk to me while she worked. The door of the ground-floor flat was open, letting light and air into the dim kitchen, and allowing the good, but strong smells of garlic and coriander to pass out into the patio rather than perfuming all the tall rooms of the flat.

"Much better?"

"Much better to be a maid for nice people who are honorable, and I'm lucky that way. Now I can take care of my family and work, too. Come and go more or less on my own time. I can even use the phone here to check that my kids are doing their homework!"

No, she said, her husband did not help around the house, but he's "a very good man, a nice guy, honest." On Fridays, her sons help with laundry, with cleaning the house, with errands.

And she is very proud because all of them are doing well in school, and her oldest has done so well that he will clearly have a place in the university, and the second son has been recruited into the Egyptian Air Force.

"You're a good Muslim. Do you go to the mosque, Amina?"

"No, no, I pray at home. I let the men go by themselves. Then I have a little time to myself."

All of Amina's two brothers and five sisters are married, with children, and they all work, except one girl who is at home. "We have to work," said Amina simply. "How else can we live?"

And she admitted that her wages as a maid were four times what she earned as a cashier at the cloth store.

Women are also pushing at the political gates, winning elections to local neighborhood and village councils to give them the experience they say they need to run for Parliament.

"I was so struck by the number of women from all areas of Egypt that were running for Parliament that I decided to follow them on the campaign trail and see what was going on . . ." Ateeyat al-Abnoudi, a well-known Cairo filmmaker, was speaking about her new film, *Days of Democracy*. Ateeyat, a graduate of the London Film School, has made many films about life in Cairo, including the much-acclaimed *Permissible Dreams* about Egyptian women's hopes, and an earlier documentary, *Mud Horse*.

The new documentary charts Egyptian women's new struggle for political representation in the Majlas al-Shaab, the People's Assembly. The small number of women who were elected to office after 1956, when the women got the vote under President Gamal Abdel Nasser's new constitution, was seen as "shameful," and in the seventies, after Nasser's death, President Anwar Sadat decided to give women guaranteed seats in all of Egypt's public assemblies. This ploy backfired after Sadat's death, when such "appointing" was declared unconstitutional. Thus, since 1985 women, like men, have had to compete in the electoral marketplace. Women's representation in the now bicameral legislature, thus has declined in both the Majlas al-Shaab (People's Assembly) and in the Majlas al-Shura (Consultative Assembly). Out of a total of six hundred seats, women held only fifteen in 1990.

It is true that women have served as cabinet ministers since 1962 when Dr. Hekmat Abou Zeid was appointed minister of social affairs. And the first woman ambassador from Egypt, Dr. Aisha Rateb, was appointed in 1979.

But only a small minority of women actually hold seats in the legislature. Thus, when eighty-seven women, the greatest number in history, filed for candidacy in the 1995 elections, many Egyptians expressed surprise. What was also interesting was that many of the women ran as independents, not as nominees from a political party. "Why not? An Egyptian citizen should be able to run," said one candidate, who had taken out a loan to pay her campaign expenses.

Ateeyat's film also demonstrated the diversity of women who decided to run—women in Islamic dress, women in secular dress, a popular television screenwriter, village women in the same black garments seen in Huda Sharawi's old portraits. Dr. Negla Kaliouby spoke in the film about the need for a return to first principles, i.e., Islam. In her white head scarf and white full-length dress, she and her three similarly attired female campaign workers were the only women in the room where her campaign speech was given. But the men listened attentively, and one young man asked the players in the back of the room to "stop the dominoes so we can hear what the doctor says." Housewife Amal Rashad told her audience she was there to serve the community. Women in Sinai, Ismailia, Port Said, Minya, Suez, Alexandria, and Zagazig spoke about the need to provide basic services for everyone, all over Egypt: paved roads, better schools, fertilizer, clean piped water.

"The people who lost their houses in the earthquake must be given real houses, not promises on a piece of paper," said candidate Fathiyya al-Essal, a well-known Cairo television screenwriter. And Nafisa Hamed Hassan of Edfu said, "I am running especially for the poor, those who need services and aren't getting them. My symbol," she added, smiling broadly, "is the Gun." In Upper Egypt, women discussed the need for coalitions between Christians and Muslims to avoid tragic violence.

Some of the men who followed the filmmakers asked Ateeyat, "Why are you just making a film about women running for Parliament, and not men?"

Ateeyat replied, "Well, when they are represented in Parliament in the same numbers we have them in Egypt—fifty percent—then we won't need to make films about them anymore."

But only ten women emerged victorious after the long and stormy campaign, one marked by threats of intimidation and violence as well as rigged voting in the booths. The public outcry was so great that the government scheduled a runoff, and in that contest the women fared even worse. Just eight women were finally elected and are serving in Parliament today.

The losers appeared undaunted. Several said they planned to run again, in the year 2000, when the next five-year election will be held. "And we'll win," they insisted, "but we will have to keep working—and working hard."

The first Arab Women's Book Fair, held in Cairo in November 1995, was of greater significance than if it had been held in America. For here the feminist issue was the appropriation (by women) of the written word, a crucial appropriation indeed when one understands the elevated position which the written word holds in the Arab world, both the holy word and the secular word. After all, the very first word of the Qur'an is an admonition to the faithful to read! An ideal Arab leader is brave, religious, kind, powerful—and a poet. The ability to create an elegant poem or a finely crafted bit of elegant prose is valued across gender and class lines, both in the oral as well as the written tradition. Traditionally, the only person allowed to interrupt a national leader is a poet; Berber women in the Atlas mountains of Morocco speak out against personal injustice through public recitations of their own poetry; my friends in Al-Nahra, in southern Iraq, wrote and recited couplets about their inmost feelings; Bedouin women from the deserts of Egypt and into Arabia speak their minds in established poetic forms. And people listen.

In the past women tended to write at home, far from the public arena where their fathers, brothers, and husbands conducted business. Thus the Arab Women's Book Fair was a dramatic demonstration of a real sea change. The time had come for recognition that women's writing was out in public life and ready to be taken seriously.

I went over the day before the opening to watch the twenty-six publishers from ten countries setting up their wares in the Hanager Center, the cultural complex that also houses Cairo's splendid new opera house and the Museum of Modern Egyptian Art.

"So," said Hesna Makdashi, "what do you think, B.J.?" She was holding up the fair poster, specifically designed by Adly Shukrallah, an image of a lush palm tree loaded with golden fruit.

"A pregnant date palm," laughed Ferial Ghazoul, one of the judges for the three prizes to be awarded at the final session of the fair. "Are we talking about literary creativity here, Adly, or what?"

"But a very nice poster," I put in, and wandered about the booths—admiring books being set up on the shelves, books by and about Arab women in Arabic, French, and English.

"Fifteen hundred titles," said Hesna, following me about, then skittering back to help Ferial and Adly hang the posters—in the corridor, in the café, and in the room leading to the auditorium where the opening ceremony and the evening panels and discussions were to be held.

Ferial explained that a committee of independent writers, editors, and social activists spent two years putting the event together, and raising money from local businesses as well as international agencies to pay for the installations, rental of the space, publicity, and the three literary prizes.

I came back the next evening, when four hundred guests crowded into the auditorium and sat in red plush seats to hear the keynote address by Dr. Salma Khadra Al-Jayyusi, Palestinian poet and critic. She spoke of the number of countries represented by the women at the fair; "an Arab literary alliance," she said, and cited Arab women's "achievements in education, science, politics, as well as in arts and literature, their contributions to the development of Arab society."

But the audience was most attentive in the working sessions, when visiting writers, from Moroccan Leila Abouzeid to Lebanese Hoda Barakat, spoke about their work, their personal goals and problems. Students, literary critics, media, men and women, listened while Radwa Ashour, the Egyptian novelist, talked of her early fear of putting words on paper. "Like many people who have read the great classics, I suppose, I doubted I was capable of producing anything of real literary value," she said.

Fawzia Abu Khaled's poetry is considered so avant garde in form and so outspoken in content that she has been hounded out of her teaching job at the women's college of a Saudi Arabian university. "I'm still at the university, but in curriculum planning," she explained.

"And of course I continue to write, though much of my work doesn't appear in my native land."

Ahlam Moustaganami, an Algerian writer, spoke against censorship. "Silence is terrible," she said. "We must fear silence." She reminded the audience that more than fifty writers have died or been assassinated in the recent past in Algeria.

"But self-censorship," shouted one young woman in jeans and tunic and head scarf, standing up and interrupting Ahlam's speech. "That's just as bad, and women do it all the time! We shouldn't!"

A gentleman asked politely whether the fair did not do a disservice to the authors.

"Disservice?" echoed Hesna, in some amazement.

"Yes," he said. "A woman's fair—doesn't it just marginalize and ghettoize women's writing, keep it out of the mainstream?"

"No, no," protested Makdashi. "None of us is interested in segmenting our society, separating one group from the others. Women's work should be judged like all literary work, in terms of its quality."

Reports were presented about the achievements of women's movements—in Bahrain, Morocco, Palestine, as well as Egypt. The discussions went on, drifting into the smoky café, where television producers from Italy, Spain, and the Netherlands piloted one writer after another into far, quiet corners where they could be interviewed on camera over the babble of intense conversation.

And there were dramatic and poignant moments, when poets and novelists from different countries who intimately knew each other's work but had never met were introduced and spontaneously embraced.

Judges Edward Kharrat, Ferial Ghazoul, and Latifa Zayat awarded first prize to Radwa Ashour for her historical trilogy of life in Andalusia after the 1492 expulsion of Muslims and Jews. Ahlam Moustaganami received second prize for her daring novel, a love story, *Memory of the Body*. Third prize was awarded to Bouthaina al-Nasseri for a collection of short stories about life in Baghdad and Cairo.

Practical sessions on the problems of writing, editing, publishing, and distribution were also included. Having difficulty getting your work published because mainstream houses insist there is no market for women's writing? Start your own press, advised Mai Ghoussoub of Al-Saqi Press, London; Laila Chaouni of Dar el Fennec, Morocco; and Hesna Makdashi herself, whose publishing house produces not only the magazine *Nour* but novels and other specialized books on women. All agreed that the route was not an easy one, but, said Chaouni, "We're still in business and making ends meet, at least."

Nour hopes to sponsor a women's book fair every two years as part of a broader marketing strategy of highlighting women's work and making it generally available to the public, Makdashi said. "We want to reach into the schools, too," she added, "so that children growing up in the Arab world today can understand women's growing contribution to their literary heritage." By the end of 1996, the book fair committee had budgeted funds to distribute copies of the prize-winning women's books to high school libraries in Egypt, Lebanon, Syria, and Morocco.

"Not bad for a first effort," said Hesna. "We wanted to showcase women's achievement, and I think it was a good, constructive step in that direction."

"We're all meeting for dinner at Le Grillon in honor of Ahdaf Soueif," said my friend Ferial Ghazoul, professor of comparative literature at the American University in Cairo as well as founder and current editor of the bilingual (Arabic and English) literary journal *ALIF.* "We always do it when a visiting Arab woman writer is in town."

At least I thought that was what she said, as I was having some difficulty keeping up with her seemingly random, but clearly sure-footed progress. We had come out of the university's side gate and Ferial was jaywalking, very quickly, dodging in and out between the cars and buses and taxis pushing along as Muhammad Mahmoud Street came to life in the lengthening April evening.

"A new restaurant?" I ran after Ferial to reach the curb of Midan al-Tahrir, just as the traffic light turned green and the cars and buses, five lanes deep, crammed into the four-laned street, roared into the central circle.

"Ful! Ful!" The young boy dangling a few strings of fragrant jasmine blossoms on his wrist was trying to tempt the pedestrians heading for the subway entrance, but he turned to us for a moment and smiled. *"Ful,"* he repeated enticingly. The heady fragrance of the jasmine reached me through the acrid odors of dust and sooty exhaust fumes, a fragrance familiar from days past. Jasmine heralded the onset of spring, and was the traditional accompaniment to the delights of evening—tea by the Nile, parties, dinners, and the theater. But I did not remember Le Grillon.

"It's not really a very new restaurant," Ferial went on, putting her hand on my arm to keep me from plunging into the crowded Rue Talaat Harb just as the light turned green once more. "You have to be careful, B.J. Cairo is not the calm peaceful city you lived in years ago.

But Le Grillon must have been here even then—it's been a gathering place for writers and artists as long as I can remember."

The red light seemed fixed in place, and the sidewalk peddlers became more insistent, men in shabby jeans and tee shirts, women in black milayahs, begging us please to buy new ballpoint pens, shoelaces, yellow-boxed Chiclets (from America!), socks, hair ribbons, old copies of *Time* magazine, cassettes, and piles of Duracell batteries. Ferial must have felt that insistence as well for she took my arm again and steered me up Rue Talaat Harb, away from the corner peddlers, past the shops banging open their shutters for the after-siesta hours. The evening business was just beginning.

"Ful! Ful!" Another boy ran down the street, close to the curb, barely avoiding the moving wheels of cars and black-and-white taxis, vying with a small boy hawking boxes of Egyptian-made Kleenex to catch the eye of any passing motorist.

"We meet regularly, this group of women writers, and we always meet here. It's central and people are polite." We had made it as far as Rue Kasr el Aini and now stood in a small passage, leading off the street, where a neon sign above a red door blinked "LE GRILLON."

"And tonight is a very special occasion, honoring Ahdaf. I'm happy you were able to be here, too." Ferial knocked at the red door.

Ahdaf Soueif, acclaimed Arab-British novelist, had spoken earlier to Ferial's class in gender and literature, and the students had not exactly been polite. They asked her why she wrote in English, not in Arabic, why her highly acclaimed novel *(In the Eye of the Sun)* was so incredibly detailed, and whether she considered herself Egyptian or British.

"Well, I have a flat in Cairo, it's my natal home, my mother still lives here," Ahdaf had replied carefully. "But of course I was brought up in England and went to school there, so my home is there as well!"

Daughter of Fatma Moussa, longtime chair of the Cairo University English Department, Ahdaf has been touted both in East and West as a gifted writer who is concerned with identity, particularly women's identity, in a world where multiple choices, residences, and identities are becoming commonplace. She is one of the first to write so frankly and explicitly and in great detail about Arab women's lives outside the Arab world. I was looking forward to talking to her at some length.

"We're not sure how many of the group will come, but I should think a dozen, B.J. The conversation will all be in Arabic, can you manage?"

"I'll do my best," I answered. "I can probably follow, but I won't ask too many questions. I'm just happy to come and participate. They're all women writers?"

Ferial nodded. "I think we're a bit early," she said, when her second knock on the red door below the flashing neon sign did not bring a response. "Yes, B.J., all women writers."

"Ah, welcome, welcome, Madame Ferial." The man who opened the door, wearing a waiter's dark pants and white shirt, smiled broadly and switched immediately to what I recognized as Iraqi dialect, to ask after her family. "He's an Iraqi exile," explained Ferial as he ushered us into the restaurant, dimly lighted like the outside passage from the street.

Le Grillon seemed to be totally empty, at least as far as I could see in the indirect lights that glimmered red and green along the arches decorating the brick walls. Large, cavernous, and multileveled, it boasted a kind of balcony wrapped around the center courtyard where a fountain splashed and a single long table had been laid with snowy-white napery, silver, and shimmering glasses.

"We're sitting in the middle?" I asked, slightly incredulous.

Ferial laughed and sat down in the chair the maître d' had gallantly pulled out for her. She had a wonderful tinkling laugh and the maître d' smiled in appreciation and nodded at me as if to say, Isn't she great?

"Yes, B.J., we're sitting in the middle, in the public eye. The thing is that women writers in Egypt today *are* in the public eye."

She settled herself, ordered "fresh lemonade, please," and asked me again whether I remembered this restaurant. "It's in the area where all the small galleries have been for a very long time, bookstores, too."

I shook my head, and looked around in some wonderment, at the balcony, and at the fountain, whose soft sound punctuated pleasantly the romantic strains of some old Italian ballad coming from speakers, hidden, like the colored lights, behind the decorative arches set into the walls. Now that my eyes had adjusted to the dimness, I could see that the place was not entirely empty. A single couple sat at one of the balcony tables, drinking beer and lemonade. The man leaned forward and stared at Ferial and me. And no wonder, I thought. Twenty years ago I would have stared, too, at the sight of two unaccompanied females, out for an evening meal, who had chosen to sit in the very center of a public restaurant. After all, it was less than two hundred years ago that the historian Abdul Rahman Jabarti chronicled the arrival of Napoleon's troops to his Egyptian readers, and was stumped for a polite Arabic translation of the word "restaurant." Why? Because the idea of eating in public, outside the family circle, was incomprehensible to the average Egyptian. Eating outside meant that your family could not feed you or wished you out of the house!

"Hello! Hello! Ferial, hi, how are you? How do you do, B.J.!"

The members of the writers' circle were filing in, taking places at the snowy central table, talking excitedly to Ahdaf Soueif, tall, slim, and dark. She had come in with Randa Sha'ath, the photographer.

"I really don't know why I'm here," said a middle-aged woman in a smart black pants suit and violet-toned scarf.

"You're a writer," I said, trying to be polite, though I had no idea who she was.

"Yes, I write, but it's all in drawers. It's not good enough."

"Oh come on, my friend," said a woman with short dark hair who sat next to me and turned out to be Salwa Bakr, well-known novelist and short-story writer. The University of Texas Press had published a translated collection of her work. "Publish! Go on! Try! What are you afraid of?"

Across from me a young woman was looking worshipfully at Salwa Bakr, watching her light a cigarette and order beer.

"She's writing her M.A. thesis on Salwa," explained Randa, who had spent the afternoon taking portraits of Ahdaf for her next novel's dust cover. "But she's also interested in Ahdaf."

I looked down the table, all seats filled: twelve women writers and editors sitting in the center of the room. Food came, and drink—lemonade, beer, olives, tahina, *lebna* with crisp toasted squares of flat bread. After a few moments of pleasantries the conversation focused in on the subject of censorship. One of the writer's works had just been banned on the basis of one story, a tale of a woman's desperate loneliness in the distant Cairo suburbs.

"But I can understand that loneliness," said Ahdaf. "Why do you think I write about women the way I do? In England I am lonely, too, I am totally denuded of my taken-for-granted support systems. But I don't take them for granted any more."

"Makes a good novel though, doesn't it?" chirped Salwa Bakr. "Here we work on other kinds of loneliness and alienation."

"All are important," said Ferial, ever the mediator.

Family and support systems have their downside, too, pointed out an older woman in a colorful striped sweater. "Children," she said.

"They're wonderful, children," shouted someone from the far end of the table. "Like gold."

"Yes, like gold, but too many children, like too much gold, weighs you down so you can't move."

Laughter. Denial.

More restaurant customers were coming in through the red door, past the arched niches where the colored lights glowed, past the fountain splashing in the center space, past our table to which some curious glances were directed. Several people stopped and spoke to Ahdaf, Salwa, Ferial. The conversational level in the restaurant had risen so that it was difficult to hear the Italian ballads in the background.

Bouthaina al-Nasseri, a prizewinner at the book fair, came in late and sat down beside me. She had, as she explained, "children to attend to, two boys, before I could come out with friends like this."

Salwa talked about the writer Alifa Rifaat, respected and admired for her finely crafted stories and for her personal charm and courage. Alifa had died recently, and been much mourned.

"Read what you wrote for *Nour* magazine, in her honor—come on, Salwa," suggested Ferial.

Up to now, most of the Arabic conversation had been comprehensible to me, but when the table fell silent and Salwa read her memorial essay, I found I was missing the nuances of her work. But I listened, as the rest of the women listened, and when she had finished, the unpublished writer at the end of the table wiped her eyes. Two women jumped in to make suggestions to Salwa about "a better choice of words" (I got that one clearly) but Salwa shook her head. "Thanks, but I like it the way it is."

"It will be published in the next issue of *Nour,* B.J.," explained Ferial, "the same one where we have a review of one of your books!"

I felt honored to be in this company, and said so. The food came and went, and the conversation drifted to lighter topics. Someone told a joke about an Egyptian male writer whose new collection of erotic poetry was making waves. But, it seemed from my sense of the rapid-fire Arabic exchanges, it was not such a funny joke after all. "Men can publish erotic poetry," said one woman rather bitterly, I thought, "but if we as women tried, we'd get banned."

"Banned?" I echoed, not sure I had understood correctly.

"Banned," repeated the woman. "You see, women writers still have problems here."

We exchanged cards, shook hands, left our central table at Le Grillon. The restaurant was now crowded with men and women. Randa pointed out a well-known painter and a columnist for a daily newspaper and said good-bye.

"This wouldn't have been possible twenty years ago," I said to Ferial, as we headed out onto Rue Kasr el Nil to look for taxis in the nearly dark street.

"Of course not. But think of the changes since then, B.J.," Ferial answered. "Education, lots more education, which means not only women writers, but women *readers*. And this is an area where the written word has status and power. It's not a joke, or insignificant, to be able to handle words with such felicity as the writers you've just met. Why do you think L—— is banned? Her words are powerful— and dangerous!''

The gathering of women writers at Le Grillon gave me some perspective on the groundbreaking event I had witnessed earlier—the Arab Women's Book Fair. For that was an affair which had drawn women from all kinds of artistic and social movements. Ferial Ghazoul was there, pleased with the prizewinners for whom she had judged: Radwa Ashour, Ahlam Moustaganami, Bouthaina al-Nasseri. So was Safinaz Kassem, in a new cotton peasant dress and a matching head scarf, attending to the needs of a very old woman in a wheelchair. When I asked the identity of the white-haired lady, Ferial said, "I have no idea, let's ask Safinaz." But Safinaz did not know either. "We assume she must be somebody important," she answered, "but whoever she is, she wants to hear about women's writing. Don't we all?" She cast an eye around the crowded room, where I saw students in jeans, fashionable women in silk suits and turbans, diplomats, actresses, students in Islamic dress.

Hala Shakrallah was there, with her eleven-year-old daughter. "We've got a special booth at the fair," she had told me. "We're distributing free material to women about their rights." But Heba Raouf Ezzat was not there. I was told that, with her husband's blessing, she was in London to complete a Ph.D. in political science. Ateeyat al-Abnoudi was in the editing studio, but people talked about her forthcoming film in excited tones. Salwa Bakr was mischievously baiting everyone—me, Ferial, Safinaz. Marie Asaad was there, with women from the Cairo Committee on Human Rights. Iqbal Baraka, in a beautiful new blue suit, greeted me warmly. She told me there were representatives from Alexandria present, but I did not see any of my acquaintances from the Home Economics Department of the Agricultural College. Salwa, Nadia, and Kawthar were obviously at home on the farm, tending to daily chores. Anne Johnson, who had come to the opening, told me that Salwa's claim for redress of her stolen irrigation pipe had been approved by the court. "Now we have to get the money out of the guy," said Anne, "and that's not easy. But knowing Salwa, she'll do it." Randa Sha'ath was there, taking pictures for *Al-Ahram,* which was doing a full-page feature on the fair. And when Salma Khadra al-Jayyusi, in her keynote address, stated that "one of the best events of the twentieth-century Arab world was the emergence of women in all areas of life," it was true that a few distinguished gentlemen rose and left. But most of the men, and all of the women, stayed on and applauded Dr. al-Jayyusi's sentiments. She stated, eloquently and clearly, what the book fair demonstrated: despite recent setbacks, Egyptian women, like all Arab women, were moving in new and important directions—to improve not only literary work but their lives, the lives of their families, and the state of their nations. Family feminism, definitely.

SIX

囗囗囗囗囗囗囗囗囗囗囗囗囗囗囗囗囗囗囗囗囗囗囗囗囗囗囗囗囗囗囗

Iraq

I'M ON Saddam Hussein's side, no matter what anyone says," said Nejlah.

I could hardly conceal my astonishment at this announcement and the other women at the table looked equally surprised. It was February 1991. We were lunching together at a Washington, D.C., restaurant to honor Nejlah, a distinguished Palestinian lawyer, and a strong advocate of women's rights who had just accepted a post with the International Lawyers Association in Geneva.

"Saddam Hussein? Nejlah, how can you? He's invaded Kuwait. He's a . . ."

Nejlah waved her hand. "I know, I know, B.J. He's a ruthless tyrant who heads a repressive political regime—yes, I agree."

"So how can you be on his side?"

"Because, my dear, he has done more for women's rights than any leader in the Arab world."

"Saddam?"

"Yes, Saddam. Lots of Arab leaders are tyrants and run repressive political regimes. So I look at what they are doing in the area that means most to me. Women's issues. And he wins by a landslide."

I found it hard to believe Nejlah. Everyone knew that Saddam ruled with an iron hand, eliminated his opposition without mercy, conducted brutal surveillance on the activities of his people. Torture was mentioned, and he was reputed to be developing chemical weapons. In the nine-year Iraq-Iran war, a million people died on both sides. For nothing. Now, apparently not satisfied with that expedition, he had moved into another conflict—with Kuwait. And Nejlah, whom I respected, supported him.

Lunch was delicious—grilled chicken with garlic sauce, one of my own longtime favorites—but I had difficulty finishing my portion. Nejlah must have realized how dismayed I was.

"I know you care about Iraqi women, B.J.," she said. "I've read *Guests of the Sheik*. It's a nice book, but it's about the past. Things are very different in Iraq now, especially for women. When were you there last?"

"Nineteen fifty-eight," I almost whispered, realizing how ridiculous it sounded. Thirty-three years is a long time. Many things obviously had changed. "But of course," I added, somewhat defensively, "I've tried to keep up, readings, and so on."

Nejlah looked at me. "Reading? Do you think the Western media, including academia, is open and unbiased in its treatment of Iraq, or any Arab state? You should go back. Because if you look at the record, you'll find out I'm right."

"Theory or practice?" I returned. "Lots of countries, including the United States, have great laws on the books. What happens to women is another matter."

But Nejlah would not give in. "Go back, B.J. Theory and practice are both working well in Iraq. You'll see."

Look at the record. Go back. See for yourself. Nejlah was right to chide me, for *Guests of the Sheik* was indeed a chronicle of a time now past, of people who had aged or passed away. More than a generation. And the image of Iraqi women which is presented in the book was, I realized, the memory that remained in my mind, despite my reading through the years, an image of women who lived apart from men, covered themselves when outside their homes, had little apparent personal freedom or choice, let alone power. For two years, I myself had lived as they lived, worn an all-enveloping abbayah, visited only with the women and learned about a woman's culture. And that image, I told myself sternly, had become the image of Iraqi women that lived in the minds and hearts of the thousands of people who had read *Guests of the Sheik* during the thirty years since its publication. If Nejlah was right, I needed to go back, to reassess those old impressions, to bring the past up to the present.

The question was, how to get to Iraq? Westerners were not welcome, and travel there was frowned upon by the United States government. Over the years, we had both tried to return. Bob had made it to Baghdad briefly in 1964, and again in 1967, but I had never returned. Family responsibilities had kept me home in the sixties; politics intervened in the seventies and eighties, with the rise of Saddam Hussein, and the Gulf War ended the mid-eighties thaw in Iraqi-American relations. In the years since the end of the Gulf War, a trip to Iraq seemed an unlikely possibility. The ideas about Iraqi society presented in *Guests of the Sheik,* my book, and in *Shaykh and Effendi,* Bob's book, would, it seemed, have to remain unqualified and unchanged, and nobody else's reports were likely to replace them.

But some surprises lay ahead. Bob and I were given the opportunity to update our joint book, *The Arab World,* and once more applied for Iraqi visas, without much hope that they would be granted. Then they arrived in our Austin, Texas, mailbox! Now what could we do? We had already finished our research travel—a trip to Iraq at this point seemed out of the question, it was so expensive! Then, just as unexpectedly, Bob was invited to give a week of distinguished lectures at the American University in Cairo in spring 1996 (travel and expenses paid for both of us). We could pay to fly on to Amman from Cairo, and travel overland from Amman to Baghdad. This fourteen-hour taxi or bus trip was the only legal entry to Iraq, under the sanctions imposed at the end of the Gulf War. We decided to go.

"But we probably won't be able to get to the village, B.J.," Bob warned. "They say the south has suffered a lot, and loyalties are probably in doubt, especially after the Shi'a uprising in Kerbela. I wonder how many people died there? Maybe some of our friends were involved, and talking to foreigners would get them into trouble."

"We should go anyway," I said.

Bob nodded. "Probably," he said, "though there's no guarantee anyone will want to see us."

So we went ahead. Bob gave his lectures in Cairo and we flew to Amman.

The trip from Amman to Baghdad was long, and hard on the back, despite the relative comfort of the seats in the old Chevrolet Caprice. We were crossing a flat, desert-like plain cluttered with black igneous rocks, empty except for an occasional green blip on the distant landscape, an oasis of palm trees which cut a sharp dark silhouette on the wide sky. I knew Bob was as full of uncertainty as I was, and that we both dreaded this trip in some way. What kind of hostility might we find in Baghdad? No room at the inn for Americans? Tom Hartwell, our photographer friend from Cairo who had come along, was much more confident that we would be okay. We would probably be assigned to the Rashid Hotel, he told us, where he had stayed many times as a photojournalist during the past ten years. But who would want to see us or talk to us?

I told myself not to expect too much. But I also wondered about Nejlah's assertions. She was right about literacy for women, for I had looked it up. Eighty-eight percent, the highest in the Arab world, up from 23 percent in 1970. Yet in the media coverage of the Gulf War, most of the women I glimpsed in the street scenes were wearing black abbayahs, exactly like the one I had worn in the village in the 1950s. Their faces weren't covered, but still I wondered. In the fifties, women were beginning to take off their abbayahs, and now they were putting them on again? Was this a return to Islamic identity as in other countries? But we knew that Saddam Hussein was a secular, not a religious leader. The Ba'athist Socialist Party he headed was secular like Atatürk's party in Turkey seventy years ago. Perhaps, I told myself, those women in the television street scenes were carrying briefcases under their traditional abbayahs and were on their way to important business meetings? It seemed doubtful, but then, what did I really know about the status of contemporary Iraqi women?

During those empty, uneasy hours in the desert taxi, bumping along with an unusually silent middle-aged driver (not even any Arab music on the radio)—Bob dozing in a corner of the backseat, Tom dozing in front—I tried to focus my scattered thoughts and fears, gather up my bits and pieces of research, to prepare myself in some way for what was to come. We knew the Iraqi people had suffered terribly during the war and that even now, in 1996, five years after the end of hostilities, food and medicine were scarce except for the fortunate members of Saddam Hussein's elite Republican Guard. We had brought gifts, as per suggestions from Iraqi exile friends: medicines for children, vitamins, coffee, aspirin, chocolate. We felt we were prepared for some eventualities, though I wondered whether Bob was not indeed right, that no one would want to talk to us. Tom thought otherwise. "They want to tell their story in the West," he said. "Why not to you guys, who've written well about them in the past?"

In the fifties Nazik Malaikah, the famed Iraqi poet, wrote "Who Am I?"

> The self asks who am I?
> I, like it, am bewildered, gazing into shadows
> Nothing gives me peace
> I continue asking—and the answer
> will remain veiled by a mirage
> I still keep thinking it has come close
> but when I reach it—it has dissolved,
>   died, disappeared.

The sentiments of Nazik's poem mirrored my own. Who was I to come back to Iraq after an absence of forty years, and presume to try to update the record on the basis of a short visit. I told myself that perhaps Nejlah was right in her estimate of the new status of city, if not rural, women. Even in the 1950s, things were beginning to change. Though there still was only a girls' primary school in the village of Al-Nahra, in Baghdad women were graduating from universities and taking their places alongside men, though they were limited in their job options. Nazik Malaikah herself was already famous for her pioneering role in the new free verse movement when I interviewed her in Baghdad in 1958.

Nazik, with two other Arab poets, both men, had challenged the hallowed patterns of traditional Arab poetry, and forged a daring style to articulate the new realities facing the Arab world. World War II had ended, Israel had been declared an independent state in 1948, and throughout the area protests were in progress, the rumblings of revolt against the last vestiges of Western colonialism. The year we arrived in the Middle East, 1956, President Gamal Abdel Nasser nationalized the Suez Canal, to the dismay of European shareholders and the delight of Arabs everywhere, who saw him leading the way to area-wide independence from European rule. The emergence of nonaligned nations, owing loyalty to neither East nor West, was heralded in the press, a new bloc that was quickly termed the Third World.

"When I went to Cairo last year for a poetry conference, everyone was writing political poetry," said Nazik, that day in 1958 as we sat in the cool tall rooms of her family's Baghdad house. I took a photo of her on the porch, with the whispering garden greenery in the background. Though it was a long time since that afternoon, I still remembered Nazik's quiet, self-assured manner, the serenity of the house, the scent of jasmine that reached us from the garden.

"Political poetry?"

Nazik nodded, and said, "But I refused. I said politics per se was not the purpose of poetry. Of course, I agreed that we needed new thoughts, new attitudes, but these should come through the *forms* of the poem, through the metaphors, the images, and rhythms, not through making up verses praising one Arab leader or another."

I remember writing busily in my notebook, a bit overawed by this young woman, who seemed so shy and so certain of herself at the same time, whose views were discussed in literary journals and newspapers throughout the Arab world.

Nazik brought us tall glasses of fresh lemonade, and said, "You probably don't realize it, but we have a name for the kind of poetry our leaders want everyone to write these days. It's exactly like the speeches I've heard in America when politicians are running for office. Except it's rhymed!" She sniffed in disdain.

"What is it called?"

"Platform poetry!"

My interview with Nazik was one of a group for *Mademoiselle* magazine's series on international women: "Young Women of Iraq" included Sabiha Daoud, Iraq's first woman lawyer; Dr. Lam'aan Amin Zaki, who was supervising new maternal and child health clinics; and Salima Shenshal, an early social worker who was setting up centers for poor migrant women in the squatter settlements of Baghdad, bustling then with new industries set up by the British-Iraqi Development Board. My article was never published, for a month after I submitted it, the 1958 Iraqi Revolution broke out, and the editors decided this was not quite the moment for an upbeat piece on Iraqi women. The King had been killed, and his British-backed locally disliked prime minister, Nuri Said, caught trying to escape in a woman's abbayah, had been cut down on the street by an angry mob. Jacobin-style trials of "imperialist sympathizers" went on for months, as did imprisonment, and executions.

The new government of General Abdul Karim Kassem at first promised rights, freedoms, and independence for all, including women.

The second stanza of Nazik's poem reads:

> The wind asks who am I?
>   I am its confused spirit, whom time has disowned
>   I, like it, never resting
>   continue to travel without end
>   continue to pass without pause
>   Should we reach a bend
>   We would think it the end of our suffering
>   and then—void.

Women in Iraq in those first heady days after the 1958 revolution might be forgiven for thinking they had neared the end of their tribulations. We were not there, but friends wrote excitedly of promised elections, increased funds to alleviate poverty, enactment of new laws. For women, the most important new laws were those which equalized inheritance for men and women, in contrast to Qur'anic law which allowed women to inherit half a man's share, the argument being that it was the man who supported the family. Arranged marriages were out in many educated urban families; young men and women who fell in love should be able to marry without parental consent, it was said,

and attitudes were even becoming more relaxed toward marriage between members of the Shi'a and Sunni sects of Islam. The new government made an effort to demonstrate this new sectarian cooperation. In
contrast to the old British policy of setting Shi'a against Sunni, Christian against Muslim, General Kassem appointed Shi'as and Christians
as well as Sunnis to important government posts. A woman was appointed to head the Ministry of Social Affairs, the first time this had
ever taken place.

But things did not work out quite as positively as our friends had
hoped. Governments rose and fell during the sixties. The inheritance
law was rescinded; the woman minister resigned. Nazik Malaikah married and moved to Kuwait with her husband; Sabiha Daoud retired;
Salima Shenshal went into exile in Beirut with her husband, like many
young people of promise and dedication who became disillusioned
with the new Iraqi state.

By the 1970s, the best way for a woman to have answered Nazik's
question, "Who Am I?" was surely to say "a member of the Ba'athist
Party, the party of Saddam Hussein." He was still in office in 1996, as
we drove on through the desert into Baghdad. The Ba'athists had
proclaimed themselves true socialists who saw women as an important
and crucial element in the formation of an independent secular state.
But what did this really mean?

From the beginning the General Federation of Iraqi Women, a part
of the Ba'athist Party, differentiated itself from Western feminist
movements. The party platform, published in 1978, stated the following principles:

> The General Federation of Iraqi Women is not a "women's"
> organization on the same line with women's organizations in cap-
> italist countries.
>
> It does not adopt the "fomentation of struggle" between the
> woman and her "antagonist," the man, as one of its objectives.
> Nor does it intend to distract half of the society from the principal
> issues. It contends that the usurpation of the freedom of the
> woman is a concomitant result of the national and class usurpa-
> tion suffered by the society and the entire Arab nation.
>
> At the top of the priority list of the responsibilities and assign-
> ments of the General Federation of Iraqi Women is: preparing and
> mobilizing Iraqi women to play their effective role in the battle
> waged by the Arab nation against imperialism, Zionism, reaction
> and backwardness.

The new Ba'athist women's movement thus directed attention away from male/female conflict. But this did not mean that the federation at the same time saw women as individuals, as public persons, in the Western sense of these words. On the contrary, the federation was careful to "glorify," as the American anthropologist Suad Joseph has written, "women's role in the family." As Article 38 of the Ba'athist Party constitution states:

1) The family is the basic cell of the nation, and the state is responsible for protecting it, developing it, and ensuring for it the condition of happiness.

2) Offspring are a trust given to the family first, and secondarily to the state. Together they must strive to increase it and to care for its health and upbringing.

3) Marriage is a national duty and the state must encourage, facilitate and supervise it.

What did these fine words mean in practice? Western observers of women's place in Soviet socialist countries like Russia and the Eastern European states have been careful to note that the so-called equality trumpeted in party platforms often turned out to be mere smoke and mirrors, that socialist women were no more "equal" in actual range of occupational choices and legal redress than were non-socialist women. I wondered whether the same might now be true in Iraq, and whether Nejlah's admiration from a distance was due less to realities in Iraqi women's lives than to theory and manifestos.

Tom woke up. "Hey, guys, we're almost there," he said.

Our fourteen-hour ride was drawing to a close, the sun was setting, and the motorist-friendly green signs above the highway overpasses began to read "Baghdad," "The South," and "To Damascus." I wondered whether I would have an opportunity in the coming days to see how Ba'athist Party ideology really affected the lives of ordinary Iraqi women.

We sat in the outer office of the Ministry of Information, not too far from the Baghdad Rashid Hotel, where, as Tom had prophesied, we had been placed by higher authorities.

"They keep all the foreigners together, so they can be watched," Tom had explained. "And we have to pay in dollars, cash, which is good for the country's depleted treasury."

Bob, Tom, and I were waiting to be summoned to the inner office, where the international press bureau chief was theoretically deciding what we could and could not do during our visit. We had handed in our wish list. Number one was "revisit Al-Nahra, in the province of Diwaniyah, to see old friends."

We had also offered, as proof of good intentions and work already completed, copies of our books *Guests of the Sheik* (mine) and *The Arab World* (Bob's and my joint volume). As I got up and wandered about, I could see those books on the corner of the chief's desk, through the window where, as his lips moved but we could not hear, we presumed he was imparting "do's" and "don'ts" to the foreign journalists sitting on the worn leather couches to his right and left: two French television reporters, an Indian and a Spanish journalist, come to cover Iraq's parliamentary elections, scheduled two days hence.

Baghdad itself had been a shock. An enormous sprawling modern city, stretching into the old palm groves, a city grown far beyond the boundaries of the small dusty capital where we had arrived forty years ago. In those days, red double-decker British-made buses trundled up and down narrow Rashid Street and into the newer residential districts of Karradat Mariam and Mansour. It was a colonial town on the Tigris. Not any more. Bob pointed out that we should not have been so surprised at the new construction, for after the 1958 revolution, Iraq had been able to bargain for and obtain a higher percentage of the profits from its own nationalized oil. Now Baghdad was a beautiful and enormous city, we saw as we toured the city with Mr. W., a businessman friend of a friend. The capital was full of parks and monuments to the party and its chief, of skyscrapers, modern boulevards, and shopping malls. We had read that successive governments had used oil revenues to improve the country. Still, the reality was amazing, particularly since we could not detect a single bit of war damage from the allied bombardment of 1991.

"That's true," said Mr. W. "He's fixed everything. You wouldn't even know there'd been a war, would you, Bob?"

Mr. W's pretty wife served us lunch and told me about the work of the General Federation of Iraqi women. "I'm a member," she said. "And I believe you will find things have much changed since your time, for the better—even now, with all the hardships caused by the recent war."

I said I wanted very much to visit the federation.

"Ask the people at the Ministry to arrange your visit," she counseled.

So we had come back to the Ministry office for a second visit, where we had been interviewed by a journalist doing a human interest feature for the party newspaper, *Al-Qadasiyyah*. "I think I will title it 'American Couple Comes to Iraq Looking for Their Memories,' " she said, a young woman with short dark hair curling over her ears, a shy smile. She interviewed us in Arabic and English.

A second reporter approached, this one obviously from television, for her camera soundman trailed behind her.

"Americans?" she said in Arabic, and without waiting for an answer, "Come with me, please."

No shy smile. No pleasant questions. It was an order. We followed her meekly into the courtyard of the Ministry and stood there, somewhat embarrassed, while the camera focused and a few men and women gathered to stare at us.

This journalist was also a young woman, but tall and dark-haired, her forehead creased in a seemingly permanent frown. She ordered the cameraman to move back a foot and turn to the side. He did so.

"And the elections? What do you think about the elections?" she asked brusquely.

Bob explained that we had not come to cover the elections, that in fact, we hadn't even known there were to be elections until we had arrived the day before yesterday. The frowning reporter raised her head peremptorily. "Cut!" she said in that international language of all photojournalists. The camera soundman did her bidding. "Thank you," she said.

We realized we'd been dismissed and headed back into the office.

"Please? Please?" It was the press bureau chief's secretary, with Tom behind him, gesturing us all into the inner office, now empty of Indians, French, and Spaniards. From Tom's smile, we decided it must be good news. It was indeed good news. We had been cleared to travel south. We could go to the village. We could stay overnight, an unusually generous gesture, the press chief said. After all these years, Bob and I would be able to go back to the village of Al-Nahra, where we had begun our lifelong involvement in the Arab world.

"Of course you will travel with a driver and representative from this office who will act as your liaison and translator."

"Of course," agreed Bob quickly.

"And you will be responsible for their expenses as well as your own."

"Right," answered Tom.

"You can begin right now. This gentleman will be your assistant."

"Good. Thank you," replied Bob.

We shook hands with a pleasant, rather diffident young man named Hadi, our "minder," and set off for a tour of old Rashid Street. There were no more creaking red British buses, in fact, no buses at all. The boulevard seemed cleaner and quieter, a far cry from the crowded old street of the days before the 1958 revolution.

"They've had three revolutions since 1958, remember," Tom pointed out. "Bezzaz, then the first Ba'athist coup, then Saddam's coup. And he's still here."

Despite fears that our presence as enemy Americans would incite the populace, no one paid the slightest attention to us, though we often strolled in pairs rather than a tight group of five. For more than an hour we ambled past shops, old and new, many closed, stopped to look at an open-air market where women in Western dress, not abbayahs, were picking through the piles of shoes and pajamas and children's underwear. The sun was warm. I suddenly realized I was not only tired but hungry.

"And aren't we due pretty soon for lunch in Azamiyah?" Bob said. He was right. Asma al-Gailani, who had kindly invited us to lunch, was the sister of my friend Lamia al-Gailani, the London-based archaeologist, "Oh yes," Lamia had said. "Do call Asma, B.J. She will be happy to see you. If something has happened and the political climate has changed, don't worry, she'll tell you."

Azamiyah was a long way from Rashid Street, in an area known in the past for large estates and gardens, the property of old Baghdadi families.

Hadi stiffened. "You are lunching with Iraqi friends?" he asked. His forehead wrinkled a bit.

"Yes," said Bob. "At the Gailani house."

"Rashid al-Gailani?"

"Relatives," answered Bob.

Hadi did not comment, but I could almost feel him memorizing the name though he was too polite to bring out his notebook and write it down. Or was this my paranoia?

"I suppose he'll be asked where we went," Tom pointed out later. "That's his job, isn't it? To tell people where we are and what we do, and to mind us while we're doing it."

So we set out with the driver and Hadi for Azamiyah. Baghdad College, the famous secondary school founded by the Jesuits, was the landmark Madame al-Gailani had indicated. But the driver seemed not to be familiar with the district, for he drove down one street and up another, past walled gardens, public buildings, long streets of shops in the process of closing for lunch. Finally, I spied a church steeple, sure sign of a Jesuit institution! The driver dropped us at a tall wooden gate, standing ajar. The brass plate affixed to the door told me this was the place. We could hear faint Arabic music, coming from the house and the garden beyond the gate.

Hadi got out with us, peered at the name on the brass plate, then bade us good-bye and promised to meet us the next day at the Press Center.

Our knocking was finally answered by a woman servant, all in black, who looked surprised.

"Are you sure the lunch is today, B.J.?" From Bob.

I nodded yes. I was sure. Then Madame al-Gailani came to the gate, a stockier version of her sister, my friend Lamia. She smiled welcomingly.

"You were supposed to be here at twelve," she chided me, still smiling. "And oh, I did not know you would bring men with you!" Another charming smile at Bob and Tom. She hesitated a moment, then said, "Come in, come in. Tell the car to leave," she instructed, "We will get you home." She shut the gate.

We passed through a free-standing outer wall of white-painted brick, a kind of loose architectural envelope for the house itself, and into a garden worthy of the charmed days of the Arabian Nights. Music drifted out the opened door, a high sweet woman's voice, accompanied by the low thrum of the *oud*, the Arab lute.

"Noon?" I repeated nonsensically. I couldn't remember that anyone ever ate lunch at noon in Baghdad.

"For the *kabul*," explained Madame al-Gailani, "The ladies' party. You must remember the *kabuls* in the old days, madame, when we women gathered at each other's houses, and told stories and sang and ate and entertained each other, and got up to other kinds of mischief."

I remembered the *kabuls* very well indeed, a very old institution from the days when Iraq was part of the Ottoman Empire. An at-home day for women, a social obligation in some circles. And I also remembered that *kabuls* were not just ladies' tea parties but networks—along which family news and political messages and warnings could be passed—even revolutionary messages.

"We're having *kabuls* again, we old ladies gather, to have fun really, now that we've raised our children," she said, an infectious smile on her attractive square face framed with graying blond hair, above a black-and-white djellaba. A party dress.

"Oh dear, I had no idea, I'm very sorry."

Tom and Bob looked at each other, at their shoes.

Madame al-Gailani laughed. "I guess men, Western men, are not, how would you say it, not very accustomed to being banned from a social occasion. But we will see what we can do." She called the servant woman, and introduced her as Um Shahid. "She will take care of you." Um Shahid gave us a quick darting smile.

"We'll leave, madame, I'm sorry," Bob began, but Madame al-Gailani raised an imperious hand, bare of jewelry. "No, no, you must not go. You were invited to lunch, you thought. Very well. We will serve you out here, separately from the ladies. And you, my dear"—pointing at me—"will eat here with the men and come see the ladies later. That will be easier for Um Shahid."

She gestured to a table and chairs, wrought iron, white, placed beneath a trellis overgrown with wisteria, the branches heavy with the violet blooms of early spring. Tom and Bob hesitated, but she was firm.

"All of you must stay," she told us. "I insist. The ladies may come and chat with you if they wish, we are much into mixed company nowadays you know, but I did promise them this day was a ladies' only party."

The music drifted out to us, in the garden, and I strained to hear the words.

"It is Widad," said Madame al-Gailani. "You must have heard of her, she is a friend of Lamia's too. Doesn't she have a lovely voice? It's an old Iraqi ballad, very romantic . . ."

She turned away, and called, "Um Shahid," then turned back with another charming smile. "Please excuse me, I'll be back."

We sat down happily on the cushioned garden chairs. The shade of the old cottonwood trees was a relief after the sunshine along Rashid Street. The wisteria nodded its violet branches over us, the dates were golden on the towering palms above, and the sweet singing reached us, even outside the house. I looked at Bob and Tom, whose faces reflected the sudden contentment I felt. Had it been only three days since we caromed down the Amman-Baghdad road, full of apprehension about what we might find in Baghdad, about how we might be treated?

"Please." It was Um Shahid, her head wrapped in the black head scarf, the *foota,* like the older village women I used to know. She bore a tray, three tall glasses of iced apricot nectar.

Five minutes later a feast was set down before us on the table in the garden, rice and meat and numerous salads, and a kind of ravioli, homemade, cooked with peas and cauliflower and spices. Homemade turnip pickles. Tahina. Egg salad, "specially made by my unmarried daughter," said Madame al-Gailani, having returned to us, her guests who had turned up unexpectedly. She smiled at our appetite, as we tucked into the wonderful meal.

"Have some more," she urged. "There's plenty, thank God. It was very hard during the war, for everyone. Not much to eat. No electricity. Now we grow a lot of our food." And then, the Arab greeting we had heard so often long ago; *Ahlan wusahlan* ("you are welcome").

The lady guests drifted out, in ones and twos, sat and talked with us for a moment, went back in to listen to the music. It was all very calm, very relaxed. What were we doing here? they asked. How did we find Baghdad after so many years? Wasn't the spring sun wonderful? Did we have children? Where were our children and what were they doing? What did Western newspapers write about Iraq these days? A brown-eyed lady in a fashionable shift of beige linen casually asked, "You don't have a copy of *The New Yorker* with you by any chance, do you?"

Um Shahid cleared plates, and Madame al-Gailani's young daughter brought out desserts. She was wearing a long flowered dress and the first *hijab* I had noticed in Baghdad. "Do have some of the meringue with jelly," she said. "I made it this morning."

"I used to visit my daughter in America regularly," said a pleasant-faced woman in a navy blue ensemble, who drew up another garden chair and sat down with us. "I got a college degree there myself. But it's hard to go now—costs a lot, and an exit visa from here is very expensive."

After lunch, Madame al-Gailani took me into the house and introduced me around. Bob and Tom stayed outside, savoring their tea. The women were all professionals from well-to-do families, now retired. Over the years they had served in ministries, schools, clinics, at the university. There did not seem to be any inequality here. Yes, they'd had government help in education, jobs, and with legal problems. Many were grandmothers, like me. They were well dressed by any standard, spoke perfect English, and were eager for news of the world. Several of them, it turned out, had read my books. Was I writing another one? What would I write about Iraq? When would it be published? Was my husband also writing a book? And the young man? Was he really a professional photographer who had worked for *Time* magazine, he looked so young.

I said how good it was to be back in Baghdad, even at this difficult time, and how much the city had grown and changed in the past forty years.

"Forty years!" echoed a tall woman in black, whose friends said she was always taken for Manuela, the heroine of a popular Mexican soap opera shown regularly on Iraqi television.

"Forty years! My God! This is a new place, compared to then, a progressive place. You know, madame, before the Iraq-Iran war, this was a wonderful country. There was enough for everybody. Equality for men, women, poor, rich. Lots of money and things to buy and enough goodies to go around. But now . . ." She gestured and left her sentence unfinished as she bade us good-bye.

When the last of the ladies, including Widad of the beautiful voice, had departed, Madame al-Gailani asked us all inside to have another tea with her, her daughter, and her niece Azza, Lamia's daughter. We admired the expanse of garden which we could see through the glass wall of the living room, the patio bright with flowering succulents, the palms and thick vines softening and cushioning the high fence at the back of the property.

"It's old land, but a new house," she explained. "We rented the old family place to the Italian Cultural Center. We grow some vegetables and herbs here. Fortunately, for us, this house was finished just before the Gulf War."

I told her that it seemed like a modern Arabian Nights house. "I like that description," she said. "Don't you, Azza?" Azza smiled and nodded. She was a very pretty girl, with dark hair, a fine face. She wore a red sweater over black turtleneck and skirt. "We worked with the architect, a relative, to do the whole thing. You like it." It was a statement, not a question.

Clearly we liked it, the old arches over doors and windows, the tiles, the oils and watercolors and drawings by modern Iraqi artists. The stained glass. "Azza did the glass," she said proudly and Azza looked pleased.

"That," said Madame al-Gailani, pointing to a piece, "is by Jewad Selim, our greatest artistic figure."

"We met him long ago," said Bob. "Didn't he die tragically young?"

"Yes, yes," she replied, and her face changed, became serious, meditative for a moment. "So many have gone." She said softly, half to herself. We knew that her husband had died suddenly during the Gulf War, of a heart attack, but were uncertain about raising the subject even after the passage of five years.

We sat quietly, drinking our tea, in this vast room that somehow, despite its size, exuded a sense of intimacy and comfort.

Perhaps it was due to the design of the arched room's end wall, which was not a clear sheet of glass, or even of stained glass, but a glass and wood mosaic of a curious and unusual pattern. Stars of red and green glass, teardrops of translucent yellow, small squares of carved wood screening had been set into or on top of the clear glass, allowing natural light to fall obliquely, asymmetrically, into the room, casting dappled shafts of different colors on the comfortable chairs and set-tees, the beautiful old carpets. "The glass is very beautiful," I said. Madame al-Gailani nodded, at us, at Azza.

"Do you have other children?" I asked.

"Yes. They're working in Abu Dhabi and Saudi Arabia."

It was four-thirty. Madame saw me thinking about leaving, and she also rose. "Let me send some dates with you back to the hotel. Ah, even at the best of times, and this is hardly the best of times, hotel food is not wonderful.

"And I am sorry not to be able to take you back," she added. "We have a car we share with other family members. I thought it would be back by now . . . But I guess I should say I feel lucky to have a car at all these days."

Amid thanks and good-byes and promises to come again, we headed out into the quiet street, where only the faint buzzing of bees and a chirping from some faraway bird broke the stillness. Everyone but us must be taking a post-lunch siesta.

After a ten-minute walk, we found a taxi, an old car with an old man driving, a small boy we assumed was his grandson curled up beside him in the front seat. He took us back to our assigned quarters—the Rashid Hotel, controlled compound for foreign journalists.

"So, B.J., Bob. Lots of changes in Iraq, right?"

It was Tom, his ironic tone back in place after the initial uneasiness at our possible reception as Americans in revolutionary Iraq. We were on our way south in our ministry-approved vehicle. Hadi turned from the front seat of the ministry-approved vehicle to hear our answer. Even Ahmed, the ministry-appointed driver who was taking us south, on orders, to Al-Nahra village, looked at us in the rearview mirror, awaiting a response.

"Amazing, really, the way Baghdad has been put together after the war," Bob said sincerely.

"B.J.?"

"We'll see," I answered noncommittally, avoiding Ahmed's question-ing glance in the rearview mirror, Hadi's expectant quiet face. "Bagh-dad is very impressive, though."

I thought again about Nejlah, and her assertion that Saddam had been good to women. Certainly the guests at Asma al-Gailani's lun-cheon-*kabul* had been women of personal as well as professional ac-complishment. But the old aristocratic families of Baghdad, I told myself, had always boasted women of such accomplishments. It was not surprising that the ladies' cosmopolitan patina of education and sophistication continued, despite war, conflict, and change of governmental political orientation. The old families had property and historic lineage, often Sunni religious lineage, with which the government might hesitate to meddle.

City women, after all, have historically been more privileged than rural women, in Iraq as in every other country in the world. All the women I had interviewed for my ill-fated *Mademoiselle* article were "advanced," by Western standards at least. That was why *Mademoiselle* magazine had been interested in them in the first place. At the time it seemed that Iraqi city women, like the poet Nazik, were becoming like women in the West, independent, free to choose their husbands. They were becoming individuals rather than submissive members of families. Perhaps, I said to myself, Nejlah, who had so praised Saddam Hussein's policy toward women, had only visited cities like Baghdad and met with women like the elegant, upper-class guests at Asma al-Gailani's beautiful house.

My own past experience was different from Nejlah's. Living in a village, learning to appreciate other kinds of women's lives, had not only changed my life but had made me doubt the universal relevance of that Western idea of women as individuals, what was then known as women's liberation, and has now become equated with feminism. Western-educated, well-to-do women in Iraq and in most of the world certainly gave the *appearance* of conforming to such feminist ideas about independence. But how much could one know from simply appearance? If dress were the measure of change, I thought, then the small number of abbayahs I'd seen in Baghdad meant things had changed in the direction of more individual choice. But when we drove around Khadimain, the sacred golden Shi'a shrine in northern Baghdad, the appearances of the people thronging the square before the shrine, shopping and browsing at the religious bookstores that lined the streets, were like those of our village acquaintances in the fifties: the women were shrouded in abbayahs, though their faces were not covered. The men wore biscuit-colored abbas over white dishdashas and dark sport jackets, their heads covered by black agals and kaffiyehs. These people lived in the city, but looked like village folk, rather than Madame al-Gailani's guests. Yet, I reminded myself, some of the women at the *kabul* in the beautiful Arabian Nights house had donned abbayahs on leaving. Tomorrow, said Bob, we would see what had happened outside the great city of Baghdad.

The four-lane highway to the south, complete with overpasses, interchanges, exits and entrances, bore no resemblance whatsoever to the old dusty two-lane road we had traveled in the past, the road so badly marked then that tragic auto accidents were a regular occurrence, especially at night. Ahmed, our driver, volunteered the information that there was actually an exit marked Al-Nahra, so we could avoid the old tortuous route through Diwaniyah, capital of the province now called Qadasiyyah, after that famous seventh-century battle when the Muslim Arabs defeated the Persians, a battle that was a turning point in Muslim history.

"I'm from a tribe, too," Ahmed said to Bob proudly. "But sheikhs were bad in the past, cruel. All over now, thanks to Saddam!"

Bob nodded noncommittally. We had been aware of that. Great wrongs and injustices had existed in the Iraq we knew; we too had hoped the revolution would right those wrongs.

"But," Ahmed added, "I would like to visit my sheikh anyway. Can we on the way back?"

"We will see," said Hadi.

Maybe those old wrongs had been righted, I told myself, the village developed and upgraded, all sins erased. But as we took the turnoff for Al-Nahra and cut through the outlying palm groves, finally bumping onto the main street, the village itself exhibited few modern improvements. My skepticism in the face of Nejlah's pronouncement welled up again as we wound down toward the bridge across the irrigation canal. There on the left was the mayor's office, whitewashed, one story, the government clinic no bigger than before, the jail, the old girls' school. No visible improvements.

"But there's a lot more traffic," said Bob, leaning forward to look at the cars, the bicycles, the donkey carts and taxis, and the pedestrians who cut in front of Ahmed's car to get to the old souk, which, I noticed, still opened out from the main street, just before the bridge, and disappeared into narrow lanes extending far back into the southern area of the village.

"Not a village anymore," said Bob. "It's a town."

The bridge was no longer new, but its ramp was still as badly angled as ever. Ahmed had to gun his motor to get up on the bridge and across the canal. The pedestrians were mostly men but I glimpsed a group of women in abbayahs ducking into the souk. Could that be? When we lived in Al-Nahra it was not considered appropriate behavior for women. If women were in the souk now, it meant village women were seen in public and that was an important change.

"B.J., look at the mosque!" cried Bob.

There it stood, but transformed from a squat square of mud-brick with a single tiled Qur'anic verse over the entrance into a structure easily recognizable as a mosque, for not only was it painted green, the Prophet's color, but a graceful new minaret of blue and green tiles rose high above the rows of houses on both sides of it, houses of cement blocks or fired brick rather than the mud and sun-dried brick of the fifties.

We were driving on the other side of the Al-Nahra canal now, and I searched in vain for the high fence at the corner of the tribal settlement where our house had stood in a lush garden of palms and figs and pomegranate trees. The corner was empty, except for a few dead palm trees which stood up crookedly in a dark, dank pool of water. I looked quickly at Bob.

"The house probably melted, B.J.," he said shortly. "In the rains. No one in it. Don't you remember how we had to always replaster the roof and the sides every time it rained?"

I had no time to mourn the lost house, for we were up the street to the tribal settlement, and here also the landscape was different. The lush palm groves were gone. And the noble mudhif, the men's guest house fashioned of arched reeds in a style traced to Sumerian times, had also disappeared. It had burned down, in the seventies, Bob was told later. In its place stood a large cement-block structure, painted white, with an arched porch flaring over its entrance. But the door was not open, as of old, but securely padlocked. What would happen now? Did our friends know we were coming? Of course not. Why should they be glad to see us, after all this time?

Ahmed parked the car, Tom and Hadi looked over the village from the mudhif's raised platform. Bob and I stood uncertainly for a moment, looking at each other in something like dismay. We should never have come back, I thought to myself. Always a mistake to go back.

Suddenly a man emerged from what I remembered as the sheikh's private house. He was aged and gray but clearly it was Nour, the sheikh's oldest son and Bob's best friend.

"Nour!" cried Bob.

"Bob!" cried Nour.

They embraced. Nour opened the door to the new mudhif and motioned Bob to enter. Then, seeing me standing there, he made a polite gesture that I might follow my husband.

But what did I do? My feminist daughters would say I reverted, and it was true. Never in all the two years of our life in Al-Nahra had I set foot in the mudhif, and now somehow did not seem the moment to begin. I turned away from the men as I had in the past and headed for more familiar ground—the women's quarters.

The door stood open, a young woman I did not recognize invited me in, and here I was, after a lifetime of marriage and children and travel and work, sitting in the new parlor of the house of the sheikh of the El Eshadda, one of the old, noble tribes of the Shammar confederation of Arabia. We knew Sheikh Hamid, our host, had died fifteen years ago, but his youngest wife, my friend Selma, survived, and I was overjoyed to see her coming toward me. And yes, she still lived in the same room off the courtyard "but the new parlor is for everyone in the family," she explained.

Selma limped badly, "from arthritis," she told me later, but remnants of her spectacular beauty remained. The voluptuous body was shrouded in black, the garments of an old woman, but her pink and white complexion was almost unwrinkled and the great black eyes that used to sparkle with laughter were even more pronounced above dark circles of sorrow and illness. She did not need kohl anymore to outline those eyes.

"Selma!" I put out my hand uncertainly, but she threw her arms around me.

"Beeja!" she cried, pulling back from our embrace. "You took a long time getting here. Look at us! We're old, but I look older than you do!"

I did not deny it—she was, I knew, younger than I, but life had been harder on her. "These kids," gesturing to a half dozen preteens giggling and staring at us, "weren't even born when you lived here."

She smiled, which lightened her face, and shooed away the noisy children just as she had long ago. "We heard the car drive up, and when we saw you and Mr. Bob get out, I thought you'd probably go to the mudhif. Women can do that now. Why didn't you?"

Why hadn't I? Old customs die hard, as my mother used to say. Just as in all the time we lived in the village forty years ago I had never entered the mudhif, so Bob had never been in the sheikh's house. Separation of men and women. Very strict then. Not so rigorous now, it seemed.

"These days people come and go," said Selma airily, raising her hand peremptorily to the young woman who had invited me in. She was introduced as Sabiha, one of the resident daughters-in-law, who was bringing us tea.

"Here, here"—Selma gestured to the carved wooden table that stood on the Persian rug, in front of the velvet sofa where we sat—"set the tray here."

"So." She turned to me. "Let's not talk about politics, please, Beeja, not the war. So many bad things, so many gone."

"I won't," I said and told her I was writing a new book. She raised a hand. "Okay," she said, "it's good to write a book but don't write about politics, please."

I said I wouldn't.

"That's clear then," she said. "Now I want to see Mr. Bob. You know I've never met him. But that was the old days. And I hear you have a cousin with you who takes pictures. I want to have my picture taken with you and Mr. Bob."

Tom was our cousin, then. Well, I thought to myself, he might as well be, we were close friends who'd lived in each other's houses off and on for years. He was exactly *like* my cousin, and I even *had* a cousin named Tom.

So Tom took pictures of me and of Selma, and of Bob, who came in, looking shy! Muhammad followed, our friend and helper, still lean and erect, but gray and smiling, and the picture became a foursome of old friends. A photo-op of Selma's oldest son, Feisal, followed; he had grown into a portly middle-aged gentleman, who wore the traditional robes, just like his father.

"He wants to be the next sheikh," she said, "but Abbas is still alive, Hamid's brother. He's ninety, Beeja! Who knows what will happen?"

It was hard to believe that the portly Feisal, fingering his worry beads, smiling self-consciously and offering pleasantries about Baghdad, was the spoiled little boy who had been the bane and the love of Selma's life in the old days, mischievous, disobedient, proud.

"Come, Feisal," said his mother peremptorily, "look at the pictures of Beeja's and Bob's children."

He came. Selma was now the senior authority figure, and clearly dominated the household, ordering about, as I watched and sipped my tea, her sons and their wives, as well as her grandchildren. A lift of her imperious hand and they rushed to do her bidding.

"You must have lunch here," said Selma authoritatively, "but I think you should have tea first with Muhammad's family."

So I rose and followed Muhammad across the back lanes behind the sheikh's house where I used to walk years ago, on my way to see his mother and sister. Here the small group of Sayids, or descendants of the Prophet, lived; in exchange for their services as mediators in tribal disputes and as religious authorities, the sheikh had given them land on which they were still living. We zigzagged to sidestep standing pools of water in all the lower hollows of the settlement. "They dammed the end of the canal," explained Muhammad. "And at first it helped, but now it's just managed to water-log the land."

Since his mother's death and his sister's marriage, Muhammad had enlarged his natal household to accommodate his wife and his eight children! He asked for pictures, too, to commemorate our visit, so Tom was sent for and dutifully came to pose us: me with Muhammad's wife and four daughters, all in abbayahs; Muhammad with his one-year-old chubby grandson; me with Bob and the daughters.

It was a large house, with many rooms opening off the central walled courtyard, chickens scratching in a corner, but the formal parlor, like Selma's, had upholstered chairs and settees, an attractive crimson-patterned rug, and, on the wall, a photo of Muhammad's father and images of the great Shi'a martyrs, Hassan and Hussein, decorated with artificial flowers.

Custom had been modified, I thought, but tradition was still here, and women's place was still fairly well defined, for Muhammad's wife and daughters all wore abbayahs, and probably, I thought, none of them would go to the souk or venture into the mudhif. I was soon to think differently. I was sitting forward on the settee, the pictures done and Tom gone back to the mudhif, stirring my tea, when a woman's voice said, in perfect English:

"You may not realize it, Madame Beeja, but times have changed!"

Who had spoken?

Muhammad told me proudly that his daughter, Jenan, seated directly across from me, was first in her class at the Higher Teachers Training College in Diwaniyah.

"When you lived here before . . ." Jenan went on in English.

"Yes?" I prompted, looking at the girl, who, in her loosely worn abbayah much resembled her sisters, but especially her father, with a thin face and high cheekbones. I noted also that she did not modestly clutch her abbayah together at her throat, as I had been taught to do long ago, but let it fall open, revealing underneath a long-sleeved blouse, a flowered skirt, and a cardigan.

"When you lived here before, fathers could make their daughters marry, whether the girls wanted to or not," she went on. "But not anymore, madame. It is against the law. I can marry or not, and who I want. My father can't do anything."

I stopped stirring my tea and stared at her.

Muhammad, who of course had not understood a word, chuckled. "Does she speak good English, Beeja?" he asked, catching his chubby grandson before he crawled out of the grandfatherly embrace and fell onto the floor.

"Yes, she speaks very good English!" I answered in Arabic. My Iraqi Arabic, never perfect, seemed to be slowly returning, in bits and pieces, every day. "Where did you learn English, Jenan?"

"In school here," she answered, with a smile. "Where else?"

Not in the old girls' primary school, surely. But Jenan had seen my disbelief, and rushed to add, "You are thinking of the past. I think then there was only one primary school for girls and one for boys here. Now we have ten schools, and one is a coeducational secondary school."

That was something new. Ten schools? And coeducational as well? Well, I thought, maybe Nejlah is right, and Saddam has done some good after all.

"In my class," went on Jenan, "we are learning to be teachers. Do you think I'd be a good English teacher, Madame Beeja?"

"Jenan, Jenan," fussed her mother good-humoredly. "Let us ask about our guest. I didn't know her personally, but we all knew who she was." She said to me, "I lived on the other side of the canal; there were a few Sayids there, too."

I wondered how much she had heard about my stumbling efforts in those early days to cook and be a hostess and learn some Arabic.

"We all knew you didn't have children, but that you did after you left here." She cleared her throat. "Are your children well?" she asked politely. I assured her they were and produced photos.

"We heard that you couldn't cook rice at all." She choked with laughter, and I bridled. Why was that so funny after all these years? "But mostly we wondered about your people, why they would let you come so far alone, with just your husband." And suddenly I found myself, after forty years, springing to a spirited defense of my family, who had let me come so far alone because they believed in the virtues of individualism, which was an important value in the United States of America. No, I heard myself saying, I had not missed my family at all, they understood I had to learn to manage alone . . . and I finally stopped, aware of the quiet stares, polite but wondering, from several pairs of eyes.

"Oh," said Jenan in English, coming to my rescue (what had come over me?), "don't be upset. I think my mother's just wondering whether you weren't lonely without your family."

No one seemed lonely in this house, I thought. They were close—perhaps too close by my standards, but they were certainly helping each other. I could not help but notice that during my outburst and all throughout the tea hour, the sisters had been passing the newest baby back and forth, while Muhammad took responsibility for the toddler. Jenan had been first, rocking the fretful baby before handing him back to his mother, Muhammad's son's wife, who nursed him briefly, and handed him on to another sister, who stood up and held the baby against her shoulder until he burped. But the baby continued to cry, so still another sister took the baby, walked it up and down the room, out into the courtyard, and back again. Muhammad, meanwhile, had continued to entertain the toddler, who had first crawled across the floor, looked up at me, crawled to his grandmother, who scooped him up and handed him back to Muhammad in a gesture that clearly said, "You handle it!" The fretful baby was given back to his mother, who nursed him, and rocked him to sleep at last.

"It's hard to live alone, but especially hard when there are babies to be cared for," Jenan said. "How do you manage in America?" I was saved from answering by the arrival of a small girl in a red sweater who announced that my old friend Basima, one of Moussa's daughters, had just returned home and wanted me to come visit—now!

"She says Beeja must come *now*," the little girl repeated breathlessly. "Her mother is up and wants to see her."

I turned to Jenan. "Her mother? How old is she?"

"Very, very old," responded Jenan in English. "And Basima is the only one at home now. She and her husband take care of her mom."

Basima caring for her mother in old age? Her sister Laila, my good friend, was supposed to be the one to do that. But Selma had told me that Laila had died many years ago. Basima's husband, I thought, must be a remarkable man to agree to live with his wife's family, since the traditional pattern is for the bride to move in with the groom's family.

"She's married to Majid, Nour's son," said Jenan. So not such a revolutionary ménage after all. Basima's husband was her second cousin on her father's side, a preferred kind of union that kept family ties and properties together.

Jenan patted my shoulder, and smiled at me. Perhaps, I thought, she had found my passionate discourse on the value of individualism amusing. Good practice for her English, though. And although I did not say so, I *had* been lonely in Al-Nahra, though I did not blame my family for not coming with me to Iraq. I was tempted to say, although I was sure Jenan already knew, that it was the women of Al-Nahra—her grandmother, her aunt, the women of the sheikh's house, and especially Moussa's daughters, who had saved me from being too lonely. I had been so naive and young at the time that it took distance and time for me to understand how much the similarities and differences between me and my Muslim women friends had been resolved in their kindness.

"And you know their father Moussa died."

Moussa's house. That was how it was known, after the father who ruled the household, theoretically. But Moussa, one of Sheikh Hamid's younger brothers, was known in the town for his bad reproductive luck. nine daughters and no sons. "No one to take care of the land " Moui had told Bob. "Yes, of course, women inherit half a man's share but with land it is difficult. A man, a son, is needed to negotiate with the father's male relatives to make sure the sisters and the mother get what they deserve."

I asked Jenan what was happening in terms of inheritance these days. "Men and women get what the law says, even the land," she said, and when I pressed her, she insisted it was true. "If the men don't agree, we can go to the Women's Federation office in Diwaniyah. They fix it up."

Was that possible? In Saddam's Iraq, were women really managing to get their proper Qur'anic legal allotment in terms of inheritance? Because this flew in the face of all the Western feminist discourse about Muslim women in general, and contradicted the received wisdom about Saddam Hussein and his totalitarian worldview. And, as one of my Iraqi exile friends had said, how can there be women's rights without human rights? But in the past women had rights at men's discretion and in modern Iraq their position had definitely improved.

Jenan stood up and offered to come with me to Moussa's house, the house that had been a refuge for me in the past. For although Moussa's public reputation may have suffered because he had no sons, the nine daughters and his devoted wife made his house a haven of order and good food and hospitality to all, even to me, the stranger.

Now I found myself once more at Moussa's house, knocking on an elegant new metal gate which had replaced the old wooden door I used to creak inward when I had reached the end of the path leading from our old house to Moussa's compound. Basima was there, in a black dress, but no abbayah or head scarf. As I stepped across the doorsill, and she embraced me gently, I felt the same sense of peace envelop me as I had in the past.

"Ahlan! Ahlan! Ahlan wusahlan," said Basima, guiding me past the fenced kitchen garden near the front door where plants moved in the breeze and birds twittered, past a series of blue doors opening off the courtyard to the back room where her mother awaited us.

"How are you, Beeja?" she quavered, as though I had been away only a few days.

I went up to the bed, carefully covered in spotless white, where Basima's mother sat, still slim and erect, eyes bright, all in black, twining a bit of yellow handkerchief in her knobbed hands. The pillows supporting her back had ruffled cases embroidered in blues and pinks and yellows. I tried to look sidewise and see whether the embroidered mottoes were there like those I had so painstakingly stitched on Bob's and my pillowcases long ago. The mottoes were indeed the same. "Sleep here and good health." That sentiment had not changed.

Um Basima nodded at me from her bed, while Basima sat me in an armchair and went out, presumably to make tea. The floor was covered with old, clean rugs, and the mirrored armoire on my left was piled from its top to the ceiling with many-colored blankets and quilts, carefully folded, mute testimony to this household's ability to sleep a dozen guests at least, if the occasion should arise (as it had, I remembered, many times in the past).

"Selma told me Laila had died. I am very sorry," I said quietly.

Um Basima did not seem to hear, but dabbed her eyes with the yellow handkerchief and kept wiping her mouth fastidiously.

"Yes. She died in the seventies," Basima said, coming back into the room. She did not volunteer the cause of death, and I did not ask.

"She was my good friend," I said.

Basima sighed as she set down the tea tray before me. Glasses, tiny spoons, sugar, Marie biscuits. That custom had not changed either.

"Yes, Beeja, she considered you a dear friend." Basima sighed again and offered tea to her mother, who shook her head. "So much has happened since you left. The war. So awful."

We sat quietly, sipping our tea, her mother twining and retwining that bright yellow handkerchief in her fingers.

"My sisters all got married, but Rajat died when her second baby was born, and Fatima had an illness for a long time." Basima was silent. "I'm lucky. My husband is a good man, we have a good son, he goes to university in the fall."

"Basima—" her mother quavered. "Someone's knocking."

"Yes, Mama, it's just Saneeya from across the way." And as she spoke a woman and her teenage daughter emerged into the room from behind the armoire. Although I had not thought of it for years, I had a sudden memory of that back door and Saneeya, a neighbor, coming into the room where the women and I sat in the evenings after the daily chores were done, sewing or gossiping or telling each other stories and poems.

"You don't remember me at all, do you, Beeja?" Saneeya asked.

It was true her face didn't seem familiar, but "I remember you coming in that back door," I said truthfully. "A secret door."

"Not a secret door," said Saneeya, laughing. "Just a little door for girls. Big men couldn't get through it." She sat down on the floor, her teenage daughter beside her, and peered up at me.

Then she burst out, "Yes, it's her all right. The children said she and her husband were here, but we couldn't believe it. A long time, huh? So why did you come back?"

"Have tea," urged Um Basima, gesturing with that yellow handkerchief. Saneeya poured a little hot tea into her saucer to cool it, slurped a little, poured it back in her glass. Basima told her about my new book, the trip, the photos we'd taken with Selma and Muhammad. "Yes, the photographer is her cousin," she added.

Saneeya mumbled something incomprehensible over her tea, held up now in one hand, and Basima hurried to reassure her. I heard the words Baghdad and government and Ministry of Information. Our bona fides were being trotted out.

Um Basima suddenly came to life from her perch on the bed. "He won't come in here, will he, that man from Baghdad, don't let him, Basima."

"No, no, Mama, don't worry, no men can come in the house that Majid doesn't allow. You know that," and she continued offering comforting phrases until her mother relaxed.

Saneeya said, "Do you remember the *krayat*, Beeja, when we read the Qur'an during Ramadan and sometimes the mullah came and talked? She was a hard one, wasn't she, Basima? And you were the only one who could read."

Basima looked pleased, but she said, "No, not just me. Mama could read a little."

"It was very good," remembered Saneeya.

"Do you still have the krayat and the other religious ceremonies in the house?" I asked.

Basima nodded vigorously. "Oh yes, and it's much better now, because all the women can read the Qur'an. I heard Jenan told you in English about the schools and inheriting and all that. And she's right, Beeja. All the women are getting educated, and we all know about Islam and about our rights. The government makes sure that the men follow the laws."

"Right! You're right!" agreed Saneeya. "But it happened too late for me. Rajaa here," with a nudge at the daughter who had not said a word, but merely stared fixedly at me throughout the conversation, "she's reading. She's growing up under the new laws. Thanks be to God."

Um Basima interrupted to ask about my family.

I said proudly that my son was selling surety bonds (I had some difficulty finding the proper Arabic word, but Basima supplied "insurance" which was exactly right); Laura Ann was working in public health and Laila was a lawyer. I said they were all married, except Laila, our youngest. "So she's not married," said Saneeya. "So what? These days lots of girls here don't get married. So many men were lost in the wars. But the girls, some anyway, say they don't want to marry."

Um Basima had receded into the past again, toying with her hand-kerchief, and Basima said, after a moment, "My husband is a lawyer, too, Beeja. He practiced in Baghdad and Diwaniyah but now that I've retired from my job as principal of the secondary schools he's rented an office here. He was a member of Parliament the last session. Elected," she added proudly.

We were all silent, sipping our tea.

Basima smiled at me. "You look the same, Beeja, but your hair's gray. I guess you're still having problems in America about women. Not like here. We can tell because we read about President and Mrs. Clinton. What is the matter with Hillary Clinton? Why doesn't she stand up for herself?"

"Politics, I guess," I offered lamely.

She paused.

"Do you find us much changed, Beeja?"

I wasn't sure what to say. "Well, our old house is gone," I said lightly. "And the mosque looks new."

"Your house, yes, in the rain, and with the canal backed up, we've got too much water. But the mosque, what's new about the mosque?"

"It's bigger, it's been tiled and painted, and it has a beautiful mina-ret."

The women looked at me, at each other. Um Basima asked what was the matter.

"The mosque, Mama! She said the mosque looked new."

"Well, yes," answered her mother surprisingly, coming back into focus. "It has a new minaret."

Basima said, "I can't remember when the mosque didn't have a minaret. Can you, Saneeya?"

"Well, as you say, times have changed," I put in lamely.

"The changes. Yes," said Basima. "And the changes are best for women. You were here before, so maybe you can see them clearer than we can—like the minaret . . ." She looked at me wonderingly. "You know, I really can't remember when it didn't have a minaret. But," she added, rising, "we've kept some of the good things." She smiled. "We don't get lonely. And we still love to have kids and take care of them. The government helps. You should go visit the Women's Federation, Beeja, in Baghdad, and see for yourself. Manyal Yunus is the head of it."

Saneeya rose, too, nodding. The daughter gave me one last fixed stare and they disappeared behind the armoire—down the rabbit hole, I thought nonsensically.

"Mama is tired," said Basima. I got up on cue and shook hands with her mother, who invited me to have lunch. "She must have lunch here, Basima, after so long."

"But, Mama, she can't, she's going to the sheikh's house."

Um Basima pulled her mouth down in annoyance. "She should come here," she repeated obstinately.

"Maybe tomorrow," I put in hurriedly, and Basima smiled and nodded as her mother subsided into the past again, old family rivalries forgotten for the moment.

"Let me show you the garden before you go, Beeja. We have dill and parsley and onions. And a fig tree and a pomegranate tree. I am so happy you came back to see us."

"I feel lucky," I said. "I wanted to come before, but I couldn't, but here I am, thanks be to God."

"God helped maybe," said Basima. "Who knows? It was fun when you were here. Doesn't seem *that* long ago."

Gifts of medicine, coffee, sweets, vitamins, biscuits. Before we left Al-Nahra the next day I presented them quietly, as one should, to Selma, to Basima, and to Muhammad's jolly wife. Small tokens of long friendships, to mark an unexpected and complex reunion after forty years, half a lifetime. Would I be able, in my writing, to describe fairly some of the changes in the lives of the women in Al-Nahra, the ones that Jenan and Basima spoke so enthusiastically about? That would be the best gift, I thought.

The General Federation of Iraqi Women occupied a multistoried glass-and-brick building in a relatively new section of Baghdad. Tom pointed out that this and several surrounding buildings stood on land cleared of old structures in the years after the first Ba'athist revolution in the 1970s. I had an appointment, with Dr. Haifa Abdul Rahman, deputy secretary of the federation. Manyal Yunus, described to me as the most powerful woman in Iraq and the one mentioned by my village friend Basima, was out of the country, attending an international women's conference.

We were a crowd. In addition to Hadi and Tom and Bob, we had been joined by Hiyam Dayif, librarian at Iraq's new Mustansiriyyah University, and Amal Khudairy, head of the Iraqi House of Arts and Crafts, where we had spent a pleasant morning. Both women were members of the federation, and I was delighted they had decided to accompany us. Bob peeled off as we headed up the stairs to Dr. Haifa's office. "I'll see you back at the hotel," he said, and went off alone.

The young woman who was secretary to Haifa Abdul Rahman did not seem at all surprised that our appointment for one person had turned into a party of five. She brought in more chairs so we could all sit comfortably in a rectangle around the deputy secretary's large gray Formica-topped desk, which stood in front of the single window and dominated the long room, bare except for Iraqi goat-hair rugs and a somewhat dusty plant on the windowsill. Decorations were minimal: on the wall hung an ornate plaque encasing the seal of the Ba'athist Party, and a large picture of a smiling Saddam Hussein in uniform; a few crocheted knickknacks (women's work) were visible among the stacks of papers and files on the desk. One telephone. A no-nonsense working office.

"Pictures? Me?" The woman who marched into the room and spied Tom's camera was clearly the deputy secretary.

"Pictures, yes. You," Tom replied in Arabic, with his sweetest smile.

Haifa Abdul Rahman smiled back. "Okay," she said. "My English not good. You want me at desk?"

"Later," answered Tom. "Let's wait for good light."

I stood up, proffered a copy of *Guests of the Sheik*, shook her hand, and thanked her for granting this interview. I explained that I was writing a book about Muslim women, and was hoping for her help in a chapter about Iraq. A hefty woman with a square, lively face framed by neat thick dark hair, she was smartly dressed in black and white, black skirt, white sweater embroidered in black. She looked at the cover of my book, looked in my face, looked down the row of visitors, came back to me.

"This kind of thing, madame, is about the past!" she said shortly.

"Yes, yes, which is why I am doing a new book!"

"What's she saying?"

Hadi explained everything rather smoothly, I thought; his own position as the official representative of the Ministry of Information; Tom clearly the photographer; the two ladies whom she seemed to know: Amal, a member of the Federation Arts Committee, Hiyam, with the university.

"These are your friends, then," she said in Arabic. "So this is not your first trip to Iraq?"

Everyone spoke up at once, except Tom, who kept walking about, looking for decent light for pictures. Hadi took the floor again, in his quiet way, talking about our mission, Bob's old book about irrigation in the village, my old book about women, our new books, our professorships in Texas.

The torrent of words from the deputy secretary that followed Hadi's speech sounded as if she had seen the article in *Al-Qadasiyyah* that morning. It had profiled Bob and me as "Americans searching for their memories in Iraq," and had featured pictures of both *Guests of the Sheik* and *The Arab World*.

"I tell you, madame," she said to me, "this book of yours is about the past! We've come so far. Iraqi women aren't like that today. You must realize that."

"Tell me about it," I said pleasantly, "and I will write what you say." Another torrent of words. Hadi translated, "She wants you to stay for the weekend so she can arrange for you to visit several important women in charge of important women's activities. She promises it will be interesting—women in arts, journalism, law, politics, work, etc."

I shook my head. If this interview had taken place a week ago, I could have amended our travel plans. But Bob and I were set to leave Baghdad in two days, drive back to Amman and then take the plane to Austin, Texas, where Bob had to resume teaching.

Haifa Abdul Rahman stared at me and exclaimed something I did not understand, then shook her head in irritation. I thought to myself how unreal it all was. We had come five thousand miles to look at the new Iraq, and could not stay over the weekend.

"You haven't seen the countryside where you lived and wrote about Iraqi women," countered the deputy secretary. "That, too, has changed, but no one will believe it in America unless, as they say, they see it with their own eyes!" Her tone was harsh.

"Madame has been there already," said Hadi.

"To the south?" Haifa looked incredulous. "They had permission?"

Hadi nodded. "And we stayed the night."

Haifa took a moment to digest that, and I inserted myself into the conversation.

"So," I said in my best Arabic, sounding out each word slowly, "I would be most appreciative if you could tell me about the achievements of the federation and of Iraqi women today. My friends in the village speak very highly of the federation!"

"Ha!" Haifa extended her arm to Hadi. "See! I am right! . . ." What followed was spoken so fast it was difficult for me to follow, but I heard those words that had recently been added to our Arabic vocabulary in the days we had been in Iraq, words like "embargo," "economic sanctions," "General Schwarzkopf." I did not understand fully what was said and I certainly did not want to get into a long discussion of America's evil intentions against Iraq, since I believed that Saddam was as much a part of the problem as my own government (and the Iraqis in the room wouldn't be able to agree with me, even if they wanted to). But Hadi was saying, diplomatically, that we were academics, not government representatives, and hence had about as much control over our government as Iraqi academics had over theirs. Etc. The pleasant-faced young secretary opened the door from the outer office, very quietly, and presented a tray of tea (in tiny glasses) and a plate of Marie biscuits (shades of British influence). We clattered our tiny spoons in the glasses, mixing sugar lumps into the dark golden tea.

"So!" declared Haifa Abdul Rahman. "And what do you want to know?" She did not wait for me to reply, but launched into a lecture. I focused on her face, my pencil poised over my notebook, while she spoke and Hadi translated.

I decided to just write as fast as I could and analyze and think about what she was saying later. Could what she was saying possibly be true? A million and a half women members of the federation, spread out throughout the several provinces of Iraq, 222 sub-branches of the federation throughout the country. That meant a lot of women in organizational positions, a lot of women poised to carry out the political as well as social aims of the federation. All part of the leader's plan, I thought, not pleasantly.

"We *elect* our officials, the women *elect* their own leaders," went on the deputy secretary, as though to deny my unspoken words, with a glance toward Hadi, who was nodding and translating. I glanced once at Hiyam and Amal, who were also listening to her intently.

"So," she said, "It is women themselves who plan the campaigns for literacy, child care, maternity leave, wages and promotions within the economic sector, as well as political participation." At the phrase maternity leave I interrupted.

Haifa Abdul Rahman smiled at me, a knowing sort of smile, but when she spoke, I realized why. Maternity leave, she obviously knew, was a real issue in Europe and the United States, as well as in the Arab world.

"We know," she said, "that feminists in America are still struggling for compulsory universal maternity leave. Here in Iraq we have triumphed on this issue. We are ahead of all countries, even Sweden!"

Hadi was translating faster now, and I found I was understanding the sense, if not the actual details of what, in my own mind, I was calling a feminist discourse. But, I asked myself, is she a feminist? What did she mean by the term? And what did I mean?

"So how much maternity leave does an Iraqi mother get?" I asked, trying to keep my voice neutral.

"One year!" Madame Haifa rose from behind the desk, moved a chair from the wall, and sat down closer to me, as if to stress the importance of her message. "One full year. Six months with full pay, six months half pay, plus six weeks at the beginning!"

"Very good," I murmured sincerely.

"One year," she repeated, "and double for twins." She looked at the audience for approval and Hadi broke ranks to contribute an opinion of his own. "Right! Right. Yes, madame, when our twins were born, this is what my wife received."

Hadi explained that it had been a big shock, twin boys following on an older four-year-old son. "Three boys! Too many!"

Amal said, "This is the first time I've ever heard a complaint about too many boy children!"

The company broke up into laughter, which lightened the rather tense atmosphere in the stuffy office.

"And," Haifa raised her voice again, "every family receives coupons for free milk and orange juice, plus a payment by the government when the new citizen of Iraq is born, a future member of the Arab Socialist Party." She was called out to the phone, and in her absence, Hadi, Amal, and Hiyam rushed to reassure me that I was not being given a snow job, that what the deputy secretary was saying was all true.

Was my skepticism so evident? Probably. My mother had always claimed that she could tell exactly what I was thinking by the look on my face. My children say the same today.

"Well then." Haifa breezed back into the room, accompanied by the shy secretary, bearing an armload of printed materials, both in English and Arabic. Materials documenting our conversation, with statistics on women's participation in the labor force, on their participation in Parliament (ten this session), on wages (equal pay for equal work) on health benefits (generous). She went on and on, flipping pages, pointing to the columns that I should note particularly. My side glance toward the audience indicated that Tom was falling asleep in the face of the standard rhetoric. But there were still questions to be asked.

"The law, then," I opened, signaling to Hadi, whose eyelids also seemed to be drooping. "When I was here before, the family law was Islamic religious law."

"That was long, long ago," said Haifa, a bit scornfully, trying I thought to be polite while still wanting to register on my consciousness the fact that I was hopelessly out of date. "As you would say in English, the dark ages."

"And now?" I said quietly, refusing to be drawn.

And I got another lecture, this one delivered not only with rhetorical flourishes, but with resounding slaps on the Formica-topped gray desk to emphasize her points. Tom woke up with a start and Hadi translated very quickly indeed, with occasional promptings from Amal.

While I listened, I thought back to Jenan's remarkable speech in Al-Nahra, and to Basima's statement that the federation ladies "helped" men to abide by the laws. This was certainly new. But now, "No more Islamic family law here," Madame Haifa was saying. A modern secular code (she was very insistent on the word "modern" and made Hadi repeat it twice, to be sure I got it). She was quite right to point out that the only other countries in the area with such codes were Turkey (since 1924) and Tunisia (since 1956). But I kept wondering about whether a secular code was really in force here.

"This does not mean that we are not good Muslims," she was saying, and was careful to add, "and we have good Christians here, a small number. The legal code we have, promulgated by our great leader, is the only logical way to give men and women equal rights."

Yes, well, maybe, I thought. A law is on the books, but is it implemented? "Two questions," I said. "The code is impressive. Does it specify that polygamy is illegal?"

Haifa looked at Hadi, at Amal, at Hiyam, as if to ask what I meant. A rapid exchange followed, which I did not understand.

"We are only trying to make sure that we know what you are asking," said Hadi smoothly. "You mean a law limiting a man to one wife at a time?"

"Yes."

Haifa stood up, pulled down her black shirt, pushed up her sleeves of her black-and-white sweater, sat down once more. "That is the law," she said. "I repeat, the law. Man is allowed one wife only. But . . ."

Aha, I thought to myself, it's not quite so clear after all.

"But if the first wife is ill or cannot bear children, after it having been ascertained by a doctor that she is infertile, then a man may take a second wife, but only with his first wife's permission, and the permission of a judge in a proper court of law."

"And if there is a divorce, the children stay with the mother?"

"Yes."

"What if the mother marries again?"

"Ah!" Haifa looked pleased again. "You mean, as is the case in the law recently reformed, so they say, in Morocco, whereby if the mother remarries, the children go to the father?"

I nodded.

"The child can choose," said Haifa.

Amal said, "Yes, B.J., I think that is the way it works."

"My cousin had that experience," said Hadi, "and my wife's sister, too."

I stood up as if to go, then realized that in this blitzkreig of information which I had been offered and had dutifully transferred into my notebook, I had found out nothing whatsoever about Madame Haifa personally, and scarcely a word had been said about my perennial interest, feminism. And Tom still needed to take her picture!

"Madame Haifa, if you please," he said, and she stood up dutifully, smiled as the flash went off. "Let's try you against the books—no, not the window, the light is not good."

"You are married and have children?" I asked.

She shook her head. "No, I'm not married," she said. "It is difficult for an independent woman like me to find a proper mate."

She smiled slightly, a smile rather different from the professional cheery expression with which she had greeted me and with which she had prefaced most of her answers to my questions.

"Is the federation against marriage?" I asked.

"No, no, one searches but does not always find a perfect mate. And a child? Yes, I would like to say I have a child, but 'my child' is really the federation, which I see as very important. I have worked for them for eighteen years, I was a student in those earlier times, at our new university of Mustansiriyyah, named after the famous medieval university."

Everyone was standing up now. Tom was storing the film into his pack, Amal and Hiyam were talking about how to transport me and Hadi and Tom to different parts of this crowded city of four million people.

"Would you call yourself a feminist?" I asked, as I shook her hand in thanks.

Hadi, Tom, Amal, and Hiyam—stopped talking.

"Feminism," she proclaimed in ringing tones. (I could understand this well enough.) "Feminism has different meanings in East and West." She stopped and took a deep breath, then proceeded to speak loudly in Hadi's direction, while looking at me, a difficult maneuver, but she managed. "Here in Iraq," Hadi translated, "we think of 'feminism,' Western ideas of feminism, as dividing women from men, separating women from the family. We think that is bad, bad for everyone—man, woman, child. We want to *support* women to be equal with men, but within the family itself."

Amal interposed, first in Arabic, then at a nod from Haifa, in English. "You know, B.J., the family is the basic thing here in the whole society. No one wants to get rid of it. You have to begin your writing with this idea."

"But rights in the family *must* be the same," said Haifa forcefully, pounding on her desk again to emphasize the point. "And wages and salaries *must* be the same." Another pound on the desk. I steeled myself for more thwacks, but they did not come. The interview was over. She was heading for the door.

Said Hadi to me, "I think you will find out that Madame Haifa is right."

"Thank you for your time and for the information," I said in English and repeated it in Arabic.

"Ah, well," said Madame Haifa. She smiled a broad smile, and put her hand on my arm in a sisterly way. "Are you sure you can't stay the weekend? We would make some interesting excursions and your Arabic would become much better by the time you got back to America . . ." I said that I was sorry I had to leave so soon, but my husband . . . She nodded, to indicate that she knew I was ruled by my patriarchal American husband, rather than by a more generous-spirited Iraqi mate. We were already in the outer office when we heard her exclaim and then come after us.

"I have been remiss in my duties," she said, and Hadi dutifully translated. "We have not discussed the war and the terrible plight of Iraqi children since they have been deprived of medicine and food because of the sanctions the United States has imposed on our country. You must say that to your fellow citizens when you return to America. We have suffered, and we need to have those sanctions lifted so we may live again."

"Yes," I said. "Yes. I will. But my interest in this book has been primarily on women's issues and you have helped a lot."

"Remember what I have said." She wagged a finger at me.

I promised to remember, but she had not yet finished.

"On your primary area of interest—you must say in your book . . . that there is no division of opinion in Iraq, among any person, male or female, about women's needs and rights. In the United States we hear there is discrimination according to sex as well as race. Not here. I believe, madame, that I may say with pride that we are ahead of you in such matters, in fact, we are ahead of most of our fellow nations in the Arab world, thanks to the far-seeing goals of the party and the hard work of the one and a half million women in the federation."

"I will write that in my book," I said.

"Your *new* book which will erase the image you gave in the *old* one about the past. Don't forget to send me a copy." She waved and was gone into her office, slamming the door behind her!

Tom started down the stairs, muttering, "That woman is a power-house. Are they all like that, Hadi?"

Hadi looked as if he might chuckle, but thought better of it. "Yes, Tom, many of them are just like that. They work very hard for women in Iraq."

My long-ago conversation with Nejlah about Saddam Hussein's at-titude toward women's issues came back to me. I thought she and he would both be pleased with Madame Haifa Abdul Rahman, deputy secretary of the General Federation of Iraqi Women. But what was I to make of it all? Could I believe all she had said?

Amal said, "I will leave you now, B.J. The only thing I would add to Haifa's comments is that it has not been possible to give orange juice and milk and vitamins to the babies since the war. There isn't enough."

I wrote that down, and she bade me good-bye, as did Hiyam.

"We've both been to the Women's Museum," said Hiyam. "I think you will enjoy it."

Amal said, "Come back soon."

"Thank you, Amal. We loved your Iraqi House of Arts and Crafts. Wasn't it once occupied by the British?"

"Yes, a British governor of Baghdad lived there. He said he liked to look out at the Tigris and think of the great ancient civilizations that had risen and fallen here. But after 1958 we took it back. We like to look out at the Tigris, too."

"And all through the war you were there?"

"No. It was destroyed by U.S. bombs that took out the Jumhiriyah Bridge. We rebuilt it. It's only now finished. A lot of time and energy and money were needed to bring it back to its original state—an old Ottoman-style house."

"I'm sorry, Amal."

"We will hope for better times," she said enigmatically, and was gone.

"Well, this is the museum, B.J., what shall we photograph?" asked Tom.

Hadi had excused himself to finish up some paperwork with the federation secretary. Amal and Hiyam had departed for home and we had been passed on to the official translator for the Women's Museum, a new building near the federation office in Waziriyah. A cheerful young museum guide introduced herself.

"You look nicer than in your picture," she said to me in rather stilted English.

"My picture?"

"In the paper this morning," she said, producing a copy of *Al-Qadasiyyah*. "I wondered whether you might not turn up here. We're very proud of the museum. It's a first in the Arab world!"

We were taken around the spacious structure, filled with ancient and modern objects, from cylinder seals of Sumerian times, 3000 B.C., to modern dioramas illustrating Iraqi women's lives through the ages.

"Sitt Sajjida, wife of our President, came to the opening," she told us proudly. Tom dutifully took a picture of the picture of Sitt Sajjida, cutting the ribbon opening the museum.

"We are beginning to work with children and teachers," continued our guide, "so they will know the history of their mothers and sisters and wives. We are planning what I think are called field trips?"

Some of the exhibits were what one might expect from a museum financed by the Ba'athist Party: these were units on women's contributions to the modern Iraqi Army, rooms dedicated to women's education, legal and social rights, with tables and maps like those Haifa Abdul Rahman had given me. Our guide pointed out a new display of women's calligraphy, that ancient and hallowed art of the Islamic world. Poster-size blowups pictured Iraqi women smiling with other international women leaders on the *Peace Ship*, Iraqi women at the United Nations.

"That was before the Gulf War, of course," said our young guide softly.

But clearly the designers had studied modern educational museum practices around the world, for a sophisticated series of timelines wound through the rooms, charting women's history in Iraq. From Sumeria, Akkad, Babylon, came representations of Inanna, goddess of love and fertility. Impressions made from cylinder seals, greatly enlarged, showed Sumerian men and women, in distinctive garments of overlapping skins, their eyes outlined heavily in black kohl, hunting, worshiping, feasting, playing musical instruments. Tom took a photo of a fine bust of a Mesopotamian woman from Tell Omar, Diyala Province, (circa 200–300 B.C.) Iraqi women poets, both past and present, were prominently featured.

"So you see we have the whole panorama, from glorious Sumeria until now," said our young guide, and when I turned to her, it seemed as though her wide eyes, outlined in black, resembled very much those ancient figures from 3000 B.C., the years when human writing was invented here, in Iraq, then known as Mesopotamia. "The General Federation of Iraqi Women built this museum, madame, and in a time of trial for our country. We opened last year only."

"Very impressive," I murmured, and meant it, but also wondered whether it would survive a change in governmental leadership.

Tom said later, "Of course it would. It's an investment. All they'd need to do is change the picture of Sitt Sajjida in the central gallery, or just move her over!"

It had been quite a day. The Iraqi House of Arts and Crafts, renovated since the devastation of war; lectures on women's new rights, rural and urban, by the deputy secretary of the General Federation of Iraqi Women; a guided tour of the Women's Museum, the only such museum in the Arab world. Clearly *Guests of the Sheik* as a picture of Iraqi women was very passé and had long needed to be updated. Perhaps I could begin the task of revision although I felt I needed more documentation to present an accurate picture.

Before we left Baghdad, our friend Asma al-Gailani invited us to a farewell lunch, and she also urged us to visit the Gailani mosque, built by one of her own ancestors. "Men and women go to the mosque now. Did you visit it when you were here before?"

"No," said Bob and I together. We did not add that we had never visited any Iraqi mosque, since in the 1950s they were off limits to foreigners like us. But I had once, years ago, stood with my friends Basima and Laila, covered in our abbayahs, and peered through the grilled window of the little mosque in Al-Nahra.

"This one is a real Baghdadi mosque, dating from early Ottoman times. It's grown much larger over the centuries," said Asma, "and the library is celebrated all over the Muslim world. Azza can take you after lunch. Come at one—" She paused, half-laughing on the phone. "No *kabul* today. Men most welcome!"

We traveled once more to the beautiful Arabian Nights house where the light came through the living room window in those enchanting colored patterns. And we enjoyed seeing Asma's niece Azza again, who was partly responsible for that unique mosaic window. She nodded her head in a pleased way when we again congratulated her on the overall effect. She had recently been given two new design commissions she said, but added that the special paint she needed for glass surfaces was difficult to find in postwar Iraq.

Asma's daughter, who had elected Islamic dress, said, "Mama, if she goes to the mosque, B.J. must wear abbayah. She must."

"You can borrow mine, madame," offered Asma. "I won't go. And just give it back to Azza."

So, after another delicious lunch, we set out, and I was wrapped once more in a black abbayah, as I had been long ago. At the mosque, Azza introduced us to her uncle, the muqaddam, or official guardian, and asked for permission to take pictures. "Library, yes, mosque, yes, but mausoleum, no," he said, a white-haired old man, polite, but pale and distant. We shook his hand and thanked him for the privilege.

It was nearing five o'clock when we finally entered the Gailani mosque's spacious lower courtyard, which was nearly empty. The crowds for the sunset prayer had not yet gathered. A round man in a turban and full-length robes read his Qur'an as he ambled slowly, back and forth, the length of the courtyard. And a woman with a small child stood, weeping, before a tall sheikh who was nodding and speaking gently, his hand on her shoulder. Birds circled above us, dipping down to the courtyard, climbing up again over the minarets, then gliding to the mosque's upper level where a group of schoolchildren walked with their teacher.

"Why does your aunt call this a real Baghdadi mosque?" asked Bob.

Azza thought a moment. "Maybe because it reflects different styles of art, from the dynasties and empires who've ruled Baghdad. Yes, maybe that's it. See that minaret, for example. It's Turkish."

She pointed to the tall, slender spire, tiled in green and pale gold, which glistened in the sun. "And there, where the family is standing," she added, "you can see the clock high up on the second minaret; it's not at all like the Turkish one." Azza was right. The second minaret, with its square tower and clock face near the top, was very different, reminiscent, in fact, of a southern Mediterranean campanile, or church tower.

A young mosque employee, in turban and reddish beard above his plain blue dishdasha, walked with us, delegated by Azza's uncle to give us the tour of the mosque complex. But when Azza invited me to go into the family mausoleum with her, the young man in the reddish beard led Bob and Tom to the upper courtyard, to oversee their picture-taking.

The door to the mausoleum was so heavy it took both Azza and me together to push it open. We walked up two short stone steps to the enclosure where stone rectangles lined the walls, filling every foot of space, rectangles of different sizes, tombs built around each long-deceased member of the Gailani family—men, women, children. They lay side by side, under the stone coverlets, in their final resting places. Azza paused by one of the smaller tombs. She prayed to herself for a moment, and I stood beside her, clutching my abbayah under my chin, as I had in the past, and saying a few prayers of my own for our children and grandchildren, for relatives, and friends, both those far away in America and here in Iraq.

When we reemerged from the quiet of the mausoleum and the heavy stone door boomed shut behind us, the courtyard had become more crowded; people were hurrying through the last light of the day, speaking to each other urgently as they moved forward to the mosque itself, to be in time for the sunset prayer.

"That was my great-grandmother's tomb," said Azza. "She died young. I always feel close to her in there. I don't know why. It's my past, I guess. It's part of me."

I did not answer, out of respect for her feelings and because I was struggling to make sense of my own complicated reactions to this return visit to Iraq, the Iraq of 1996, not 1956.

In the library, Bob and Tom and I listened while the assistant conducted a short tour of the well-kept and orderly collection of books, medieval manuscripts, rare antique maps.

"I want you to see one special book," said Azza. "It's a book that someone pulled out of the river Tigris in the thirteenth century, after Genghis Khan ransacked Baghdad."

She walked us down the rows of illuminated Qur'ans in glass cases, past the texts of science and philosophy in Arabic and Persian, past the exemplary calligraphy in different historical styles, to a glass case, locked, that stood in a far corner. The guide opened the case and pointed to, though he did not touch, an ordinary-looking book with a worn and spotted brown cover and no spine at all.

"Not a very valuable book maybe," said Azza, almost apologetically. "Not a rare manuscript or a Qur'an or anything like that. A book of geography, I think, but see, it is there, someone rescued it, rescued the past, rescued the heritage of Baghdad. Saved it from destruction."

She looked at me intently, her abbayah clutched around her finely chiseled face, the dark eyes sad.

"People do care," she said. "I believe that. Despite everything."

I suddenly felt impelled to tell her about my village women friends' apparently improved new status under the law, and how bad we felt about the effects of the embargo on Iraq, on Iraqis. I told her what my friends in Al-Nahra had said about the great benefits of women's education and how it had changed their lives.

Bob and Tom were outside by now, Tom still taking photographs in the fading light, but Bob waving at me, to say that it was time to leave, the light almost gone.

"Yes," Azza replied. "Yes. I think what your friends in the village say is all true. We were lucky here, for a while. Education, yes. Enough to eat. Health care. But today many things are on hold. Now we are unlucky. I'm not even thirty years old, but my generation has been left behind. The world outside Iraq has passed us by. Other things may improve with time, Iraq may be lucky again. Who knows? But for me and for those my age it will be too late."

"Oh, Azza . . ." I began.

"It's true. We must remember the better past, I think, and hope that things will improve for the next generation."

On the street outside the mosque, we looked for a taxi, and as it drew up, I quickly took off my abbayah, folded it up, and handed it to Azza, who was going back in her car to her aunt's house. At that, the crowd descended on us, children, women, men, their hands out, begging.

"Please! Alms! For the love of God!"

"Give us alms! We beg! Give us alms."

"We are hungry! Money! Food! In the name of the Prophet!"

"Shut the door," Azza shouted to the taxi driver over the noise of the crowd. "Good-bye," she said to us. "Good-bye!"

"Good-bye, Azza. Take care."

The taxi pushed through the crowd and we sank back on worn plastic-covered seats.

"Wow," said Tom. "That was not fun. The mosque was so beautiful—"

"And these people are so unhappy," Bob finished.

"Bob," I said, "I told people in the village that you thought the embargo would be lifted, come summer. Do you think that will actually happen?"

"There's a chance it might," Bob answered. "Iraqi oil coming onto the market would lower world oil prices, and it's always good to bring down gas prices before a presidential election."

"And the embargo isn't hurting the leader of Iraq."

"Not at all," Tom agreed. "Like our friend the businessman said, the embargo helps Saddam to stay in power. He can blame everything on us evil Americans, and make money off smuggling on the side."

I decided to write a thank-you letter to my friend Nejlah in Geneva, for shaking up my long-held ideas about what was happening to women in the Arab world. I had come to the reluctant conclusion that she was more or less right: Saddam Hussein, despite his horrendous reputation in the West, had the best record on women's rights in the Arab world today. But, the words of my dear friend, an Iraqi exile, still echoed in my head. "What good," she had cried, "are women's rights without human rights?"

SEVEN

¤ ¤

Saudi Arabia: A Brief Visit

T HE KINGDOM of Saudi Arabia occupies most of the Arabian Peninsula, the birthplace of Islam. Thus it has become the official guardian of two of the sacred places of this worldwide religion— the holy cities of Mecca and Medina (Jerusalem is the third). Saudi Arabia is also widely perceived to embody the conservative values of Islam, including a patriarchal tradition that grants men authority over women. Hence, Muslim women friends who had been following my book project said, "You should go to Saudi Arabia, B.J., and tell your readers what's happening there."

I pointed out that was nearly impossible, since Saudi Arabia does not welcome tourists, and no lone women, even on official business, are granted entry visas without Saudi male sponsors. I doubted that any Saudi official would find the project title of my book, *In Search of Islamic Feminism,* appealing enough to endorse a visit. "But many Americans confuse Saudi Arabia with the whole of the Islamic world in its attitude toward women. You must write something, B.J., to explain that's not true," a Muslim friend said.

I knew they were right. For many in the West, Saudi Arabia is synonymous with Islam, with Arabia in general, a template on the basis of which Westerners think of all Islamic countries and judge the realities of the lives of all Islamic women. But in the forty years Bob and I had been living in and out of the Arab world I had never visited Saudi Arabia, so from my own observations I could not in good faith challenge this generalization. And in the courses I teach I have always cautioned my students to be critical of generalizations not based on the writer's own experience. In fact, the majority of the comments about women's lives in Saudi Arabia have, until quite recently, been written by Western men who travel to the Kingdom on business or as journalists, but seldom if ever are invited into the private world of the family, the secluded world of women. I personally believed most of these accounts to be flights of male imagination, presenting Saudi women as stereotypical figures; rich, gorgeous, idle, passive creatures, the prisoners of men.

But I was in no position to verify my belief. No, it seemed a Saudi chapter would sadly have to be left out of my book. And that was that.

Then, as I was working on the book in the fall of 1996, I unexpectedly received an invitation to visit Saudi Arabia as a member of a delegation of American academics sponsored by the National Council of U.S.–Arab Relations. It was too good an opportunity to miss. We were fourteen in all, including seven women, an unusually high number of women for such a group, we were told by our sponsors. Of the women, two were professors, one a chaplain at a small Catholic college, one involved in educational exchange, one in cross-cultural training, two officers in the U.S. Armed Forces. We were all on a first-time visit to the Kingdom; the cross-cultural trainer and myself had spent time in other parts of the Middle East. But the other five women believed, like most Americans, that what went on in Saudi Arabia was what went on across the Muslim world as far as women's status was concerned. The template was in place.

Saudi Arabia is an incredibly rich country, thanks to its possession of about 25 percent of all the world's proven oil resources. This is ironic, given the nation's history. For in the late eighteenth century, Great Britain, in building its worldwide empire, chose not to colonize Saudi Arabia because of what were believed to be its skimpy natural resources; they chose instead to take and keep the Red Sea port of Aden, as a safe pass-through for British ships. By the end of the twentieth century, countries all over the world depended on Saudi Arabia for oil. The United States alone buys a quarter of its total supply from the Kingdom.

To us, as special visitors, Saudi Arabia appeared to be very rich, indeed; on that count the general public view is correct. Luxury. Comfort. Glitter. Flash. Consumerism at an unprecedented level. This was evident in the five-star hotels where we were lodged: the Jeddah Holiday Inn; the Riyadh Sheraton; the Omni Dammam. As for food, a few gentlemen in our party were disappointed not to find whole sheep roasted and served over a table-sized bed of rice, like the feasts pictured in movies such as *Lawrence of Arabia*. However, we all made do with well-stocked buffets, including marinated and grilled baby lamb chops, preceded by such starters as smoked salmon (from Scotland), and followed by desserts like chocolate mousse (prepared by a Swiss chef). The bottled water generously placed in our rooms came from France, the lavish fruit baskets from Lebanon. The only recognizably non-European foods were dates and a Saudi-style coffee, tasty, a dark green color; it was available twenty-four hours a day in the hotel lobbies.

From the windows of our air-conditioned tour bus, we saw fleets of luxury automobiles careening at breakneck speed down brand-new four-lane highways. (The area of the paved road system has jumped in the past twenty-five years from five thousand to forty-three thousand kilometers.) I noted a profusion of Jaguars, BMW's, Porsches, and Mercedes-Benzes.

"So there are no poor people in the Kingdom?" inquired one member of our group.

Our guide smiled indulgently. He was a pleasant young man in an immaculate white dishdasha and kaffiyeh, or head scarf, the kaffiyeh rolled back carefully over the black *agal* rope which held it in place.

"Almost none," he said. "This is a good country, even for the guest workers."

"How many of those?"

Our young guide consulted a notebook. "Three or four million in our total population of eighteen million."

"Fast growth," commented another member of our group, a demographer. "Your people have nearly doubled in a generation. High birth rate."

"Yes. We love children here. My own," he smiled again, "are my greatest joy—and of course my wife's as well."

"Poor people?" Our inquirer would not let it pass. Further discussion elicited the information that the only really poor people were those citizens of less fortunately endowed Muslim nations who stayed on after the days of the annual pilgrimage or *hajj* were over, and hoped to take up residence in the Kingdom. "Not too many, maybe," said our guide. "We have a lot of pilgrims—two and a half million each year—and maybe some hundreds of poor Muslims try to stay. It is a shame. But we must deport them."

"You deport them?"

"Yes." He turned back to the driver.

Our bus continued on through the wide streets, past emporiums displaying in their shining plate-glass windows French Empire furniture reproductions, crystal chandeliers, designer bedding, English china, television sets, stereo combinations, computers.

Academic studies inform us that Saudi Arabia has managed a tremendous improvement in its standard of living in the past twenty years. This certainly appeared to be true. In addition to the luxury goods available in the stores, we saw elegant housing which the government had provided for, among others, university faculty and government retirees. But while the telephone system, the libraries, and the bookstores appeared excellent, sources of information and communication on the Internet, the World Wide Web, were not yet available to the public, our guide said. Why? He smiled and shrugged. We learned later of the conservative opposition to such international links, which would bring uncensored and inappropriate news of the world into the Kingdom. Control was clearly the issue. Central control. In Dammam, in the "mother of all shopping malls," goods on display ranged from clothing by Liz Claiborne, Gap, and Versace to antique art objects and Häagen-Dazs ice cream. On the mall's second floor, a cozy café curtained in flowered chintz allowed women (with their children), to eat ice cream sundaes and drink coffee in peaceful seclusion, properly hidden from the madding male crowd. A branch of Toys "R" Us stood a block away from the Riyadh Sheraton and I wandered over one day, hoping to find some locally made toys for my grandchildren. No such luck. The merchandise was exactly the same as that in our Austin, Texas, store. A Saudi friend quipped that Toys "R" Us in Arabia meant really Toys "R" U.S. (all imported from America!). The same could be said for much of the goods in the malls. U.S.A. all the way. American businesses were clearly favored importers.

We visited schools and universities, and all of us came away, I think, with admiration for the Kingdom's achievements in education. In 1970, Saudi Arabia had one of the lowest literacy rates in the Middle East (15 percent for men, 2 percent for women). After a quarter century of dedicated effort, the country had raised that level to one which is competitive worldwide. The 1990 figures are 73 percent literacy for men, and 48 percent for women.

When I remarked about this achievement, however, in an audience granted to us by Prince Saud el-Faisal, Minister of Foreign Affairs, he said, "Thank you for your good words, madame, but I myself am not pleased with our facilities for *women's* education, especially in Riyadh. We have made great strides, it is true, but there is more to be done. And," he smiled at us, "in case I forget this need, I have a very vocal daughter who keeps reminding me!"

We all returned his smile. We were trying to be polite guests, knowing that on a junket not widely available to Americans we were the fortunate recipients of traditional Arab hospitality. We dined with princes, lunched with members of the Gulf Cooperation Council (oil), had audiences with government officials. We were treated with courtesy and respect—wherever we went.

Except. There was one big exception. For in this pageant of modern Arabia unfolding before our eyes, we did not meet any women. No one seemed surprised. We had all read academic studies and news reports about the Kingdom. "We must remember," said one of the men of our party, "that Saudi Arabia abides by Islamic principles, and this mandates the segregation of men and women."

"Please! What Islamic precedents are we talking about here?" replied another American gentleman. (He was also a professor.) "I think we need to remember that we're only talking about Wahhabi precedents within Islam, which follow the Hanbali rites. Not all Muslims follow those rules!"

He explained to the group that the Wahhabis were an eighteenth-century reform movement, dedicated to purifying Sunni Islam of practices which its charismatic founder Muhammad ibn Abdel-Wahhab perceived as non-Islamic: the veneration of Muslim saints, luxurious living, ostentation in worship. Saudi Arabia was the site of Abdel-Wahhab's early preaching, and the Wahhabi interpretation of Islamic texts on which current Saudi law is based is usually associated with Ahmed Ibn Hanbal, the famed ninth-century jurist, who has given his name to one of four schools of law within Sunni Islam.

"But it's not really according to Ibn Hanbal, either," put in a third professor. "I've been talking to people here, and the interpretation in use is a Wahhabi *interpretation* of Ibn Hanbal. Not the same thing elsewhere. Particular to Saudi Arabia."

Whatever the origins of the local laws, women were certainly invisible to us, just as the media and academics had said. We had been told that if women do have to appear in public, they must wear all-enveloping black abbayahs like the one I donned long ago, when Bob and I lived in a southern Iraqi village. The Saudi *mutawa,* or self-appointed morals police, are on the streets to deal with women who, by chance or design, show too much ankle, or leave their hair uncovered. We saw no *mutawa,* but then we also did not see any women on the streets.

No women on the streets. And in the hotels, the people who made our beds, operated the elevators, carried our bags, were men, as were the waiters who tended to our tables. (As women, we were directed to eat apart from men, in an alcove of the dining room, which was tastefully protected from prying male eyes by a screen.) For the interviews and audiences with government officials (all male), we women were treated in a courteous fashion that might be described as gender-neutral. We had been asked to dress modestly, yes, but not to bother wearing abbayahs or veils. In trying to explain to my co-travelers the apparent contradiction between what we had all read (all women must be covered to the eyes) and our own day-to-day experience, I resorted to an old story about our Iraqi experience forty years ago.

"What about your wife?" Sheikh Hamid, our village host, had asked Bob.

"My wife?" Bob returned. "She will be coming from Baghdad soon."

"Yes, but what will she wear?" the sheikh had persisted. "Will she be like Miss Bell" (Gertrude Bell, a British official), "wearing riding pants and sitting in the mudhif with the men, or is she a real woman who will wear an abbayah?"

Bob had said he would see. (I chose to be a real woman!)

Here in Saudi Arabia we were being treated like Gertrude Bell, in the tradition she established, the tradition of honorary men.

"Then, B.J., why do we have to dress modestly at all?" one lady asked.

Why indeed. "Well, er-uh, times have changed, and now visitors dress modestly, because . . ." (suddenly I had it) "because both Saudi men *and* women dress modestly." Which was true.

But we were not always treated like honorary men. One morning while the men had an audience with the Emir or governor of Jeddah, the women were taken shopping. We visited King Abdul Aziz University as a group, but the men were dropped off at the men's section, while we women were guided out of our bus and into a narrow passageway off the street, a passageway that led to the women's faculty. Here, at the entrance, while we were being formally welcomed by Dr. Haifa, the female vice rector, I noted neat bundles of clothing, scores and scores of black, dark blue, and gray bundles reposing in a long row along the high wall that shielded the spacious women's college campus from public view.

"Abbayahs," answered Dr. Haifa. "For later on, when the girls leave. They don't need to wear them here—since we are all women."

Our official program included two other special women's visits, to girls' primary schools. If we had been confined to that program, we would probably all have come back to America with impressions that confirmed media and academic accounts; Saudi Arabia was a rich country, but segregated, where women are left alone, idle and passive, their every move controlled by men. We were being welcomed into the public spaces of Saudi Arabia, the spaces designed for guests, strangers, non-Muslims. But of course other important spaces exist, spaces where family life goes on, where women and men negotiate for power. We would never have been fortunate enough to be invited into this part of Saudi society, if Saudi women themselves had not intervened and changed our agenda.

This happened rather unexpectedly at a lunch in Jeddah. For women only. Arranged by Lora Berg, the American consul, and given by the beautiful American-born wife of a distinguished Saudi architect. We sat at round tables covered with hand-loomed Saudi folk textiles in stripes of crimson and gold and green. We were, in this setting, introduced to a remarkable group of Saudi women who did not fit any stereotype at all: businesswomen, artists, translators, professors. In answer to questions, we described our program.

"But hardly any women!" exclaimed one tall young girl wearing a denim dress and a black velvet vest.

"Something must be done!" suggested another.

So these good women proceeded to telephone their relatives and friends in other parts of the Kingdom, and as a result, we found when we left Saudi Arabia that we ladies had been the fortunate guests at several other "women's spaces." At an art gallery in Al-Khobar in the eastern province we met women painters and sculptors and printmakers; we had tea privately with women writers; we were entertained at dinner by the women of the family of the chairman of the Riyadh Chamber of Commerce. (This was the occasion when the younger members of our group proceeded to demonstrate the macarena, but given the agility with which the steps were imitated, I had the feeling it was well known to the company already!) And we were welcomed at the El Nahdah Philanthropic Foundation for Women.

Thus, thanks to women's intervention, we saw a side of the Kingdom ordinarily closed even to invited strangers, and as a result we began to question ourselves and each other about our prior assumptions.

Does seclusion mean, for women, complete loss of agency? Are women's activities performed out of the public eye any less important than those available for everyone to see? For example, in the light of new information from Saudi women, we had to revise our earlier reactions to the session on Saudization of the workforce that we had attended, in which women were not even mentioned in the labor projections for the next decade. Said one of our new acquaintances, "But women are going to be involved. A delegation of women petitioned the ministry, and asked for recognition. The men agreed but they just didn't happen to mention it to you."

The Saudi women we met in these encounters bore no relationship whatsoever to the stereotypes we had brought with us. They were not idle and passive, though they were fashionably and attractively dressed. We met business women who had banded together to invest ten million dollars of their own money in a women-only shopping mall. We were told that women's private assets in Saudi banks alone totaled at least seventy billion dollars. We met women university professors and secondary school teachers who were training thousands of other women in science, medicine, social science, humanities. They told us that of the 175,000 students in Saudi universities, half were women. Of course, they added, women were being educated apart from men, and this was difficult, especially at the graduate level, where more laboratory spaces (for scientists) and better library materials (for all) were needed. "But what will these women do when they graduate?" I asked.

"Teach in the segregated primary and secondary schools as well as in the segregated universities."

"What about the future, when those jobs may be filled?"

Polite smiles greeted such queries, followed by comments such as, "We will see. It is important for girls to be educated so that they can educate their children. But *all* women want to learn. The Qur'an tells us we must be educated."

I met the sociologist Dr. Saleha Mahmoud, current editor of the important academic journal *Islamic Minority Affairs,* published in London. I interviewed Cecile Rouchdi, Lebanese educator who had come to Arabia long ago to keep house for her widowed father and been asked by the King, with encouragement from his wife, Queen Iffet, to open a school for girls, the first in the Kingdom. I dined with Asma Bahormuz, a former Texas student, whose textbook on operations research, a theoretical branch of computer studies, was the first such work published in Arabia. (It was later on display at the 1997 Cairo International Book Fair.) We talked with Rajaa Alim, novelist, short-story writer, essayist, who was now writing, in English, a novel about a woman's experience of the pilgrimage to Mecca. Her sister Shadya, a painter, designed the covers of her sister's books. We met Soad Bassam, a filmmaker in the audiovisual unit of the American Arabian Oil Company's public relations department, the one workplace in all of Saudi Arabia that is not sexually segregated.

And finally, near the end of our stay, we met Princess Sarah, sister of the King, and her niece, Princess Moudy. Princess Sarah and Princess

Moudy bore no resemblance whatsoever to media stereotypes about the royal family of Saud. They were neither idle nor bored. They were the moving forces behind the success of the El Nahdah Philanthropic Foundation for Women, which occupied several dozen square meters in the Sulaimaniyah section of the capital city of Riyadh. El Nahdah means "advancement" in Arabic, and the foundation, which began as a center to educate handicapped and Down's syndrome children, had now expanded and offered a variety of learning and leisure activities for women, as well as children. We toured down the spacious halls of El Nahdah's new quarters, past classrooms filled with women, young and old, working on different kinds of computers; we were shown well-equipped studios where women were glazing pottery, mixing oil paints, shaping stone into sculpture.

"We have more applicants for these classes than we have places," said Princess Sarah, a dark-haired, middle-aged woman of modest mien. "We are surprised at the response we have received." She wore not dazzling chiffons and satins, but a simple dark brown suit of slubbed natural silk.

I asked who had designed the building, its wide corridors of large classrooms alternating with pleasant open spaces furnished with comfortable chairs and tables, and hung with women's art.

Princess Sarah merely smiled.

"She is the one responsible," said Princess Moudy, in dark blue jacquard silk, high-necked white blouse, and a single gold chain. "She is too modest. It's her design."

As a group, we found ourselves finally in an exhibit space cum museum shop where mannequins modeling traditional Saudi costumes stood against white walls faced with colorful wooden doors.

"Antique doors from our cities," explained Princess Moudy. "They are beautiful, aren't they?"

Princess Sarah said, "We are trying to encourage the preservation of traditional Saudi arts and crafts, as you can see. And some of our members are taking those decorative motifs and utilizing them in new ways." She leaned forward to one of the center tables filled with hand-crafted objects and took up a large china plate adorned with golden and orange circles and dots reminiscent of those on one of the old hand-painted doors.

"Very beautiful," I said, and fully meant it.

We offered our thanks, and went on our way, laden with generous gifts—handcrafted pots, vases, and colorful posters depicting the doors of Arabia. (The mounted poster hangs in my office at the university today.)

Toward the end of our visit, we were entertained by a Saudi newspaperman who was a well-known popular dissident, our guide whispered. After we had feasted on the homemade delicacies generously spread out on the tea table, including a marvelous guava cream, our host offered to answer questions.

"Interview me," he said. "Ask anything you'd like to know, but haven't yet heard about our society." He added, "And I prefer provocative questions."

After two or three queries had been handled deftly, he said goodhumoredly, "Come on! You're all intelligent Americans, I'm told. These aren't provocative questions. What's the matter? Are you afraid to ask?"

Stung by his remark (for indeed I had been afraid to ask what I was dying to ask), I cleared my throat, and said, "Well, here's a provocative question, one which my Muslim women friends in Morocco and in Egypt asked me to ask."

"Yes?" Our host was smiling.

The room suddenly seemed to fall silent and I began to lose my nerve. "With all due respect, sir," I said, somewhat sententiously.

"Yes, yes, what is your question?" he replied, a trifle impatiently.

I came to the point, more abruptly than I had intended. "What is it in the Qur'an that mandates the sexually segregated society we have seen during our visit to Saudi Arabia, the complete covering of men and women, the refusal to allow women to drive. We know women drive in the desert," I added, though I had not meant to do so.

The leaders of our American group, both men, looked a bit startled, I thought, but our dissident host took the question in stride.

"Nothing," he said firmly. "Nothing in the Qur'an mandates such practices. No, madame, it is custom and tradition in the Kingdom that prescribes this attitude toward women, not the Holy Book." He raised his hand in case I felt like interrupting. (I didn't.) "I wish to say that my wife and I, like many Saudi citizens, see this present situation between men and women as a transition period, a phase that will, we hope, pass away slowly as our society develops and adapts to the world in which we find ourselves."

There was a short silence, while our group digested this response.

Nothing in the Qur'an. Nothing at all. An important statement, for the Qur'an is fixed and stable, the reference point for all Muslims, a work believed by Muslims to be literally the word of God, revealed to the Prophet Muhammad. The Qur'an does not change. But tradition and custom do change, in every society including Arabia.

Currently, Saudi Arabia has enough wealth to be able to resist pressures for change in the status quo, to reject the entry of women into the mixed labor force. In other Muslim countries, this entry, prompted by economic need, has tended to alter older cultural attitudes about the place of women. On the other hand, the Kingdom has committed itself to "Saudization," which means placing Saudi citizens into all jobs currently performed by foreign workers. In this push for national self-sufficiency, it seems defeatist to ignore the trained workers from the other half of the population—the newly educated women who are now emerging from universities. When we posed this question to officials, some argued that women were not going to be ignored at all; they could participate in the labor force without upsetting the policy of sexual segregation. Women would work in offices separate from men, or work from home, as some do now, linked to male co-workers only by computers and television projections. Women could serve each other, as they do now, in schools, banks, medical and dental clinics. (A whole chain of women's banks is in operation, we were told.) But is this going to work out for the greater good of the nation in the long run?

Current demand is already eroding strict enforcement of the ban on women driving. For we had indeed seen women in the desert, piloting pickup trucks over the dunes, speeding away into the distance. Why are they driving? "Their husbands maybe need their help with the animals," was the answer. Is it the city which is conservative, the place where historically men have demonstrated their wealth and social class and power by secluding their women? And therefore will change come from rural areas instead?

My short visit to Saudi Arabia confirmed some assumptions but challenged others. Saudi Arabia is rich. Its per capita income is among the highest in the world. Saudi Arabia has achieved, in one generation, an incredible material improvement in the lives of its people. Saudi Arabia is also a sexually segregated society, in which women have little freedom of public movement and are indeed subject to the control of men. But Saudi women, we found, are certainly not all the idle passive creatures portrayed in media accounts and in ghost-written novels and memoirs. Within the limited spaces available to them, many if not most Saudi women were taking advantage of the opportunity for education, of control over their inherited wealth (rights granted by Islamic law). They were working to improve themselves, their families; those who were able were giving generously to charitable projects (as mandated by Islam as well). They were also investing their capital in future development. And, in contrast to the assumptions of some of my traveling companions, Saudi Arabian women's lives were not representative of the Arab world. In the Muslim world today, they were an exception, the only group of women so strictly covered and segregated and controlled, so invisible to the public eye.

The Kingdom's officialdom continues to enforce gender segregation, and many citizens are said to support this state of affairs, arguing that it is required of them by Islam. Public opinion is not unanimous on the issue, as our dissident host suggested. But Saudi Arabia is still a kingdom, directed and controlled from above; it is not a democracy in any sense of the word. The current status quo remains in place.

Western feminism is clearly not present, but at least a breath of Islamic feminism is slowly sweeping through the elegant homes, the schools and universities, the mosques and shopping malls, the suburbs and the deserts of Saudi Arabia. When the powers that be see fit or can no longer resist, public changes in the position of women may come very swiftly indeed.

EIGHT

¤ ¤

Israel/Palestine

THE MAPPA MUNDI, the first Western European map of the world, was created in western England in the twelfth century, by an unknown monk at Hereford Cathedral. The map pictures the world as a great flat plate, bordered by Africa, the British Isles, Europe, and Asia. (The New World had not yet been discovered.) In the precise center of the map the unknown monk placed Jerusalem, the polestar around which, in medieval times, all other countries and continents clearly spun.

Even in the twentieth century, Jerusalem remains the center of the religious world for more than two billion Jews, Christians, and Muslims, some of whom live in the city, others who make regular pilgrimages to the shrines they revere (the Wailing Wall for Jews, the Church of the Sepulcher for Christians, the Al Aqsa mosque for Muslims).

Jerusalem is also the center of the patriarchal tradition of the three monotheistic religions; this is a tradition that gives man pride of place as head of household, and sees woman as his less than equal partner, a tradition currently being challenged all around the world. But in Jerusalem, the tradition has not changed. Family affairs like divorce, marriage, child custody, and inheritance continue to be regulated, not by civil law, as in the United States, but by religious law. For Christians, the different sects (Armenian, Eastern Orthodox, Roman Catholic, Greek Orthodox) interpret family law differently; some do not allow divorce, for example. For Muslims, (Sunni, Shi'a), sharia law grants men greater access than women to divorce; for Jews, the Orthodox rabbinate governs all marriage and divorce, and the state does not recognize even the authority of Reform or Conservative Judaic congregations.

A casual observer might say, "Given this situation which affects all women, why don't they join forces and try to change it?" But women's common interests are lost in the complexities of the society that occupies this religiously charged and surprisingly small piece of Middle Eastern land. Israel is only about the size of New Jersey, but it is home to five and a half million people—Ashkenazi or European Jews, Sephardic or oriental Jews, new Jewish immigrants from Ethiopia and the former Soviet Union, and over eight hundred thousand Arabs, Palestinians who stayed put in 1948 and now hold Israeli citizenship. And in the West Bank and Gaza, with a combined area about half that of Israel, two and a half million Palestinians live, mostly Muslims, though a significant Arab Christian minority is still present, a group with deep historic roots in Palestine.

Most important of all, after fifty years of conflict, most Palestinians and Israelis see each other as enemies.

Thus feminists or women's activists, both Israeli and Palestinian, have tended to organize separately, creating women's centers in their own communities, establishing societies to aid the poor, helping women deal with legal and employment problems. Which is why their sudden cooperation in 1987 startled many Western observers.

For a brief period in the 1980s, and again after the signing of the 1993 Peace Accords, Israeli and Palestinian women interested in peace, as well as in a more egalitarian society, made common cause. The most dramatic example of their cooperation was the organization known as Women in Black.

Hannah Safran, coordinator of the women's center in Haifa, said in a 1991 interview that Women in Black "was not really an organization, in the sense that there were no address or telephone lists or even a central office. No traditional symbols of an organization." She said she thought the time had come when women should stop "imitating men's organizations, meeting in the evenings [when men were free but women had children to care for], electing officers in a hierarchical way, and so on. It was time," she insisted, "to create a new kind of organization, more geared to the realities of women's lives—cooking, working, taking care of the family."

Women in Black was one such group flexible enough to allow many kinds of women to participate—poor, single, married, working, non-working, with or without children.

"Every woman who felt that she wanted to voice her protest against the occupation just had to choose, depending on where she lived, the place where she wanted to join a vigil of Women in Black, every Friday between one and two o'clock," said Hannah.

"And who keeps the signs?" I couldn't resist asking, for the women who wore black and stood together silently at crossroads and in city squares throughout Israel all carried small signs. Banners, cardboard cutouts in the form of the dove of peace, round "hands," these signs bore similar messages in Hebrew, Arabic, English: STOP THE OCCUPA-TION.

"The signs?" Hannah, an attractive mother of two with a mop of unruly black hair, laughed. "No one has ever asked, but it's done in two ways—here each woman brings her own, but in some cities women take turns keeping all the signs and then distributing them at the vigil sites."

Critics termed Women in Black "a publicity stunt for the left," a cover for "illegal PLO connections," and "totally ineffective as a polit-ical movement." Yet, between 1987 and 1993, the years of the intifada or uprising of Palestinians against Israeli occupation, the Women in Black continued to stand vigil; before the Gulf War, women estimated that groups were standing in more than twenty towns and cities throughout Israel.

Naomi Raz, of Kibbutz Shomrat, who stood near Akko, said she believed Women in Black was more effective than people realized. "One could tell by the violence of the opposition," she said. "After all, what were we doing? Just standing there quietly. Why the hostility? At the very beginning of our demonstration in Akko, a group of thugs even tried to run over us."

Women in Tel Aviv and Jerusalem had not only taunts and curses leveled at them but eggs and tomatoes! "I think they were also cursing us because we weren't behaving like proper Jewish women should. Some shouted, 'Why aren't you home preparing Shabbat?' And worse."

In Jerusalem, the situation became so dangerous that by 1991, a group of concerned rabbis organized themselves to accompany the women to their homes after their vigil, as protection from possible attacks.

Women in Black, according to Aliyah Strauss, who lives near Tel Aviv, provided a forum for Palestinian and Israeli women to join to-gether in political protest but also in friendship. "But you must re-member, B.J.," she said, "that most of the Palestinians we stood with are Israeli citizens, not Palestinians from the West Bank. It would be dangerous for them."

Aliyah was almost right. Only a few West Bank women are said to have participated in Women in Black vigils, and they were indeed, as noncitizens, subject to police harassment and possible imprisonment.

These two groups of Palestinians have essentially grown up in different cultural environments, Palestinian sociologist Salim Tamari pointed out. "We in the West Bank have been socialized in our old ways, learning Arabic in school, but Arabs who live in Israel attend Israeli schools and learn to deal with the world first in Hebrew, and after that in Arabic. It makes a difference."

After 1993, some of the women from Women in Black formed the Jerusalem Link, an association of Israeli and Palestinian women that saw itself as forging ties across old enemy lines, working together for the future, the common good. But by 1996, the Jerusalem Link had frayed considerably. Bat Shalom (the Israeli Hebrew group) had an office separate from El Markus el Quds (the Palestinian group). Judy Blanc, one of the founders of Women in Black and a pioneer peace activist, talked somewhat sadly about the breakdown.

"I guess it was bound to happen," she said, almost resignedly. "Since Netanyahu was elected, any official cooperation between Palestinians and Israelis is suspect. What can you expect after the tragedies we've witnessed recently, beginning with Rabin's assassination? Violence on both sides. Trust has evaporated. The communities are working on their own now. We hope it's only a transition period."

Israeli and Palestinian women have different histories of relationship to the patriarchal tradition. For Palestinians, the aftermath of the establishment of Israel in 1948 is called *al-nakbah* ("disaster") and *al-ghurbah* ("exile"). Since 1948, Palestinian women have been called upon to sustain and uphold the patriarchy, as a sign of their commitment to a national Palestinian state; only after that state is a reality, women have been told, will their specifically women's agendas merit consideration.

Israeli women have watched this process take place in reverse. The first Jewish European immigrants looked to Israel as an escape from the constraints of the old patriarchal family, with what they saw as its dire effects on women, children, and the group. Thus, with socialist zeal, they set out to create a new form that broke apart that old system: the *kibbutzim,* agricultural cooperatives where men and women were equal in work, under the law, and in decision making. However, as early as the late sixties and early seventies, these old ideals were fading, as the Israeli sociologist Yonina Talmon demonstrated in 1975. More recently Michal Palgi has charted the decline of these old patterns of "total equality."

By 1996 Israeli women found themselves divided, between secular and religious Orthodox, between poor and rich, between the small number of remaining "kibbutzniks" and urban dwellers, between Ashkenazim and Sephardic. In response, women's groups are reorganizing, rethinking their priorities.

"The political alliance for peace did some good," said Yvonne Deutsch, current director of the Kol-Ha-Isha (Woman to Woman) Center in Jerusalem. "But because of that political link, we were perceived by some traditional women as anti-Jewish or at least anti-Israeli. We have changed direction slightly—to focus on the Jewish women who need us—poor immigrant women without resources, Orthodox women stuck in bad marriages, women who suffer from low status because they are divorced, and so on. From politics to social services, I guess," she added, smiling a little. "It seems necessary at this time in our nation's history."

"What about Palestinian women who are Israeli citizens?" I asked. "Muslim women, for example." I had read that the move to Islamic revival was also evident in Israel, where, particularly in the northern city of Nazareth, an Islamic party had competed peacefully in local elections. In travels throughout the country, I had seen Jewish settler women covering their heads properly, according to religious requirements, but also Muslim women doing so, just as in other parts of the Middle East. Ms. Deutsch said, "Well, you know Muslim women are subject to Muslim religious courts here, just as we are subject to Judaic Orthodox courts. We haven't much information about the groups in the north. But we haven't completely forgotten Palestinian women."

Kol-Ha-Isha operates a resource and information center for all women, Muslim, Christian, and Jewish," she explained, "and part of it is a support group and workshop for young Palestinian women coming from outlying areas to study at the Hebrew University in Jerusalem." These women, she believes, are caught between two cultures.

Many Israeli feminists think the vigils of Women in Black also served to draw public attention to women's vulnerability. Thus new programs in women's centers in Jerusalem, Tel Aviv, Haifa, and other smaller towns have taken on the responsibility of educating their constituents about crimes in which women are victimized, such as rape, and battering. Attacks on women are routine, some say, and recent statistics support that view. In two months during the fall of 1996, seventeen attacks on women were recorded, attacks on Jewish women by Orthodox Jewish men for "dressing immodestly." Yvonne smiled wryly. "And one of those women was saved from harm by a group of Palestinian men. Ironic, no?"

Other organizations working with women, many calling themselves feminist, are the Israel Women's Network, the Jerusalem Rape Crisis Center (founded in 1981), and the Israel Association for the Advancement of Women's Health (which produces informational materials on menopause, breast cancer, and other health issues). Dr. Amy Avgar, IAAWH director, has pointed out that the Israeli state spends far more money on men's health than on women, even though women report more health problems, see doctors more frequently, and take more medication. I found it hard to believe that in this proclaimed "equal" state, only 12 percent of the nation's doctors were women.

"We have a long way to go," Dr. Avgar admitted.

But many women stated that the base of the problem lies with the religious law, and its unequal treatment of men and women.

"Are they still protesting on that front in front of the Ministry of Religious Affairs?" I asked, remembering the work of Anat Hoffman. Hoffman, a peace activist and an elected Jerusalem city councilor, had spearheaded women's marches each Friday to the Ministry of Religious Affairs, to demonstrate against the unequal laws.

"Anat has more or less stepped down," said Yvonne Deutsch. "She has a new baby, you know, and wants to give her family all her time." Judy Blanc felt that the legal situation had improved with the appointment of a Minister of Religious Affairs who, she said, "considers himself a democrat and is taking a second look at all the family law legislation and the protests by men and women surrounding that legislation."

The idea of civil, rather than religious-sanctioned marriage, has been floated many times in Israel by women's rights activists, but particularly by longtime feminist Shulamit Aloni, until recently head of the liberal leftist party Meretz, and once a member of Shimon Peres's cabinet. Aloni, who is viewed with mixed feelings by many Israelis (too American, too radical feminist), was soundly criticized for even suggesting that civil marriage might be appropriate in a society like Israel, which views itself as religious in base and origin.

Hannah Safran and her colleague Dalia Tzachst in Haifa have taken on the religious establishment by forming a new group, Women Against Fundamentalism, dedicated to fighting extremist religious sentiment as well as legally empowered Orthodox control in Jewish, Muslim, and Christian communities. Response to their new initiative has been mixed, even among women themselves. Some have applauded Safran's move, others feel it is counterproductive, since it sets religious women against less-religious or secular women.

"Closing off the connection to religious women is not a good idea," said Simona Sharoni, who now lives in the United States but spent many years as a feminist activist in Israel. "It just buys into American feminist goals, which do not necessarily work in Israel. And it isn't an either/or situation. Many Israeli women consider themselves religious, but do not go along with extreme views."

Judy Blanc is not as depressed as some of her younger friends about the way Israeli feminists are proceeding. "Old feminist tactics are giving way to new approaches," she said over dinner at her modest apartment in West Jerusalem. "That's as it should be. The younger people are less interested in ideology. They're much more practical."

"Working on specifics like rape and battered women and so on?"

"Yes, but also going at the law, and showing some long-overdue concern for oriental Jewish women, the Sephardim, and for Arab Israeli women and their low status. That's been an unforgivable lapse in our program over the years, I think. These people are, after all, Israeli citizens, and they're beginning to take part in women's groups."

And the future?

"I see some signs of hope," said Judy carefully, "but then I've always been an optimist. At Bat Shalom, our half of the Jerusalem Link—we're still meeting and talking. Seventy-five women turned up for the last session on Palestinian women prisoners."

"What will you talk about next?" asked Tom Hartwell, who had come along to dinner and also to photograph Judy at home.

Judy smiled. " 'What is a just peace?' "

We rose. Time to go. Tom began packing up his gear; it was dark and late, and we had to go across town to our hotel, the American Colony, which stood on the border between West Jerusalem (Israeli) and East Jerusalem (Palestinian). "I'll call a cab," offered Judy, "and come down with you. Often the drivers don't want to take you to what they call the other side, particularly late at night."

But the taxi driver turned out to be a jolly burly fellow who was fascinated by our pickup place in West Jerusalem and our destination in East Jerusalem, but mostly by Tom's camera. He turned out to be a freelance photographer on the side. "Do this to keep my family together," he said. "Life is expensive here, and getting more expensive all the time. I thought peace was going to make it better economically."

"Well, if it were a real peace, it would," said Tom, as we disembarked under the stone archway of the beautiful old American Colony Hotel.

"You think so, eh? Economics the base of it?"

"Good part of it," answered Tom.

□ □ □ □

Israeli women may feel the need to battle their own conservative patriarchy on the legal front, but Palestinian women told me they must now fight patriarchy on two fronts: against the Israeli Defense Forces and against the Palestinian Authority headed by Yasir Arafat. I was shocked to hear this sentiment echoed across the West Bank towns of Ramallah, Nablus, and even in East Jerusalem. I found it difficult to believe that the women expressing these views—active, educated women, some of whom I had known for years—were the same women who had greeted Arafat's return in 1994 with enthusiasm and acclaim, who had welcomed the Peace Accords as a beginning of new possibilities within Palestinian society.

"The official documents say it all," said Eileen Kuttab, a member of the new women's studies program at Bir Zeit University in the West Bank town of Al-Bireh. "You don't even need to know what the authority itself is doing and saying, B.J. Just read the materials."

And I did. The 1988 Palestinian Declaration of Independence, penned one year after the beginning of the intifada, stated, "Governance will be based on principles of social justice, equality and non-discrimination in public rights of men or women, on grounds of race, religion, color, or sex, and the aegis of a constitution which ensures the rules of law and an independent judiciary."

To Palestinian women, that declaration seemed only just reward for years of working through women's committees in the refugee camps, in the towns and cities of the occupied territories, taking part in the intifada not only by keeping schools and health care going but by putting together popular local committees to organize economic and political activities.

But things have not worked out as expected. Since the 1993 Accords, and the establishment of the Palestine Authority in Gaza and Jericho, a draft constitution has replaced the original declaration. This constitution, published in 1994, does not include the passages about gender equality that caused such euphoria among Palestinian women.

"Not at all," said one woman, who preferred to remain anonymous. "Not only have the passages about gender equality been eliminated, but the constitution reads as though it were written by men, for men, and probably for men with more than one wife."

Rita Giacoman, director of Bir Zeit's community health program, said, "Through the grass-roots movements of the intifada, we grew to taste and understand the flavor of democratization, and to recognize our rights. Now we feel cheated."

Samiha al-Khalil, indomitable founder/director of In'ash al-Usra in Al-Bireh, felt so cheated that she decided to challenge Yasir Arafat in the presidential election. She was the only opponent of PLO Chairman Arafat, and she lost, but she garnered 10 percent of the vote, running on a platform which lambasted the Peace Accords and championed the need for reestablishing the family.

"Why did you run?" I asked Madame al-Khalil, in the front office of her expanded center for women and children. She had aged considerably since I interviewed her in 1981. She wore glasses and her gray hair was pulled tightly back from a face that betrayed no joy, only tension and concern.

"I didn't like what I was hearing and seeing," she said. "I live with the people whose houses continue to be demolished. And I smelled blood. I don't want another river of blood in this country, either Israeli blood or Palestinian blood. So I decided to take a chance and run against this peace, which is not a real peace."

When I asked her to elaborate, she took off her glasses, and rubbed her tired face with long, expressive hands.

"Well," she said. "Let me just pose a few questions. What about all the Palestinian prisoners that haven't been released? Especially the women? What about our roads, still patrolled by Israeli police? Don't you know that women are praying every day in Halhoul and in Hebron that there won't be more violence? This must stop, madame."

"But how?" I asked.

Samiha al-Khalil spread those long hands. "You are asking *me*? Ask your government in the United States. Do they care? *We* have given, and given. We have nothing more to give."

"But the violence on both sides," I ventured, "contributes to the problem. Israelis also feel threatened."

Madame al-Khalil took a deep breath, as one might do when trying to control one's temper in dealing with a stupid child. *"Why* is there so much violence? Does anyone ask why? Our young people have no future. They have no hope."

"The politics of despair?" I offered.

She paused, leaned forward. "What did you say?"

I repeated what Bob had said, long ago, about terrorism. "It is the politics of despair."

Madame al-Khalil stared at me. For a moment she did not speak. Then she banged a small bell on her desk.

"Yes," she said. "Your husband is probably right. But he has the pessimistic view. I cannot give way to such views. We must work against falling into the trap. So now . . ." She paused as a young woman entered, small, dark-haired, in flowered skirt and black blouse. "Yes, Dina. These are our guests. Professor Fernea. Mr.—"

"Hartwell," answered Tom, shouldering his camera.

"Show them everything in the center. Let them take pictures. Who knows, one of these reports some day may be of help to us."

My heart sank, but I knew she was absolutely right. We were just another in the long series of writers and journalists who came to the troubled area of Palestine/Israel, published their work, and nothing, absolutely nothing changed.

For the next hour, Dina, who was pleasant and knowledgeable, shepherded us around the complex, much enlarged since 1981. Samiha al-Khalil had established her Society for the Preservation of the Family in 1965 in answer, she had written, to "expressed need." The wars of 1948, 1967, and 1973 between Israelis and Palestinians had left orphans, and widows, and families without resources, often without homes or means of earning a livelihood. For thirty years, the society, a nonprofit organization that subsisted on philanthropic donations, had provided housing for orphans, child care for working mothers, and most recently vocational training for young girls whose parents were either dead or unwilling to allow them to attend the West Bank coeducational public schools. We were shown the workshops in secretarial skills, computer basics, weaving, embroidery, sewing; we watched girls preserving and canning food to be sold in the society's gift shop—olives, dolma, jam. The hairdressing salon was full, and a girl under the dryer giggled when Tom stuck his head around the door.

"Don't worry, I won't take pictures unless you want me to," he said.

The day was sunny and pleasant, and the young women in the training programs seemed eager to learn; they even smiled at us as we were paraded by. Why had In'ash al-Usra, this seemingly innocuous institution, so incurred Israeli wrath? For I knew that Madame al-Khalil had been jailed six times by Israeli Defense Forces. "One day, two days at a time," she had said long ago. "Why? Who knows? Perhaps the idea of preserving the family in the face of an occupier is seen as a revolutionary or dangerous activity?"

"But they must have told you," I had insisted.

"I was never in front of a judge, if that's what you mean," she had replied. "The longest time I was incarcerated was in 1970, when George Habbash flew those airplanes to Jordan. One of the members of my family was with him, so the Israelis jailed us all—mothers, sisters, and so on."

The center boasted a library now, and a museum of traditional Palestinian folklore, which, I noted, reinforced the historical pattern of a sex-segregated society. The diorama presented the viewer first with a "women's room," where mannequins in beautiful embroidered dresses and head scarves carried in their hands the tools of their daily tasks: the spindle (for spinners and weavers), the wide sieve (for cleaning flour and rice), and the brass coffee grinder (to prepare cups of Turkish coffee for guests). In the "men's room" mannequins in traditional costumes of baggy pants, shirts, vests, and turbans sat on cushioned banquettes, enjoying the tray of tiny coffee cups that had clearly just been prepared and delivered by the proper women of their households.

"We had a big folklore festival in Jerusalem in 1982," said Dina, "and Madame al-Khalil wants to have another one when peace is really here."

"What's that marvelous smell?" asked Tom. It was past noon. We had breakfasted early.

"Cinnamon buns!" announced Dina, and took us to the new bakery, which offered catering services for teas, parties, weddings. "More money for the women," she added, while we chomped happily on the fresh products of the society's recently purchased ovens.

"We also assign piecework," added Dina, guiding us down the stairs and into the sunny courtyard where children were romping after their naps. "Many women can't leave their homes, you know, so we distribute piecework—embroidery, and also precut uniforms for schools in the territories."

"A few women?" I said.

"Over five hundred women are involved," responded Dina. "As I said, lots of traditional families still don't want their girls to go out and work in public."

"What about you?" asked Tom.

"My family is more progressive," replied Dina sweetly. "And I am from Al-Bireh, so I live at home."

Time to leave. We headed back to thank Madame al-Khalil, but as we approached the central suite of offices, we heard shouting and weeping, a long-drawn-out sobbing. What was happening? Samiha al-Khalil's office was so crowded with men and women they were spilling out into the corridor. And the weeping went on. Dina signaled us to wait. But we could not help overhearing.

"They came in the middle of the night, they took him, they took everything. We have no house, no place to go." Fresh sobbing.

"What about the rest of your family?"

"They're far away."

A child began to cry.

"Help us, please, Samiha," begged one of the men, stocky, his hair slightly gray, his back stooped. "Please, Samiha, we beg you!"

"What can I do?" shouted Samiha back, then spied us around the corner.

"So!" she called to us. "You see what I have to deal with every day? What am I supposed to do? We are already helping more than twenty thousand folks whose families are without housing, without food. Where? In Gaza, Hebron, Nablus. And I have nothing to give. Nothing to give!" She gestured and shouted as Tom and I stood transfixed in the doorway.

We looked at each other, dug in pockets and purses. "Can we offer something? Fifty dollars is what we have," Tom said, and we both felt embarrassed that it was so little.

The room had quieted and everyone turned to stare at us.

"Americans!" hissed the gray-haired man. His tone was bitter. We stood there uncertainly for a moment until I stepped forward to press our contribution into Samiha al-Khalil's hand.

"Thank you!" I said. "Good luck with your work."

"Yes, of course, you are welcome," she returned. Her voice was flat. Solidarity phrases, automatic in this society, but meaningless in the situation. We were not welcome at all, for we were identified with our government, the American government, which was seen as hostile to the problems Palestinians faced—or at least indifferent to them.

Even as we walked out the door, the shouting began again, and the weeping. What good was our fifty dollars?

"Well, it'll feed a few people tonight," pointed out Tom. "What else could we do?"

As we headed back to Jerusalem, our taxi was stopped by the long lines of cars and trucks and motorcycles ahead, waiting for the Israeli border guards to pass them through from the West Bank (Palestinian) into Jerusalem (Israeli). After an hour sitting in the sun we got out of the taxi to wait. The driver got out, too, scratching his head.

"Something going on?" asked Tom.

"Who knows?" the driver answered. "It happens every day."

He spat in the road. "How can we make any money when it takes us two hours to do a twenty-minute run?"

When we finally made it through the gates at the checkpoint, the driver volunteered that he thought the size of the backup meant another bomb scare.

"Those kids are nuts, making bombs in their houses," was his opinion, well considered. "But they don't have any work. The Israelis won't let them in to work. They sit around all day, getting madder. I guess I might go nuts, too."

Rita Giacoman had invited us back to Bir Zeit to see firsthand the public health program she was putting together. So Tom and I set out once more from Jerusalem, in a stream of traffic that seemed to move much faster than before.

"Welcome!" Rita smiled from behind her desk. In contrast to Samiha al-Khalil's halfhearted response, this seemed sincere. "Let's go out into the courtyard to talk. It's such a lovely day, why not?"

I returned to our earlier conversation. "You, like all Palestinian women, feel cheated by this peace?"

"Yes. We worked very hard during the intifada. You know that, B.J., you made a film about it, didn't you?" Rita did not wait for an answer but went on to say, almost passionately, "And as women we did not get our reward, which is to share power! Look at the Palestinian Authority! Almost no women in the managing body."

"Hanan Ashrawi . . ." I began.

"Hanan refused that one post that was offered to her, but rumors are that she may become the Minister of Education. Meanwhile, she's formed her own group, a kind of watchdog on human rights, an excellent idea, by the way."

Rita believes that the snubbing of women by the new authority is totally unacceptable.

"So what's your solution?"

"Solution?" she repeated. With an edge of sarcasm in her voice, she said, "I doubt very much that all by myself, B.J., I can manage the Israeli side of the equation. On the Palestinian side, I think it's important for us to keep an eye on the larger issues of freedom and equality, but not to give up . . . to keep working on other crucial issues, like health."

I said, "I read everywhere about your new department of community health here at Bir Zeit. But I have to confess that I thought that was what you were doing when we first met in 1983."

Rita smiled. The sun was warm. A young girl brought a tray of coffee, the traditional offering to visitors. A slight wind moved in the acacia trees that bordered the walled courtyard, wafted past us toward Rita's small suite of offices, the public health library, the conference rooms. The wind also ruffled her hair, glossy dark brown, and her earrings, crescents hammered out of some old silver, as she talked, animatedly and with enthusiasm. Her work was clearly a crucial part of her life, had been for many years.

"You're right, B.J. We were established as a formal part of Bir Zeit that year, 1983, but of course we'd been working informally since 1979."

"So what's new?"

Rita laughed. "You should know. Remember, no one took me seriously in those days. I was very young, to begin with. And age is a very important indicator of status in Palestinian society. And I didn't have a Ph.D., either."

But now she had a degree from Exeter University in Britain, and her book about health conditions in a group of Palestinian villages had been published and was quoted constantly in the West, as it was one of the few such documents available to an English-speaking audience.

"And since then," she put in, smiling broadly, "I've gotten married—to Mustapha—and that gives me status too, and now—with my daughter . . ." She stopped and shook her head happily. "Why didn't anyone ever tell me how wonderful it would be to have a family?"

"But you live in a society where it's supposed to be the be-all and the end-all of life," I protested.

"Yes, yes." Rita considered a moment. "I think I only saw the problems before."

Now, with a trained staff and a reasonably funded department, she directed a broad program of policy-oriented research. "That's the new fashion in the public health field these days, but we were doing that kind of work long before it was the fashion," Rita said.

Health, Rita believed, was a basic right of all peoples, and she had worked hard, channeled her energy and that of her staff into establishing an innovative program for her Palestinian community that combined theory and practice. Training health workers, fielding outreach programs into remote villages and refugee camps. This was common in America, my public health–involved daughter Laura Ann told me, but was relatively new in Palestine.

"Not so long ago people ridiculed us," said Rita, "because we focused on family care, but then everything was seen in biomedical terms. When I talked about the social construction of disease, everyone laughed at me."

While we were talking, the high door to the courtyard had opened twice, admitting a woman with a briefcase, who waved at us as she passed across the courtyard, and another woman in traditional embroidered Palestinian dress, who stood uncertainly near the door holding a small girl by the hand. The little girl's white hair bow was large and lovingly puffed up. Rita rose and found a staff member to answer the mother's questions. "About tetanus shots," she called.

"So!" She turned back to me. "I think we've won. They don't laugh at us anymore, and we're beginning to work on disability rehab and on garbage. Garbage! No one likes to talk about garbage, everyone politely uses that word 'sanitation,' but garbage is a huge problem here and affects everything else."

And then? "We work on tradition, good and bad," said Rita without a moment's hesitation. "Tradition decrees that women should bear children. And that's great, none of us would be here if women didn't have that wonderful capacity, but it's not the only thing a woman is capable of."

"What I'm saying," went on Rita, "is that our health and personhood are defined not only by being mothers and agents of reproduction. Sure, it's important for us, but that's not the only dimension of our life. Women must have the right to choose when to have kids, how many, and so on."

Like many concerned and dedicated health professionals, Rita saw the long-term health of mothers as closely related to the health of children and thus to the mental and physical health of the next generation. She insisted that "Palestinian society needs a holistic approach that looks at children, at women, and at men in a way that is compatible with the World Health Organization's definition of health, which is the physical, social, and psychological well-being of all people."

"Most American feminists would agree with your approach."

"Really?" Rita was amused. "Well, our society is very different, we have different problems and issues, but I suppose the idea of holistic health might be said to cut across cultural and geographical boundaries. We may not need the same kinds of laws and customs, but we could certainly all get along better with healthy citizens worldwide!"

A woman with a mission. Rita excused herself, for she had two meetings to attend (one with her training class, the other with the trainers themselves). And an international delegation of women had come out from Jerusalem to look at this small, modest center of community health, behind the windy walled courtyard that faced a cobbled street in Al-Bireh.

I had also made an appointment at Bir Zeit to visit the new women's studies program which I'd heard about in Cairo, at the Arab Women's Book Fair. Eileen Kuttab, who taught women's studies, had given an eloquent presentation about the plight of the Palestinian women's movement, for which she had received sustained applause.

"Despite all the official setbacks, we can't stop now," she had insisted. "We have to work harder. And a women's studies program is part of it!"

Eileen, Lisa Taraki, and Ilham Abou-Ghazaleh were members of the steering committee of the new program. With Hanan Ashrawi, who also taught at Bir Zeit, they formed a committee in 1989, wrote a proposal. But the committee never met. The university was closed down by the Israeli government, the Gulf War began, and Hanan Ashrawi went on to appear on Ted Koppel's *Nightline* and eventually became a major spokesperson in the historic Madrid peace talks.

"But, as you see, our program is going on, we are doing it," said Eileen, as we sat in the program's small office, crammed with papers, books, and too many desks, drinking coffee served in mugs on a table made of an overturned cardboard box that had clearly held books rather recently. (No luxurious guest reception room here.)

Ilham said, "We're struggling to do too many things at the same time—teaching, research, helping draft a new document of basic women's rights to submit to the authority—Al Haq is helping with that."

"And teaching is hard," said Eileen, "because most of the women's studies materials are geared for a Western audience. We have to translate these new ideas to our students. Not only the language but the ideas themselves into concrete examples that will make sense in women's lives here. Takes time, and money, and cooperation." She added, "We have the cooperation, certainly," smiling around at her colleagues, who were coming in and out, off to class, back from class, filing, telephoning, crossing through the cramped space surrounding our makeshift coffee table.

"I was surprised to hear in Cairo that you had a women's studies program at all," I confessed, and went on for a moment about the difficulties of starting our Texas program in 1978. "Some of our faculty wanted us to be just academic, others wanted activism included, and the dean of the College of Liberal Arts thought we were trying to destroy the American family."

No one laughed or even smiled. "We didn't have any of those problems," said Eileen. "What stopped us were the objective conditions."

"What do you mean?"

Ilham said, "Objective conditions like the Gulf War and the bombs, and the closing of the university . . ."

"And the women who were supposed to be in the program," went on Lisa, "were busy with other things—like getting their teenage children out of jail for violating the Israeli-set curfews—problems most

American women's studies programs wouldn't face." It was said pleasantly enough, but the message was clear: there are things you in the safe haven of Texas don't even think about, and of course she was right.

"But now things are moving along?"

"Yes, the administration, especially Ibrahim Abu-Loghud when he was here, is behind us. And we're getting good reports from students, so the university is proud of us."

"Though I am not sure they really understand what we're doing," put in Ilham.

As we rose to leave, Tom asked about yesterday's roadblocks at the checkpoint between Jerusalem and the West Bank. "They say maybe there'll be another one today. What do you think?"

The women looked at each other. "Maybe protests about the Israeli-proposed building near Jerusalem?"

"That particular situation looks bad," said Tom. "Yes, maybe."

"A bad situation for everybody is the impression we get," I offered, "but especially for women."

Eileen shook her head. "It's not as bleak as it looks from the top," she insisted. "Lots of determined women—and men, too—working for change in policy. The law, the passport issue . . ."

"Passport issue?"

"Yes, a man must still sign if a woman wants to get a passport."

"I don't believe it," said Tom. "Or maybe I do. What next?"

"Well, this debate is serious. Arafat has gotten into it. The word is he agrees that women should be able to get their own passports. His wife Soha agrees with us. The passport issue is a big first step."

"A first step?" I repeated slowly. "And after that?"

The women all began talking at the same time, to each other, to us.

"The whole women's rights issue. Reversing the policy in the draft constitution."

"Returning to the declaration."

"Teaching our students about it, men and women."

"Campaigning in people's homes."

"In Gaza women are being secluded again, forced to marry whoever their father chooses. Can you imagine? After all this?"

"Big plans, as you see," said Lisa. "We have to think that way."

Outside the office, on the newly paved walkways around Bir Zeit, students had set up booths to raise funds for refugees, for the families whose houses had been most recently demolished. They were selling earrings, embroidery from Samiha al-Khalil's workshop (at least the place mats and guest towels looked the same). And tee shirts, white and black, bearing the emblem of the university. Young women and young men, together and separately, sat on the walls bordering the new stone buildings, flirting, going over their class work, laughing. They wore shirts and jeans, and dresses, and I noticed an occasional head scarf—white, blue. At that moment they did not look like young people in the middle of ferment, of a sustained struggle for political rights. But the roadblock was up again when we reached the checkpoint, and it took so long to get into the environs of Jerusalem that our taxi driver refused to be side-tracked to visit the new women's legal aid center. "Lunch," he said curtly. He was round and sported a skullcap on his balding head, and he pointed out that it was two-thirty in the afternoon, and most people, most civilized people, he said sarcastically, "are hungry by this time."

Thus I called the legal aid center and made an appointment for the following day. But the following day the news was not good. Those calm-looking students we had seen at Bir Zeit University yesterday were today blocking the main roads to Jerusalem, holding placards, shouting and protesting.

"What are they protesting?" asked Tom. No one was sure.

The hotel personnel looked worried, not surprisingly, for this was the major tourist season, the time of the great religious festivals. And in 1996, for the first time in many years, the Jewish Passover and the Christian Easter were taking place during the same week, which meant double the usual number of tourists. We heard conflicting reports at the travel agency, and at the nearby branch of Barclays Bank; when I called Eileen to thank her, she cautioned that this was not a good time to run around the area.

"No one knows what will happen, B.J.," she said. "The students are out there, and more are joining the crowd all the time."

The next piece of news came from the desk clerk at the hotel, who reported that, given the tense situation, the Israeli government was planning to close the Allenby bridge—the main entryway to Jordan— and keep it closed until after the holidays were over.

When I finally got through to the legal aid center, Maha Abu Dayeh, the director, suggested that we not come out to her office "at this precise time."

So we conducted a long-distance interview.

"We're part of the new movement of Palestinian women who are determined to gain our rights," she said over a phone line that crackled in and out. "Women don't know their legal rights, even under sharia religious law, so our first job is to tell them what they can and cannot expect in the present situation. The men are so upset with the way things are that they can scarcely keep going, let alone be fair to their wives. So we're doing a lot of counseling of both men and women. It's free."

"What's the most important new program you've introduced?"

Maha's voice faded out, came back strongly.

"The hot line," I thought she said.

"The hot line?" I responded, raising my voice to make sure she could hear me.

"Yes, we helped the women to do it themselves. It was their idea. And a good one. In the past six months, we've had two hundred and eighty-three calls on that line, and a hundred and fifty cases taken to court. Domestic violence mostly. Some were settled out of court . . ." Her voice was fading out again.

"Good-bye," I thought she said.

"Good luck," I shouted back, though I was not certain she could hear me.

"Start packing, B.J.," said Tom, knocking on my door. "They really are closing the bridge, and we don't want to be stuck here for another week—or ten days or whatever time the Israelis decide to keep it shut."

The protests at Bir Zeit, we heard from the French passengers in our oversized taxi, had turned into a riot. But it was not about the building in Jerusalem after all.

"*C'est le problem avec Monsieur Arafat,*" said the French woman sitting next to me in the backseat. She had come from Amman to take her elderly Parisian mother to the Easter services in Jerusalem, but they had been advised to leave before any trouble erupted.

Problem with Mr. Arafat? Yes, it seemed that the rioting students were not protesting building in Jerusalem at all, but the recent actions of the Palestinian Authority in jailing dissidents and critics, including Jonathan Kuttab, a journalist-activist, longtime supporter of Arafat, and tireless worker for Palestinian independence. Palestinian police had been called in to put an end to the melee.

The unconfirmed reports cited many hurt, some jailed.

What was it I had been told upon my arrival in Jerusalem? "We now have to struggle against two patriarchal authorities, the Israeli Defense Forces and the Palestinian Authority?" I had been shocked at the time. But I was no longer shocked.

On the way to the Allenby bridge, our taxi was stopped three times at checkpoints on the outskirts of the city, checkpoints complete with bulldozers and armed police trucks as well as Israeli guards. At the last point before reaching the Allenby bridge, the guards flicked shiny wands under our taxi, two-sided wands, which, I noticed, had mirrors on one side so that any questionable object (a bomb?) attached to the car's undercarriage would be visible. But I also noticed that the guards did not flick those wands under the car in front of us, which bore a yellow Israeli-registered license plate. Our plate was blue, indicating registry in the area of the Palestinian Authority or the West Bank, still considered the Occupied Territories. We were, like all Palestinian-registered cars, suspect.

On the other side of the bridge, the taxi driver stopped and offered all of us, his passengers, soft drinks from the roadside vendor. He was sweating, I noticed, but now, as he guzzled Jordan's generic equivalent of Sprite, he seemed to relax. We stood around the car for a moment, thankful to be out of Jerusalem, and on our way to Jordan.

We were out, we were strangers, we could leave. Most of the people in both Israel and the Palestinian Authority did not have that luxury. Given the fear, the growing paranoia, I could only marvel at the tenacity and strength of the women on both sides who continued to try to improve their situation, continued to struggle for rights. Jerusalem, Jerusalem. Center of the world, and of male domination. What kind of feminism was it going to produce?

NINE

¤ ¤

The United States:
Coming Home

I HAD, I estimated, already traveled more than forty thousand miles in search of Islamic feminism. Eight countries. Kuwait and Saudi Arabia on the Gulf. Uzbekistan in Central Asia. Morocco in North Africa. Egypt, Iraq, Turkey, and Israel/Palestine in what is called the *mashraq,* the Fertile Crescent of the Middle East. All these countries are part of contemporary Dar al-Islam (literally, the house of Islam), places where Islamic majorities rule. Even in Israel, where a Judaic majority rules, Muslims have their own religious courts. In Dar al-Islam, a Muslim is supposed to be able to live according to his or her religious principles. Jews and Christians live in these countries, too, but they are considered People of the Book because they believe in the same God; their belief systems spring from the same sources as Islam: the Prophets Abraham and Isaac, the Torah, the New Testament.

But how do Muslim peoples, and particularly Muslim women, manage to practice their religion in countries which are not part of Dar al-Islam, countries where, unlike Israel, they do not even have their own religious courts? How do they accommodate themselves to states in which they are in the minority? And how do Muslim women's issues play out in a predominantly Christian country like the United States? For women's issues, I had found in my two years of travel, were controversial even in the countries which are part of Dar al-Islam. So what about America?

Historically, the problem of maintaining strict adherence to religious principles in a secular society like the United States has been faced in different ways. The early Amish and Shakers closed in on themselves, formed self-sufficient communities of their own; the Mormons for many years kept legal control over their members; Catholics and Jews have frowned on mixed marriages, creating real obstacles to such unions. But by 1996, most of these groups had been integrated into mainstream American life. I wanted to see what was happening to the growing Muslim community, which was now larger than the Episcopalian population, an estimated six to eight million people. Of the 1,200 mosques which now stand in towns and cities throughout the United States, 80 percent are said to have been built in the last twelve years. This burgeoning of the American Muslim population came home to me dramatically in the spring of 1997, at the time of the Muslim feast, the Iid al-Adha. For in Austin, Texas, where Bob and I have lived for thirty years, so many of the faithful turned up for prayers that a large ballroom had to be rented to accommodate the overflow crowd. The ballroom stands next to the rodeo grounds in the nearby town of Manor.

Thus, to try to find out what was happening, I headed out across my own country, and I started in Portland, Oregon, where I grew up, went to high school, graduated from college.

When I was a child in Portland fifty years ago, the term Muslim was not in use. If the followers of the Prophet Muhammad were mentioned at all in the ancient history books I studied at Jefferson High School, they were called Muhammadans. Miss Doris Euler, our teacher, drew the parallel between Christians, as followers of Christ, and Muhammadans, the followers of Muhammad. "They also worship a different god," Miss Euler added. "A god named Allah." And in our youth fellowship discussion group at St. Andrew's Roman Catholic Church, this meant that they—those Muhammadans, that is—had nothing to do with us and our faith. They were strange people who lived far from Portland, far from the United States. How could we possibly have anything in common with people who worshiped a different god?

By 1996 things had changed. Interfaith workshops had managed to educate some Americans, and it was generally recognized that Islam was one of the three Abrahamic religions, following Judaism and Christianity. These people wished to be called Muslims, not Muhammadans, for they did not worship Muhammad any more than Christians worshiped the Virgin Mary or the Jews worshiped Isaac. And

Allah was simply the Arabic word for God; an Arab Christian prayed to Allah in the same way that an American Christian prayed to God.

In this changed climate, friends from college days who knew about my projected book suggested I should visit with women in the growing Muslim community of Portland. Three mosques were active, they said, and the *Oregonian* reported many activities (with Christian and Jews as well as separately). So here I was again in Portland, and, wonder of wonders, it was not raining.

I headed up S.W. Tenth Avenue toward my first appointment, with Wajdi Said, a member of the board of directors of the Muslim Educational Trust. Over the phone, Mr. Said had given me the address, the corner of S.W. Broadway and Montgomery streets, which, according to what I remembered, would be near the campus of Portland State University. A fledgling downtown college when Bob and I were attending Reed in the 1940s and 1950s, Portland State had become a university with fourteen thousand full-time and thousands of day students.

It was a perfectly beautiful spring day, with real sunshine, a gift to be treasured in Portland, which Bob and I both remembered as a city of eternal rain, of swishy shoes and dripping umbrellas from September until May. And here was sun in *April*. Along the avenue in front of the venerable public library, people sat out on the "literary" benches, eating their lunches, benches where I, too, had once sat, during my summer tenures as a teenage library minion; one day the pages (us) would sit on the bench inscribed "George Eliot" to eat our tuna fish sandwiches; the next day we would choose "Victor Hugo." Ahead, the street opened out into a double-sided boulevard, complete with overarching trees, glimmering green in the welcome sunlight rather than dripping wet in the routine rain. Here, too, in what we used to call the park blocks, many of the benches were occupied by happy lunchers, several of them seniors taking the sun, celebrating the break in, if not the end of, winter drizzle and chill.

Well, here it was. S.W. Broadway and Montgomery. All four corners. Which one was a possible site for the Muslim Educational Trust? Had Mr. Said said that his office was on the campus? It seemed a bit unlikely. Muhammadans on the PSU campus?

After making a tour of the four corners, I focused at last on the large black-and-white marquee which announced the presence of the Campus Christian Ministry. Yes. The Christian Ministry. That would obviously not include Muslims, but maybe they could help me find them. The marquee bore the following announcement:

Catholic Mass, Wednesdays 12:45 P.M.
Episcopal—Lutheran Worship, Sundays 7 P.M.
Ask About Others

And then, to my surprise, at the bottom of the marquee hung two square signs, side by side, smaller than the marquee, true, but still clearly visible. One announced the presence of the Society for Values in Higher Education, and the other, a translucent green, the color of the Prophet Muhammad himself, proclaimed in neat black letters the presence of the Muslim Educational Trust.

I stared at the sign for a moment, then mentally shook myself. Why shouldn't there be a Muslim group situated in the same building as the Campus Christian Ministry? Was I stuck in the past? Even after all our years in the Muslim Middle East, was I still making a distinction between there (them) and here (us)? What nonsense! Muslims had immigrated to America in the past from all parts of the world, just as everyone else had. Before, there had probably been Muslims living in Portland, but I didn't know any, and they no doubt had kept a low profile, a wise move considering the general opinion of them as strangers and infidels.

"Could you direct me to the Muslim Educational Trust?" I asked the young student at the reception desk of the Campus Christian Ministry. He wore a black tee shirt and had blond hair. "Oh," he said, "you mean Wajdi? He's up there on the second floor at the top of the stairs. But," he added, "I don't think he's in."

The young man was correct. Wajdi was not in, but would be right back, said the young woman in a blue chambray dress, with long sleeves, her head covered in white. "I'm Gail Ramadan, the associate director. Please sit down. I know he's expecting you. Dr. Fernea, right?"

"Right."

"I've read some of your books." Pause. So what did you think about them, I was dying to ask, but didn't.

Gail turned back to her computer. I found myself fidgeting. "Am I late?" I asked.

"No, you're early." Gail smiled. "He should be back soon." Moments passed. I admired the posters on the walls, noted the framed art calligraphy—it was a verse from the Qur'an, something that is often found in Muslim homes and offices. Gail continued to work, below the single window which was screened in green by the burst of new foliage on the tall trees outside. I also covertly studied Gail's garb, which certainly resembled the *hijab*, or Islamic dress, I had seen in

Egypt, Kuwait, Morocco, even in Turkey. But her head scarf was different. White and crisp and full, but pinned over an underscarf, and this underscarf was decorated with lace. A half circle of white stylized lace leaves framed her pink and white skin, complemented her blue eyes, but also seemed to serve as an anchor for the top scarf. I wondered how it was fastened, remembering my own long-ago efforts in a village of Iraq to keep my silk abbayah under my chin to keep it on. Here was Gail, unconcernedly entering data into her computer, with no apparent worry about the stability of her head covering.

She turned and smiled again at me. "We are glad you are here," she said. "We know and like your work. I hope Wajdi will tell you all about the things Portland Muslims are doing these days. Ask him if he doesn't."

Another pause. I could resist no longer. "I know this sounds like a silly question, but how does that underscarf work? I mean, it seems to stay firmly on your head." I rattled on about my own past difficulties with unfamiliar garb.

"Oh, it's great, let me show you." Gail stood up, unpinned the wide voluminous overscarf, and proceeded to enlighten me about her head gear.

"These things are just wide elastic headbands," she said, showing me how it held her hair in place. "They're made in Damascus and someone here in Portland orders them for us. The cotton has just enough rough surface to keep the other scarf in place."

"So, Gail, you are a convert to Islam, I presume?"

"Yes, I am. Since my kids were small. My husband's a Muslim from Zimbabwe, but it was only when I'd take the kids to religion classes that I began to think about it myself. I went to high school here in Portland—Islam was something I hadn't even heard of. My daughter was three then, learning the basics; she's almost fifteen now, so it's been about twelve years."

"Is the head covering really required?" I asked. "People I've talked to overseas seem divided about it."

"Many people believe it is required," said Gail. "It took me a while, but I feel good about it now."

"And your daughter? Will she cover her head?"

"It's a big problem," agreed Gail. "But she's tough, tougher than her older brother. She's thinking about it."

"But—" I interposed.

"There are rules," said Gail. "Some people interpret them differently than I do. I have chosen to abide by them. But it's hard for Muslim kids. They know they're minorities, so they tend to hang out with minorities. My son was once asked by a teacher 'Don't you feel bad at Christmas?' And you know what he answered?"

"No."

"He said, 'Most of my friends are Jewish and they don't get presents at Christmas either.' "

The knock meant Wajdi was back. "Let him tell you about our program," she said.

"You have programs for women too?"

Gail looked scandalized. "Of course. We have women on our board, all volunteers. Women are half of the Muslim world. They are crucial."

"And feminism?"

Gail shrugged. Wajdi came forward, a dark-haired young man with a dark mustache and a pleasant expression. He had heard my question, apparently, for he answered it.

"During the time of the Prophet," said Wajdi, "women were very important. Aisha, particularly, was very influential. But cultural influences where Muslims live have discouraged women from claiming their full rights under Islam. If by feminism you mean the Western definition—men and women in conflict, then I would say we differ. We would say *complementary*, not equal."

He and Gail proceeded to put together a collection of materials for me: newsletters, schedules of religion classes, notices of conferences, even a copy of a new glossy magazine *Sisters*. "It's published in Seattle, and is directed just to Muslim women, you might like to see it," said Gail.

"And you should stay for this conference we're having," suggested Wajdi, "on 'Islam and the American Dream.' "

I obediently glanced over the forthcoming conference schedule, noticing that no session was directly concerned with women's issues. But Wajdi, as though reading my mind, pointed to the bottom of the flyer, where a discreet notice in smaller type indicated that "Sister Ama Shabazz will be available for free and confidential marriage and family counseling." Sister Shabazz was identified as a member of the Council of the Islamic Schools of North America and was also scheduled to speak on a panel, "Muslim Identity and the Challenges for Assimilation."

"Naturally," said Wajdi, "she will talk about women's place in American Islam, but we do not see women as separate, nor men as separate, but both as part of the overall community."

I put the folders and flyers into my bag and stood up to go.

"I do have one more question," I said. "How did you manage to get an office in the building of the Campus Christian Ministry?"

Gail smiled and turned to Wajdi.

"Let me take you to a very good coffee place nearby, madame, if you have the time," he suggested, "and I will tell you about our work."

Over excellent cappuccino, Wajdi held forth on the past and future of the Muslim Educational Trust of Portland. "We are lucky, I think," he said. "The people of Portland are good people. We've worked with the media, with the schools. We have, as I think you say, paid our dues. I'm proud of this book especially," and he opened a large illustrated book for children, *Sacred Myths: Stories of World Religions*, published locally. "I worked with this author for quite a while. We try to be good citizens and show that we're not all terrorists. It's not been easy, either within the Muslim community itself, or in Portland. Lots of new immigrant Muslims feel like pariahs, they've read all the stuff about terrorism, they just want to isolate themselves."

"Well, I can certainly understand that impulse."

Wajdi looked disturbed. "But we can't do that. I tell my fellow Muslims, yes, we know what we believe, we have this system of values, but we have to look at the environment in which we live, and adapt it and embrace it, that's why we work so hard on the education."

"It is important," I agreed. "And I have to say that when I was growing up here, I don't think there were any Muslims around. It's a different world these days."

"Yes." He leaned forward and stirred his coffee thoughtfully. "In Portland today, Muslims are active in all fields," he said, "and many more people understand Islam than when you were growing up here. We at the trust think the issues of women and the family are very important, and we work to bring these issues into our discourse whenever we can. But you must also know that there are some Muslims, just as there are some American Christians and Jews, who do not wish to raise these issues, or think about them."

"Yes, Wajdi, I can see that."

"But I do believe, contrary to the media, that they do this first out of concern for women and their families, but mostly out of sincere belief. So they must be respected for those beliefs."

Ten thousand practicing Muslims live in Oregon, the trust estimates, "and probably more, because this is based on mosque attendance, three in Portland, one in Corvallis, one in Eugene. A few older immigrants, many born in America, some converts like Gail."

"And who finances the trust?"

Wajdi answered, in surprise, "We do it ourselves, with volunteer help. I work as coordinator of Islamic Studies at Portland State. Gail's a volunteer here in the trust office."

"Well, we hear these tales of Saudi Arabia paying for mosques . . ." I began.

"Not here," said Wajdi stoutly. "This is our own operation. You may check."

I changed the subject. "And all the women in the congregation cover their heads?"

"Most of them. But there are rules about covering, you know. One chooses whether or not to obey these rules of God, and accept reward or punishment for one's actions."

When I later interviewed Wajdi's wife, an Afghan immigrant, by phone she confided that she had begun to cover her head three years ago.

"Does that create problems for you?"

"Yes and no."

I waited.

"Well, my husband seems very happy that I am covering, but you see, I'm a dentist."

"A dentist?"

"You sound surprised, madame. But you should know that in the Muslim world most women have to work, and many are in professional positions. If they work there, why not here in America, where everything is supposed to be freer?"

Of course. Why not indeed? Why was it that I could write and speak perfectly comfortably about professional women in Cairo wearing *hijab*, but was stopped dead by the idea of one practicing dentistry in my old hometown?

"Of course I don't wear the head scarf when I work."

This threw me. Was the dental office private rather than public? Did she treat only women patients?

"I wear a paper hat and a mask, that's what dentists are supposed to do in Oregon. It is different in Texas?"

"No. No."

"It is true," she went on, "that at first when I wore *hijab*, people stared, but I don't notice it anymore. It was a problem when I was in group practice. But I opened my own practice last year and things are okay now. Just fine!"

In the evening, I was to interview several Muslim women who had lived in America for many years. My friend Carmen Kasrawi had arranged the session at a restaurant called AbouKarim. The guests included Farida Derhalli, who immigrated from Jerusalem in 1969 and manages retail stores which sell uniforms for medical personnel; Nilge Emre, who trained as an architect in Turkey, practiced in Portland, and had recently acquired her own construction firm; and Lena Bargouti, the youngest, an optometrist in Portland. They were all friends of Carmen, Puerto Rican-born artist and wife of Nofal Kasrawi, and they had agreed to talk with me about my project.

The women assembled at the restaurant were not wearing head scarfs or any suggestions of *hijab*. They were all dressed in suits, fashionable trousers, turtlenecks, discreet jewelry. It was immediately apparent that they were not close friends, for they began by asking each other questions.

"Have you found a mosque community where you are comfortable? Anyone?"

"No."

"Not me."

"I go once in a while, but I don't really feel part of it."

One of the women turned to me. "You see, the strongest part of Islam, the most important for me, is the community. It's hard for me to be without that community."

"But there's an active and large community here," I countered. "Three mosques. I spent the day at the Muslim Educational Trust."

The women smiled politely. One said, in the awkward pause, "But those groups are from a younger generation. They are creating communities for themselves—good for them, but not for me. Head scarves!" She pursed her lips.

"But not everyone covers her head," I insisted.

"It is a different generation, though," said Nilge. "Things have changed in our own lands even while we have been here. I know it, because when my parents come visit, they pray more than they did when I was a child in Turkey and they're upset that my daughter does not seem pious enough."

"That's what I mean," went on another. "And so it is hard to find any community in which I can wholeheartedly participate."

Farida, dark-haired, wearing dark-rimmed glasses, cocked her head to one side and asked mischievously, "Then why not become a Christian or a Jew? It seems to be the fad these days to turn into something new."

Her companion's intense reply silenced the slight laughter that rippled around the table. "No," she said firmly. "I could never do that. I will always be a Muslim in my heart. But I am spiritually alienated from these new Muslim groups. I read the Qur'an. What does it say about head scarves? Nothing. It says be modest. Well, I'm modest. We're all modest, don't you think?"

I agreed that everyone looked modest. "Try the *babaganouj*," suggested Carmen, the mediator. "It's supposed to be good here."

We all tucked into the meze, the traditional Middle Eastern starters. These had been prepared, it appeared, to near-perfection by the cook in AbouKarim's restaurant, one of the new fashionable ethnic restaurants that had replaced the old chop suey places in the upgraded Portland waterfront district. When Bob and I were at Reed, this area was considered dangerous at night, and the nearby streets held burlesque houses, Salvation Army kitchens, and gypsies, who lived in abandoned storefronts, covering the plate-glass windows with drapes of orange and cerise satin. Those glorious colored drapes, often strung across the windows on visible clotheslines, intrigued my brother and myself when, as children, we peered out the window of the old trolley busses that traversed those dangerous streets, passing the street people and the gypsy lairs en route to more conventional downtown emporiums: J. K. Gill Books, Meier and Frank, Lipman Wolfe, the post office.

My mother, in whose veins ran the blood of a committed middle-class social reformer, must have sensed our fascination, for she always said, as we went by, "You must feel sorry for those poor Gypsies. No real home. They have to move all the time."

"Pretty curtains, though," I remembered murmuring.

I do not think my mother deigned to reply, but in her silence as she looked straight ahead, I somehow received the impression that she did not think they were very pretty curtains. Cerise? Orange! *Satin!*

"The *babaganouj* is not bad," opined Farida.

"Let's see how they do with the *shish taouk*," said Nilge.

"There was no Middle Eastern restaurant here when I was growing up," I put in.

"Even when I came," said Farida. "But now they've done the waterfront up, it's quite gentrified."

Yes, I thought, and the gypsies are long gone, as well as the burlesque houses and what the town fathers might term "the other riff-raff," headed east, away from the new historic district that had been created. Antique stores, pedestrian walkways, ethnic restaurants like AbouKarim, a Saturday market, and riverside parks had risen around the beautiful Skidmore Fountain, a late-nineteenth-century neoclassic monument. Its base was inscribed with the motto, "Good citizens are the strength of the city."

Lena burst into my musing saying, "Being a Muslim is no big deal, but I get it from all sides because I'm a Palestinian. That seems to be much more of a problem."

"Why you?" Farida looked puzzled. "You look quite American, my dear. Pale skin, nice brown hair, green eyes, no head scarf."

"It's my accent," she replied and now that she had spoken, I realized she did have a very slight accent. "I brought it with me when I came here from Qatar to go to Beaverton High. What a shock that was! I hated it."

Nilge looked sympathetic. "High school students can be very cruel," she said.

"So none of you go to mosque," said Carmen.

"On the feasts, yes," answered Lena. "Who has time to go every week? Children, full-time job, cooking, keeping house."

"Child care?"

"I'm lucky." Lena's smile flashed, dispelling the tension on her face. "My mother-in-law lives in town. I take the kids to her house, and my husband picks them up." She turned to the others suddenly. "You really should all go to mosque sometimes. There are nice Muslims around, you'll see."

The others looked dubious. "Feminists?" said one. "Interested in women's rights?"

"Yes," said Lena. "Yes. Islam is all for women's rights, you know that . . ."

Nilge said, "It's our cultures that have gotten it all wrong. America is just as bad. They think we, as Muslim women, are downtrodden. Let me tell you about some of my American colleagues. They say they're feminists, but no Muslim woman would put up with some of the stuff they take!"

"Like what?" I asked.

"To begin with, they don't get equal pay for equal work and they sort of don't even try for it. They're afraid. And their divorced husbands don't pay child support! And some even don't have their own checking accounts, but have to ask men for allowances!"

Lena said, "They talk about feminism and equal rights, but what they really mean is their own personal rights. Kids aren't considered, and neither is the family."

We had all dined well on good *shish taouk, fattoush,* dolma. The Turkish coffee and tea were served. "Well," I said, "if the Qur'an doesn't say women should wear head scarves, why are people doing it here, in America?"

"To make clear they're different maybe."

"To show they're Muslims."

"The converts want to prove something to the other Muslims, so they overdo it."

"Some people do say it is in the Qur'an."

"But that verse can be interpreted many ways—cover up your adornments, your beauty. What does that mean, your breasts, your jewelry, the rest of your body?"

The women looked at each other, at Carmen, and then at me.

Lena said, "Every woman has to decide for herself. And I decided no."

"Religion to me," said Farida, "is the Ten Commandments. They apply to Christians and Jews and Muslims. I've been raised in all three religions, since my dad was Muslim, my mother was Jewish, and now I'm living in a Christian country."

Nilge added, "But they don't call it that. America calls itself a secular state. But it is not really secular, I think. It's a very religious place, even more religious than Turkey."

"I have enjoyed being a Muslim here," said Farida finally. "Before I ran the uniform stores, I owned two very successful boutiques. Telling people I was Muslim made me feel good, it was a chance to point out that not all Muslims are dangerous people, terrorists. We're good people and bad people, too, but all of us, as you see, are independent women. We could have been successful in the Middle East, and we're even more successful here. And feminists? Yes, I think so."

The morning I left Portland it was raining. Sort of reassuring. The real surprise had been the sunshine that first day, the sunshine that followed me as I walked back from interviews to McCormick Pier on the waterfront, where I was staying in the pied-à-terre apartment of old friends Dick and Pat Ivey. The sun had burnished the greenish-bronze public drinking fountains on street corners that had been installed in my grandfather's day; restaurant owners in the new historic district had even put tables and chairs out on the street. A few customers took advantage of these impromptu sidewalk cafés.

"Come on, B.J.," said Pat, who had offered to take me to the new Portland International airport for the next leg on my journey. "We'll be late."

I let down the venetian blinds to cover the window in my ground-floor guest room, which overlooked the Willamette River. This was the river that nineteenth-century historians had described as "a veritable forest of masts," of ships coming and going from ports north and south and across the Pacific from Asia. No masts were visible on the gray river today, but the freighter *Nol Halaaran* (South Asian?) had drawn up on the opposite shore, to unload conveniently in the center of the city, in the shadow of the old steel bridge. The same ugly black metal pillars I remembered from childhood supported the complex webs of dark iron that constituted the span, which still provided safe river crossing for cars and trucks and an occasional freight train. The trolley cars were gone. New bridges had been built. New groups were fitting themselves into the old cultural mosaic of Portland.

The *Shasta Daylight,* a Southern Pacific special, used to make daily trips from Portland to San Francisco. We would leave early in the morning, my parents, my younger brother, and myself, and the train would chug slowly enough so that we could admire the dark woods of southern Oregon and the mountains of northern California (including majestic Mount Shasta) and swiftly enough so that we would be in San Francisco in late evening. Very exciting indeed to arrive in the dark, the lighted streets of Baghdad-by-the-Sea beckoning us, the cable cars swinging around to carry us triumphantly up the hills of San Francisco, the city which one of my friends used to refer to as "a dear person."

In 1996, I flew over the woods from Portland, topped the peaks of the California mountains, and within two hours was met in San Francisco by our oldest daughter Laura Ann, and her daughters, baby Maya in arms and four-year-old Isabel pronouncing, "You're late, Grandma!"

I had come to interview Asifa Quraishi, a member of the Muslim delegation to the 1995 Beijing Women's Conference and also of KARAMAH, a new informal group of Muslim women lawyers. It was an added pleasure to be able to visit my family, and I invited everyone to dinner with Asifa, who had suggested we meet at Palermo, a Palo Alto Italian restaurant. She had been described by a mutual friend as an "intellectual rising star," and I was not certain what to expect of the encounter. The family dinner turned out to be a good idea, for within moments, the young people were into the problems and politics of the Bay Area, particularly for first-generation immigrants and new citizens. Alberto, our son-in-law, is one of them, a public health specialist who does outreach in the Latino community about AIDS and domestic violence.

"Domestic violence?" Asifa echoed. She was a slight young woman with finely chiseled features, a huge black beret covering her hair, fashionable silk pants and tunic, and a sideways smile that immediately endeared her to Isabel, who was patiently waiting for her dinner, and Maya, happily mouthing a breadstick in her father's arms.

Asifa and Alberto were already exchanging business cards when I repeated, in some surprise, "Domestic violence? That's your job, too?"

Alberto nodded. Asifa nodded. "It's a big problem for our community," she said, "and we are already trying to find some religiously viable solutions." Religiously viable? What does that mean, I wondered to myself. But as I listened to Laura Ann, Asifa, and Alberto, it seemed that solutions to the problem, whether in Latino or Muslim settings, sounded much the same: care, counseling, workshops.

"Mama, where's dinner?" Isabel asked politely, and as if on cue, the waiter appeared and greeted Asifa as an old friend.

"This is my favorite restaurant," she explained. "And all the specials are good," she added with a glance at the middle-aged waiter, who smiled at her delightedly.

She was right. Everything was good at Palermo: the wonderful smells of homemade pasta and sauces and fresh grilled fish wafted to us from the trays held high above the waiters' heads, the spirited conversations at nearby tables, the bursts of laughter. Isabel looked around her and then smiled contentedly as the waiter set a plate of spaghetti in front of her and dusted it with freshly grated cheese.

Asifa was saying to Alberto, "You see, I was born in Palo Alto but people treat me like an immigrant. They say where are you from and I say Palo Alto and they ask where I went to high school and I say Palo Alto and they ask where my mother is from [Medford, Oregon] and my father? And when I finally say that my father came here from India forty years ago, they smile knowingly and say, oh yes, of course, you're Indian! I'm not Indian, I'm American!" Asifa bit off a mouthful of good Italian bread and nodded her head to make her point. She looked at me. "That's the way many of us first-generation American Muslims feel," she said.

Alberto nodded, too, and smiled as he skillfully prevented baby Maya from upsetting the water glass on the table in front of him.

"You are far ahead of me, I'm afraid," he said to Asifa. "I was born in Veracruz and I have this accent, so I must be an illegal *something!*"

We were all eating by this time, Isabel tucking into her pasta with gusto, sitting up straight next to Grandma (me), behaving as though she was enjoying herself. She listened to the adult conversation, which ranged from identity politics to public health woes on the Peninsula to local elections to Proposition 187. The young people exchanged background and education, placing each other in the complex world of 1990s San Francisco. A long way from *Shasta Daylight* times. And no opening yet for me to introduce Islamic feminism.

Asifa must have sensed my concern, for as Laura Ann and Alberto prepared to depart to put the children to bed (kisses and hugs for Grandma and Grandma's friend in the beret and beige and black muted silks), she suggested we go around the corner for coffee.

"I'll bring your mother home," she promised Laura Ann.

In the upstairs lounge of the coffee shop, sipping tea out of Italian oversized blue-and-yellow pottery cups, I learned that Asifa was indeed an intellectual legal presence with whom one must reckon. She was the death penalty specialist for the judicial council of the Ninth Circuit of the U.S. Court of Appeals. Her card bore the gold seal of the United States courts.

"Death penalty?"

Asifa said, "I don't decide about the application of the death penalty in any particular case. My job is to continually inform the judges about the complex capital punishment law and assist them in making policy on how to administer the capital cases in the circuit. It's a good job and an important one and I enjoy it."

In answer to my interest, question finally posed, Asifa explained that Islamic feminism was not, she believed, an illusion or an oxymoron. "Not at all. Islam holds the potential for a really vibrant kind of feminism," she said. "The basis of egalitarianism is there in the Qur'an. What different cultures have done with it is another matter."

"In other words, like many of my Muslim friends, you would argue that if you look deep into the spirit of the Qur'an, you will find equality."

Asifa shook her head vigorously. "No. No. No. Not the *spirit*. The *letter*. These days Muslim women, and men, too, are reading the texts in light of their current situation and they're finding empowering responses to their questions and problems: in fact, a lot of this is there in traditional jurisprudence itself, but has just fallen out of use."

"Fallen out of use?" I echoed.

"Yes, or if you like, fallen out of popular discourse," answered Asifa. "A lot of Muslims are also analyzing the context and the reasons behind traditional Islamic laws that look unfair or oppressive—analyzing, that is, with an openness to change."

"In other words, what's happening today is new and different."

Asifa nodded. "But the word feminism to most Muslims means a Western—almost an imperialist—movement, which seems to be attacking Islam and destroying Muslim women's identity, replacing it with a secular identity and agenda."

"But there is more to feminism than that," I protested. "I consider myself a feminist, certainly, and I think the movement has many positive aspects."

"Yes, but the Muslim community doesn't see that side," said Asifa. "I'd say that Muslims have about as much understanding of the real meaning of feminism as Americans have of Muslims and Islam."

Touché, I thought, and wrote that down.

I asked about Muslims in the Bay Area, and Asifa talked about the different mosques and political organizations but seemed especially proud of the young, decidedly *American* Muslim group she helped found.

Asifa said, "I guess you'd call it a forum for American Muslims who don't feel comfortable in the existing more traditional Muslim organizations and mosques here. Our group is called AMILA."

"Which means?"

"American Muslims Intent on Learning and Activism," Asifa announced. "How's that for a name? It's in its fifth year now. We meet at least once a month, in each other's homes, have speakers, discussion, study groups, all that. There's an ethnic mix—most of us are first- or second-generation children of immigrants, and American converts. And there's no dress code or segregation enforced." She smiled and sipped more tea, though I thought that was more a gesture than anything else, since her tea must have been as cold as mine after an hour and a half of conversation. The waiter came and she ordered more hot tea, looked around her at the walls covered with plates and platters of that distinctive blue-and-yellow Italian pottery.

"I really love this place," she said. "I've spent a lot of time in a lot of cafés over the years, in college, in law school."

Married to an engineer of Iraqi origin, Asifa has two sisters, one at university, one working in human rights. Her brother just finished film school. "The difference between my family and my husband's family was difficult at first—ethnic, and Sunni-Shi'a—but it didn't take long to resolve itself," she said. "We were both raised to believe—and practice—that what was most important was the religion itself, Islam, not the variations in sectarian theological differences. We were both raised here, so we're both more American then Iraqi or Indian. But parents like ours, newcomers to America, are afraid of the word 'Americanized.' To them, it means their kids will lose their culture and their religion and become part of a homogeneous mass that doesn't have any values at all."

I said that my own mother, daughter of a Polish Catholic family, had the same problems with her parents, but they came around too, and were proud of her education and her achievements, even her marriage to a Protestant Scots-Irishman.

"They're proud of me, yes," said Asifa reflectively. "I think so. I've done well, in their eyes. But my parents may wonder about me, from time to time."

"Tell me more about your work on domestic violence," I prompted.

Asifa explained her association with the group of Muslim women lawyers called KARAMAH. "Azizah al-Hibri founded it," she said. "A friend of yours, I think."

"Yes."

"We're working with one particular group in one city that is setting up services for victims of domestic violence," she explained. "As soon as we started, we heard more and more about it—about Muslims' need to internally address the issue in an organized way. Domestic violence is all of a sudden more of an issue than I'd imagined."

"Will you expand your work to other communities?"

Asifa paused, then added, "Maybe eventually, but it would have to be tailored to meet the needs of each community, its demographics, its environment."

"And other issues?"

"Education, legal education of the American Muslim community. What should an engaged couple do to protect their marital rights under both U.S. and Islamic law? What are your rights if someone accuses you of being a terrorist? What does the new antiterrorism act mean for you? And so on. People are scared. You can't blame them, really."

I nodded.

"Muslims, Arabs, become the scapegoats for everyone," she said, sadly. "I can't tell you how we felt after the Oklahoma tragedy, and how sorry we felt for the victims and how guilty we felt to be relieved that it wasn't an Arab who did it. It's not easy being Muslim in this country."

I knew that it was late, and that Asifa had to drive me home to Laura Ann's and Alberto's house and then drive herself all the way back to San Francisco and get up early in the morning to be at the courthouse promptly. But it had been such a wonderful evening and such a good hopeful kind of conversation that I was hesitant to end it. Into the silence Asifa suddenly said, "And then there is the problem of rape."

"Rape?" I was startled into attention.

"Different cultural views. I just finished writing an article about it."

"Yes?"

"It's coming out in May in the *Michigan Journal of International Law*. I'll send you a copy, if you'd like."

"Yes, I would like. What is the title of the piece?"

Asifa said, "I called it 'Her Honor: An Islamic Critique of the Rape Laws of Pakistan from a Woman-Sensitive Perspective.'"

The proprietor put his head around the entrance to the upstairs parlor where we sat. "We're closing," he said. "You're the last customers, ladies."

"I've enjoyed this evening very much," said Asifa.

"I have, too. Thank you for coming."

We set out along El Camino Real, where my family lived, and Asifa mentioned that her husband was getting into the theater. "He's very good," she said, "and he's bored with his engineering job and wants to go to drama school in New York. And I'd like to go back to school for a graduate law degree and eventually teach law. So who knows? We might move."

I explained that Laura Ann and Alberto lived near a motel complex that looked like a fairy-tale castle, the Glass Slipper Inn.

"Oh yes," said Asifa. "I remember that place from when I was a child. When we were little, my sisters and I liked to think it was Cinderella's house."

"My granddaughter Isabel thinks it's Cinderella's house, too," I answered. "But her mother—my daughter, whom you met—told her it's not really—she has to grow up and build her own house."

Asifa turned into the driveway, let me out. We shook hands.

"Good luck with everything," I said. "Sounds like you're doing good work."

"Enshallah," said Asifa, and smiled that sideways smile that had so entranced Isabel and Maya. "Good-bye. I had a great evening. Oh, I said that."

"Good-bye," and I waved as she headed back—down El Camino Real past the Glass Slipper Inn on the way home to San Francisco.

After "terrorist," the image most closely associated with Islam in America is the Nation of Islam, headed by Louis Farrakhan. The Nation of Islam is often perceived as the organization which enfolds all black Muslims, but many members of the larger Muslim community told me they felt the American public viewed Mr. Farrakhan's group as representative of all U.S. Muslims. The name itself evokes the idea of a separate community, a *nation* of Islam. And in speeches and interviews, Louis Farrakhan has positioned himself as head of that nation, the man who has assumed the mantle of Elijah Muhammad; Elijah Muhammad himself became the leader after the disappearance, in the 1930s, of Wallace Fard, founder of the Black Muslim movement in America. Mr. Farrakhan states that the Nation of Islam has a clear and simple goal—to better the conditions of black people in the United States, by fighting racism and the white status quo. He has, he asserts, cleared up the confusion in the teachings of Malcolm X, who, before he was gunned down in New York in 1965, had begun to advocate that Black Muslims in America should become part of the international Muslim community, rather than remain a separate group.

Louis Farrakhan gained national attention recently with his Million-Man March on Washington. The effort to reenlist men in their roles as fathers and thus reenergize the black family was one commended by all Americans. But for me, looking still for Islamic feminism, the actions of Mr. Farrakhan were problematic. Where was Mrs. Farrakhan? Only men were invited to the march. What about women? The move suggested that the Nation of Islam did not see women as full and equal participants in the family, but rather as important assistants to men, who were, in this march, encouraged to accept their power and their dominance along with their responsibilities. Such ideas are close to those of Christian white fundamentalist groups, with the Promise Keepers as an obvious extreme example. My fruitless efforts to find and interview a woman member of the Nation of Islam only supported that perception.

But as I traveled and read and interviewed, I found that many of my original assumptions about Black Muslims were dead wrong. The Nation of Islam is not the majority movement of Muslims in America or even of black Muslims in America. Louis Farrakhan, according to many sources, can count perhaps twenty thousand followers within the six to eight million people in the United States who identify themselves as Muslims. Even among black American Muslims, Farrakhan's group is seen as a fringe movement, outside the mainstream groups of Wurth ed-Din Muhammad, with two million followers, and Jamil al-Amin, with ten thousand. (Jamil al-Amin was known as H. Rap Brown before his conversion.) Wurth ed-Din's and Jamil al-Amin's groups actually are members of the American *Shura* council, an umbrella organization representing Muslims in the United States. The *Shura* council meets regularly and speaks publicly as one voice on issues facing Muslims in America in coordination with the Islamic North American Council (ISNA). But the Nation of Islam is not part of the council as it is not considered by these other groups to be truly Muslim.

To the average American, this is a nonissue, but for Muslim Americans, it is crucial. In the 1950s, when Bob and I were working and studying at the University of Chicago, on the city's South Side, we knew something about the Black Muslim movement because we lived right around the corner from one of the temples. I remember the women of the congregation, for in those days they were hard to miss. In their long white garments, their heads and throats wrapped in white like the nuns at nearby St. Thomas the Apostle Church, they marched their well-scrubbed children along the streets of Hyde Park, on the way to and from services in the temple.

But when we spoke about the movement to our Muslim Arabic teacher, he dismissed them as "not real Muslims."

"Why?" Bob asked.

"Because these people believe," he explained patiently, "that Muhammad was not the last Prophet of Islam, but the next to last." They believe Wallace or W. D. Fard, later known as Master Fard Muhammad, to be the last Prophet, he said. Mr. Fard was supposedly an Arab from the holy city of Mecca, who had come to America on a mission from God to find and bring His lost tribe back into the Muslim fold. These people were African-Americans, the tribe of Shabazz, who had been stolen by Caucasians (blond, blue-eyed devils, in some accounts) and forcibly transported as slaves to America.

"An appealing message," Bob had said. "I mean, many of the slaves that came over were Muslims, you know, and I've heard many gave their children Muslim names, even in slavery days."

Our Arabic teacher, an Egyptian Sunni Muslim, was not impressed. "The people of this group are simply not Muslims," he said, clearly and unequivocally. And, almost in exasperation at our stubbornness, he added, "Look, you know how important the *shahada,* or declaration of faith, is. This is the first duty for every Muslim. Well, these people say the *shahada* but they say 'There is no God but God and Wallace Fard is His Prophet after Muhammad.' That's blasphemous!"

But I remembered responding even then in some fashion. "Whoever they are," I think I said, "those dignified black ladies in white should be given credit for keeping their kids on the straight and narrow, and cleaning up some of drugs and violence in Hyde Park. We can now walk on the street by our house, thanks to what you call non-Muslims."

My sarcasm had not made any difference, I recalled. "I told you, B.J., these people are not Muslims." And that was that. "Now, since you are paying me for Arabic lessons, we'd better get back to the *masdars.* You and Bob seem to have trouble with these particular grammatic constructions."

Later, when we lived in Cairo while Bob was teaching at the American University, we kept meeting young black Americans who were studying at the theological university of Al-Azhar. David Du Bois, son of the famed black sociologist W. E. B. Du Bois, was frequenting the old cafés around Al-Azhar (cafés people said had been there since medieval times) along with many other black Americans, searching, they said, and learning about Sunni Islam. Were they not Muslims? Or at least learning about what it meant to be true Muslims?

The 1965 assassination of Malcolm X was the tragic evidence of basic disagreement within the community about the direction of the American Black Muslim movement. Was it a black nationalism movement? Or was it part of Dar al-Islam, the international Muslim community? For Malcolm X, the appointed first assistant to Elijah Muhammad, had shifted ground. After making the *hajj* or pilgrimage to Mecca in 1964, he changed his mind. His words, as recorded by Alex Haley in *The Autobiography of Malcolm X,* are worth quoting.

On the *hajj,* he saw, "The brotherhood! The people of all races, colors, from all over the world coming together as *one!* It has proved to me the power of the one God!"

His experience led him, on his return to America, to urge his followers to replace their "hate whitey" approach with one that recognized the common struggles of all peoples and to join with other Muslims worldwide in that recognition. This was not a particularly popular view, given the continuing racism with which most black Americans had to deal—in education, in the workplace, in political life.

The basic controversy (inclusion or exclusion) simmered, however, until 1975, when Elijah Muhammad died, and designated his seventh child, Wallace M. (Wurth ed-Din Muhammad), as his successor. The organization was then still called the Nation of Islam. Wurth ed-Din soon decreed that all black American Muslims should eventually become orthodox mainstream Muslims, as Malcolm X had urged ten years before. No violence erupted, but after two years of infighting over decentralizing the economic enterprises which actually belonged to the Nation of Islam, the group split. Louis Farrakhan reestablished, around 1977, a new Nation of Islam. Wurth ed-Din opted for inclusion in the larger Muslim community, and carried the majority of black members with him.

In the accounts of this tangled history, little mention is made of women's issues, to say nothing of possible Islamic feminism, but the pattern of the past has been to place great emphasis on the stability of the family. The ladies in white on Chicago's streets in the 1950s were a living demonstration of this. Women are the center of the family, but not the dominant figures. When I asked about the division in the American Muslim groups, and especially about their attitudes toward women's roles, I was met with a curious but certainly understandable reticence, by both Muslim men and women in many communities. They preferred to remain anonymous, but the tone of their comments was very different from the scorn of our Arabic teacher forty years ago.

"There is nothing but praise to be given for the social services which the Nation of Islam tries to provide."

"No Muslim would ever be put in the position of criticizing Farrakhan. He does good for his people."

"We differ with Mr. Farrakhan in his belief that Wallace Fard is a Prophet. That is not acceptable."

"Mr. Farrakhan is filling an important need."

"We, as the Muslim community, however, would not agree with him that the white man is a devil, and that racism is the overriding goal of Islam. We believe that this kind of racism is a disease of the United States, because of its history."

"Perhaps the message of Master Fard and Elijah Muhammad was important to African-Americans in the beginning, but no longer. Imam Wurth ed-Din has said no to violence and hatred, and we are with him."

The real issue within the Muslim community today seemed to be not who or which group was right or wrong, but what good could be done as a community, working together. As for women's issues, and specifically the possibility of Islamic feminism, my question was greeted with amusement on one occasion.

"Have you interviewed American Muslim women of the mainstream?" one woman asked.

"Yes," I had responded.

"And have you interviewed women who belong to Mr. Farrakhan's group?"

I confessed that I had not been able to manage that. Was it because women's rights were not viewed the same in the different communities?

"Partly that," one woman suggested, "but then think for a moment."

I thought, but could not seem to come up with a reasonable reply.

"Well, B.J.," said another woman, "if Farrakhan's group sees the white man as a devil, how do they view you?"

One of the young men of the group laughed. "It's pretty obvious, isn't it?"

"Well, I'm white and middle class, if that's what you mean. And an infidel to boot."

"But if the white man is a devil, the white woman is clearly the devil's wife. So of course they don't want to talk to you."

Me? The devil's wife? I quickly cast through my mind for any childhood religious teachings that would have discussed the devil's wife. What did she look like? What did she do all day? The only thing I could remember was an old saying of my aunt Rose: "when it rains and sunshines at the same time, the devil is beating his wife." But of course it did not matter what I thought or remembered; what mattered was the way the Nation of Islam viewed me.

"Yes," I said. "I think I see."

I was then given a lot of written material, which I dutifully read, and was particularly struck by one passage in a speech of Louis Farrakhan: "When you see a real man you are looking at God." He had gone on to assure his listeners that "there's no woman on earth who would not be happy with a man who is a reflection of God."

In that same speech, Mr. Farrakhan told his audience that "real men" did not beat their wives or commit adultery, and that clearly "not all black men are gods," but they "have the potential to evolve into gods."

My search for different expressions of Islamic feminism then turned toward the communities outside the Nation of Islam.

"You should talk to men and women who are part of the communities like the people in Portland," said Salam al-Marayati, director of the Muslim Public Affairs Council.

The Council occupied a two-story building in the heart of what natives call "the religious mile" along Wilshire Boulevard, where the historic early churches stand—Catholic, Lutheran, Baptist.

"We're just like the Jewish Federation," said Salam, "and I'm not joking. The only difference is that we have a place of worship in the center, whereas Jewish people would not include the synagogue in a center like ours."

"But we have lectures, child care, youth activities," put in his wife, Laila, a gynecologist whose offices were down the street from the Glendale restaurant where we were lunching with her mother, Jane El-Farra, American-born wife of a Palestinian physician.

Salam added, "And don't forget our magazine, the *Minaret*." A slim good-looking young man who came to the United States from Iraq to study engineering, Salam left a successful career as an engineer to get an MBA at UC-Irvine and assume his current position as paid director at the Council.

"You must realize," went on Laila, "that things are very different these days for Muslim men and women in America. Maybe it's because many of us like me were born here, we've grown up here, we realize we must participate in American life and politics, and we're doing that.

"We consider ourselves Americans and Muslims simultaneously," she continued, "just as in the same way Christians and Jews consider themselves. Muslim, Christian, Jew, it becomes, for me at least, what we can do together, not separately. Don't you think so, Salam?"

Salam, dipping his foccacia into the herb-flavored olive oil in the center of the restaurant's table, paused with the bread in midair.

"Of course," he said. "You're right, Laila."

"I am," she continued, "an American Muslim, just like Salam, just like the Muslim colleagues I meet in schools, mosques, and homes throughout America. We have to keep explaining this to our fellow Muslims."

"Why?" I asked, thinking that it seemed obvious.

"Because a lot of Muslims in America," said Salam, "are in denial about the fact that they are actually living in America. They're still struggling for inclusion . . ."

I nibbled some foccacia, too, but my doubt must have been evident in my silence.

"Yes, inclusion," said Salam. "We're still struggling to demonstrate that we are a positive element, not a terrorist threat, in American society. I mean, when our community's media stars are Saddam Hussein, the Ayatollah Khomeini, and King Fahd, with an occasional positive story about a basketball player, we know we have a long way to go."

I had actually wondered about this, for the address I had been given turned out to be a local post office. I could not get a phone number listing from Information, so I assumed they were keeping a low profile to avoid unpleasant freak attacks by people who saw "Muslim" as a code word for terrorism. But it turned out that I was using the wrong name. Salam finally called me, at my daughter's house.

"And," Laila's voice broke into my reverie, "we know you're interested in women's issues, because we've read your books, my mother and I."

I smiled, pleased, and attacked my scallop and greens salad with ginger-flavored dressing. It was delicious.

How to proceed? I knew Laila had taken time off from her practice to talk to me over lunch and patients would be waiting for her, beginning in an hour, so I wanted to waste as little time as possible. I looked up at her, dark eyes, short curly black hair, a pleasant, questioning expression. No head scarf. Very like her mother, a slight woman with a small face and wide eyes, also, I thought, with a reserved and questioning expression.

I made a quick decision. No questions.

"Why don't you just talk to me about the position of women in the Muslim community here, how they feel about the role of women, and particularly whether they think at all about feminism."

Salam cut into his pasta lunch, I nibbled another scallop, Laila considered me across the table. She took a deep breath.

"Okay, feminism. This is a bad word among some Muslims both here and overseas, as you probably know. It's often associated with other movements—imperialism, colonialism, to some, even Zionism. Among Muslims here it's a kind of buzzword that we try to avoid because of the perception that feminism is somehow about depravity, particularly sexual depravity, birth control, individualism, no family concerns, no morals."

"So women's issues are complicated?" I said.

Her mother looked at her quickly. Laila said, "Yes, very complicated. Because Muslims come to America and they bring their own traditional cultures and attitudes—from Afghanistan, Iraq, Lebanon, Yemen, Pakistan, wherever. So they're trying to make sense of themselves and their culture in relation to American society and guess what?"

"What?"

"The confusion gets played out, argued, discussed, negotiated mostly in terms of the issues relating to women—like segregation of the sexes, veiling, honor crimes, mobility of women, the double standard, and so on."

We had been eating our way through a delicious lunch and the waiter now stood inquiring about dessert. We all declined, but ordered coffee and Laila looked at her watch.

"I do appreciate your giving me the time," I offered. "I know how busy you are."

"We're all busy," said Salam, "but let's get back to your interest. *Hijab,* for example. Wearing a head scarf is mandated by law in some Muslim countries, like Iran. But here no . . . so . . ."

"So we have the freedom to choose." Laila finished his sentence for him. "What was the *hijab* for? In the Qur'an, to keep women modest—and also *safe*. For some women the head scarf has a protective effect, for others it's the opposite."

Salam broke in again. "Yes, we often have cases on our hands of Muslim women who've been discriminated against, or even harassed, for wearing head scarfs. Why?"

"Well," I suggested. "Maybe because Americans tend to be obsessed with the veil—they have this hate thing going. Look at those French schools which have forbidden girls to wear it!"

Laila nodded. She folded her napkin, checked her bag, prepared to rise. "Muslim women should not be harassed for wearing—or not wearing—a head scarf. We need to focus on other issues—like abuses of marriage and divorce laws, domestic violence, access to mosques and to decision making. Muslim women in America have to be active, just as they are in other countries around the world. The Qur'an tells us we must be educated and active men and women to make a difference in our society. Now I must run—patients waiting!"

We exchanged greetings, smiles, she slipped out of the booth, and Laila's mother, Salam, and I sat back down to finish our after-lunch coffee and tea.

"What are the most important things the Council here is doing?" I asked.

"Education," said Salam promptly. "Our own community first—we have three private schools, the New Horizon schools we call them, in Pasadena and Santa Monica as well as in central Los Angeles. Our motto? A value-based education system within the American context. . . . The Islamic Information Service originated here, and now it has a program on the access channel—fifty affiliates—there are over forty-five mosques in Los Angeles alone. We try to involve as many Muslims as we can. . . ."

Laila's mother, who had been silent throughout our discussion, suddenly broke in. "You know, Hillary Clinton visited the Muslim Women's League last year," she said in a pleased tone. "The first time anyone of her national stature has done so. It was really wonderful. . . ."

Salam nodded. "It was an important moment for us," he agreed.

"So," I said to Laila's mother, Jane, "you must be happy to have your children close by."

"Oh yes." Her face broke open into a happy smile. "All but one of my five kids are in the Los Angeles area. And of course lots of lovely grandchildren. Salam and Laila have two boys. Show her pictures, Salam . . ."

Salam looked slightly embarrassed, but produced his wallet, and then of course I produced mine, and we sat, for several moments, in parental and grandparental infatuation, admiring the pictures of the next generation we had all been part of producing.

"Thank you for your time and help," I said. "My daughter Laila is coming to pick me up outside, so I probably should go."

"Laila? Why did you call her by a Middle Eastern name?" asked Jane.

"After the area, I guess, where Bob and I lived so many years. She didn't like the name when she was little, not wanting to be different, but she does now."

We shook hands all around, and Salam walked out to the curb where Laila was already waiting. "Our generation really does want to be part of America," he said earnestly, "and to help in making America better. I sincerely believe that, and most Muslims I know do, too . . ."

"As long as you're not connected with foreign governments, that'll work," I said. "I know some groups here are connected to Iran or Saudi Arabia."

Salam turned serious. "Our center's policy concerning funding is very clear," he said. "No money from foreign governments. That allows us to have the political and ideological independence to develop a healthy *American*-Muslim identity. Most of the mosques in the Los Angeles area are small, have grass-roots origins, and pay for themselves."

"And the big ones?"

Salam said, "Look around you in Los Angeles. There are lots of rich people here. And lots of them are Muslims. They give money for mosques and education in the same way that Christian and Jewish groups do. Write that. It's true."

I promised that I would.

The Sisterhood Is Global Institute, established in 1984 as an international independent nonprofit organization, is the brainchild of Robin Morgan, then an editor of *Ms.* magazine and still a member of the board. Morgan and other American feminist activists have said they had become concerned in the eighties about the relation of American feminists to women around the world. And, as a demonstration of that concern, Robin Morgan edited the massive volume *Sisterhood Is Global,* an anthology of writing—prose, poetry, essays, by women from seventy countries.

The institute, an outgrowth of Robin Morgan's volume, is now based in Bethesda, Maryland, and its stated goal is "to improve women's rights on the national, regional and global levels." Women from seventy countries are listed as members.

It was perhaps surprising to find that the current executive director of this U.S.–based international organization was Mahnaz Afkhami, an Iranian Muslim woman who was for three years Minister of State for Women's Affairs in the prerevolutionary government of the Shah. Or perhaps it was not so surprising, given the association of the prerevolutionary Iranian government with Western feminist views, with secularization, with women's rights defined by Western standards. But Mahnaz Afkhami objected to such a simplistic view of the institute.

"I took the job in 1993," she said, "because I believe in what I have defined as global feminism in my talks and writings and also because I think it's important for a Muslim woman to be in this position. A lot of the destiny of the Middle East is tied to what happens in the West. Our images of ourselves as Middle Eastern women are influenced by what happens here—money, resources, political decision making. We can't ignore it, even if we want to."

Afkhami believes that the Sisterhood Is Global Institute can be an important bridge across the East-West feminist divide. "We can offer women of the Global South (non-Europeans, that is) access to funding sources for women's projects," she said. "And we can offer Western women access to information about what is happening overseas.

"Let's face it, stereotyping is a two-way street," she stated, sitting behind a neat desk in her small office on Montgomery Avenue. "The East has a caricature of Western feminism in its collective mind—the devil's work, some say—but the West also has its own caricature of Muslim women—oppressed prisoners of religious dogma."

"No problems for women in Muslim lands, then?" I asked ironically. I had known Mahnaz for several years, and worked with her when she was director of the Foundation for Iranian Studies. In 1980, after the 1979 revolution and the subsequent demonizing of Iran by the United States, she put together an informational packet on Iran's history and culture for public schools, one that continues to be useful.

She smiled. "Come on, B.J., you know better than that. Of course we have problems as Muslim women. A major area of our work is designed to correct stereotypes." She turned to the well-stocked bookshelves to give me pamphlets and Xerox copies of news stories about the institute, as well as videos and books.

"This, for example." She showed me the stories that appeared in the *New York Times,* about the first SIGI conference on Muslim women, held in May 1996, with speakers from more than twenty countries.

"MUSLIM WOMEN'S MOVEMENT IS GAINING STRENGTH" trumpeted the four-column headline over the story and an appealing photo of four of the participants: Mahnaz herself, Yasmeen Murshed of Bangladesh, Fatima Mernissi of Morocco, and Deniz Kandiyoti of Turkey. Sub-headings within the story, such as "WOMEN'S RIGHTS GAIN ATTENTION IN ISLAM," indicated, Mahnaz believed, that the Western world had a very dim image of the Islamic world in general, and women's role in particular. "After all, women's rights have been an issue since the very first days of Islam," she pointed out. "It was the emphasis on women's rights, especially women's rights to own, inherit, and manage property, that distinguished the new religion from its two monotheistic predecessors, Christianity and Judaism. You yourself have written about it, B.J. . . ."

I nodded. She was referring to my books but also to an old article of mine, about Lady Mary Wortley Montagu's amazement at Turkish women's wealth. "They are the only free women in the empire," noted Lady Mary in 1711, more than a little enviously. She was quite right to be envious since she, a free and emancipated Englishwoman of the eighteenth century, the period of Mary Wollstonecraft and *The Vindication of the Rights of Woman,* had not a penny to her name, and was dependent on her husband and son for her livelihood.

I said, "Well, let me rephrase the question. Does the institute support the idea that one set of universal rights for women applies across geographic and religious boundaries?"

Mahnaz looked at me hard. "Look at the list of rights here. These are the topics of our new human rights educational manual for women in Muslim countries. It's called *Claiming Our Rights.* Are there any rights here you think women shouldn't have?"

I looked at the list:

Women's rights within the family;
Women's rights to autonomy in family-planning decisions;
Women's rights to bodily integrity;
Women's rights to subsistence;
Women's rights to education and learning;
Women's rights to employment and fair compensation;
Women's inter-related rights to privacy, religious
    beliefs, and free expression;
Women's rights during wartime;
Women's rights to political participation.

"How do you think that's going to play out around the world?" I asked.

"We don't know. That's why we're doing this, to see the relation between what we understand as basic human rights and the practices of indigenous cultures."

"And if there are differences?"

Mahnaz smiled and handed me the manual. "We'll deal with that when we come to it. But look at it yourself and then maybe we can talk again."

I accepted the materials with pleasure, and also Mahnaz's invitation to lunch at a local Persian restaurant. Like all Persians, she is proud of her national cuisine, often described as one of the world's greatest.

"B.J.," she said to me as we climbed into her car in the windy, cold parking lot outside the SIGI headquarters. "I need to talk to you about something. We're learning a lot from each other in this North-South dialogue. I think women from the South appreciate Northern women's sense of self-sufficiency. But there's so much the North can learn from the South in family relations, in feelings, in a sense of community. Food is a good example."

"Food?"

"Yes, food. I love to cook, and I love to cook for my husband and my grown-up son and for guests, for all kinds of people! Some of my feminist friends object to that."

"Object to food? All the feminists I know are very fond of food, or they are worried about eating too much or too little."

Mahnaz shook her head. "Fasten your seat belt, B.J." I did so obediently. "No, I mean about *cooking* food."

"I cook, too! I love to cook!" I answered. "So what's wrong with that?"

"Some of my American feminist friends equate cooking with women's subservient role and so on."

We sat down in the softly lighted and comfortably warm restaurant, and were quickly served hot thin round bread. "That business about cooking is one of those indigenous cultural differences you have to factor into your project, Mahnaz," I suggested.

She laughed. "But how? How can I explain to them? Tell me!"

"Have everybody in your focus group cook a dish, and then talk about food as exchange," I suggested. "That's what my husband Bob the anthropologist would say—cooking is a gift, and the recipient should offer a gift in exchange. He sees marriage as a system of exchange, not as capitalism."

"Like the non-cook cleaning up afterward?" said Mahnaz.

"Why not? That's what Bob does, and I am happy with that. Maybe your feminist friends would see the wisdom of such an approach. Of course I don't know about their husbands."

Mahnaz was silent. So was I. One sensitive issue, the place of religion in the institute's program, had yet to be raised and I found I was reluctant to raise it in the pleasant ambiance following our delicious lunch (*sebsi,* wonderful rice, marinated grilled chicken). I admired Mahnaz for what she was trying to do—bridge an old and contentious rift between Western feminists and Middle Eastern women's rights activist-feminists. Perhaps SIGI was the way to try to do it, but problems remained, according to Muslim friends in America, friends who had called me in some dismay after the famous spring 1996 conference. No religious women were represented, my friends had insisted. How could the conference then be representative of the Muslim world, where religion was a basic strand in the fabric of life in every country, whether Muslims were in the majority or the minority. No women in *hijab*, or Islamic dress, were on the program. Why? And the conference did not include any criticism of Western feminist views, views which many Muslim women found insulting and arrogant. "The American commentators even said how surprised they were to find that Muslim women could be so articulate! Imagine!"

I cleared my throat. "Religion," I said. "What about the place of religion? And Western feminist views?"

Mahnaz squeezed lemon into her tea. So did I. The restaurant was nearly empty, an impression heightened by the sudden absence of the soft background music that had accompanied our luncheon talk.

"It's not easy, B.J. I don't know what to say exactly. Except first, we don't need to spend our time insulting each other anymore. Women have problems. We need to try to help each other, in any way we can."

"Yes, I see that, Mahnaz. But the religion issue seems important."

Another pause. "Well, of course it's important. That's why our manual is focused on religion. Let me say that as an Iranian, I am almost always into religious dialogue with others, including people of my own community. I don't mean dialogue about what some ayatollah may have said about a particular point in Islam, but rather about the place and role of religion in society. We can't help but be affected by the events before and after the 1979 revolution, and our attitude toward religion is part of that."

"What kind of attitude? You are Muslim yourself, aren't you?"

"Yes, yes, of course, but we take our religious belief for granted. We don't want to inject it into everything, the way some Muslim groups, even in this country, want to do."

"But they would argue that it is there anyway, as a basis of life, and must be part of any equation that tries to define or test or study human rights."

"Yes," she said. "That's why we spend so much time and energy focusing on religion. Many women who took part in the 1995 conference, including myself, are religious. We didn't choose our speakers on the basis of how they were dressed, but there were women speakers who wore head covering. We didn't spend time criticizing Western feminists. Why? Muslim women are, I think, past the stage of defining themselves for or against Western feminism. They're looking for their

own ways to deal with their society and women's place in those societies."

"And they all agree?"

"Of course not. You have probably noticed yourself, B.J., how Muslim women are more and more interested in the *diversity* within Muslim cultures—they find this an important factor in dealing with
women's issues. For example, a number of feminists, both East and
West, objected to our conference's stress on religion, on Islam."

We left it at that, with my promise to try to look at the manual and
ask the students in my graduate seminar in Middle Eastern Studies to
evaluate it. I thanked her for lunch and for the work she is trying to do.

"Much needed," I said in parting.

"Thank you, I think so, too, or I wouldn't be spending my time on
it," she replied.

I remembered her other work, editing the volume *Faith and Freedom,* the proceedings of a 1994 conference on "Religion, Culture, and
Women's Human Rights in the Muslim World," held at American
University, Washington, D.C. She had also put together a collection of
memoirs by women in exile. Both books had been well received. Despite objections in some quarters, the selection of a Muslim woman of
dignity and capability like Mahnaz Afkhami as head of SIGI seemed a
real breakthrough in the tortuous efforts at communication between
feminists in East and West.

Historic Richmond, Virginia, is home to two Muslim women who
called themselves feminists: Amina Wadud Muhsin, author of the acclaimed book *Qur'an and Women,* and Azizah al-Hibri, whose book
Women in Islam I reviewed ten years ago. Azizah met me at the train
station in Richmond, where she is a professor in the T. C. Williams
School of Law. It had been twenty years since I'd known her in Texas;
she'd come there with her faculty husband. She went on to the University of Pennsylvania, received a Ph.D. in philosophy, and taught
briefly at Texas A&M. Her first marriage ended in divorce and she
headed back to Philadelphia. There she was the founding editor of
Hypatia, the journal of feminist philosophy. She then went to law
school—and practice in a Wall Street firm.

"Seven years on Wall Street was enough for me," she told me. "I
learned a lot about the corporate world, about deals and packages and
decisions, and then I woke up one day and said, what about ethics,
what about morality, what am I spending my time doing?"

She wrote a widely praised article, "On Being a Muslim Corporate
Lawyer," which was finally published in the *Texas Tech Law Review.*

"If you read that, B.J., you will understand where I am coming from, in terms of my concern about religion in public and private life," said Azizah, as we skirted the old historic center city and headed for her house in the beautiful suburbs of Richmond, past magnificent dogwoods, pink and white, which were blooming not only in cultivated gardens but flashed white deep in the woods, "like snow," I said aloud. Azizah smiled. "Not everybody thinks snow," she said. "My neighbor says her husband calls them the salt in the woods."

In her article on being a Wall Street lawyer, Azizah had written, "I have denied the impact of my faith on my professional life because I am a good American Muslim. Yet, as every religious person will readily admit, being religious is central to one's life. You cannot, for example, decide to be dishonest in the office and a good Muslim, Christian, or Jew at home. Religion just does not work that way. It provides you with a worldview, complete with a set of moral and other rules that are supposed to permeate every aspect of your life and inform your daily practice."

The response to her article, said Azizah, was overwhelming. "So many people, Christians and Jews as well as Muslims, wrote to me, called me. It was clear I had hit a nerve."

Azizah al-Hibri was one of the Muslim women who had some problems with the Sisterhood Is Global Institute.

"The institute is basically secular," she said. "And as I've said already, religious belief is central to all Muslims' sense of identity. I don't object to the institute's secular stance—they obviously can adopt any position they wish."

I broke in to say, "But they also see religion as an important dimension in women's lives, Azizah. They are focusing on religion, at least that's what it looks like to me."

"Yes, yes," Azizah answered, "but what I see is they are adopting religious discourse—including Qur'anic verses—as a *tool* to achieve *secular* goals. That's what I object to."

"Why?" I asked, puzzled.

"It demeans Islamic revelation and thought," she said quickly. "It's paternalistic."

"Paternalistic?"

"Yes, because their human rights manual uses religion as a *means*. It's not central to the project in the sense that religious belief is central to the very Muslim women the institute claims it wants to 'liberate.' "

"I do believe the institute is making a contribution," I insisted, "and they are trying, I think, to heal the breach between Eastern and Western feminists—personally, but also in theory."

Azizah bristled slightly. She was good-looking, in her jeans and yellow polo shirt, with brown hair and a slight, but proud carriage, large searching brown eyes, a rare smile that transformed her face, banished the intensity of her usual expression. There was no doubt that Azizah knew who she was and what her rights were.

"A change of attitude is what is needed," she said crisply. "A little less of this 'you-need-to-learn-from-us-the-superior-secular-West' bit and a little more interest in learning about alternative ways of the world."

Azizah had been teaching in Richmond for five years, "and I really love it." She had married again, and she lived happily with Ahmad, a computer whiz, in a beautiful colonial house with a garden that sloped downward into a hollow and climbed up the hollow, masking the neighboring house with flowering shrubs and a curtain of trees. From my spacious guest room window, I could see the dogwood again, stark white against the new green of the foliage.

Azizah's and Ahmad's house was full of flowers, fresh flowers in vases, flowers painted on the tall glass jar of fruit drops in the kitchen, still-life wreaths of dried flowers on the doors of the downstairs bathrooms. Dried petals of flowers reposed in the bowls of potpourri that subtly scented the rooms. I said how much I was appreciating dipping into the dishes of nuts, raisins, and apricots covered with Damascene-flowered napkins, the snacks usually found in hospitable Arab households. Ahmad, Azizah's charming Saudi husband, looked pleased.

"Azizah's personal little touches are everywhere," he said. "And you see there are even flower designs in the old Persian rugs that came from her father's house."

After dinner, we talked in earnest about her commitment.

"I've had to get involved in religious dialogue," she said, "and these days that means interfaith dialogue—conferences about the place of religion in American life." She handed me articles from the conferences, including one on "Family Planning in Islamic Jurisprudence." For Bill Moyers's book *Genesis,* which accompanied the PBS series, she was interviewed about the biblical figure of Hagar in the Old Testament; her remarks interested the Jewish women's journal *Lilith,* which asked her to contribute an article. She wrote, "I personally identify not with Hagar, who was a stranger, nor with Sarah, insecure because she was barren, but with the Queen of Sheba, a strong, capable and intelligent leader who, according to the Qur'an, negotiated with King Solomon and consulted her people before taking major decisions."

"So what does all this have to do with feminism, and particularly my subject of interest, Islamic feminism?" I asked the next day.

Azizah said, "Let's start back a way." She had come back from teaching her classes and we were having tea in the sunroom, its wicker chairs cushioned in green-flowered chintz, the view of the dogwoods and the azaleas filling the windows.

The trouble with many American secular feminists, Azizah believed, was that they did not look at themselves in relation to the whole, something that should be obvious in a democratic society. "I think they have abandoned feminist principles in their international activities and adopted a patriarchal ideology. What I mean is, they've abandoned democratic relations on a global level.

"Maybe it's because I came from Lebanon, a democratic society, that I see things in this way," she allowed. "I am happy to be part of a democratic society, and what that entails, I honestly believe, is taking all people's rights into account."

"So?"

"Some secular American feminists only look at themselves. Themselves!" Azizah punctuated her point.

"If you want to liberate women," she said earnestly, leaning forward so that the white wicker rocker creaked, "or help them achieve their full rights, you have to worry about the *whole* of society. If any one part is denied democracy, it reflects on the entire society."

I reminded her about the American idea that each person is expected to fulfill his or her own individual potential, and how for some American women, this ideal sometimes seems to conflict with the family ideal.

But Azizah shook her head. "I'm not talking about a 'family ideal,' " she said. "Women's rights aren't achieved in a vacuum, they need a healthy democratic society to prosper. So, if we demand full rights for women, we must demand them for everyone."

Azizah, as Asifa Quraishi had told me in San Francisco, was one of the founders of KARAMAH, an informal group of Muslim women lawyers. "It's a non-member organization," Azizah stressed. "Hundreds of volunteers, not members, all over the world. A board of directors, yes, an advisory board. Members in the accepted meaning of the term, no. It's *really* informal."

"A new *kind* of women's group?" I suggested.

"Maybe," said Azizah. She smiled. "No dues at least. It's basically a networking organization, writing and communicating about common problems. Each of us has a different conception of the group, I think. We really came together at Beijing—adopting a platform that, by working it through together, was adopted by almost all of the Muslim women there."

KARAMAH had already begun to fill an important function in the United States, acting as consultants in legal cases when misunderstanding existed between American civil law and the Muslim religious sharia law by which most observant Muslims are bound.

Example? "Divorce cases," said Azizah, "in which we try to advise and inform judges and lawyers. We don't operate to *change* or *challenge* American laws, state or federal, but to inform."

Example? Financial assets reckoned at time of divorce by lawyers for husband and wife. The American pattern is to add up all the couple's assets, divide by two, and allot accordingly.

"But this practice punishes women," Azizah said.

"Punishes them? How?"

"You know, B.J., that under Islamic law, women are entitled to keep income or other assets they have acquired for themselves during the marriage as their own property. So it's not fair to make women throw these assets into the pot if they divorce, or ask the divorced wife to pay maintenance to her former husband—that happens sometimes in U.S. courts, as you know."

"Confusion. Misunderstanding. I see," I put in.

"Yes," she answered, and added earnestly, "In some cases judges actually see the existence of separate bank accounts and separate assets as an indication that the couple was not serious about creating a real marriage in the first place!"

I reminded her that it was very recently indeed that Western women had been given rights to their own assets.

She nodded. "Yes, yes, I know."

In Azizah's garden, the petals of the dogwoods seemed to flare, luminous and white in the fading light, against the darkening trees. Somewhere a dog barked—joyfully, it seemed. Azizah looked at her watch. I nibbled absently at the nuts and raisins in the china bowls between us on the wicker table, topped with glass.

I contemplated my old friend. She was wearing her lawyer-teaching clothes, a slate blue suit and a pale yellow silk shirt that complemented her fresh pink and white skin, her dark thick hair cut carefully to just below her earlobes. A gold Qur'an on a discreet gold chain and her wedding ring were the only jewelry she sported.

"You must realize that Americans are also a religious people," I said.

Azizah nodded, putting her head to one side. "Of course they are, a God-fearing people. My research, my interfaith dialogue, is based on this assumption. But secularists in the United States seem to minimize this fact. Secular feminists in particular often present America to the world as secular, and even modernity as a secular concept. Not true."

"Not all of them do so," I put in.

"Many, though." Azizah was firm. "Read those documents, those international instruments about rights, and so on. Nothing about religion."

It was past tea time. A long time to be talking. Now we were waiting for Ahmad to come home. He drove a punishing hour each day to the train station in Fredericksburg, from which he traveled to his job outside Washington.

"We've had this argument before," I returned. "You have to remember that in America we talk about the separation of church and state—the founding fathers were very clear about that."

Azizah seemed to be agitated. She stood up and walked back and forth in her pleasant sunroom. "Ahmad is late," she said, then, suddenly, forcefully, she added, "But the separation of church and state: what does that mean? That we drive God out of our daily lives? No. It means that the state does not favor one religion over another. It's to keep one religion or sect from persecuting another. It was not intended to persecute or ban *all* religions. We are all free to worship as we wish. Right, B.J.? Think about it."

We heard the car drive up onto the circular driveway. Azizah's agitation suddenly ceased. She smiled, moved forward. "It's Ahmad," she said happily. "Let's go to dinner."

The next day, we were talking about KARAMAH's mission. "We have long-term goals," Azizah told me. "First, developing an Islamic jurisprudence which takes into account the American experience and the twenty-first century. We have a large American Muslim community which needs answers to new questions, and to old problems, too. And don't forget that American civil law is said to be secular, but of course its assumptions are based on Christian customary practices."

I admitted that I had never thought of that, though she was clearly correct. "Two, dispute resolution in the Muslim community to train people to resolve their differences amicably. And three, establish Islamic courts—arbitration bodies—using the model of rabbinical courts; courts that would deal with the Muslim community's problems, such as divorce and commercial disputes."

I wrote busily.

"And of course, the most important of all is to develop a marriage contract that will be clear and also one that will be difficult to challenge by either party in an American court. It's not easy."

"But I've seen sample contracts," I replied, "in that new Muslim American magazine *Sisters.*"

"Yes, yes, but those aren't adequate to protect women's rights in U.S. courts. More needs to be done. But we've started. You see, family law is state law, so we need to create contracts for the fifty states. It's not going to happen tomorrow, but eventually, we'll do it."

"Are the KARAMAH lawyers working as volunteers?" I asked.

Azizah laughed out loud. "Who would pay us for the billable hours we put in? No, we do it because we feel it must be done for our community, if it is to prosper as well as survive."

"Isn't there opposition to women lawyers working on the sharia law?"

"Of course there's opposition, B.J. While I was on Wall Street, I tried to form an American Muslim Bar Association, and then a man walked in and took it over."

"Tell me more."

"No. Past history, long ago, no point thinking about it," Azizah said. "I didn't feel it was worth fighting about. KARAMAH is actually more effective. We meet once a year. The rest of the time—e-mail."

What KARAMAH was doing was revolutionary, for they were working with sacred texts, something that had always been the province of men. Although nothing in the Qur'an actually prevented women from interpreting the law, cultural practice has meant that men were in charge. Jurisprudence? Mediation? Writing marriage contracts? Never in the past was this women's business. And not only were women lawyers reading, learning, and interpreting, they were doing so in the United States, where they held positions of legal credibility in American society. This gave them an advantage they might not have had in some of their own societies, such as Saudi Arabia.

"A lot of Muslim men in this country help and support us, many of the younger generation, but also some older religious men, trained to think in traditional ways about men and women and law. These are the people I thought would be against us, but they aren't! So we are hopeful for the future."

The other Muslim feminist who lived in Richmond was Amina Wadud Muhsin, assistant professor of religious studies at Virginia Commonwealth University. An African-American divorced mother of five children (twenty to seven years), she had carved out time to talk to me, and I had invited her to come to Azizah's house, which was near her next appointment. She came in, casting aside her head scarf and black overgarment. She sat down in Azizah's kitchen and I made tea.

"I've used your book in class," I said to open the interview. *"Qur'an and Women.* The students find it challenging."

"How do they find it challenging?" Amina was interested.

"They question whether the Qur'an actually gives the kind of picture you suggest."

Amina smiled. "Well, maybe they should read the Qur'an again. It's all there, I think. We just have to learn to work on it, with it. I talk about that in one of my courses here, 'Islam and Gender,' and also in 'Introduction to Islam.' "

"I've been told you spent three years in Malaysia, teaching at the Islamic university there."

"Yes, it was a wonderful time. I met Muslim women who were beginning the organization known as Sisters in Islam. They were working hard. One of the things they did was to produce a series of small booklets, inexpensive, to distribute to women all over Malaysia."

"I remember seeing them," I replied. "On subjects like 'Does the Qur'an allow a man to beat his wife?' That sort of thing."

Amina said, "And that particular booklet was helpful in passing the domestic violence act in Malaysia—after ten years. . . ."

"Real grass-roots activism," I commented.

"Yes. That was a good moment, for I suddenly saw the theological notions of equality which I find in the Qur'an successfully translated into practical uses."

"You still have connections with the Malaysian group?"

"Oh yes. We do e-mail all the time and as Muslim women in America, we are always in touch with Muslim women worldwide. Many of us met at the Beijing conference."

"So would you describe your religious commitment as a combination of belief and action?"

Amina considered. "Maybe," she said. "I guess I am a seeker at heart. My father was a Methodist minister in Baltimore, and I had a positive experience as a Christian, but Islam made more sense than any other spiritual approach. I felt as though I'd finally found the path to the way home. Islam has become a motivating factor for all I want to do in life."

I mentioned my Turkish acquaintance Ayse Sasa, who said that Islam saved her life.

Amina, interested for a moment, shook her head. "Not the same. She came to it from a negative basis, I approached it from a positive one. It makes a difference."

I told her that her book was being discussed on the internet by a group of Muslim women who had developed a web site called "Sisters." "That's good," she said. "And it's been translated into Turkish and Indonesian, too. But I really wrote it for myself. Though of course I'm glad it's making an impact."

"So tell me what you think about this 'Islamic feminism' I'm searching for."

Amina pondered for a moment. "We need to think of the issue in community terms, our Muslim community that is, and not see it as a factor in the discourse of East-West difference and conflict. I get very tired of the ideas that come to us in so-called global dialogue. Most of that discourse suggests that we should put religion aside so we can get real women's problems on the table. As Muslims we can't do that, religion is the base. As for me, too, I can't separate religion from my identity. It's just not possible."

"So how is Richmond in the good old U.S.A. after Malaysia?"

"You really want to know?" Amina looked at me hard. "Malaysia," she said, "is a truly multicultural, multilinguistic, multireligious place. Unlike this so-called democracy of ours. My kids have had a rough time here in Richmond. Here they all ask them, 'Hey, you black or white, or what?' Since they're all different shades of brown, all five of them, they are puzzled by the question."

"So what do your kids say?"

"They develop their own answers. Most of them are tough. I've told them the question means different things in different places. As Malcolm X said himself, "If somebody in the U.S. says he's white, it means 'I'm the boss,' but if someone in Africa says he's white, he just means his skin is that color. But my kids are learning to deal with what goes on here."

Amina is less optimistic than Azizah about the unity of the Muslim communities in the United States. "There's lots of ethnocentricity in the various immigrant establishments—Arab, Persian, Pakistani, whatever. I have to say"—and she smiled grimly—"that the African-Americans like myself are the most gracious in overlooking sectarian and class differences."

"Some of the people I've interviewed have insisted that the overriding basic principles of Islam serve to unify you all."

Amina was tall and slender, and sat upright in one of Azizah's well-designed chairs. "Questionable," she replied. "I've seen individual communities in the United States shift points of view in short periods. When I was at Michigan the Muslim student group changed from liberal Libyan to conservative Saudi, and they added a special door so women could come into the mosque separately. What kind of overriding principles were operating there?"

I mentioned racism, which one of my Muslim friends in Kuwait had described so eloquently as, "an American disease." And we were not yet rid of it.

"We have to keep working against it now," Amina said, standing up and retying her print scarf over the black tunic and black pants. "I have to go talk to my youngest kid's teacher. She's in special education and I've been trying to get over there for three or four days."

A smile. A firm handshake. "I like your watch, B.J."

I looked at her wrist. We were both wearing Mickey Mouse watches.

"A gift from my youngest daughter," I said.

"My kids gave me mine, too," she answered and was gone.

From Richmond I planned to head home to Austin via Chicago, where I still hoped to interview a woman from the Nation of Islam or from Wurth ed-Din Muhammad's group; friends had offered to help intervene on my behalf. Then, unexpectedly, Azizah offered another alternative. Bekirah Muhammad, daughter of Wurth ed-Din Muhammad himself, had recently moved to Richmond, Virginia. How was she related to Louis Farrakhan and the Nation of Islam?

"Ask her," said Azizah. "I've been working with her group on some other projects here in Richmond, and I'll try to set something up."

Thus it was that I found myself, the next evening, in a fish restaurant called Skillealley's, ushered into a padded seat in a booth across from Bekirah Muhammad, small, dark, attractive. Azizah sat next to her and they both stared at me while I spoke my piece, explained my project, Azizah with a friendly smile, Bekirah measuring me with large eyes. She wore a navy blue dress of silky and subtle pattern, her dark hair was swept up, and delicate gold earrings swung against her smooth young face. What were her feelings about her religion, about her father's split from Louis Farrakhan when she was a little girl?

Her face was reserved; she was keeping her counsel. Azizah had introduced me as an old friend, one of her professors who had written many books about Muslim women in the Middle East.

"I appreciate your willingness to talk to me," I said.

Azizah broke in to say how grateful she had been for Bekirah's father's help during a recent crisis. She did not identify the crisis and I did not inquire.

Bekirah nodded. The tiny red stones set into her golden earrings glinted in the dim light of the restaurant. She smiled slightly and waited. Over to me.

"Somehow," I said, "I thought I'd find you in Chicago."

"Well, you were nearly right," answered Bekirah. "I was born and raised in Chicago, went to school there on the South Side. My husband and I only came here to Richmond six months ago. I like it, though."

I said, "I lived on the South Side, too, when I was first married and my husband and I were students at the University of Chicago." I paused, then said in a rush, "I got married in Chicago actually, but I used to visit my aunt Rose in Chicago when I was small and we'd come down State Street on the old street cars and I'm old enough to remember bad days on the South Side."

Poverty. Hard times. When we were there, I went on to explain, the Woodlawn Conference was trying to improve things between black people and white people, working to upgrade the neighborhood.

A very slight quickening of interest. "And did you ever go to the Hyde Park art fair?" asked Bekirah.

"Oh yes."

"Me, too," said Bekirah. "My mother is an artist, and she was always there, doing portraits of people in charcoal, and when I was a little girl, I'd sit on a stool beside her and watch the folks go by. Maybe we saw each other and didn't know we'd meet again." She smiled, a warm smile, the reserve lifting slightly.

I smiled in return. "Maybe. Who knows? And you worked in Chicago, too?"

"Yes, I've been working with my father since I was out of high school," she said. "Doing his books, running his office, things like that. My father is a quiet man, not like Mr. Louis Farrakhan, so the media doesn't pay him much attention."

"What about Mr. Farrakhan? Do you see much of him?"

"He's a close friend of all of us," said Bekirah pleasantly. "He does a lot for black people. I think he's different from my father though. He's more interested in social improvement, not so much in religious issues."

"How about women's place in Mr. Farrakhan's group?"

Bekirah did not answer. She went on to say, "You would like my father, Imam Wurth ed-Din. He has always encouraged women to think and act equality. You know, I believe that all women, but particularly black women in this country, are very insecure. In the Muslim circles, women are hesitant to get involved in religious affairs. In my mother's day, women reading the Qur'an was almost unheard of."

"And now it's different?" I queried.

"Oh yes. My father tells all women to learn the basics of their religion, just like men. We have a lot of women's organizations now, the Muslim Women's League, Muslim Women United. We have Qur'anic study groups just like yours, Azizah."

Azizah looked gratified.

"My father encourages women to get involved in small business, to be independent economically. That's what my husband and I are trying to do. He has a jewelry store, me a small restaurant. We have women in our group who design clothes, who get into computers and real estate. Beekeeping. Local politics. All on the local level."

"Grass-roots enterprises," prompted Azizah.

"Yes, but they're going beyond that, Azizah. We have people in Congress now. And one woman's leather bags are being sold in Neiman-Marcus, all over the country. It's happening, just like Malcolm X wanted it to. But we have to *work*."

"How does your dad feel about the *hijab* for women?" I asked.

Bekirah took a moment before replying. "Well, as you see, I am not covered this evening. Azizah here is uncovered as well. My father always told me it was my choice. A lot of men are not as balanced as he is."

"Yes, indeed they are not." From Azizah in a strong voice.

"But it *should* be a woman's choice," insisted Bekirah, still in that quiet tone. "I was born Muslim, raised Muslim. I never covered my head, but I used to go around with my grandma and we'd often visit Muslim groups where all the women were veiled. The way those covered ladies behaved, they didn't seem like they were following the good ways of the Prophet Muhammad. And these were the ladies always telling me to cover my head. I guess I've been through all that, and come into my own."

"How do you mean?"

"I don't *always* cover my head, but sometimes I do, during Ramadan, and when I'm praying."

Azizah interrupted. "The head cover is a big issue for Muslim women in this country, B.J., as you already know."

"But there are more important things for women to worry about, don't you think so, Azizah?" Bekirah asked.

"So what do you think is most important?" I asked.

"Education," she said. "We need more schools for kids, like the Clara Muhammad schools, the ones my grandma started."

I was silent, recognizing with a start that this quiet, extremely pretty young black woman in the restaurant booth opposite me was not only the daughter of Imam Wurth ed-Din Muhammad, but the granddaughter of Elijah and Clara Muhammad, early leaders of the Nation of Islam. An impressive lineage for one so young and unassuming. The lineage of an American branch of Islam, one which had split during Bekirah's own lifetime. One group had decided to follow the example of Malcolm X and embrace the world Islamic community; the other had chosen the minority path, that of Louis Farrakhan, and the Nation of Islam, focusing on the American black community alone in conflict with whites. Here she sat, in a Richmond fish restaurant, an intimate part of all that history. I had not really considered the cross-currents, the family struggles that must have been involved. Her father was Elijah Muhammad's child, and it had clearly taken courage and strength for him to break with that legacy. And it clearly had also taken a particular kind of vision to break with the old legacy of women's traditional role and argue that women should "think and act equality." Here was Bekirah, a living embodiment of the change in point of view from the older patriarchal pattern, as she was not wearing a veil or otherwise signifying her Muslim identity.

Azizah was saying, "We need to become involved in some joint projects. Really, Bekirah. Why not join KARAMAH?"

Bekirah looked pleased, but she shook her head. "I'm not a lawyer," she said gently. "I couldn't do that."

"But you're a bookkeeper. We could maybe raise money for a Clara Muhammad school right here in Richmond."

Another pleased look. "Maybe," said Bekirah. "Maybe we could meet together and talk about the schools . . . at Starbucks next week?"

"And we need to talk about domestic violence too, battered women shelters, about opening one here."

Bekirah looked a bit startled at Azizah's sudden display of energy. "Yes, those are women's issues, too. Plus the children—we have to think about the next generation. You are right, Azizah."

To me, she said politely, "I am happy to have met you, B.J."

I said, "Good luck with the Clara Muhammad schools."

"I want to make my grandma proud of me," she answered with a shy smile, as she retrieved her umbrella and black raincoat from the restaurant's closet and headed for her car. "I'm driving to D.C. tonight," she explained. "We have an important meeting tomorrow." That energy belied her shy smile.

Washington, D.C., the nation's capital, is also the headquarters of the North American Council for Muslim Women, which has four hundred professional members. Sharifa Alkhateeb, its vice president, has been involved in Muslim women's issues for thirty years. She maintains a schedule of meetings, writing, research, family care, and volunteer work that would make any woman's—or man's—head spin.

"We've spent the last few years helping build women's self-confidence," she said over the phone. How? "Education, working to shift the public image of Muslim women, both in the U.S. and overseas, from negative to positive. We believe in the family, and we believe that strong women create strong families."

Muslim women in America, Sharifa continued, "have been doing their theological homework for at least ten years. They now feel strong enough to stand up for themselves when some practice or other is presented as 'religiously correct.' Whether it's at home or in a religious gathering, they say, 'Okay, where's your proof?' "

"Well," I put in, "I've met a lot of academic women who—"

"Not just academic women," interrupted Sharifa, "women in the trenches, high school girls, college graduates, and even older home-makers who'd never before have dared to challenge their dads or husbands on anything."

"Why now?" I persisted.

Sharifa believes the new openness is a response to American society, "where ideas are weighed, and not often accepted without question. That's why we at the Council work with other organizations both religious and secular, to effect legal change, to improve the way Muslims are viewed and treated in public. Public respect," she said firmly, "has an immediate effect on private roles. I honestly believe that."

Sharifa was a member of the Coalition for the Free Exercise of Religion that worked with sixty-five other American groups—Jewish, Christian, and nonreligious, as well as Muslim—to get the Religious Freedom Restoration Act passed by Congress in 1993.

Has the law been helpful to Muslim women?

"Oh yes!" she responded. "It's helped create an atmosphere of respect for all religions. But," she added, "we didn't stop when the act was passed." With other coalition members, the North American Council for Muslim Women helped produce guidelines for religious practices in the workplace. This was extremely important, Sharifa said, because many Muslim women (some of whom cover their heads and wear *hijab*, or Islamic dress) face job discrimination.

"So we were all thrilled," Sharifa said, "when President Clinton unveiled his executive order in August 1997." This order guarantees every American's constitutional rights, and mentions, for Muslims, "the acceptability of reading the Qur'an during private time at work and also wearing Islamic symbols, like head covering, if the person so chooses." A big step, and an important one, given the hostile attitude toward Islamic dress in some European countries, where young girls have been forbidden to wear headscarfs to school.

Sharifa also offers a regular course on Middle Eastern culture for teachers in the Fairfax County, Virginia, public schools; and she produces a half-hour monthly television show on Middle Eastern parenting.

When we finally met in person, Sharifa was wearing a long skirt, a fashionable green silk jacket with covered buttons, and a subtly printed headscarf.

"Is that head cover necessary?" I asked.

"Absolutely," said Sharifa, without hesitation. "There are three verses in the Qur'an that mandate it."

I demurred. "Not everyone would agree with you."

Sharifa smiled. "Yes. Everyone has their own interpretation of the verses. I consider them binding. But covering is an individual decision; no one should be forced to wear it or take it off, either by the family or the state. Islam practiced freely, without force—that's real Islam." She added, "I ask one thing of you, B.J."

"Yes, Sharifa."

"Don't put all Muslim women in one box and assume they'll all live, act, and react in the same way. Would you do that with non-Muslim American women? Of course not. Grant us the same possibility of diversity within our belief."

Diversity. Yes, indeed. If there was any single generalization to be made about the Muslim women I had interviewed, it was that because of the diversity, there *was* no generalization possible.

"And that diversity was so clear at the Beijing Women's Conference," said Sharifa. "So clear. The Muslim caucus presented six panels. I was honored to serve as Muslim chairperson at that tremendously exciting gathering. But there's still more to be done."

She described the Muslim Women's Georgetown Study Project, which works on the relation between UN Declarations of women's rights and the rights guaranteed to women under Islamic law. "We're just beginning," she said. "We're playing catch-up with years of secular feminism."

"Any final thoughts about Muslim women in America?"

"We're lucky," she said promptly. "Very lucky. Here in America we can discuss, research, publish anything we want to. And without fear of being arrested. Our ideas can spread throughout Muslim circles and into the wider Muslim world." Sharifa paused. "Really," she said, looking directly at me, "for freedom of Islamic thought and expression, there's no better place to be than in America."

Dr. Amira al-Azhary Sonbol is one American Muslim of Egyptian descent who is trying to help her Muslim women students "make sense" of their new position in the world. She is also helping to change the way Western feminists and feminists in the Middle East thought about the position of women throughout history. A member of Georgetown University's faculty, she teaches both in the history department and in the university's new Center for Muslim-Christian understanding.

"We're beginning to look at the past differently, I think," said Dr. Sonbol. "All those documents from the seventeenth and eighteenth centuries that had to do with women's legal rights, their health. For too long we have accepted what Westerners have written about us and not checked back into the original records."

Dr. Sonbol was particularly intrigued by Egyptian documents about the position of women in the health professions before the arrival of Napoleon's army in Egypt in 1798. "The documents show clearly that women—*hakimas*—were performing operations in Egyptian hospitals, were viewed as equal with doctors. But what happened when the French and British arrived?"

"I can imagine," I said, "given the nineteenth-century European view that men, not women, had the key to the new antiseptic medicine. Midwives were primitive and backward, of course."

"Yes, yes." Amira had a wonderful bubbly laugh. "That's just what Lord Curzon, who governed Egypt, said. 'Who needs women doctors, we need nurses, civilized nations have nurses.' And we've been following the British policy ever since. To our loss."

This confusion of reality with colonialist ideas about "civilization" was a real injustice to women, Aziza believed, as was the current battle over the civil marriage contract in Egypt. "There are historical precedents for the contract. It's nothing new. Look into your own past, I tell my students. Don't use the West as an example."

That advice was taken seriously by the young women and men who signed up for her controversial seminars and tutorials, some focused on gender in history, some on women and health.

Dr. Sonbol said, "We're in a new era, B.J., all women, I mean, not just Muslim women. But what I see among my Muslim women students is something rather exciting. As educated women, they are claiming their own spirituality. This means they're actually inventing a new set of social relationships, a new concept of women's role in the world. Is that what you would call feminism?"

I thought for a moment before answering. "Yes, perhaps. Women accepting responsibility for defining their own selves, their own future. I would say that's a kind of feminism."

☐ ☐ ☐ ☐

The problem, of course, as I had put it to myself before starting the American leg of my journey, was how these women were managing to live as Muslim believers in a secular society like the United States. I found that most of them were indeed creating spaces for themselves within the larger national context. But a few Muslim men and women have established self-sufficient communities, which at first glance look like those of the American Shakers and Amish of long ago.

One, founded in 1986, and actually named Dar al-Islam, is located on two thousand acres in the heart of the old Spanish-settled country-side of New Mexico. It does not appear to be a player in American social and political life, or a separate nation which challenges the status quo, but rather a retreat from the status quo. The residents live in small houses along the mesas that border the Rio Chama, just outside Abiquiu. But the center of the community is a complex of beautiful whitewashed adobe buildings—a domed mosque and several interconnected structures: a library, classrooms, a kitchen, a cafeteria.

Designed by famed Egyptian architect Hassan Fathy, the complex is situated so that the distant Sangre de Cristo mountains are visible on the clear desert horizon. Hassan Fathy himself came to Abiquiu from Cairo several years ago and brought two Egyptian Nubian artisans to teach local workers the art of building a free-standing arch in mud brick.

Dar al-Islam stands in an area with other religious groups. An American Sikh community has been set up in the nearby town of Espanola, and Ghost Ranch, a Presbyterian-affiliated retreat that is associated with Georgia O'Keeffe, is just up the road. The Christ in the Desert monastery is also nearby, and so is the famous sanctuary of Chimayo.

When Bob and I visited Dar al-Islam in 1997, we asked whether the choice of Abiquiu as a site had anything to do with its proximity to Chimayo (twenty miles northeast), which touted itself as a "pure" Spanish community dating back to the 1500s.

"Why do you ask?" queried Hakim Archuletta, Dar al-Islam's director of community relations. A native of New Mexico, he converted to Islam twenty-eight years ago.

I explained that Chimayo was one of the places in the New World, where, to this day, the great historic battle between Muslims and Christians was reenacted every year. The participants wore medieval costumes, they performed on horseback. The annual presentation of *Los Moros y los Christianos* drew spectators from all over the United States, to commemorate the 1492 triumph of Christianity, and the subsequent expulsion of Muslims and the Jews from Spain.

"Perhaps," I said in the silence, "the founders wanted Dar al-Islam to present the image of a peaceful, not a warlike community?"

"Yes, that must be it," answered Hakim politely. "But everything here has changed in the last ten years." He smiled, and added, "We're still peaceful, as you can see, but our focus is on education now."

"All the residents are involved in education?" This from Bob.

Hakim looked at Karima Diane Alavi, in whose pleasant house we sat, drinking Turkish coffee and admiring the view over the hills. "Well, I am," she answered. "I do a summer workshop for teachers, but there are only six resident families now."

"Only six?" My tone of voice must have betrayed my surprise, for Hakim took that up and explained that times and needs had changed, "not only for American Muslims," he said, "but for all Americans."

"We decided the best way to use our resources was to serve as a kind of bridge between Muslims and non-Muslims in America," he continued. "And to do that, we had to change course. We sold off some of our land to finance the new ventures. Karima and I both do a lot of speaking. I spent this morning at a conference of the National Association of Ecumenical Councils."

Most of the men and women residents worked outside Dar al-Islam, in nearby towns, but they lived a life guided by Islamic principles. Men seemed to be in charge and modest dress was the norm. The women members included a librarian, a social worker, a real estate agent, and two teachers. Yes, they covered their heads with scarves. But what did that mean?

Karima said, "Well, for many Americans a head scarf on a woman seems to equal oppression. When this came up at a recent conference, I found myself replying, 'So what? My scarf doesn't suck my brain cells out!'"

"What did the other person answer to that?" I queried.

"Nothing," Karima answered. "What could she say?"

Karima and Hakim exemplified the new approach of Dar al-Islam— out of self-containment and into the wider American community. Through generous gifts from Muslims all over the world (but not from any government, Hakim stressed), the community was able to offer its educational sessions free "to facilitate the growth of accurate and authentic knowledge of Islam among the American people." He stated that the community had a commitment to "build bridges among Muslims and non-Muslims of America." By the end of the summer of 1997, the summer program alone would have reached nearly two hundred teachers. "We were lucky to get an initial grant from the

National Endowment for the Humanities for the pilot summer session in 1994. Since then, we've been on our own."

Dar al-Islam's sale of some of its original gift of land raised eyebrows among some Muslims in America, and abroad, said Hakim, for this was the event that changed the original focus of the community.

"But we had to," said Hakim. "We had eighty-five hundred acres, much of it without roads or other facilities. Selling sixty-five hundred acres of the land grant gave us enough money to establish a permanent endowment. Now we don't have to depend so much on annual giving, but can get on with our mission of education, which we see as crucial."

Karima brought impressive credentials to the summer education project; she had been teaching for nineteen years in Quaker schools, for eight of those years at Sidwell Friends in Washington, D.C., the highly respected Quaker school from which Chelsea Clinton recently graduated.

"I was raised a Quaker," Karima said, "which I still believe offers an admirable set of values. But when I married my Iranian husband, I became a Muslim." (She and her husband were recently divorced and she has married one of Dar al-Islam's administrators.) At Sidwell Friends, over the years, Karima developed a popular course on "Peoples and Cultures of the Islamic World," but soon she would be leaving to take up a permanent post at Dar al-Islam.

"I shall miss the Friends school," said Karima, "but I'm looking forward to the new job. We bring Muslim speakers from all over the world to instruct the American teachers during the summer sessions. The teachers themselves are full of questions, and we get into some interesting debates about faith and belief systems."

And what would happen to the course on Islam at Sidwell Friends?

"I'm afraid it will disappear," answered Karima sadly. "They've decided to replace it with a course on the modern Middle East, with a focus on the Arab-Israeli conflict." She paused. "Not the same thing, of course. Not the same thing at all."

"What about women living in Dar al-Islam? I've heard they're restricted?"

"No more." Karima assured me that at Abiquiu she will not be subject to any segregationist rules. "Times are changing," she said. "I am a Muslim but I am also an independent woman, even if I do cover my head. I made that clear from the beginning, and that is acceptable." She added, "Come back and see us if you're in the Santa Fe area. It is a beautiful and peaceful place, Dar al-Islam."

¤ ¤

Conclusion

FEMINISM, to the young women I interviewed in Kuwait, was synonymous with America, with fast food. Feminism indeed crosses boundaries these days; it has become transnational, like fast food, and like music, films, blue jeans, the ideas of democracy. It is reaching the far corners of planet Earth, through videos, cassettes, television, radio, faxes, e-mail, the World Wide Web. But like music and films and fast food, feminism and democracy are not digested whole. People in other countries, with other traditions, react to and sometimes reject these ideas, and often shape them to their own needs. Frantz Fanon, the Algerian revolutionary, said of freedom that "what is given is not the same as what is taken," that is, people must themselves act to earn their freedom. The same might be said of feminism. But first, as my friend Um Zhivago, woman activist in the Palestinian refugee camp of Rashadiyah said long ago, "a revolution is like cooking; before you begin, you have to look in the cupboard to see what ingredients you have at hand to work with." This is what women in the Middle East are doing, evaluating their strengths, calculating their resources.

Democracy is not an easy sell around the world, for it challenges established autocratic governments, which are unlikely to cede power to anyone. But feminism has an advantage; it can take many forms, it can be fought on many fronts, in both public and private life. What I discovered in my travels was that feminism seemed alive and well in many countries of the Middle East and North Africa, but not in the forms I expected. Everywhere I found women reordering their activities to meet new challenges from the old order. The tradition of God the Father, the tradition that men rule, is the order faced by all women who have inherited the paternalistic, monotheistic religious tradition of Judaism, Christianity, and Islam. This tradition is now being contested on a daily basis as women move into the public workforce beside men, and expect recognition, respect, and power.

I found I was having to recast my own definition of feminism, as a movement for equality between men and women, a way for women to share the world which has been until recently the sole prerogative of men. "We see feminism in America as dividing men from women— separating women from the family. This is not good for anyone," said Haifa Abdul Rahman, deputy secretary of the General Federation of Iraqi Women. The Iraqi approach with its support for maternity leave, child care, and other needs which are shared by *both* women and men might be called family feminism, a term with which Haifa Abdul Rahman seemed to agree. Yes, I thought to myself, a good approach, remembering how in America the feminist emphasis on the individual woman had allowed the religious right to appropriate family values. I hastened to explain to my Iraqi friends that American feminists now recognized that the majority of American women still want to marry and have children. This has led to new initiatives, pressure for new laws about child support and family leave, and conferences with titles like "Feminism and Family Values." My Iraqi friends merely nodded and smiled.

I have also viewed feminism as a movement to allow women to develop a sense of their own worth and value, a more positive sense of themselves. "Yes, of course," said Marfua Tokhtakhodzhaera, an Uzbek feminist. "But first one must take care of the conditions which prevent women from doing so—conditions like poverty, illiteracy, lack of contraceptive methods other than abortion." When those obstacles were overcome, one could "nourish the self," said Marfua. And I thought of my friend Aisha bint Muhammad in Marrakech, who was old and unemployed and had trouble finding enough money to feed herself and her son, let alone improve her "sense of self."

On the travels I have described, I often asked myself what I meant by a term like Islamic feminism, the stated goal of my long search. Was it a militant fundamentalist movement which denigrates Western methods to improve women's lives and argues a return to older ways— women in the home, center of the family unit, but veiled and secluded from public view? This is what many Western reports have suggested and there is some truth in that view. But I found that such a view, to the extent it exists at all, does so in the minds of some men, and is part of their fantasies; it also exists among a minority of women who see their roles exclusively as homebodies, hidden jewels of the family. In this small group, many feel that the beliefs of their male relatives are the same as God's will.

But to my surprise, Islamic belief is also the stated basis of most of the behavior I felt to be "feminist."

This was quite different from my understanding of Western feminism, which has defined itself over the years as solidly secular, a movement set apart from religion. Spirituality, yes; religious establishment, no. This Western position does not work for Azizah al-Hibri, Lebanese-American lawyer and feminist who said, "As a Muslim, religion is part of my life, and cannot be divorced from it." She also believes that most secular feminists in America operate in a legal and social environment which is shaped by religion—Christianity—even though they may not be aware of it. For, she stated, all of the so-called secular laws in America are based on Christian ideas about morality. My Jewish feminist friends in the United States agree.

In Egypt, Turkey, Kuwait, and in the United States, Islamic women begin with the assumption that the possibility of gender equality already exists in the Qur'an itself; the problem, as they see it, is malpractice, or misunderstanding, of the sacred text. For these Muslim women, the first goal of a feminist movement is to re-understand and evaluate the sacred text, and for women to be involved in the process, which historically has been reserved to men. As Heba Raouf Ezzat in Egypt said, "This will provide us with a more just society for all—men, women, and children, and that is a goal of Islam." And Islamic feminists strive to create equality, not for the woman as individual but for the woman as part of the family, a social institution still seen as central to the organization and maintenance of any society.

Other women who are Muslims and feminists, but who do not call themselves "Islamic feminists," question the legitimacy of this movement for re-understanding the Qur'an. They argue instead that women must work with the existing situation. But they are in accord when it comes to insuring equality for women within the family, about which the Qur'an is quite specific. And no women *I met* doubted the basic message of the Qur'an: men and women are equal in possibility and potential. (Some men felt differently!)

To achieve different forms of parity for both sexes, Islamic feminists and feminists who are Muslims, Christian, and Jews are using a variety of strategies. Some of these strategies are familiar to American women. The first step for many Western feminists has been to document women's condition, to provide a data base for proposing changes in policy, and in Turkey, the new women's library is doing just that.

"The most important thing now is the research and documentation," said Sirin Tekeli, one of the library's founders. Moroccan women are also engaged in a documentation project. Other strategies I saw in action were grass-roots women's groups organizing, networking, protesting, petitioning the nation's leaders. In Egypt, women's groups and human rights groups have joined forces to fight female circumcision, which has increased rather than decreased in recent years. Certainly local controversy over this practice has increased. "But it is a long and hard battle," said Aziza Hussein, president of the Cairo Family Planning Association, who has been campaigning against female circumcision for thirty years. "It's a custom that predates Islam, a cultural practice," added Marie Asaad, who heads the task force which is involved in nationwide workshops, data collecting, and lobbying of national leaders to end the practice.

The Union de l'Action Féminin in Morocco organized a drive to reform family law, which legislates basic issues affecting women: divorce, child custody, inheritance, polygamy. They gathered one million signatures from men and women on a petition submitted to King Hassan II. In response, he created a commission to recommend changes. Some improvement has been achieved, "though not all, not yet," amended Latifa Djebabdi, one of the members of the union.

Throughout the area, women are also clamoring for more participation in the public political process, no surprise for American women, who are still struggling for greater representation in Congress. Eighty-seven women ran for Parliament in the 1995 Egyptian elections, but only eight won. "We must work harder," they said. And three hundred professional Kuwaiti women, who still do not have the vote, recently staged a sit-in strike before the House of Parliament, just as American and British women have done in the past.

Literacy classes for women were offered by the Women's Cultural and Social Society in Kuwait, several years before passage of the nation's compulsory education law for both sexes. Business women in Saudi Arabia lobbied the Riyadh Chamber of Commerce and won the right to be included in the nation's new job training programs for Saudi citizens. Palestinian women at Bir Zeit University and Moroccan women at Muhammad V University have raised funds for women's studies programs in the past three years, programs based on Western models, but adapted to local needs, with translations of texts and ideas to make Western feminist paradigms meaningful to non-Western students. And although Middle Eastern feminism, like American feminism, is middle class, a responsibility to include all women in the movement is widely accepted. In Turkey, the Foundation for the Support of Women's Work is, they say, an example of practical feminism, providing child care, counseling, and income-producing activities for the thousands of poor women in the *gecikondus,* or squatter settlements, outside Turkey's burgeoning cities. Women have thus taken seriously the Islamic injunction to help those less fortunate; in Kuwait, Islamic feminists offer free counseling and literacy classes for women guest workers, who are often neglected in the national plans. In Saudi Arabia, Princess Sarah Abdul Aziz and her niece, Princess Moudy, have established the El-Nahdah Philanthropic Foundation for Women, which provides schooling for the disabled, and for Down's syndrome children, as well as many other kinds of educational opportunities for women.

But the women I met are also utilizing strategies that are related not to Western practices, but to their own indigenous traditions. Dr. Rasha al-Sabah in Kuwait is adapting an old social pattern—the diwaniyah or social council of men—to fit modern needs. In Dr. Rasha's diwaniyah men and women sit together weekly to discuss issues of importance to all Kuwaitis—such as the problem of censorship and the relationship of the nation to its neighbors. She is providing a forum for the development of new male/female ties, a forum based on an older established all-male model. Sufi ritual tradition is being transformed in Turkey, with integrated rituals rather than separate male and female rituals. Ayse Sasa, a Turkish film theorist who has recently "become an Islamist," is utilizing religious perspectives in her work, writing and publishing what is called by some critics "the cinema of the unseen, the cinema of Sufi metaphysics." These women are taking older ideas and practices and refashioning them for different times.

But new ideas are surfacing as well. Hannah Safran of the Haifa Women's Center in Israel, was one of the moving forces behind the vigils of Women in Black, an innovative political movement of Israelis and Palestinians that utilized women's informal networking to achieve its aims—drawing attention to what it perceived to be the unjust occupation of the West Bank. "It worked," said Hannah, "because it was not modeled on men's bureaucratic organizations, with lists and evening meetings, but tailored to women's schedules."

Women's appropriation of the written word is another important strategy that is recognized by Western feminists, but is of far more importance in the Middle East because of the high status of the written word in all of these societies. Women's magazines are proliferating, from Egypt's *Hawa* (for the general public), to *Nour* (for literary-minded women), and Morocco's *The Eighth of March,* (for the politically active). And the 1995 Arab Women's Book Fair, held in Cairo, was a milestone, marking a shift for women writers from the privacy of the home to the center of public attention. Publishers from fourteen countries brought fifteen hundred titles in Arabic, French, and English—no mean achievement for a first-time event, said Ferial Ghazoul and Hesna Makdashi, who helped raise money and organize the fair.

Agriculture, seldom recognized as important by Western feminists, is also an area where women are making strides. This is particularly true in Egypt, where one thousand women have been granted title to land, through the Mubarak New Lands program. And the women's home economics faculty at the College of Agriculture, University of Alexandria, have launched a support project, providing business training, small loans, animal health care classes, and pesticide education to help the new women farmers make the best of their opportunity.

The many successes of the General Federation of Iraqi Women in establishing and implementing new guarantees of gender equality raise the old question of whether the end sanctifies the means. For it was a fiat from above, from President Saddam Hussein himself, that made such a state of affairs possible. Does that mean that this achievement has been sullied by its association with a tyrannical leader? Iraqi women seemed delighted with the new laws and claimed greater achievements than other Arab women. But an Iraqi woman exile said, "There can be no women's rights without human rights." If one agrees with this, then it is logical to agree with Palestinian and Israeli leaders' insistence that women's rights in their countries must wait until full political rights have been achieved for all citizens. Is this a reason or an excuse?

Are all of these activities in progress throughout the Middle East, North Africa, and Central Asia, as well as in the United States to be classified as feminist activities? Does it matter? And if so, to whom? "Feminism is not a word in my vocabulary," said one of the members of the Kuwaiti Women's Cultural and Social Society. "But women's rights and freedoms are. Aren't they the same?"

Yes and no, I'd answered. Certainly women's rights and freedoms are a fundamental goal of the feminist movement, but feminism has developed different elements as the years have passed: the idea of gender as a continually constructed identity; and the idea of the legitimacy of a female view, a view that sees the world differently from the male, and can point to new directions in human thought, a woman's view that seeks to restore women to their place in history.

When I asked Moroccan women about gender, they seemed puzzled, but Moroccan women writers like Leila Abouzeid document, in their women characters, a "contextual self." This idea, that a woman constructs a self according to the company she keeps, the place she lives (at home, in a foreign country, as a wife, mother, sister, or daughter), challenges Western ideas of the self as a bounded entity, ideas that have been important in Western philosophy and psychology, particularly since the Enlightenment. The Moroccan woman novelist's presentation, however, is not so far from new directions in Western women's studies, particularly in the work of Nancy Chodorow, who sees a flexible, rather than a fixed and bounded self as an advantage for women (and also for men) in a rapidly changing world like our own. Flexibility for all these women does not mean waffling, but adapting, which is an important human survival strategy.

My attempts to talk about a female viewpoint generally drew blank looks until a woman in Saudi Arabia answered, "What's so new about that? In our society, we've always had a female perspective. In the world of women of course." At that, I began to wonder whether this particular element in Western feminist thinking was ignored in Middle Eastern societies because it was already present there, and taken for granted. Moroccan sociologist/feminist Fatima Mernissi pointed out long ago in her work that Muslim women had a strength and independence in their own female society which made them appear dangerous to men. Dr. Mernissi never states that the female gaze had any *recognition* within the society of men, the patriarchs who wielded the ultimate power. But that strength existed, and was utilized in the power plays of family life that included men. This strength, this female independence, remains in abeyance—in storage—sometimes, like the figs and walnuts and eggplants that women preserve against the cruelties of winter, like the wild greens that Turkish women gather in villages to supplement the drought-ridden diet of their families. Strength stored to be used when the time is right. And now is the time, Dr. Mernissi believes, to take the talents honed in private life into public life.

Why do Western feminists overlook or undervalue this hidden aspect of Muslim women's lives? There is clearly a good deal of ignorance. But over the years, I have pointed out to Muslim women friends, that we Western women are brainwashed from childhood into believing that the only important acts are those that men perform and that women must replicate those acts if they are to gain power or agency. This leads us, I believe, to downgrade any activities and evidences of agency that take place outside the public, i.e., male orbit. In doing so, we are buying into the old public/private split. This is the paradigm developed by male anthropologists, who, when faced with the need to study a sexually segregated society, and the fact that one half of the society was closed to their (male) eyes, implicitly judged that hidden half to be the less important one.

Social class is an issue that in different ways is a sore point with feminists everywhere. Most international movements for women's rights seem to have begun as class-based movements, rich, upper-class elite ladies with the leisure and the means to help those less fortunate than themselves. This is also true in the Middle East and Central Asia, where class remains an important index of people's status. As Leila Abouzeid said, "I would rather be an upper-class woman here than a working-class man," and marriage, job promotion, and wealth still are influenced by class, by family status. The Islamic feminist movement is the only women's movement to cross over lines of class and color, and thus appeals to many women—and men—who are not part of the old status quo.

North American feminists are in a different position than their Middle Eastern cousins, for they are in the minority rather than part of the majority. But they live in a democracy and as citizens of that democracy have certain guaranteed constitutional rights. The women I met are balancing their Muslim identity with their responsibilities as citizens. And some, like Azizah al-Hibri, Sharifa Alkhateeb, and Asifa Quraishi, are contributing new insights to American feminist concerns about the relation between religion and the state.

Finally, a word about the veil, which has for so long been a focus of Western interest, and seems to be equated with oppression in the Western mind. Is that what the veil means to Middle Eastern women? On the basis of my interviews and travels, I would say generally no. Cover or *hijab* is an important *new* development in Muslim countries, where it is equated with piety and belief. But as Karima Alivi in Abiquiu said so eloquently, "The veil doesn't suck my brains out." Sometimes women are forced to cover, as in Iran and Afghanistan, and that is certainly a restriction. But in other countries, *hijab* appears to be a matter of the woman's choice, of her own decision based on her reading of religious texts. Sometimes this dress gives women extra authority as they struggle with male Muslims to achieve gender equality. Thus we have diversity in attitude, strategy, and dress, which might be said to characterize the entire area.

Feminism then has many faces in the Middle East. The woman question is a central question everywhere, and women are active in all the countries that I visited. They are regrouping and utilizing a variety of methods to achieve goals of gender parity, dignity, public power, goals that have been challenged by the ruling patriarchal traditions. Many are rejecting the Western feminist label, while at the same time employing some of the ideas, some of the same strategies as Western feminists. For some, religion is a given in the feminist/womanist movement, the path to equality; of these women, a minority do indeed call themselves Islamic feminists. Some Muslim women believe that women should cover their heads and dress modestly, and they find justification for this in the Qur'an; the focus of their efforts is not the veil but the evaluation of sacred texts, with an eye to reforming the law, and "creating the just society propounded by Islam." A few women like the Egyptian feminist Hala Shakrallah object to the use of the term "Islamic feminist." Why? "Because I'm a Christian," she said. "Is there something special that applies only to Islam?"

Hala believes that a wider movement is in progress, a movement that includes secularists and Marxists who were born Christians and Jews and Muslims, all of those who adhere to the monotheistic religious tradition. Poverty, domestic violence, political participation, female circumcision, literacy, social class, discussion of the veil, appropriation of the written word, legal equality—these are all aspects of this wider movement, in which Islamic feminists are also involved. The strategies these women are using to address their problems, though often different from ours in the West, merit our respect, and offer us a new source of inspiration. They are creating something new and powerful out of bits and pieces of Western ideas and Middle Eastern traditions. In their struggles for legal and economic equality they stress the viability of the family group, a sense of responsibility to the wider group, the importance of religious values. Muslim, Christian, and Jewish women are combining elements of both East and West to develop several feminist ideologies of their own.

Index